# Starting & Runn
# Restaurant For D

C000162684

## Must-Have Personality Traits for a Successful Restaurateur

- ✔ Tolerance
- ✔ Business sense
- ✔ Positive energy
- ✔ Ability to hold (or hold off) booze
- ✔ Leadership skills
- ✔ Schmoozability
- ✔ Passion
- ✔ Presence
- ✔ Persistence
- ✔ No life (outside the restaurant)

## Numbers and Reports to Track Your Success

- ✔ Daily business review
- ✔ Income statement
- ✔ Cash flow analysis
- ✔ Menu mix analysis
- ✔ Cost of goods sold report

## Tips for Making Your Restaurant a Great Place to Work

- ✔ Educate employees about your products and concept.
- ✔ Let them taste the food on a regular basis.
- ✔ Praise, praise, praise them.
- ✔ Encourage communication.
- ✔ Carry yourself well.
- ✔ Encourage staff camaraderie.
- ✔ Run targeted incentive programmes and contests.
- ✔ Cross-train your staff to keep it interesting. Cross-training gives you a lot of flexibility as the manager, and it keeps staff members engaged and interested about new areas of your business.
- ✔ Be consistent. Your staff should know what to expect from you *and* what you expect from them. Apply policies and procedures consistently across the board.

## Identifying Unsatisfied Guests

- ✔ **Human periscopes:** Look for people looking up and around and then back down. Typically, people do this because they don't have something they need.
- ✔ **Leaving food on the plate:** Maybe the customer plans to box it up to go home, but confirm this. You want empty plates going back to the dish area.
- ✔ **Waiting on a refill:** People like full glasses of drink, especially nonalcoholic drinks, so replenish the water, pop, and iced tea regularly.
- ✔ **Watch gazing:** Customers who keep looking at their watches may not be wondering where their food is, but investigate the situation anyway.
- ✔ **Waving and snapping:** If you see any of these gestures, it's not good. Try to get to the customer quickly and sort the problem before they leave.
- ✔ **Safe orders:** If customers order chicken in your seafood restaurant, they may be afraid of the menu and simply need some educating. Don't let them miss what you do best.

# Starting & Running a Restaurant For Dummies®

## Key Steps for Resolving Customer Service Issues

1. Listen. Let them talk and don't interrupt.
2. Apologise or thank them, depending on situation.
3. Rectify the current situation.
4. Develop a long-term solution to avoid future customer service problems. This step also reinforces to your diner that you heard their issue and acted on it.

## Tips for Staying Competitive

- Play up your strengths and make them matter to your diners.
- Analyse your competition, determine their deficiencies, and exploit them.
- Close the gaps on your own deficiencies.
- Continually create new points of difference.
- Know your audience, how your points of difference matter to them, and how to reach them.

## Menu Lingo that Sells

- **Many great menu-item names start with the preparation method.** Words like *braised, seared, pan-fried, oven-roasted, wood-fired,* and *poached* lend a level of prestige to a dish that increases a diner's perception of its value.

- **Incorporate reasons the dish is special, different, or unique into the name.** Is your beef *aged to perfection?* Are your eggs *farm fresh?* Is your bread *baked in-house each morning?* Is your produce *locally grown* or *organic?*

- **Great ingredients make for great descriptions.** Are there any oustanding or hard-to-find items? Does a dish contain seasonal items that you should highlight?

- **Highlight where the ingredients come from.** *Scottish* beef and *Roscommon* oysters mean something to people.

- **Be more specific.** Of course you're serving *pasta,* but what kind of pasta? Tell the guests whether it's *fettuccine, linguine, capellini,* or *fusilli.* And that sauce you're serving tonight is probably great, but be more descriptive – *ragout, coulis, demi-glace,* or *reduction,* for example. Getting down to specifics has the dual advantage of providing more information and enhancing the diner's perception of the dish.

*For Dummies: Bestselling Book Series for Beginners*

# Starting & Running a Restaurant

## FOR

# DUMMIES®

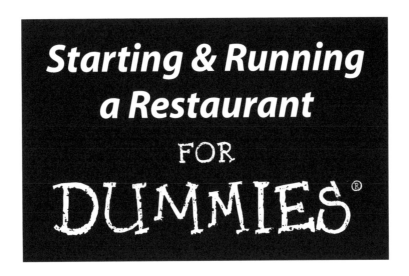

# Starting & Running a Restaurant

## FOR DUMMIES®

by Michael Garvey, Heather Dismore,
Andrew G Dismore, and Carol Godsmark

John Wiley & Sons, Ltd

**Starting & Running a Restaurant For Dummies®**

Published by
**John Wiley & Sons, Ltd**
The Atrium
Southern Gate
Chichester
West Sussex
PO19 8SQ
England

E-mail (for orders and customer service enquires): cs-books@wiley.co.uk

Visit our Home Page on www.wiley.com

For general information on our other products and services, please contact our Customer Care Department within the U.S. at 800-762-2974, outside the U.S. at 317-572-3993, or fax 317-572-4002.

For technical support, please visit www.wiley.com/techsupport.

Wiley also publishes its books in a variety of electronic formats. Some content that appears in print may not be available in electronic books.

British Library Cataloguing in Publication Data: A catalogue record for this book is available from the British Library

ISBN: 978-0-470-51621-8

Printed and bound in Great Britain by Bell & Bain, Ltd., Glasgow.

10  9  8  7  6  5  4  3  2  1

WILEY

# About the Authors

**Michael Garvey** was, at one time, an unassuming if not innocent soul from Brooklyn before he was grabbed by the clutches of the evil shadow known simply as the restaurant business. Starting as a resort waiter in the Poconos of Pennsylvania, he quickly became smitten by his new work and found himself a genuine masochist at heart. Garvey delved into other facets of the industry, from bartending in saloons to waiting in fine dining atmospheres. He also found time to volunteer in the kitchen of the Marist Brothers in Esopus, NY, manufacturing meals for handicapped and underprivileged children and adults. In 1994, he returned to New York City for some real brutality. He latched on to a small three-unit outfit by the name of Mumbles as a manager. After seeing action in their other locations, Michael landed a job as floor manager at The Oyster Bar in Grand Central Station owned by famed restaurateur Jerry Brody.

The Oyster Bar was a wonderland for the then medium-rare manager. Garvey took advantage of many opportunities including wine cellar stewarding which led to sommelier certification. He was part of the management team that rebuilt the institution in 1997 after a devastating fire. In 1998, he was offered the General Manager position and added President to his titles in 2000. Today, in addition to running the day-to-day operations in Grand Central, Michael has led efforts to franchise The Oyster Bar concept. While writing this book, he organised the first franchise in Tokyo, half a world and a culture away. Michael currently resides in Long Beach, NY, with his beautiful (and understanding) wife Vicki and their ridiculously cute daughter Torrance.

**Heather Dismore** is a veteran of both the restaurant and publishing industries. She has published works including such titles as "Indian Cooking For Dummies," part of the compilation *Cooking Around the World For Dummies All-In-One, The Parents' Success Guide to Organizing, The Parents' Success Guide to Managing a Household,* and *Low-Carb Dieting For Dummies,* all published by John Wiley and Sons. This is her fifth published work.

A graduate of DePauw University, she succumbed to the restaurant business in Denver, Colorado while applying to law school. She rapidly rose to management at such regional and national chains as The Italian Fisherman, Don Pablo's Mexican Kitchen, and Romano's Macaroni Grill. She orchestrated the openings of 15 new restaurants and developed the training, procedural, and purchasing systems that were used as the gold standard in numerous concepts throughout her tenure. She currently lives in Missouri with her husband, co-author Andrew Dismore, and their daughters who are her first loves, inspiration, and never-ending source of new material.

**Andrew G Dismore,** one of the catering industry's premier chefs, joined the food service marketing agency Noble & Associates in 2003 after amassing critical success and national recognition as Corporate Executive Chef/General Manager of Chicago's uber-posh Calihan Catering, Inc.

In a career spanning some 15 years, Dismore has amassed an expertise in the catering field few can rival. His experiences are a study in dramatic contrast. He has prepared seated dinners for over 10,000 guests, designed highly profitable operations that have fed over 200,000 diners in three weeks, overseen the execution of over 2,500 events annually, and directed the culinary operations for such mega-volume events as the Indianapolis 500, The Brickyard 400, The NCAA Final Four, The RCA Tennis Championships, and Formula One. He has participated in over 20 openings and has independently designed 12 new food service concepts. Yet he has catered intimate events for many of the world's social, political, and culinary elite.

**Carol Godsmark** was smitten by restaurants and their culture at an early age having moved from Canada, aged eight, to Europe where she lived in a Communist hotel for six months and chomped her way through goulash, schnitzels, and *kapr na cerno*, Christmas carp with black sauce. She later advanced to lighter, rather more fabulous food, as she travelled the world, eating in all styles of restaurants and seeking out local markets.

Chef and owner of a classical French-influenced restaurant in Sussex which has had entries in *The Good Food Guide*, *The Michelin Guide*, and has gained two AA Rosettes, self-taught Carol turned to journalism after returning to college. She somehow became a restaurant critic, chef interviewer, and food writer for national and regional newspapers and magazines, and a restaurant consultant and teacher. She returned full circle as a chef educator in Eastern Europe, updating Polish chefs on lighter-style cooking techniques. Revenge is sweet.

Her books include *Starting and Running a Catering Business* and *Starting and Running a Successful Gastropub and Brasserie.* She edits *Savour,* the Guild of Food Writers' publication. When not cooking for friends and family, she plays an erratic violin with an amateur London orchestra, sings with the Portsmouth Festival Choir, and is mad about film of any genre. She travels extensively, trying to winkle out the best, small, family-owned restaurants along the way, never tiring of the thrill of the chase, the bonhommie, shared meals, and the conviction that simple is often best. She lives in West Sussex.

# Authors' Acknowledgements

**Michael:** The crews I've worked with over the years, big and small, for standing together in the trenches. Jerry Brody for acting on a feeling and giving me an opportunity. Marlene Brody for continuing to give me opportunities. The night manager who chopped open the door that pointed to the future. Craig Harrison for being a kind and understanding chef while still kicking ass. Jonathan Young for taking the training wheels off and making me laugh whenever I fell (even now). Tracy Boggier, Mike Baker, and the Wiley staff for pushing us with a patient stick. Dave Mazzorana, a fine technical reviewer. Wine salespeople for walking the tightrope of keeping me up to date without nagging. My Mother for giving me my first *For Dummies* book. Hiro Nagano, Ai Ito, Ishii Hideo, Master Toda, and all of the WDI staff for showing me while I showed you. Mark Abrahamson for letting a cellar rat run with it. Don and Debbie Richter for keeping me behind the bar and adjusting on-the-fly. Austin Power for showing me how to have fun waiting tables. My co-authors for keeping me up at night and bringing back a lot of memories. My current staff for helping through another gut checking year. Vicki for leaving the light on so many nights.

**Heather:** A special thank you to Mike Baker, Project Editor Extraordinaire, who kept this project on track despite Murphy's Law, an influenza epidemic, and intercontinental communication challenges. And to everyone else at Wiley who made this book a success, including Diane Steele, Joyce Pepple, Kristin Cocks, Tracy Boggier, Tina Sims, Holly Gastineau-Grimes, Jennifer Ehrlich, Christy Beck, and many other behind-the-scenes folks in the editorial and production departments. Thanks for the opportunity to work with the best in the business. Thanks to Dave Mazzorana for a stellar technical review. Thanks for keeping us on our toes! Thanks to Mike Garvey, who managed to juggle writing this book, running a 500-seat restaurant, opening a new restaurant in another continent, and an NYC commute; just another day in the life. Finally, thanks to my incredible family for their patience and support during the never-ending writing schedule.

**Andrew:** Thanks to my family for your love, support, and much deserved kicks in the butt. I am truly grateful to all those that, without whom, I would never have made it out of the pantry: Chefs Dominic Menna, Scott Brittingham, Charlie Trotter, Dave Mazzorana, Todd Rogers, Frank Terry, Gabriel Viti, David Danielson, Mike Cansler, and the entire staff at Calihan. A very special thanks to Chef Tony Hanslits, whose tireless dedication to pure cuisine continues to be an inspiration. I especially need to thank Kurt Layer. You are the greatest caterer in the business. You will never know how much you taught me or how often I recognise it. Special thanks to Bob Noble, Judy Sipe, and everyone at Noble & Associates. I have never worked with a more driven, dedicated, and visionary group of professionals. I am truly honoured to be a small part of your team.

**Carol:** My heartfelt thanks to Jason Dunne of John Wiley who has been an inspiration and delight to work with and to Simon Bell, also part of the Wiley team, for his remarkable, erudite editing. Thanks also are due to family and friends who recognise the enthusiasm for this all-enveloping subject and who are more than happy to share in this, well, obsession.

## Publisher's Acknowledgments

We're proud of this book; please send us your comments through our Dummies online registration form located at www.dummies.com/register/.

Some of the people who helped bring this book to market include the following:

**Acquisitions, Editorial, and Media Development**

**Project Editor:** Simon Bell

**Commissioning Editor:** Jason Dunne

**Publisher:** Jason Dunne

**Executive Project Editor:** Daniel Mersey

**Cartoons:** Rich Tennant
(www.the5thwave.com)

**Composition Services**

**Project Coordinator:** Erin Smith

**Layout and Graphics:** Carl Byers, Rueben W. Davis, Alissa D. Ellet, Joyce Haughey, Melissa K. Jester, Ronald Terry, Christine Williams

**Proofreader:** Laura Albert

**Indexer:** Claudia Bourbeau

**Publishing and Editorial for Consumer Dummies**

    **Diane Graves Steele,** Vice President and Publisher, Consumer Dummies

    **Joyce Pepple,** Acquisitions Director, Consumer Dummies

    **Kristin A. Cocks,** Product Development Director, Consumer Dummies

    **Michael Spring,** Vice President and Publisher, Travel

    **Kelly Regan,** Editorial Director, Travel

**Publishing for Technology Dummies**

    **Andy Cummings,** Vice President and Publisher, Dummies Technology/General User

**Composition Services**

    **Gerry Fahey,** Vice President of Production Services

    **Debbie Stailey,** Director of Composition Services

# Contents at a Glance

# Table of Contents

# Introduction

*T*he restaurant business is an exciting one, full of challenges and opportunities. We're glad you're interested in finding out more about it, and you've definitely come to the right place to get started. Years ago, going out to eat was truly an event – reserved for weekends or special occasions. Today, however, even a Tuesday, just another day, can be an occasion to eat out, especially when busy careers and overloaded family schedules leave little time to cook. Fortunately, consumers have more restaurant choices than ever before. And opportunities in the industry have never been greater. This book can help you minimise the challenges and overcome the obstacles before they overcome you.

We've managed, worked, eaten, mopped floors, run bars, learned to repair equipment mid-shift on a Saturday night, hired, fired, trained, and checked stock in some of the best (and worst) restaurants in the world. We've worked in ultrafine dining, fast food, catering, and everything in between. We've worked dining rooms that sat 30 and catered events that fed 5,000 diners in a single day. Certainly, each of these situations is somewhat different, but many aspects of running a restaurant transcend restaurant size, location, or dining style and fall under the category of universal restaurant truths. We do our best to bring all that information to you in this book.

Whether you're a seasoned restaurant veteran or just out of catering college, we believe that if you're reading this book, you have the *desire* to run a restaurant. After reading it, you should know if you have a *passion* for it – or what we sometimes call The Sickness.

## About This Book

Success in the restaurant business is the dream of many and the achievement of a few. Often, would-be restaurateurs have misconceptions about what running a restaurant is really like. Some folks are quick to see the glitz and glamour without also having the opportunity to see the anxiety and effort that accompany it. Others have seen the business from the inside and are sure that they can do it better than the people they've worked for, without feeling the true weight and complexity of the tasks and decisions that face The Boss everyday. On the other side of the coin, you find people who could do very well in the restaurant business but stay out because of the horror stories they've heard.

We want you to see the full picture – the good, the bad, and the absurd – so that you can make an informed decision about your place in this business.

We wrote this book because no Ministry of Restaurant Operators exists to test your knowledge and skills on the open road to determine whether you have what it takes to get into the business. After you've read the pages between these gorgeous yellow and black covers, you'll have a good idea whether this is the racket for you – and the knowledge to get started on the right foot.

You can find plenty of books that tell you how to open a restaurant, but you won't find many about how to *keep* it open. This book does both. Why? Because even after opening day arrives, you can never stop improving your service, evaluating your product, scoping out the competition, or researching opportunities in the marketplace. Change is the only constant in the restaurant business. To succeed, you must anticipate and act on new trends, new pressures, and whatever else the market throws your way. The spoils go to those who see opportunities before they happen.

Please don't mistake our realism for cynicism. We want you to be in the business. But we're going to make sure that you have the information you need to be a success. We show you many everyday realities that people don't always consider, but should. We hope that you take the information and use it to be wildly successful. You can do this, but you have to look at this business the right way. If you do, save us a table!

# Conventions Used in This Book

To help you navigate through this book, we use the following conventions:

- *Italic* is used for emphasis and to highlight new words or terms that are defined.

- **Bold** text is used to indicate keywords in bulleted lists or the action part of numbered steps.

- `Monofont` is used for Web addresses.

- Sidebars, which look like text enclosed in a shaded grey box, consist of information that's interesting to know but not necessarily critical to your understanding of the chapter or section topic.

# *Foolish Assumptions*

Just as owners have to make assumptions about the customers who will be eating in their restaurants, authors have to make assumptions about their readers. If one or more of the following descriptions hits home, you've come to the right place.

- ✔ You're thinking about opening your own restaurant, and you want practical, how-to advice to accomplish your goals.
- ✔ You've worked in the business, and now you're thinking about getting in on the ownership or management end of things.
- ✔ You've never worked in a restaurant but you've met with success in other professional endeavours and possess skills that may be applicable to this business.
- ✔ You're fresh out of catering college and thinking about putting those skills to work in your own place.
- ✔ You buy every book that sports a yellow and black cover.
- ✔ You currently own or operate a restaurant, and you're seeking advice, tips, and suggestions to keep things running smoothly and successfully.

# *How This Book Is Organized*

This book is organised into five separate parts. Here's what's on the menu.

## *Part 1: Getting Started*

In this part, we give you a crash course in the business, including tips for getting started, understanding your options, creating your concept and picking your name. We help you research the marketplace to determine whether your concept has a shot at success, and provide information on how customers approach the buying decision. We include a detailed timeline from idea to grand opening to get you up and running. We also help you decide whether you have what it takes to make it in the business.

# Part II: Putting Your Plan in Motion

In this part, we focus on acting on your idea. We take you through the critical steps, like writing a business plan and getting financing. We work you through the ins and outs of finding the right location or making an existing location work for you. And we wrap it up by dotting some i's and crossing some t's, including help on getting the right permits and licences, getting up to speed on the law and the powers of your local authority, and legally protecting yourself, the right way.

# Part III: Preparing to Open the Doors

Here, we detail all the tasks you need to do to get up and running. We walk you through hiring and training your staff and developing your menu and beverage programme. We show you how to set up your kitchen and dining room for the best flow of food and people. We also give you concrete tips for purchasing and managing your inventory, which can take you a long way toward profitability. And finally, we cover two often-neglected areas of the business: operating your office and promoting your business.

# Part IV: Keeping Your Restaurant Running Smoothly

This part is for anyone running a restaurant today or tomorrow or considering doing it in the future. We show you how to maintain and build on your current operation, including tips for managing employees, keeping your diners coming back, and handling customer service situations. We explain how to keep your place spick-and-span and ensure food safety. We show you how to get great information about what your customers want. And finally, we wrap it up with a lesson in watching your numbers, with tips on what reports to run, how to analyse the numbers, and how to make changes to your business when necessary.

# Part V: The Part of Tens

Here, we dispel the common myths about running a restaurant. We give you resources to help you take the next steps when you're ready. And finally, we give you some of our favourite only-in-the-restaurant-business stories.

# Icons Used in This Book

Icons are the fancy little pictures in the margins of this book. Here's the guide to what they mean and what the icons look like:

The Tip icon marks ideas that can make your job a bit easier and help prevent problems from happening. The tips are often hands-on ways to improve your business today.

The Remember icon points out ideas that sum up and reinforce the concepts we discuss. In fact, if you're in a time crunch and can't read it all, you may want to go straight to this icon. It's your choice – read it as you see fit.

We use the Warning icon to alert you to potential pitfalls and to give you a heads-up on what mistakes to avoid. Pay particular attention when this fella rears his head.

Think of the Technical Stuff icon almost as bonus material. Usually, the info gives you some background about the subject that's not critical. We think it's interesting, so we include it, but you don't have to read it to get the ideas and concepts.

# Where to Go from Here

We think that you'll find the information in this book valuable enough that you'll want to read it all. Doing so provides you with a strong, general foundation for starting and running a restaurant.

But one of the great things about a *For Dummies* book (among the hundreds that we can count) is that you don't have to read it word for word, front to back, cover to cover. If you're more interested in one particular topic than another, that's fine. Check out the corresponding part, chapter, or section and read up on that issue. You can find out about it without first having read the information that precedes it – get-in-and-get-out convenience. Interested in tips to create or improve your menu? Turn to Chapter 9. Are you currently looking for a location to plant your new shop? Check out Chapter 7. Is sanitation your thing? Chapter 18 has your name written all over it.

You can jump around, start wherever you want, and finish when you feel like it. So tie on your apron and get going.

# Part I
# Getting Started

# In this part . . .

You're standing on square one. In the chapters that follow we introduce you to the business and help you determine if you have what it takes to make a go of it in the restaurant world. We give you the big picture, including a detailed timeline that takes you from today through to the day you open the doors of your place for the first time. We also help you nail down your concept, come up with a name, and start researching everything from your potential customers to the competition.

# Chapter 1

# Grasping the Basics of the Restaurant Business

*In This Chapter*

▶ Understanding the basics of the business

▶ Deciding whether you have the necessary skills

*R*estaurants are fun. Whether you stop by to celebrate a special occasion, grab a quick bite for lunch, meet friends for a drink, or pick up dinner for the family on the way home from work, the experience is usually enjoyable. (At the very least, it's more enjoyable than not eating or being forced to cook!.) Just about everyone associates restaurants with having a good time. If people didn't enjoy their experience, they wouldn't come back. So it's natural for people to think, 'I enjoy going to restaurants, so I may as well get paid to do what I enjoy – hang out in bars and eat at great restaurants'.

Living the restaurant life is fun. We've been doing it for many a year, and we love it. But the problem comes when people see only the fun and never the struggle. Viewed from the dining room or bar stool (or from the kitchen, the stockroom, or anywhere else other than the seat marked 'Proprietor'), it's difficult to see the 95 per cent of the picture that's pretty tough work. It's like wishing every day was Christmas and actually getting your wish. In the restaurant business, you have so much fun that you can hardly stand it. You get tired of wrapping the presents, preparing the mulled wine and checking that the elves are on time for their shifts, and if you have to look at any more roasted chestnuts, you'll die. The restaurant business quickly becomes more work than fun, so don't be fooled.

In this chapter, we take you on a quick tour of the business. We introduce you to all the work that you must do on paper before you can even think about picking up a pan or laying down a place setting. We move on to the physical preparations that will consume your every waking minute on the way to opening your doors. Then we remind you that the work has only begun after you first open your doors. Finally, we help you examine your motivations and expectations for pursuing your dream to determine if both are rooted in reality.

# Getting a Feel for the Restaurant World

The restaurant world is more than glitz and glamour. It's truly a business, and if you don't look at it that way, you won't succeed. Ultimately, being a restaurateur is being a manufacturer. You're producing a product (food) from raw materials (your ingredients) and selling it to a customer (your diner). You're competing with lots of other 'manufacturers' for that same diner. So you better do it better than the bloke across the road, or you'll be out of business.

## Laying the foundation

Sometimes the business of *the business* is hard for people to relate to. It's a hard concept for many people to get because your product isn't packaged in a box that sits on a shelf. Your product is packaged in many layers – including your exterior, your lobby, your staff's attire, the music playing, the aromas coming from the kitchen, the friendliness and knowledge of your staff, your silverware, your china, and your glassware. All these things make up your packaging, affect the costs of doing business, and affect your diner's decision to come in and, ultimately, to come back.

As with any business, the planning stage is crucial, and you have to survive it before you can enjoy any of the fun. Right off the bat, you have to create a timeline for getting your business up and running (see Chapter 2), develop your restaurant's theme and concept (see Chapter 3), research the market (see Chapter 4), develop a detailed business plan and use it to find and secure financing (see Chapters 5 and 6), and find the best location for your new restaurant and get the right licences and permits (see Chapters 7 and 8).

Buy your products at the right price and sell them at the right price. This simple tenet can make or break your business. Check out Chapter 14 for tips on getting the best price and look to Chapter 9 for pricing your food and beverage menus right from the start.

## Setting up shop (with a little help)

Depending on how new you are to the restaurant biz, you may need accountants, attorneys, contractors, and host of other characters, all at the ready and working with you at various stages of the project.

Hire an accountant early in the process of setting up your business. She can help you get your numbers together for your business plan, which is a must if you're trying to get financing for your venture. Chapters 5 and 6 can give you the details. After you're up and running, you'll analyse your monthly financial reports and look for ways to improve the numbers. A good accountant, preferably one with restaurant experience, can help.

When starting any new business, you'll need to review contracts, get premises and alcohol licences or maybe incorporate your business. Depending on how you set up your business, you may need to draft a partnership agreement or two. Before you sign franchise agreements or vendor contracts or sack your first employee, make sure that you're working with a good lawyer, who can help you with all these tasks and more. Watch for details in Chapter 8.

Most people starting a new restaurant, or taking over an existing one, change a few things (or a few hundred things) at their new location. Maybe you need to set up a new kitchen from scratch or improve the air flow of the hood over the cooker. Maybe you want to upgrade the plumbing or install air filtration in your bar. Contractors can save you lots of time and trouble. Don't hesitate to ask them questions and check their references.

Check out Chapters 10 through 12 for the low-down on designing your exterior, dining room, kitchen, and bar – with or without the help of contractors, designers, and architects. Interior designers and architects come in very handy around renovation and revamp time. Sometimes they can come in and give your place a face-lift for much less than you might imagine.

## *Welcoming the world to your restaurant*

All the hard work that's required to get to the point where you can open the doors will mean absolutely nothing if no one shows up. You have to start thinking about how to draw customers way before you open your doors (and every day after that). Develop your marketing plan based on what's special, unique, or different about your restaurant. Maybe it's the food, atmosphere, price, or value. Study your competition, watch what they're doing well (and not so well), and understand where you have the advantage.

Different groups respond to different messages. Decide what works for the diners you're going after. Check out Chapter 16 for details on telling the world about your place and getting them to beat a path to your door. After you get the customers in the seats, you have to keep them there. We've heard that you can't use handcuffs for some reason, so you do have to let them go and hope they come back. We want you to do more than hope. Chapter 19 gives you concrete tips for building your clientele and ensuring that most of them come back – and bring their friends.

To be successful in this or in any business, you need to take care of your business today, tomorrow, and years from now. Stay up on trends in your sector and the restaurant business as a whole. Watch for information about shifting dining preferences and behaviour in trade magazines, print publications, television news and magazine shows, the Internet, or anywhere else you get information. And always keep an eye on your competition. Don't copy them, but know what they're up to. See Chapter 4 for information on how to conduct a market analysis. And check out Chapter 20 for ways to maintain what you create, using feedback from financial analysis and operational reports.

# Discovering Whether You Have What It Takes

Culinary prowess, a charming personality, and an ability to smile for the cameras. That's about all you need Isn't it? Wrong. Take a step back. It takes much, much more to run a restaurant successfully. And that's what we all want: anyone can run a restaurant, but not everyone can run one well. (In fact, we should've titled this book, *Running a Restaurant Really Well For Dummies,* but the publisher wouldn't go for it.)

## Monitoring your motivations

This is a tough business, and if you want to succeed, you have to have the inner motivation the drive – to sustain you through all the downs that accompany the ups. This isn't a venture for the faint of heart. If you want to own a restaurant to have a place to hang out with your friends and get free drinks, we say pay the bar bill and avoid the hassles.

The first thing you need to do, before you invest any additional time or money in this venture (besides buying and reading this book, of course), is to examine and understand the factors that motivate you. Be honest with yourself.

There are lots of great reasons to want to run a restaurant. Here are a few of our favourites:

- ✔ You love an ever-changing work environment.
- ✔ You love taking on a challenge.
- ✔ You're passionate about the business.
- ✔ You have a passion for food.
- ✔ You hate having any free time (including the holidays).
- ✔ You're continuing the family tradition.

And the following list contains a few reasons that should send up a red flag in your mind:

✔ You think it will be fun.

✔ You want to be a celebrity chef.

✔ You want a place to hang out.

✔ If Gordon Ramsay can do it, so can you.

✔ You're tired of having a 'real' job.

✔ You've always wanted to run a restaurant after you retire.

If one or more of these reasons sounds familiar, don't be completely discouraged. Just make sure that motivations such as these aren't your only, or even your primary, reasons for wanting to get into the business. And do some further investigation before making the financial, personal, and professional commitment to the business.

## *Evaluating your expectations*

Running a restaurant, either yours or someone else's, is a huge commitment. It requires long hours, constant vigilance, and the ability to control potentially chaotic situations – on a daily basis.

Running a restaurant shouldn't be a leap of faith. You need to go into this with your eyes open. Just as we suggest that you carefully consider your motivations (see the 'Monitoring your motivations' section, earlier in the chapter), you also need to make sure that your expectations are firmly planted in reality.

Take out a pen and some paper. Divide the paper into two columns. In the first, list all of your expectations for the future business. From the profits you expect, to the lifestyle you hope those profits will support, to newspaper reviews or the customer views you hope to elicit, list it all. This is your chance to put your dreams on paper. Then, in the second column, write down what you expect out of yourself to make this thing happen – your contribution in terms of time and money, sacrifices you'll have to make, and anything else that you can think of.

Then it's time to determine whether the expectations on your lists reflect the reality of the situation. Reading this book is a great place to start – this book is a balanced look at the joys and pains of running a restaurant. (If you want an instant reality check, skip over to Chapter 21, where we confront ten common myths.) But don't stop there. As we state in Chapter 2, you have to start researching every aspect of the business on Day 1, and you don't get to stop until you close your doors for the very last time. So you may as well start now. Minimise the mystery by getting out in the restaurant world – talk to owners, managers, waiters, and suppliers about their experiences and what you can expect. (Chapter 22 provides you with additional industry resources that you can consult.)

# Tracking key traits

Based on our experience in the restaurant business, successful restaurateurs exhibit a few common traits. We list them below. Don't worry if you possess more of some traits than others. Just being aware of them is a great step toward making them all part of your world and succeeding in the business.

### Business sense

This is probably the single most important trait. For all that the restaurant business is, it's still basically a business, subject to the same pressures as any other. Keep that thought in mind going into your arrangement. If you don't, you'll be hard-pressed to succeed. Skills that you've learned, developed, and honed in the real world can apply in this business, like buying skillfully, managing tactfully, and negotiating shrewdly. But many different facets of this business are tough to pick up.

### Tolerance

The ability to keep your cool under pressure, thrive in chaos, and handle multiple points of view and personalities will serve you well in the business. Whether you're dealing with customers, employees, suppliers, changing trends, or a fickle clientele, you have to develop a thick skin. The inherent stress of the restaurant makes for short fuses. Your job is to dampen those tempers, smooth the rocky waters, and calm the storm.

### Flexibility

The environment changes from minute to minute. You have to be able to adjust and think on your feet. You have to have a good balance of process- and product-motivated people. Process-motivated people micromanage what's going on in their organisation. Product-minded people focus on the end result. Sometimes you'll wear both hats.

### Creativity

Infuse creativity into every facet of your business from how you approach your customers and your food, to how you promote your business. That creativity affects how your business performs.

### Positive energy

Whenever you're in the restaurant, you have to be 'on' – all the time. Restaurants that have a positive vibe are the ones that make it. Positive energy is *the* differentiating factor, as intangible as it is, between the winners and the losers in this business. And your restaurant can't have it if you don't.

### Ability to hold (or hold off) alcohol

Coveted by many, achieved by few, the ability to handle drink has been the downfall (physically, financially, and spiritually) of many a restaurateur. Per capita, no industry drinks more than the restaurant business. For some people, managing a restaurant is like getting the keys to the grown-up sweet shop, and the temptation is too much to resist. As a restaurateur, you often drink as part of your job. No matter what the circumstances, you still have to count the money at the end of the night, or you have to be ready to go first thing in the morning.

### Leadership skills

**Restaurateur** /REST-o-ra-tor/: n. doctor, babysitter, marriage counsellor, parent, mediator, conscience, seer, sage. *See Winston Churchill,* Gandhi*, et al.*

Being a leader in this industry is being able to balance an entire range of different management approaches, knowing when to lead by example, and knowing when to give the troops their marching orders. Most importantly, a successful restaurant leader is able to find her own leadership style and deal with employees fairly, consistently, and with respect.

### Schmoozability

People like to feel important. They want to be part of the inner circle of the restaurant, no matter how large that circle may be. It's cool to say, 'I know the manager' or 'The chef's a friend of mine.' Nothing gets return business like calling a diner by name. That's why you put up with the pictures of grandchildren, whines about their big project at work, or not-so-interesting travel tales. Always make the customer feel welcome, at home, and at ease. Turning a good mood into a bad one is incredibly easy. Turning a bad mood into a good mood is exponentially more difficult.

### Passion

We call it The Sickness. To succeed, you have to have it. Running a restaurant is a business that eventually chooses you; you ultimately can't choose it. If you don't have passion for the business, you can't sustain, maintain, and overcome the obstacles that crop up.

You can't teach it or learn it; you have to feel it. If you don't have the passion, your task of becoming successful will be exponentially harder. You have to connect *everything* to your passion. You have to get waiting staff enthused and passionate, because they're selling your vision to the customers. You have to get kitchen staff buzzing, because they're working on a tough schedule, without the natural excitement of a restaurant full of people. You have to get the kitchen porters psyched about cleaning the dishes, because the dishes frame the experience for the customer. Diners should experience a buildup of expectation for their experience from the first time they come into contact with anyone from the restaurant (whether on the phone, in person, or online). Imagine doing all that without a passion for your restaurant, and you see why passion is mandatory.

### Presence

Being there day in and day out has no substitute. Absentee landlords need not apply. Just stopping in to say hello or giving off an aura that you know what's up ultimately won't allow you to run the restaurant. If you're not there, those who are there in your stead will be the de facto rulers, and it won't be the same. If you're not physically present in the building most of the time, the schmoozing, the energy, the passion, and so on can't get to your staff and ultimately to your diners. You can't positively impact your restaurant if you're not there.

# Chapter 2

# Getting Everything Done before Your Grand Opening

*In This Chapter*

▶ Setting up your overall timing

▶ Checking things off your master to-do list

*I*n this chapter, we help you plan for your restaurant's opening with a time-line of all the tasks you need to accomplish and track before you serve your first meal. Everything on the list is covered in detail in this book, so we include lots of references. From writing your business plan to opening the doors to the public, if it happens in the start-up cycle of a restaurant, it's on this list.

Every restaurant is different, so every opening-timing varies. Even if you're part of a chain, your timing may be different from another unit's based on what side of the street you're on. This list is a guide. Check with local govern-mental and regulatory offices to determine how long it takes to get the paper-work you need to open the kind of restaurant you want, keeping in mind that the processing time may be longer than quoted. And if we include things that don't apply to your restaurant, feel free to ignore them.

## Working Out How Much Time You Need

Early in the planning stages, you may need to adjust your timing and go with the flow, accepting the fact that timing isn't always set in stone. For example, you may not need to have your business plan completed nine months before your opening if you're taking over an existing, established restaurant and don't want to make any changes. But, as you get closer to opening day, create and stick to a firm schedule to get everything completed on time.

If you're terrible at keeping to timing, add some extra time your schedule. This approach is similar to setting your own clocks 15 minutes ahead to be on time. But in this case, time is money. If you hire the chef a month earlier than scheduled, it's an additional expense you'll absorb before you're even open. You may have a very good reason, and it may be the right thing to do. Just be sure to factor the time and money adjustments into your schedule and expense projections.

In the checklist that follows, we group together similar tasks at each time interval. Use these categories to stay organised and eventually to delegate to the person who will handle the functions permanently. Here's the list of categories we use, shown in the order they appear in each time interval:

- ✔ **Administration:** Administration tasks include paperwork, phone calls, planning activities, and so on.

- ✔ **Construction:** Construction tasks consist of work related to designing and building your restaurant.

- ✔ **Human resources:** Human resources tasks involve hiring, training, or managing your employees.

- ✔ **Buying:** Buying tasks include choosing equipment, supplies, and just about anything else your restaurant needs to get up and running.

- ✔ **Front of the house (FOH):** This term refers to any place a diner can be in your restaurant, including the dining room, toilets and bar area. Tasks under this heading include organising your bar, setting your dining room tables, creating and maintaining a floor plan, taking reservations, establishing your hours of operation, and all forms of customer service.

- ✔ **Back of the house (BOH):** This term refers to any place a diner can't be, including the kitchen, storage areas, the delivery entrance, the employee personal belongings area, and the managers' office. BOH tasks include cooking, setting up a cleaning programme, organising your storeroom, and placing and receiving your first food orders.

- ✔ **Advertising and promotion:** This category includes any publicity, advertising, and public relations duties you should do.

- ✔ **Research:** Research is ongoing and forever. We list ideas to help you stay competitive and to reform and refresh your plans as you go along.

# *T-Minus One Year or More*

Here's your chance to create the business you've always dreamed of. Use this time early in your schedule to thoroughly research your ideas, talk about and write down your concept and vision, and put together a comprehensive plan for achieving it. Network with other restaurateurs and talk to everyone and anyone about the business, but keep the details of your plan (like your restaurant's name, menu specifics, and key points of difference) close to your chest. The first thing on your to-do list is one of the most important:

❑ Buy a copy of *Running a Restaurant For Dummies.* Use Chapter 1 to consider whether you have what it takes (and want to put forth the effort) to succeed in this business before you invest the time and money.

### Administration

❑ Write a detailed and professional business plan. See Chapter 5 for all the forms and lists you'll ever need.

❑ Develop and write down your vision for the restaurant's physical layout, both the interior and exterior. The more detailed it is now, the better you can communicate it to designers, architects, and your general contractor as needed. Take a look at Chapters 10 through 12 for information on the physical layout of your restaurant.

❑ Develop your logos, trademarks, and brand identity. Chapter 3 helps you narrow down your theme and concept.

❑ Put together your team of advisers, including an accountant, solicitor, estate agent, designers, partners, and so on. See Chapter 8.

❑ Join trade organisations or local business organisations. Chapter 22 contains resources. to help you.

❑ Check with the local governing agencies to confirm the timing of your applications for your permits and licences, especially your alcohol licence, if you need one. See Chapter 8 for details on how (and where) to get started.

### Research

❑ Formalise your process for conducting market, trend, and competitive research. See Chapter 4.

From this point forward, you have to continuously perform market, trend, and competitive research.

❑ Get a job. If you've never worked in a restaurant, now's the time to get started. Get a job doing whatever anyone will hire you to do, either in the kitchen or the dining room, and learn everything that you can. (We've done just about every job a restaurant can offer, including the less glamorous ones – taking out the rubbish, cleaning greasy ovens, cleaning toilets, shovelling snow, and the ever-popular dishwashing.) Any experience in the business is better than none. Use this time to look at how other people run their restaurants. Make lists of things you'd do differently and note things you'd like to implement in your place.

# T-Minus Nine Months

At the nine months and counting mark, you should have your business plan in hand and be shopping for money. You can also begin researching specifics for your business, such as looking at prospective locations and researching your computer systems.

### Administration

❑ Start meeting potential investors. Explain your concept, business plan, and financial forecasts. Check out Chapter 6 for more information.

### Research

❑ Shop for a location. See Chapter 7.

❑ Start researching point-of-sale (POS) systems. Much more than a simple cash register, a POS system can help you track and analyse just about any type of data you can think of. Check out Chapter 15.

# T-Minus Seven Months

Around this time, your plan starts to become reality. Finalise your choice for a location and sign your lease. Get your money together and set up your bank accounts, credit card processor, and develop your other financial systems.

### Administration

❑ Sign a deal with the landlord. But take a look at the chapters in Part II and Chapters 10 to 12 first to make sure that the location meets all your objectives and requirements for your concept and sales projections.

❑ Finalise your financing. Skip to Chapter 6 for the full story.

❑ Set up business bank accounts to pay deposits, rent office space, and deposit your investors' money. See Chapters 6 and 15 for help.

❑ Decide how you get cash from the restaurant to your account. You may wish to use a security company or make daily deposits yourself.

❑ Establish a plan for regular financial reporting. Create the reports you'll use on a regular basis, such as an income statement and Cost of Goods Sold report. Check out Chapter 20 for what numbers to watch and why.

### Research

❏ Research credit card processing systems. Kindly turn to Chapter 15.

❏ Check out payroll companies. Weigh your options for contracting with a company or doing it yourself. Chapter 15 can get you started.

# T-Minus Six Months

Your biggest task at this point is to get – and stay – organised. Get your permits, licenses, and other legalities straightened out. Set up your temporary base of operations. And do your homework to figure out what equipment you need and whom you should buy it from.

### Administration

❏ Set up water, electricity, gas, and other required utilities. Make sure that the billing is set up and the utilities are on *before* construction begins.

❏ Complete paperwork for permits and licences. Figure out which permits your contractor will handle and which you must apply for on your own.

You may have to apply for your alcohol licence even sooner, especially if your concept depends on it. You'll need the restaurant's permanent address. If you change locations, you'll likely need to reapply for your licence. Check out Chapter 8 for details.

❏ Set up your temporary office space. Use a space in your restaurant that's away from the construction noise or work out of your home or even a caravan outside the restaurant while it's under construction. You need a space with electricity, lights, some form of climate control, desk space, a land-based phone line, and Internet access.

Get a fax machine for exchanging plans with architects and designers and other documents, such as specifications for equipment and CVs from management candidates. If you don't have a computer, get one. It's essential for doing research, ordering, creating your manuals, and developing your menu. Chapter 15 has info on equipping your office.

### Construction

❏ Interview your-builder candidates. Check out Chapters 10 and 11 for information on working with a builder and architect.

Make sure that you give your builder your full specifications and your schedule. Make him or her commit to a detailed schedule in writing to confirm a completion date, with a financial penalty attached for not meeting the deadline.

❑ Meet with your kitchen and interior designers. Give them a tour of the rough space and discuss your ideas for final changes. Chapters 10 through 12 are your source for additional info.

We say 'final changes' but realise that circumstances can arise that require changes later in the process. At this point the plans should be as close to final as they can be.

❑ Review your kitchen layout to make sure it fits your actual space. Take a peek at Chapter 11 for great ideas on ensuring an excellent kitchen flow and planning adequate storage.

❑ Review your dining room layout to make sure it fits your actual space. Chapter 10 gives you excellent hands-on advice for creating a dining room that flows well and captures the atmosphere you're striving for.

❑ Review your exterior requirements to make sure they fit your actual space. Sneak a peek at Chapter 10 for the lowdown on the exterior.

### Purchasing

❑ Start researching equipment suppliers and sourcing equipment. Consider new versus used equipment, and buying versus leasing options. You have to know your menu mix (see Chapter 9) to ensure your equipment provides enough capacity for your needs. It may seem early, but doing this step now is important, especially if any equipment needs to be special ordered or customised for your space. Do you need a chef? If you've done your homework and you know what you're doing, involving a chef may not be necessary. If you don't feel comfortable taking this step alone, consider bringing your chef or a consultant on earlier to help with this and other BOH functions. Take a look at Chapter 13.

# T-Minus Five Months

Building begins on your new site! Interview candidates for your key positions, such as your general manager (GM) and your chef, assuming that you're not either or both of them. Use any available time to work on manuals, job descriptions, and anything else you can get out of the way early.

### Building

❑ Begin building. This schedule may be too soon or too late, depending on your operation. Take a look at Chapters 10 and 11 for more tips on working with contractors.

❑ Make sure that you and your contractor are still on the same page regarding the concept, design, and schedule and that anyone else involved with the process (such as designers) share your thoughts.

### Human resources

❏ Interview general manager and chef candidates. Flip to Chapter 13.

❏ Develop job descriptions, pay rates, and benefits packages. Take a look at Chapter 17 for help.

### Purchasing

❏ Order your kitchen equipment.

This stage is a great opportunity to get to know your business from the ground up. Don't pass it up by giving it all away to your chef. If you need help, definitely tap him as a resource, but stay actively involved. Know what you're buying and why. Look at Chapter 11 for details.

❏ Order your tables, chairs, and fixtures. Specify delivery for 30 days before opening. This schedule gives you time to allow for shipping and delivery delays. Review Chapter 10 for dining room layout and design.

❏ Purchase a POS (point of sale) system.

### Research

❏ Research your drinks list. Take a look at Chapter 12.

❏ Investigate phone systems and phone service companies. All systems are not created equal. Check out Chapter 15 before making your selection.

# T-Minus Four Months

Building is well under way. Use this time to work on employee and operational manuals and create your drinks list. Check out the sidebar 'Things to do in your free time' in this chapter to find things that you can complete now to save yourself time later.

### Construction

❏ Check in with your builder to make sure that building is proceeding according to schedule.

❏ Finalise exterior construction.

### Human resources

❏ Create employee and operational manuals. Spend some time in Chapters 13 and 17 for some direction on what to include in your manuals.

❏ Finalise job descriptions and pay rates. Chapter 13 can help.

### FOH

❑ Finalise your drinks list. Create a drinks menu. Chapter 12 can help you with the details.

❑ Finalise your hours of operation. Do so before you hire your staff so they can coordinate their lives outside work with the restaurant's opening hours.

### Research

❑ Research pest control companies. Set up a regular schedule for treatment once you're up and running. Take a look at Chapter 18 for staying on top of your hygiene programme.

# T-Minus Three Months

Ideally kitchen construction is finished, and you can get a jump-start on cleaning it and placing equipment. If you haven't hired your general manager and chef by the end of the third month till opening, you'll definitely be behind. Delegate duties to your new managers, when possible. It's a great way to see how they work first hand. Taste and test the menu to make the final selection. Firm up your drinks menu and start interviewing suppliers.

### Administration

❑ Activate the phone lines in your restaurant. You may choose to do this later in the month, especially if you have office space somewhere else. Just make sure that your phone numbers are set and the lines are up and running when you're ready to begin pre-booking parties and accepting reservations. Choose an on-hold message. Chapter 15 gives you a great checklist for selecting all the features of your future phone system.

### Construction

❑ Your kitchen construction should be in progress.

❑ Review your final kitchen layout, including the eventual placement of all equipment. Look to Chapter 11 for tips.

❑ Dining room construction may be continuing. Check out Chapter 10.

Don't install your FOH floor until the end of construction. Putting off the installation until as late as possible in your construction cycle minimises construction-related dirt and damage. If people are wheeling heavy equipment through your dining room or banquet room, you may be able to save yourself some hard-core wear and tear. But you probably want to have the floor finished before you set up the tables and chairs. They're a huge pain to move while your flooring is being laid.

### Human resources

❏ Employ your general manager and your chef (if they're not you).

❏ Start training your general manager and chef. Bring them up to speed on your plans and your progress. Set up your expectations for the rest of the start-up period and for the regular business period.

❏ Review CVs for supervisors and managers.

### Purchasing

❏ Start sourcing food and drink suppliers. Check out Chapter 14 for tips on negotiating the best deals and working out what you need.

❏ Order printed supplies.

### FOH

❏ Review your drinks programme. Take a look at Chapter 12 for details.

❏ Develop your reservation system. Investigate online systems, phone systems, and computerised systems. Check out Chapter 10 for help.

❏ Start up your reservation system.

### BOH

❏ Review final kitchen layout, including eventual placement of all equipment. Chapter 11 is a great resource if you need help.

❏ Test recipes. Review Chapter 9 for help tweaking and cutting.

### Advertising and promotion

❏ Begin pre-selling banquets, parties, and VIP functions. Make sure the phone numbers and reservation methods are in place.

If you're going to take early reservations, make sure that you're open when you say you will be.

❏ Revise the advertising and promotion plan you developed for your business plan. Work with a public relations firm as appropriate. Check out Chapters 16 and 19 for info on advertising and building a clientele.

### Research

❏ Research your music options.

# T-Minus Two Months

It's time to turn your attention to hiring your staff. At two months, create your plans for hiring, training, scheduling, and retaining your new team. Your menu should be set at this point. Hopefully, you have your alcohol licence in hand. You should also be working on any purchasing tools, like ordering procedures and forms, that you'll use after you're up and running.

### Administration

❑ Make the final menu adjustments. See Chapter 9.

❑ Approve the opening menu items.

❑ Approve your menu design, layout, and fonts. Consult Chapter 9 to help you decide whether to print the menu on your own or outsource it.

❑ Follow up on any outstanding permits or licences. Check out Chapter 8 for info on licences, and other legalities.

❑ Commission someone to create your Web site. Consider implementing an online reservation system, online ordering, and e-mail. Even if you can't support the cost for all features right away, make sure that your Web site is flexible and can handle changes when you're able to add them. Look at Chapter 16 for more info on inviting the world to your new place.

❑ Finalise your music programme.

❑ Finalise your operational manuals. Chapter 13 shows you how.

❑ Set up your rubbish services recycling, and pest control services.

### Construction

❑ All FOH areas should be completed at this time.

❑ Your kitchen construction should be complete.

### Human resources

❑ Hire any other supervisors or managers.

❑ Create a blank interviewing roster for both the FOH and BOH. Look to Chapter 13 for details on the hiring process.

❑ Schedule times and dates for these hiring milestones:

  • Initial interview

  • Second interview

  • Hiring

  • Orientation

❑ Create a training schedule, including these specific training sessions:

- Steps of service (what you do when a guest sits down, when you offer bread, or how you present the menu)

- Product training (menu, drinks, concept, and so on)

- POS

- Menu tastings

- Equipment training (dishwasher, food processor, slicer, coffee and espresso machine, and any other equipment you have)

Coordinate BOH and FOH job-specific training. Both teams should train on similar concepts at the same time. When you have your menu tasting, your kitchen should already be able to cook the food, and your waiting staff should have an understanding of what your concept is. When it's time for your dry runs, everyone should be on the same hymn sheet. If the kitchen is ready but you haven't hired your waiting staff, you've wasted kitchen time.

❑ Finalise employee manuals. Chapter 13 is a great resource.

❑ Coordinate outside as necessary such as your payroll company if appropriate

### Product buying

❑ Create buying sheets with exact specifications of all products. Chapter 14 can give you a head start on buying.

❑ Review all printed materials, trademarks, and proprietary marks. Approve the specifications on all signage, business cards, menus, advertising, takeaway bags and containers and your letterhead. (Chapter 8 contains trademark advice.)

❑ Finalise all purchasing agreements with suppliers.

❑ Work with BOH to finalise smallwares order list and quantities.

❑ Create your purchasing manual.

❑ Create your purchase order for linen.

### FOH

❑ Develop your floor plan (sections, table numbers, and section sizes). Chapter 10 can help you coordinate your furniture, your new dining layout, and your required sales projections to opt for the best setup.

### BOH

❑ Finalise your small order list and quantities. See Chapter 11.

### *Advertising and promotion*

❏ Finalise your campaign. Look at Chapter 16 for help.

❏ Finalise plans for your pre-opening party. Create a guest list and invitations for your pre-opening party.

❏ Provide tours to groups such as businesses in the area, corporate clients you're courting, and other VIPs. Tours can help you book and pre-sell banquets and can also give a kick-start to sales of gift certificates.

# T-Minus Six Weeks

Use this time to make sure that you have all the paperwork, training materials, and schedules ready when your prospective employees walk through the door. Set the expectation that you run a professional, organised, and well-run business and that you expect nothing less from them.

### *Construction*

❏ Create a snagging list of unfinished items that must be completed before opening.

### *Human resources*

❏ Print and collate your final employee manual.

❏ Make sure that you have all hiring paperwork in house, including applications, uniform agreements, emergency contact cards, training materials, and so on. Check out Chapter 13 for the details.

### *FOH*

❏ Finalise your opening floor plan (including sections, table numbers, and section sizes).

❏ Review FOH controls for maintaining optimum inventory levels while maximising cash flow, and for minimising your risk of theft. Take a look at Chapter 14 to get the full story.

# T-Minus Thirty Days

The last month is a hectic one. You clean every square inch of your new restaurant. You set it up exactly the way you want it to look. Take pictures because you'll be setting the standard for how both the BOH and FOH should look before and after every single shift. You hire and train most of your opening staff during this mad time, so make sure that you've set up your interviewing and hiring systems in the weeks beforehand to minimise the chaos and maximise the information transfer.

### Building

❏ Follow up on outstanding snagging list concerns.

### Human resources

❏ Start the hiring process for general employees. Place your ad and set up interviews at your location. Chapter 13 guides you through the process of hiring and training your employees.

❏ Hire new employees.

❏ Begin training new employees.

❏ Set up new employee files.

❏ Add new employees to the payroll systems.

### Supply buying

❏ Place food order for delivery two to three weeks before your opening. Coordinate the delivery so that you have time to train employees on food prep and menu tastings. See Chapter 14 for tips on buying right.

### FOH

❏ Thoroughly clean all FOH spaces, including toilets, dining rooms, the entrance hall and the bar to get rid of any lingering building dust and dirt.

❏ Set up all furniture and fixtures.

❏ Set up the managers' office. Check out Chapter 15.

❏ Finalise the table settings. See Chapter 10 for more info.

### BOH

❏ Run a final test of all equipment (assembled as it comes in).

❏ Clean the kitchen, storerooms, and refrigeration to get rid of any lingering building dust and dirt. Chapter 18 covers your hygiene system.

❏ Unpack, wash, and store all small pieces of equipment.

❏ Set up all storerooms. See Chapter 14 for tips on setting up your storerooms to keep the flow of inventory moving smoothly.

### Advertising and promotion

❏ Get your signage in place.

❏ Send invitations for your pre-opening party.

❏ Continue to provide tours to groups, like businesses in the area, corporate clients you're courting, and other VIPs. Tours can help you book and pre-sell banquets and kick-start gift-certificate sales.

# T-Minus Ten Days

More of the same. You may be "just" the project manager at this point, overseeing the schedule to make sure that everyone is doing his or her job (rather than doing any of the jobs yourself). All employees should be hired by this point. Engage your staff's help in setting up your bar and assembling your menus. Continue to train and test your staff to make sure that they know your menu and processes in time for opening day.

### Construction

❏ Follow up on outstanding snagging list concerns.

### Human resources

❏ Continue setting up new employee files.

❏ Continue adding new employees to the payroll systems.

❏ Continue training and testing employees on products, processes, and procedures. Test all FOH employees on menu knowledge, steps of service, table numbers, and so on, and test all BOH employees on station-specific menu items, station setup and tear down, and sanitation.

### Buying

❏ Place your drinks order.

### FOH

❏ Receive your drinks order.

❏ Set up your bar.

❏ Print and collate your final menu.

# T-Minus One Week

The one-week-and-counting milestone marks the time when you want to have your restaurant completely assembled and in working order. Employees should be tasting the menu by this time and should be able to identify all dishes on sight. Each section cook should know the ins and outs of his station. All FOH employees should be role-playing and practicing mock service.

### *Construction*

❑ Follow up on outstanding snagging list concerns.

### *Human resources*

❑ Continue training. Look at Chapter 13 for tips.

❑ Continue menu tastings. Chapter 17 gives great ideas for selling your employees on your restaurant. Start a tradition of tasting every dish and continue it as you change or add items to the menu.

❑ Work on mock service. *Mock service* lets staff wait on 'guests' (other training employees), go through the steps of service, and practise fielding menu questions. Just like athletes actually practise how they want to play, you want your team to take this seriously and understand your systems and processes. You'll add real guests and real food very soon, so go through the drill to start working out the kinks.

❑ Continue setting up new employee files.

❑ Continue adding new employees to the payroll systems.

# T-Minus Three Days

In the past four days, you've been focusing on developing your staff. Now it's time to see how they fare in an almost-like-real-life-scenario, the trial run.

### *Building*

❑ Follow up on outstanding snagging list concerns.

### *Human resources*

❑ Continue setting up new employee files.

❑ Continue adding new employees to the payroll systems.

❑ Conduct your first *trial run*. Some people call them *dry runs, soft openings*, or a host of other names. Before you open, invite employees' families, friends, investors, advisers, consultants, and others to eat in the restaurant. Treat them just like regular diners. They order off the menu, and the kitchen prepares the orders. Everything is the same as a real dinner shift, except the customers aren't paying. This is a chance to go through a practice shift and see how everything works together. You'll probably have a few things to iron out between your trial run and opening day, which is why you do it. Every restaurant should do at least one dry run, but do as many as you can afford to schedule in terms of time and money. Trial runs aren't cheap, but they're well worth doing.

---

## Things to do in your free time

Okay, we know free time in this business is a contradiction in terms. Some tasks associated with opening a restaurant can really be done earlier or later in the process, depending on when you have time. It's simply a matter of choice. Consider getting some of these out of the way early. Your to-do list can quickly become unmanageable if you leave them all until the last couple of months.

✔ Develop your drinks list.

✔ Set up your training schedule. You probably can't know that on March 23 next year you'll be doing drinks training. But you can develop rough estimates and outlines for what new employees should do on Day 1, Day 2, Day 10, and so on.

✔ Establish your internal control mechanisms, such as procedures for cash handling, ordering, requisition, and receiving.

✔ Set up your credit card agreements.

✔ Figure out how you're going to get your money into your account. Are you going to schedule a security company to collect your money or deposit it yourself everyday?

✔ Develop your preferred reporting systems. Develop your specific income statement format. Create your cost of goods sold report. See Chapter 20 for tips on which reports to use to evaluate your business.

✔ Research your music programme.

✔ Develop your reservation system. Check out Chapter 10 for help.

✔ Interview pest control companies. They're one of those unmentionable necessities.

✔ Investigate phone companies and phone systems. Check out Chapter 15 for can't-miss tips.

✔ Research printers for letterhead, advertising or promotional materials, matches, napkins, and anything else you'd like to print with your logo.

✔ Develop your employee manual.

✔ Write job descriptions and establish pay rates for each type of job.

✔ Pick your payroll company unless you're doing it yourself.

# T-Minus One Day

Hopefully, you're having a fairly relaxed day. You may have your pre-opening party tonight, but your to-do list should be under control at this point.

### Building

❏ Follow up on outstanding snagging list concerns.

### Human resources

❏ Continue setting up new employee files.

❏ Continue adding new employees to the payroll systems.

# Chapter 3

# Deciding What Kind of Restaurant to Run

*In This Chapter*

▶ Working out where to begin

▶ Picking the right restaurant for you

▶ Selecting your concept and restaurant name

*I*f you're thinking about getting into this business, and you're like most people, you probably have an idea of what kind of restaurant you want to run, and you're looking for a way to get started. But before you run out and print your menus, think about your options. Better yet, take your time and research your options to set up the best plan for you and your restaurant.

In this chapter, we show you different ways you can get your business started, and give you some pros and cons for each. We walk you through the different styles of services you can offer. Finally, we help you finalise the theme and concept for your new restaurant. Your concept ultimately shapes all your research, planning, and design, so spend some time developing it.

## Working Out Where to Start

For most restaurants, you have several possible starting points, including going with a franchise, taking over an existing restaurant, or starting from scratch. We give you the pros and cons of each in the following sections.

# Buying into a franchise

In the restaurant business, buying a franchise is buying a licence to sell a restaurant's food and use its brand, logos, and name. McDonald's Burger King, and KFC are examples of restaurants often sold as franchises. The company who sells its franchises is called a *franchiser*.

Not all chains are franchises, but all franchises are chains. A *chain* of restaurants simply means that there are more than one just like it. Many chains, such as Wagamama's, Starbucks, and Hard Rock Cafe, are chains all owned by a parent company, not by independent *franchisees,* people or companies who buy into a franchise. The terms *chain* and *franchise* aren't synonymous.

Buying into the franchise is the closest thing there is to a 'sure thing' in the risky restaurant business. The pros of buying into a franchise are:

- ✔ They typically have a proven track record and have worked out the difficulties.

- ✔ Franchises have a consistent product, a set menu, huge brand recognition, and a built-in customer loyalty.

- ✔ Franchises help you with marketing, realistic sales projections, market research, and market analysis.

- ✔ You get a jump-start on all human resources (HR) and administrative issues, because franchises come equipped with all their own forms, policies, and scheduling philosophies.

As good as all that sounds, most of the cons of buying into a franchise are closely associated with the pros:

- ✔ You have to pay franchisers hefty set-up fees and significant franchise fees monthly, usually a percentage of sales.

- ✔ You have to follow their rules, meet their numbers, and serve their menu. If you're the creative type, the franchise mould may be the wrong size or shape for you. Love it or hate it, when people see the golden arches, they know what to expect, and they don't want you messing with it.

- ✔ Because franchises are fairly lucrative, franchisers are very selective about whom they franchise to. Often you have to have a significant amount of money to invest and agree to open multiple units.

## Taking over an existing restaurant

You may have an opportunity to take over an existing business, either one you've been a part of or one that you're completely new to. Maybe your boss wants to sell and you would like to buy the business. Maybe you're walking by and see a For Sale sign in the window of your favourite restaurant.

The primary positive and negative aspects of taking over an existing restaurant are relatively straightforward, but it all boils down to discerning the owner's motivation for selling.

- ✔ If the restaurant is relatively successful and the owner is retiring or moving, or has health concerns, taking over may be a head start. It presents you with instant client base that you can build upon.

- ✔ Often, though, restaurants are sold for reasons that paint a much bleaker picture of future success. The owner may be trying to pass along a loss-making enterprise.

Your job is to work out which of these scenarios is more likely. Before signing on the dotted line, work your way through the following list:

- ✔ Ask to see the books and get the full financial picture at an early stage. Chapters 5 and 20 cover what numbers to look at and information to gather.

- ✔ Find out the history of the space *and* the current concept. Just knowing it was a restaurant isn't enough. If it was a shop before that, why did it stop operating? How does the neighbourhood work? Before you sign the lease, it's good to know that every three weeks the first floor fills up with water. Check out Chapter 7 for details on choosing the best location.

    A common reason why people sell a successful business is that the landlord intends to raise the rent. If you're buying the business, you may also be *assuming* the lease or be required to agree to this increase. Talk with the landlord and the business owner about future plans for the space.

- ✔ Decide whether you're going to take over the business or just the location and equipment to open your own business. If you're buying the business, you probably want to keep the name the same. If you do change the name, you'll probably be hurting yourself, at least in the short term. However, if the restaurant you're taking over was a failing one, you'd definitely want to change the name so that you're not associated with it.

If you determine that the current business is working well, you may want to keep quiet about the fact that new ownership is in place. Don't mess with success. Your regulars will know, but for customers who come in only occasionally, why bother notifying them about the change? The idea of new ownership or management can affect people's perception of the place as they fall into the 'back in the good old days' mentality. Suddenly, their old favourites don't taste the same, or the waiting times are too long.

You may incur lots of unforeseen costs when you take over an established restaurant, including repairs to older equipment and facilities. Work with a reputable builder and inspector to thoroughly go through the restaurant from top to bottom before you finalise your deal. Check out Chapter 10 for tips on working with a builder.

## Becoming a partner with your current employer

If you're considering becoming a partner with your current boss, our advice is to look this gift horse in the mouth. When you buy into a restaurant, you buy into its profits *and* losses and its assets *and* liabilities.

If the restaurant is a profitable business that's well run, consider why someone is giving you a piece of it. Why is someone letting you buy into it? A couple of legitimate and potentially profitable motivations exist:

- Reward for your hard work
- An owner who wants to retire

However, other, less-positive motivations may be behind the offer:

- The operation is leaking money like a sieve. If someone wants you to put money in right away, you should be wary. This is the one situation to immediately be very concerned about.
- The owner's attention is being diverted to another business, so he's giving you an incentive not to rob him blind while he's distracted.

Whenever you consider entering into a partnership, you want to see the books before you hand over any money. Make sure that you get involved with a financially sound business that offers the potential for success.

When getting involved in any partnership, get definite answers about how much and what kind of say you're going to have in day-to-day operations and long-term planning. Clearly define on paper who gets what, including compensation, profit sharing, the best parking space, and Christmas Eve off. If it's important to you, write it down and make sure that everyone signs it.

## Starting from scratch

We can quickly sum up the pros and cons for this one: Starting from scratch is exciting and scary. You have a blank canvas: It's your baby from the start. You may be taking over an existing space that's been abandoned for years, or you may decide to convert a shop or a house into a restaurant. (Take a look at Chapter 7 before you sign on the dotted line for any space.) Either way, you'll have limitations for what your space can do, but you can get very creative with the obstacles in terms of layout and flow. It's like putting together a puzzle – rebuilding the pieces to fit your concept.

Taking this road can involve a lot of work. Very few spaces are ready and waiting for you exactly as you want them. And implementing your idea isn't as easy as saying, 'I want to make this bar 40 feet long and 4 feet high mahogany with a marble top'. You actually have to work out how to build it and work out all the details. Work with a builder to implement your vision because the devil is in the detail. You'll face the fun of electricity, plumbing, heating, ventilation, air conditioning, placement of everything from ovens and refrigerators to the waiting-staff stations . . . the list goes on. Check out Chapters 10 and 11 for info on laying out the front and back of the house. And get a surveyor to come in and evaluate the space, just like when buying a home.

When you're starting from scratch, now's the time to plan ahead for the future. During the rebuilding after a fire, co-author Mike left extra plumbing under the floor in the middle of the lounge so he could add a sushi bar later if he wanted to. Always add more power outlets than you think you'll need, even in the office. Extra cable and wires for electricity are handy in case you have to move something around later.

# Choosing the Best Type of Restaurant

Forty years ago, going out to dinner was an event. Now it's more routine, and the number and variety of restaurants that you can find illustrate the change in Britain's eating habits.

As a general rule, the atmosphere defines the type of restaurant more so than the food does, but they usually go hand in hand. The atmosphere of each venue is very different, though, while some menu items may be similar.

There's no magic formula or amount of money that you need to start a restaurant. The cost varies based on such things as the concept, size of your space, size of your menu, location of your space, number of employees you'll need to hire, and cost of insurance in your area. You need to do your homework to work out how much money you need to spend and why. Chapters 5 and 6 can help you with the nitty-gritty details.

## Dining in style

*Fine dining,* dining with the highest quality food, service, and surroundings, usually includes the highest prices as well. If you choose to run a fine dining restaurant, your restaurant needs to cater to the guest's every need.

### Soaking up the atmosphere

When they walk in your door, your diners should know they're in a fine dining establishment. If you choose to open a fine dining restaurant, include these factors in your plans:

- **Atmosphere:** The tables should have white linen tablecloths and top-notch dinnerware, glassware, and silverware. Choose lighting that's subtle, maybe even leaning toward the dark side. Select furniture and décor that reflect the mood you're trying to set. Decide whether you want to show the world a hip, trendy place or a more traditional restaurant.

- **Service:** The service is almost smothering. You escort guests to the toilets rather than direct them to it. Your waiting staff place napkins in your diners' laps after they're seated. You must train your staff in every service detail imaginable, such as removing crumbs from the table properly and serving plates from the correct side of a diner.

- **Amenities:** You offer amenities such as a cloakroom. You must have a reservation system. Many fine dining establishments get creative while trying to outdo each other. For example, a restaurant may offer guests a choice of 10 or 15 high-quality pens to sign their bill. Are you ready for the challenge?

### Focusing on food

If you're thinking about opening a fine dining place, spend some time thinking about what kind of food you want to serve. People have very high expectations about what they eat when they're in a fine dining restaurant. Here are a few things to keep in mind while you're mulling it over:

- ✔ **Food quality:** In your fine dining restaurant, the quality of food should be exceptional. It's characterised by top-notch ingredients, precise preparation styles, and intricate presentations, with a wine list to match.

- ✔ **Menu selection:** Your menu doesn't need to be extensive, but the items should be intricate.

- ✔ **Alcohol:** Your alcohol list should be high-end with an extensive selection of cognacs and brandies. The wine list is perfectly paired with the menu items and includes selections of superior quality. Some of these wines might be quite expensive, but a well-balanced list includes options in all price categories.

## Casual dining

The term *casual dining* is a description for anything that isn't fast food or fine dining. You can get a broad range of food and service quality in casual dining, but the dress code is consistently casual in every casual restaurant. In general, *casual* refers to the ambience or atmosphere of the place and the style of the service, rather than the quality of the cuisine. You can have remarkable food in a very casual setting. Think about a bistro concept: you can get fresh, fabulous food while wearing your jeans and trainers.

The same goes for *gastropubs* and *brasseries*, which are increasingly popular in the UK as they often offer high-quality food but in more relaxed surroundings. Gastropubs are smarter pubs with modern food, and may also offer traditional British food, while brasseries bridge the gap between the formality of a restaurant, and the casual feel of a café – though not at the expense of the food, which could be a mixture of traditional French and British.

Casual restaurants tend to be noisier than their fine dining counterparts with loud music, loud diners, and maybe even loud service,. The food is generally reasonably priced, somewhere between £9 and £14 per main dish. Guests tend to linger longer in casual restaurants than in fast food restaurants. They usually order from menus at the table rather than at a centralised menu at a cashdesk. Many chain restaurants are casual restaurants. Examples include Wagamama's, Pizza Express, Strada, and Café Pasta.

In casual dining, sometimes the food matches the level of service, and sometimes it doesn't. The Wolseley in Piccadilly has an extensive brasserie menu, with high-quality products and traditional French bourgeois dishes, but the service is friendly and efficient, not smothering.

Many diners are opting for bar service these days and casual dining is filling that need. If a diner is dining alone, or in a hurry, the bar is a popular choice. Sitting at the bar is usually good for groups no larger than three or so. Typically you can get the full menu at the bar, usually in a hurry. If you choose to set up bar service, make sure you set up an ordering system that prioritises bar orders, for this very reason.

## *Placing an order – to go!*

You can view your takeaway and delivery options as falling under one of two general categories:

- ✔ **Takeaway/delivery-only operation:** This setup is most applicable if you're considering opening a pizzeria, Chinese restaurant (or other ethnic food), or sandwich shop. You may have one or two tables with chairs or just a couple of chairs where customers can wait for their orders.

- ✔ **Takeaway or delivery as part of your larger operation:** Many restaurants, particularly Indian, Chinese, and pizza ones, successfully incorporate takeaway and/or delivery options to varying degrees. Your options are numerous, including a dedicated carry-out counter (with a separate entrance, even), ordering takeaway from a staff member, or simply permitting eat-in guests to order food to go.

  The menu for this option may be the same as your usual menu, or you may offer a modified menu. But takeaway hours are often modified if it's part of a larger operation, usually with shorter hours for takeaway and delivery.

As with any restaurant, the takeaway and delivery business has high and low volume turnover times, and they usually coincide with mealtimes. Staff your delivery, kitchen, and ordering staff appropriately. See Chapter 17 for tips on scheduling.

### *Ordering*

Make sure your customers can order in person at the restaurant or by phone, fax, or e-mail. Ordering online is also more and more common.

If you have some items on your menu that aren't available for takeaway, make sure that they're clearly marked and your order taker knows which menu items aren't available. That employee also needs to be able to answer questions about menu options and ingredients.

If your takeaway or delivery order system is integrated with your point-of-sale (POS) system, make sure to clearly differentiate the order as takeaway in the system. Otherwise, takeaway orders may get *plated,* or placed on plates for service, as dining room orders instead of being packaged in to-go containers. You can distinguish between the two types of orders by creating different POS items (chips versus To Go chips), with additions such as (chips with peas versus chips with salsa to go), or by simply noting where the order came from (dining room – section 1 versus takeaway ordering area).

### Delivery

You want to deliver a quality product to your diner's door. Establish your delivery radius by determining how long your food holds in the containers you use and how long it takes to get to your customers. You don't want to go further than your food is capable of travelling. And consider that your delivery guy needs to get back to your shop to deliver the other orders. Make your delivery area as large as you can reasonably serve. Do it well or don't bother doing it.

You will need to make sure that your takeaway menu doesn't contravene any law regarding delivering particular hot foods, such as shellfish. Check with your environmental health officer (EHO) as to what you can or cannot deliver, because the item may contravene health and safety laws. A lot of common sense comes into this and, if in doubt, take the item off your takeaway menu. Another way around this is to look at restaurants offering takeaways. What do they offer? But be safe rather than sorry and check with your EHO. You may also give advice on how to re-heat food, for example by handing a leaflet out to customers when they pick up the food,. Do add a proviso, however, that re-heating takeaway food is done at the customer's own risk.

If you offer delivery, you need transport, probably either scooters cars. You'll probably need some kind of ID (for buildings with security doors or gates) and/or a uniform that indicates that the delivery person works for you. A recognisable uniform also help keeps you in the loop on what he's doing outside the restaurant. If he's rude to people, drops litter, or rides on the pavement, you'll hear about it.

Overestimate the amount of time it will take to get orders to your customer by at least 10 minutes. Things get dropped and lost, and you need leeway. Customers almost always react better when you call them to let them know a problem has occurred and give an estimate on how long it will take to fix it instead of just showing up late.

## Selecting self-service or fast-food

Many fast-food, self-service, or *quick service restaurants* (QSR) are franchises, but you don't have to take that route for fast-food success. Pizza, Chinese food, and ice cream are all great choices for fast-food non-chain restaurants. Even an independent sandwich or burger joint can be successful.

You'll really need to hone your point of difference between you and your competition (see Chapter 4 for details). Generally, you'll need to focus on the difference in your quality because you probably can't compete, at least initially, with the big boys in terms of price.

*Fast casual* is one of the hottest emerging trends in restaurants at the moment. Fast casual takes the concept of a quick-service deli and enlarges it into a range of cuisines combining bar service, comfortable but basic furnishings, takeaway, and sometimes delivery.

## Running a bar – with or without food

Even if you're opening a bar, you'll probably need at least limited food service. Most bars offer some kind of food service even if the menu is very small and it's not available at all hours (the kitchen may close at 9 p.m., while the bar is open till 2 a.m.). The food may be something as simple as snack bar food.

Lots of people eat at the bar, not out of necessity but out of preference. More and more operations are incorporating food service in their bars as part of their regular business. Now that smoking is against the law in enclosed public places, the trend towards eating in the newly smoke-free bars will continue. If you're not serving food in your bar, take advantage of this trend by experimenting with a limited menu. See Chapter 12 for details on setting up and running a bar.

## Providing catering and banquet services

In general, both catering and banquets serve large parties, anywhere from 15 to 500 people at a single time. *Banquets* usually take place at a designated banquet hall or facility, and *catering* takes place at a customer's location. More and more restaurants are getting into the catering business, and you may want to consider it as a component to your operations (or consider basing your operations only on catering).

Catering lends itself to highly controllable costs and consequently high profitability. In catering, you generally have the luxury of knowing, in advance, how many guests will attend, exactly what they'll eat and drink while they're there, and how many employees you need to staff the event. Therefore, in theory, you should know all the costs in advance: what it costs you to produce 150 servings of chicken pie in terms of food, labour hours to produce that chicken pie, and labour hours to serve that chicken pie and clean up.

In catering, all direct expenses associated with the production of an event are transferable to the client. In other words, everything you spend for food, drinks, staffing, disposables, transportation, rentals, flowers, and décor are chargeable to the client. You only need to factor in your administrative time, overhead, and profit margin to arrive at a price. Simple, right? Wrong.

The art of profitable catering lies in understanding how to 'work the numbers' (understanding how to prepare just the right amount of food, no more, no less).

Here's an example of how to work your catering numbers. If you have a party of 500 people outside in a marquee, your prep list might look like Figure 3-1. Looking at Figure 3-1, you may say, 'Gosh! That doesn't add up! You've got 408 pieces of flourless chocolate torte (34 tortes × 12 pieces per cake) for 500 people.' See, we know that in one hour, the average guest consumes four canapés. We know that on a buffet, only 80 per cent of guests have salad, and those who do have an average of 80 grams of greens. If you have two types of salad dressing and specify 60 per cent of the guest count for each, you'll be fine. (Here's the calculation: 80 per cent of 500 guests = 400 guests having salad. Then take 60 percent of 400 to decide how many 30 ml servings of each dressing you need, and you get you 240 portions = 7.2 litres.) We know that an average hotel pot of food feeds 25 average people (less if they're rugby players or more if they're ballerinas). And we know to always have vegetarian meals available for 5 per cent of guests (in this case 5 per cent of 500 is 25), whether the customer orders them or not. These tricks of the trade can make the difference between having too much food and wasting profits, and having just enough to cover the count and maximising your profitability.

Learning what to charge and where the opportunities are for increased sales is the trick. Do you only sell food and drink, or do you become an event planner and coordinate the flowers, décor, china and linen rental, and the like? You need more info and experience to do this effectively, but the profits are huge because you're simply the middle man for some of the services, coordinating them for a more-than-fair mark-up.

---

### Catering Event Order Sheet

**Client:** National Association of Sleep-Deprived Restaurateurs
**Attendees:** 500                **Date:** December 15
**Location:** Marquee (Kew Gardens)    **Time:** 6 p.m.

| DINNER MENU | PREP QUANTITY |
|---|---|
| **6:00 – Canapes** | |
| | |
| *Bruschetta alla Caprese* | 300 each |
| *Seared Tuna on Wonton Crisp* | 300 each |
| *Selsey Crab Cakes with Spicy Aioli* | 300 each |
| | |
| **6:30 – Client's Award Presentation (15 minutes)** | |
| | |
| **6:45 – Buffet Dinner** | |
| | |
| *Tossed Mixed Green Salad* | 13.5 kg |
|     *Balsamic Vinaigrette* | 5.6 l |
|     *Mustard Dressing* | 5.6 l |
| *Seared Organic Salmon with Herbed Potato Crust* | 27 kg |
| *Carved Beef Fillet with Horseradish Cream* | 40 each |
| *French Green Beans with Tarragon-Shallot Butter* | 57 kg |
| *Roasted Garlic Potato Galette* | 57 kg |
| *Flourless Chocolate Torte* | 34 each |
| | |
| **Drinks** | |

**Figure 3-1:**
Sample of an order sheet for a catered event.

Many restaurants, such as Just St James, London, have spawned hugely successful catering operations that have become as big as, if not bigger than, the restaurant, because you can make big money feeding the masses. You get rid of the speculation of the restaurant, trying to decide how much food to prep, how many servers to schedule, and so on. Catering enables you to know there are going to be bums in the seats and about how many people will be present.

Your catering menu will be smaller than your regular dining room menu. Select items from your main menu that are easily produced in volume, don't require a lot of steps, and hold well. Your choices should embody your concept. People choose you to cater based in large part on your signature dishes. In most cases, you'll be fulfilling catering/banquet orders out of the same kitchen, so the items should fit the workflow you've established.

The scope of your catering operation varies with your own wishes. Start small and work your way up. Maybe you do small at-home parties for key guests at the restaurant. Maybe you provide off-site lunches to doctors' offices in town. Whatever you choose, remember that transporting food must be done professionally, cleanly, and with food safety as a priority.

# Putting It All Together

Make sure that your theme is consistent with your décor, cuisine, and style of service. If you have a Latin American name and theme and customers are singing along with the mariachi band, it's a good indicator that you've met or exceeded their expectations.

## Thinking about theme and concept

Just like in a film or a story, a *theme* is a common thread, idea, or image that runs throughout your restaurant. You can base a theme on many different things. Your *concept* is the whole package, including your food, menu, price points, design, décor, atmosphere, and how that package marries the theme. Here's the short list of what you can base your theme or concept on, but your imagination is really your only limit.

- **A style of cuisine:** For example, you may decide to base your concept on South African braai, a cuisine that delivers various kinds of roasted meats sliced from the spit. You're not offering the entire scope of South African food; you're focusing on a single dish.

- **An individual dish:** A pizza place isn't necessarily Italian; it may have Sicilian, Spanish, and Portuguese cuisine all on the same menu, but it focuses on pizza. Some places specialise in just desserts.

- **Ethnic influence:** Japanese, Italian, Chinese, and so on are all well-known examples.

- **Décor and ambience:** Maybe you want your guests to be surrounded by New Age music, soothing scents, sage green walls, and relaxing lighting. You then serve food that fits that environment.

- **A character from a book, film, and the like:** Maybe you want to open the Sherlock Holmes Bookshop and Café.

- **Sporting events or hobbies:** Sports bars and Internet cafes are typical examples.

- **Games:** Some restaurants offer pizza for the parents and provide the kids with flashing lights, animatronic animals, and tokens for games. Others skip the kids' stuff and focus on video games, pool, and darts for adults.

- **Geography:** Maybe you're located in a train station. Continue the theme into your restaurant via your décor, menu titling, and uniforms. Or maybe you focus on cuisine related to your area of the country, like Scottish seafood, or Cornish pasties.

If a restaurant's theme is very kitschy, it tends not to have fantastic food. Instead, it spends more time focused on the theme, décor, and look of the menu rather than the food. In these cases, a big part of their draw and of the product they're selling is the atmosphere. But for most diners, the food is always the most important thing. If the food is marginal, they won't be back, so spend some time on your menu no matter how kitschy you decide to go.

Make sure that your theme and menu match. If you open Mike's Indian Bazaar, it's up to you whether it's a bazaar or just bizarre. Just be sure to do your research (and don't serve beef on the menu; the cow is a sacred animal and is rarely eaten in India). If you open an Indian-themed restaurant, you're trying to create an atmosphere that lets diners imagine they're in India. The smells, sounds, sights, and tastes you create can do just that.

## Choosing a name

Your restaurant's name should be catchy, easy to remember, unique, and somewhat descriptive. Picking your name is fun, but don't get so caught up in it that you forget to take care of the necessary legalities (like making sure someone's not already using your favourite choice). Check out Chapter 8 for details on searching for trademarks. You may have picked out a name already, but consider these ideas before you inlay it in 24-carat gold on your signage:

- **Name of someone significant to you:** Consider your name, a relative's name, or the name of someone that inspired you. You could choose a figure in history who's been dead long enough not to have trademarked his or her own name. Examples are Gaudi, Carmen, and Napoleon.

- **Geography:** You can borrow your restaurant name from a natural formation, such as a river, lake, hill, crater, or mountain range. Or use your town's name, a street, neighbourhood, bridge, park, sanctuary, or an area of town as an inspiration. Southwark Tavern, Port Isaac Grill, Royal Buxton Brewery, and Everest are a few geography-based names.

- ✔ **Historic or traditional names and spaces:** Urban sprawl has incorporated many once-independent villages into larger cities and towns. Maybe you want to incorporate that tradition into your concept. In some areas, restaurants have taken over locations that used to be occupied by other businesses, such as banks. Those old names may be perfect for your new restaurant, especially if elements of the old business are part of your decor. At 'Bank' in Portsmouth, the wines are stored in the bank's old safes.

- ✔ **Ethnic and cultural names:** Maybe you want your name to describe the influences of your concept. Thai Garden Café, a Thai restaurant, is an example.

- ✔ **Pop culture:** Hard Rock Cafe, Planet Hollywood, and the like make their bread and butter, so to speak, by tapping into people's love of pop culture.

- ✔ **Your concept and theme:** You might include the term 'Sports Bar and Grill' in your name. Sports Bar restaurants and bars are often havens for those who love to watch football or cricket matches with like-minded people. The food is simple, and beer is the most popular drink. Waterspouts Bars are typical of these places.

- ✔ **Your preparation methods:** You may want a name that reveals how your food is cooked. Couscous Café, Gourmet Burger, La Paella, The Real Greek Souvlaki Bar, and The Rotisserie are some examples.

- ✔ **Other business in the area:** Consider a name borrowed from a nearby business. Examples include The Bottom Line Bistro in a financial district, The Green Room near the theatre district, and The Bull and The Bear near the Stock Exchange, City of London.

- ✔ **Humour and irony:** You may want to try a funny or ironic name, but be careful that the humour doesn't offend anyone. The Cellar's Market is a café. 'The Library' may work as the name for a bar on a university campus.

Certain names will alienate people. Avoid truly offensive terms at all cost. In your quest to appeal to your target market, you may ruffle some feathers – the extent to which you do so is a marketing decision you have to make.

# Chapter 4

# Researching the Marketplace

· · · · · · · · · · · · · · · · · · · · · · · · · · · · · · · · · · · · · · · · · · · · · · · · · · · · ·

· · · · · · · · · · · · · · · · · · · · · · · · · · · · · · · · · · · · · · · · · · · · · · · · · · · · ·

*C*ompetition is defined as the following:

   ✔ A test of skill or ability; a contest

   ✔ The act of competing, as for profit or a prize; rivalry

   ✔ Rivalry between two or more businesses striving for the
      same customer or market

Before you read one more page or take another step toward realising your
dream of crowded dining rooms, ringing cash registers, and holiday homes in
Spain, reread the definition of competition again . . . again . . . and again. Think
about what it means in the restaurant business.

You're reading this book because you're making a decision to enter a *competition* – the restaurant business. And this is not some friendly card game of
Beat Your Neighbour. You have a lot at stake: your business, your financial
future, and your family's sense of security. That's why you have to analyse
the competitive environment to make sure that you have a chance to succeed.

In this chapter, we show you how to investigate your competition. We give you
tips on evaluating their strengths and weaknesses. If you're developing your
concept, we help you use this information to shape your decisions about how
to develop your concept and how to position it in your market. After you're up
and running, you can use many of these same tools to constantly analyse the
market and stay ahead of your competition.

# Getting Your Mind Right: Profits Matter

To the casual outsider, the restaurant business is attractive for reasons that are by-products of success (the fun, the glamour, the status). But success, and all its trappings, isn't guaranteed – a fact lost on many would-be restaurateurs. At its core, success in the restaurant business requires you to look at the business differently than these misguided victims of their own lack of knowledge. You must understand and accept one basic concept that eludes many: A restaurant is a business, a manufacturing enterprise whose products are only as good as they are saleable.

And the only way to measure success in any business is profits. Ultimately, nothing else matters. You can have the smartest space, the hippest crowd, and the trendiest cutting-edge food, but without net profitability, you might as well close the doors and save yourself a slow death.

You're a manufacturer, so accept that fact. We know that the title of manufacturer isn't as sexy as the titles *chef de cuisine* or *restaurateur,* but it's the most accurate label. (Or, if you still insist on a cool-sounding French term, you can use *fabricant.* That's French, too – for manufacturer.)

Creativity, vision, and equipment allow you to produce a product. That product is not just the type, quality, and presentation of your food or drink. *Product* refers to the whole of your concept (restaurant), including the quality of the food, design of the space, appearance of the waiting staff, and the convenience of the location. All these factors affect the likelihood that a consumer will buy your product over the competition's product. (Check out Chapter 3 for tips on choosing and developing your concept.)

You need to embrace the fact that your success is based on producing a saleable product and turning a profit – just as it is with any business. If you create a product with no sale, you're only creating excess stock. Profits come only when you make the sale, and everyone is competing for that sale. Your job is to continually win that sale over your competition.

# The Buying Decision: The Big Question

Why does one car sell and another doesn't? Why do you buy one type of beer and not another? Why do you go to the restaurants you go to? If you think about your own actions, you can begin to understand the criteria that others use in making the buying decision. This process (whether formal or informal) is called a *competitive analysis*. How your product positively influences the buying decisions of customers determines your market share, operational cash flow, and ultimately, your success. Perform a quick competitive analysis based on your own views. Here's how:

1. **Pick five food shops and five cars.**

2. **Compare and contrast your personal feelings on each one.** Evaluate them using criteria of your choosing. But definitely include price, value, design, practicality, and service. You can't have a good competitive analysis without them.

3. **Now take those same criteria and apply them to your concept in your market.** By doing so, you begin to see how the customer views your concept when making a buying decision.

As you go through this exercise, you gain an appreciation of all the factors that influence a buying decision. But you're only you, so take it a step further. You need to understand the potential consumers and what influences *their* buying decision as it relates to *your* market.

Figure 4-1 illustrates the *competitive response cycle* – the process of research and action that you *continually* follow to ensure that your restaurant *continually* meets the needs of the consumers you're going after. You study the market-place (including customers and competitors) and changes in the marketplace (including emerging trends) and then implement responses to your findings (marketing, menu changes, and so on) to develop your business. Then you analyse how well your efforts are working, which leads you right back to square one. In the following sections we describe each part of the cycle in detail. The cycle never stops.

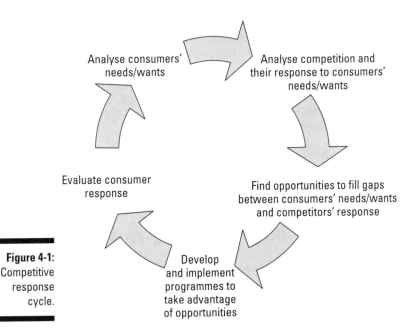

**Figure 4-1:** Competitive response cycle.

Analyse consumers' needs/wants

Analyse competition and their response to consumers' needs/wants

Find opportunities to fill gaps between consumers' needs/wants and competitors' response

Evaluate consumer response

Develop and implement programmes to take advantage of opportunities

Information is the weapon in the restaurant wars. Base your decisions on sound intelligence.

# Identifying and Analysing Potential Customers

Start by working out who you want your customers to be, and make sure they're likely to frequent the kind of restaurant you have in mind. Work out what demographic group(s) you're likely to attract. The term *demographics* describes characteristics or traits shared by a group. A demographic group includes people within a specific age range or income level, or who share other distinguishing traits like gender or marital status. Ask yourself questions, such as:

- ✔ Are you looking for a male or a female clientele, or both? If it's both men and women, are you focusing on singles or couples?

- ✔ Is your concept geared toward families, or is it not child-friendly?

- ✔ Are you targeting a particular ethnic or religious section of your community?

- ✔ Do you want to attract people in suits, in hard hats, or in everything in between?

- ✔ Do you appeal to locals, or are you trying to draw out-of-towners, including business travellers and tourists?

You're not excluding anyone from dining with you; you're simply trying to identify the clientele who's likely to visit your restaurant. You must make sure that your menu offerings, music (and its volume), entertainment choices, décor, and so on appeal to your proposed clientele.

Over time, build a profile of your wished-for diners and tweak your concept, as appropriate, to appeal to this group. Work out where they eat. Discover what motivates their buying decisions. Find out what else they do besides dine out.

## Working out what you need to know

Deciding what information you need is half the battle (the other half is actually doing the research and analysing the information, but of course you wouldn't expect us to do everything for you). Here are our tips for focusing your research on what your diners want from you:

✔ **Location:** Determine how much importance your potential customers place on location convenience and identify locations that fit. Maybe you're close to your customers' homes or workplaces, or maybe they drive past your place to and from commuting to work.

✔ **Hours of operation:** What hours are convenient to your potential customer?

✔ **Menu:** A big menu is a draw for some consumers; others prefer a short, simple format. Work out what fits your desired clientele.

✔ **Food quality:** Given your concept, what do people expect?

✔ **Price/value:** The *price* is the amount of money that someone pays for a menu item. The *value* is how they perceive what they get (usually in terms of quality and quantity) compared to what they pay. Both need to be in line with the needs and wants of your consumer.

✔ **Service:** Determine the type, style, and efficiency of service that best fit your targeted customers' needs.

✔ **Applicable trends:** Determine how conscious your potential customers are of dining and lifestyle trends and how these trends are likely to impact their buying decisions. Do they largely ignore trends in favour of consistency, or are they largely trend followers? Keep in mind that a trend doesn't have to be glitzy and hip to qualify. Past trends like wraps, frozen yoghurt, or low-carb dieting aren't especially glitzy.

Depending on your concept and the trends in question, think about how to take temporary advantage of them. Don't refashion your concept to serve nothing but trends, but you can use them as components of your concept. By watching for and interpreting trends correctly, you can either create the next trend or have a plan ready when the market is ready for it. Maybe you notice that people are going for Asian flavours. Even if you're not running a Chinese or Thai place, you can add a grilled chicken salad with coriander lime dressing and shiitake mushrooms to your menu.

Gathering this intelligence is a key component to getting your restaurant up and running, but you must continue to do so on an ongoing basis. Truly successful businesses foresee, adopt, and maximise opportunities as consumer behaviour changes. They listen, and then give customers what they want.

## *Finding resources*

In the following sections, we explain great ways to get the preliminary and relevant research information that you need. Just remember that you can read what other people have to say and listen to what experts think will happen, but none of it is a substitute for talking with customers.

### Demographic data

You can have the demographic part of your research done for you, but it may cost you some cash. Demographic research companies, establish their fee schedule based on how detailed you want your information to be. Believe it or not, this step isn't out of the realm of possibility for a single-unit startup restaurant. You can get good data, customised to your concept, for little expense. This route gives you specifics about your consumers in your prospective area including their income levels, age, ethnicity, and number of children in the family, among other information.

### Trade publications

One of the least expensive ways to find out about your consumers is to read trade magazines and newspapers. These publications contain info produced by trend watchers, industry analysts, and consumer groups. Publications like *Caterer and Hotelkeeper, Restaurant Magazine,* and *The Good Food Guide* are full of information on dining trends, culinary tips, and the business of running a restaurant (check out Chapter 22 for more information).

### Other restaurants like yours

Go to every restaurant that's what you want yours to be. Walk in and look around. Pay attention to who's eating there. Look at the ages of the people who go there. Does the clientele change at different times of the day? What are they eating? Create a mini focus group by talking to everybody you can about the food, menu, and atmosphere. Ask them questions: 'What do you like about the place? What would you like to have there?'

You need to be sensitive and subtle. For example, you may be having a meal and sitting near to other people. It's quite easy to get into conversation with them without giving the game away as to why you're there. An honest opinion is tremendously helpful and you don't need to say why you are there. A bit of detective work on the sly!

 Look outside of your geographic market as well. Look at a new successful chain that hasn't entered your market yet. What customers are they serving? Maybe you can be first to market with components of their concept and reap the success. But remember that being first to market with a concept based on something you've seen elsewhere is no guarantee of success. If you open a casual dining restaurant serving mainstay Italian cuisine, you need to be ready to compete should Pizza Express ever decide to roll into town.

### Your community

Be your own consumer. Completely immerse yourself in your local dining scene. Know your local market. Put yourself in the shoes of your patrons in order to understand what motivates them, who they are, and what their perception of dining is. Know your community as a whole as well. Read your local newspapers and watch your local news. Get a feel for local events. The more you know about what's going on in your community, the better you'll be able to work out how to connect with the people who live there.

### Consumer-oriented food media

Pay attention to the publications and broadcast media that target food fans:

- ✔ **Foodie magazines:** Publications like *Olive,* and *the BBC Good Food Magazine, Waitrose Food Illustrated* and *Observer Food Magazine* report consumer info and help shape diners' expectations.

- ✔ **Newspaper dining and lifestyle sections:** Newspapers, whether they're local or national, contain useful info about foods people are interested in.

    While you're reading these periodicals, pay attention to who is advertising there. What do you like about their ads? What can you incorporate in your own ads? What would you do differently?

- ✔ **Televised food programmes:** The ability of Jamie Oliver, Gordon Ramsay and others to reach into the British household is probably the biggest single force that's made dining, cooking, and gastronomy what it is today. It's motivated the way people eat in this country recently. It made previously unheralded ingredients popular outside their indigenous markets. Foods such as andouille sausage, couscous, and mixed 'gourmet' salad greens are now commonplace.

### Non-food TV and magazines

In all your free time, read magazines and watch popular television programmes. Your customers are, and you should, too. See what they see and hear what they hear. Checking out general interest TV shows and magazines is also a good way to get ad ideas and help you decide whether you want to advertise there.

### Focus groups

*Focus groups* are interviews with 10 to 15 people at the same time. The interviewer asks the group carefully drafted questions, and the group provides objective answers. It's a tactic borrowed from the biggest companies out there, and they're doing it for a reason. Focus groups create a forum where businesses can analyse their consumers and test new products or services. Focus group testing is crucial in making customer-centric decisions. People tend to respond to focus groups because they feel important and that their opinions matter. Typically, participants give you honest, critical opinions. Focus groups allow you to gather local customer-specific info that you can analyse along with broader, industry-specific information from other sources.

You can pay for this research. Impartial professional research teams develop well-designed, cognitively sound questions that ensure an objective, pertinent, and actionable set of results. You get the best information this way – at a hefty price. If you're a new business on a budget, do it yourself. It may not be as scientific, but you'll still get lots of good, useful info.

Create an objective cross-section of your marketplace and potential customer, including the businessman or woman, the stay-at-home mum, and the student. We recommend that you hold two to four sessions to get a large cross-section of data and to have the ability to make changes to your presentation to extract increasingly more pertinent data based on the results from previous sessions.

Identify what kind of insights you want to glean from your focus group. The more pointed you are in creating your questions, the more illuminating your group will be when answering them.

Anonymity is the key to honesty and objectivity in focus groups. Don't meet at your restaurant. Don't announce who you are. Don't give them coupons or gift certificates to your place. If they're going to recognise you, get someone else to do the screening and interviews. You can watch the video later.

Compensate the attendees for their time. The concept of making a quick £20 or so is generally motivation enough to get someone to break from their busy schedule and offer their opinion. Oh, and feed them, too.

# Keeping an Eye on the Enemy

Your competition is doing their own intelligence and implementing their own marketing strategies, just as you are. They're reaching out to the same group of potential customers. With your target customer in mind, you then have to work out who your competitors are – both your *direct* and *indirect* competition. Here's the basic information that differentiates the two:

- ✔ Direct competitors share similar prices, a similar atmosphere, a similar style of service, and similar food. If your customers see your restaurant as similar to another restaurant, you're probably direct competitors. If you're a burger restaurant, every other burger joint is your *direct competition*.

- ✔ But when people go out, they don't just go out for burgers. They also go out for curries, pizza, and sautéed foie gras. These restaurants are your *indirect competition*. Indirect competitors don't share the same food, but they share similar prices, similar geographic areas, similar styles of service, and/or a similar atmosphere.

Make a list of your potential competitors. Your research will confirm (or deny) that everyone on your preliminary list is indeed your competitor. The next few sections show you how. And remember that to be successful you must continue to do this type of research even after you open your doors. Old competitors die out and new ones are born on a regular basis. And some concepts that don't seem like competitors today may be tomorrow, depending on how you and they make changes to your businesses in the future.

Don't limit your attention to only direct competitors. Try to capture market share from indirect competitors as well. Many fast food companies have some of the most creative and calculating minds in the industry developing their marketing strategies for them, so learn from them.

You're competing not only against other restaurants; you're also competing against people eating at home. Think of all those supermarket ready meals that fly out of their outlets so that customers don't have to cook. This company and many others like them are also your indirect competition.

## Who do they think their customers are?

You can find out a lot about your competition and their perception of the consumer by studying where they choose to place their message. Every time somebody reads an airline magazine, a local community publication, a supermarket magazine, or watches TV, they're being motivated by your competition in varying degrees.

It's no secret that companies selling beer, pizza, cars, snack food, and burgers advertise during sports games. Big companies spent millions of pounds to have someone tell them what may look obvious now: There's a gathering of their consumers at a certain time on a certain TV channel, so that's a good place to place propaganda – we mean ads. These same viewers are likely customers at your pizza restaurant. Maybe you can't afford Olympics-type advertising, but you can afford to advertise on the front page of the sport section of your local paper. Chapter 16 has more on advertising.

## Shop till you drop

If you really want to know your competitors, spy on them. Be their customer, literally. Dine at their restaurants and experience their products. Take notes and share them with the other managers in your restaurant. Use them as a starting point for brainstorming sessions for new services and products. In the restaurant and retail industries, these activities are called *mystery shopping,* or more accurately, *mystery snooping.*

Don't get too caught up in the 'my duck à la orange is better than your duck à la orange' type of thinking. Be objective enough to say, 'They're beating me hands down with their salads, sandwiches, and trendy interior décor.'

Initially, you can mystery shop your competition on your own. But hopefully, you'll reach a point where you won't be able to do this on your own. You'll be so prominent in your restaurant community that the competition will pick you out like a novice restaurant critic. You may need to hire a professional mystery shopping service.

Mystery shopping services aren't always the way to go. We've had mixed luck with their results and accuracy. You can also get friends and employees to go in and spy for you. But give them the specific criteria you're looking for and remember that people you know may have a hard time telling you what you don't want (or what they think you don't want) to hear.

Examine your competitors that do it right. But looking at the failures is just as important. Spend some time thinking about why they failed. With few exceptions, they probably failed because they stopped being vigilant. They stopped being innovative. They ignored trends and failed to adapt to the ever-increasing savvy of the consumer.

Use Table 4-1 to define your direct competition (restaurants that consumers see as just like yours) and their strengths and weaknesses. We suggest using criteria, like those listed in Table 4-1, to begin to gather the facts about your competitors in the marketplace and to list your own. After you gather the info, you'll take the next step, evaluating the information and making judgments about it. (See Table 4-2 for an example.)

| Table 4-1 | Comparing Your Concept to the Competition | | |
| --- | --- | --- | --- |
| **Criteria** | **Andy's Sports Bar and Grill** | **Bave and Duster's** | **Sports Zone** |
| **Hours of opening** | 11 a.m. – 12 a.m. (7 days/week) | 11 a.m. – 11 p.m. (7 days/week) | 11 a.m. – 1 a.m. (7 days/week) |
| **Menu** | Wood-fired pizzas, black Angus burgers, chicken breasts | Burgers, wings, ploughman's and jacket potatoes | Wings, pizzas, sandwiches |

| Criteria | Andy's Sports Bar and Grill | Bave and Duster's | Sports Zone |
|---|---|---|---|
| *Price/value* | Price based on 'quality' brand costs of premium ingredients | Value-priced based on volume and lack of work required for pre-prepared foods | Price based on national brand and image; portions and quality not in line with pricing |
| *Efficiency* | Personal service and physical layout expedite service; not the spot for a quick bite; more of a stay and linger destination | Quick service of foods due to convenience preparation | Slower service due to staffing levels |
| *Location* | Across from football stadium; | Shopping centre; by big box edge of town shopping areas. | City centre corner location; difficult parking |
| *Targeted demographic* | Affluent sport fans, regulars | Mid-market sport fans | Tourists, convention business |
| *Type/style of service* | Table service | Table, counter service | Table service |
| *Novelty/other* | Sport-specific rooms; distinctive | Free peanuts | National brand image |

# Developing Your Battle Plan

How are you going to take your product, your information about your customers, and sussing out what's going on with your competition and create a plan that brings people in through *your* door, not to your competitor's door? Your plan should take the following into account:

- Your strengths and weaknesses
- Your competitor's strengths and weaknesses
- Your local marketplace

If you need information on refining your definitions of who your clientele and your competition are, check out the sections earlier in this chapter.

# Creating a competitive analysis

Start to brainstorm what it is that you sell and what you're good at. Say that you sell innovative fresh Thai food. Make a list of your strengths. Then work out what strengths are yours alone. Decide whether your competition is better than you, equal to you, or deficient compared to you in this category. Unless you're the only person in town who does fresh Thai cuisine, you don't own it. But if you're the only one who delivers, you own the delivery market for your type of cuisine. You're trying to find the things that your competition doesn't have an answer for. Your point of difference is what you see as your strength. From your customer's point of view it could be a strength or a weakness.

Use Table 4-2 to help you refine your points of difference. Your points of difference can become your greatest strengths. In Table 4-1, we focus on gathering the facts. In Table 4-2, you take the next step, evaluating the data and making judgments about the info. In the first column, we list everything that we want our restaurant to be known for. We want Thai Garden to be the market leader in each category. In this context, the market leader is the restaurant that's best known (usually measured in terms of sales and reputation) in the category. In some cases, Thai Garden is the leader; in other cases it needs to improve to be the leader (–) while in others it may actually be better (+), but not yet *known* for being better.

| Table 4-2 | Refining Thai Garden's Points of Difference | |
|---|---|---|
| **Your Desired Points of Difference** | **Market Leader** | **How Do You Compare?** |
| Innovative Thai | Thai Bistro | – |
| Fresh (made from scratch) | Thai Garden and Thai Bistro | Tied |
| Signature dish (Thai fishcakes with green papaya salad) | Thai Garden | Leader |
| Create your own Thai curries | Thai Garden | Leader |
| Service time less than 5 minutes | Thai Garden | Leader |
| Broad selection of premium and oriental beers | Thai Bistro | – |
| Authentic Thai ingredients | Thai Garden | + |
| Broad kids menu | Neither restaurant | – |
| Private-label sauces | Thai Bistro | Leader |

| Your Desired Points of Difference | Market Leader | How Do You Compare? |
|---|---|---|
| Location (across from cinema complex and close to major market) | Thai Garden | Leader |
| Low-carb menu | Thai Garden | Leader |

The most effective point of difference that you can have is one your competition can't answer. If you have a location directly adjacent to a major destination (such as a stadium, major cinema complex, or shopping centre), odds are your competition doesn't, and you can work this to your advantage.

Points of difference may be long lasting, or they may be fleeting, but while they exist, maximise them. Big companies spend tremendous effort to develop the next point of difference that competitors can't immediately duplicate or copy. The chicken nugget, the drive-thru, and proprietary recipes or products are all historical examples of this type of temporary no-response point of difference. Eventually every fast food place developed its version of the chicken nugget, but for a time, a single restaurant enjoyed it as a point of difference. (For information on communicating those points of difference through advertising, see Chapter 16.)

However, most points of difference are subtler. These are the nuances that you 'own'. In Table 4-2, for example, Thai Garden 'owns' several clear points of difference (like signature Thai fishcakes and a papaya salad and a service time less than five minutes) that its owner can use to his advantage. However, as in most competitions, his competitors also have their strengths (a broad selection of premium and oriental beers and a close proximity to the cinema complex). The process of analysing competitive advantage requires that you objectively weigh your strengths against your competitors' strengths and develop plans to simultaneously improve your deficiencies while emphasising your 'ownable' strengths.

When weighing your strengths versus the strengths of your competition, you have to again put yourself in the shoes of your potential customers and determine which criteria matter most to them. You may own several minor advantages like a, a fresh mint teapot served with every meal and free refills, but if your competition owns the categories of freshest, better-tasting foods, better service, and lower item-specific prices, you're in trouble, if that's what your consumers want.

Having a strength isn't enough; you have to have a point of difference that will be a deciding factor in motivating a potential customer to select you over the place down the road.

## Acting on your information

You should now know who your most likely competitors and consumers are, so use that information to develop your plan. Here are the high points to help focus your evaluation:

- ✔ Play up your strengths as long as you can make them matter to your audience.

- ✔ Analyse your competitors, determine their deficiencies, and exploit them.

- ✔ Continually strive to close the gaps on your own deficiencies because these are weaknesses that your competitors will counter-attack.

- ✔ Continually strive to create new points of difference. Your competitors aren't blind, so they'll develop new plans to counter your offensive. By creating new points of difference, you're always on the attack.

- ✔ Know your audience, how your points of difference matter to them, and how to reach them.

The strategy of evaluating and playing up points of difference helps smaller businesses exist in the face of competition from bigger ones. The simplest example of this is 'You may be bigger, but I'm better'. This works in all markets. Take fashion, for example. Levi's is bigger than Armani, but both companies are able to exist because they leverage their distinct points of difference to generally separate consumers.

The lines blur when businesses go after the same potential consumer. Now comes the time when the difference is in the details. All you have is small points of difference. So you must focus on the importance of these points of difference to your potential customer. For example, maybe your direct competitor microwaves all his food, while you prepare yours over a wood-fired grill. You take this point of difference and convert it into a message as to why your wood-fired cuisine is better, fresher, and less radioactive than your competition's.

# Realising that Research Doesn't End After You Open Your Doors

The minute you open your doors, you're in the battle. Every day is a battle. You can't just launch your plan and assume victory. The minute after you launch your attack, you need to analyse your competitors' reaction. You're threatening their market share, and they'll fight for it. Only by observing the successes and failures of your strategy can you implement a successful campaign and claim the market share.

Suppose that you built your strategy on your wood-fired grill products, attacking your competition on the use of a microwave. You played up your quality and your investment in equipment to ensure the quality. You're targeting a consumer who values freshness, made-from-scratch cooking, and trendy cooking methods and is conditioned to assume that microwaved products are inferior. Your plan went well for a while, until a competitor launched a two-fold strategy that included getting his own wood-fired grills and attacking your location by playing up his proximity to the cinema complex.

Now it's time to change your strategy. You must try to make the most of another point of difference. If you're out of points of difference, you need to create one. By observing and evaluating the success and failure of your marketing strategy, and noticing your competition's response, you can continually develop new marketing strategies based on your point of difference (existing or new) and continue to capture or threaten the market share of your competition.

The restaurant business is noted for its ever-changing array of new competitors, new advances in products and technology, and increasingly savvy diners. You can stay competitive only by analysing, reinventing, and re-evaluating your strengths and weaknesses and those of your competition.

Take a look at Chapter 22 for resources on keeping up with trends and making sure that your restaurant is the best it can be.

# Maintaining Your Competitive Edge

Some restaurateurs think that you can peacefully coexist with the competition because plenty of market is available. This point of view is wrong on two fronts:

- ✔ You're not accounting for new competition. The next guy might just be better, faster, cheaper, and sexier than you are. The new kid on the block steals market share, at least temporarily. And if he lives up to the hype, you're really in trouble.

- ✔ Peaceful coexistence doesn't actually exist. Think about Ford and Mercedes. On the surface, these brands cater to two different markets. But Mercedes didn't build a £20,000 car by accident. It's looking to cash in on a market it didn't have before. Mercedes made a cheaper car that's still sexy. They've targeted customers who, above all things, want a Mercedes because they get prestige they couldn't afford before.

In today's marketplace, be wary of competitive threats from below and above. Casual theme restaurants can offer a gourmet experience without the gourmet price gastropubs, brasseries and bistros are grabbing market share from fine dining. Their common point of difference from their fine dining competitors is that they too are serving innovative, hip new cuisine, but in a less stuffy atmosphere and at much cheaper prices. Fine dining has responded with the message, 'We still have better service and a proven track record of exclusivity, and we can make it accessible to you now'. Many restaurants can create and offer a fine dining experience to new customers at a lower price point.

Casual dining is caught in the middle. It's attacked from below as the fast food folk upgrade their menus. It's attacked from above as fine dining dumbs itself down, trying to grab back the market share it's lost in tough economic times. Even though casual dining is battling on both fronts, it has managed to expand.

Don't rest on your past, or even current, successes. A shark that stops swimming dies and becomes food for the other sharks. Change is the only constant in this industry. The successful restaurateur is the student of information. Research means the difference between a sure win and a bloody fight for survival.

# Part II
# Putting Your Plan in Motion

'In a previous life, before I became a lemming,
I was a small company without a business plan.'

# In this part . . .

It's time to ramp up the activity and move from idea to action. We show you how to develop a restaurant-specific business plan, and we help you round up financing and scout out the best location for your concept. Finally, we cover permits, licences, laws, insurance, and a host of other legal issues – including how and when to call on some professional help for these matters.

# Chapter 5

# Writing a Business Plan

*I*f you're going somewhere you've never been, you need a map to get there. Otherwise, you're going to get lost. If you have to stop and ask directions from strangers, doing so will cost you time and maybe even money. And who knows whether you're going to get the right information? If you're running a restaurant, you need a similar kind of map to help you reach your destination. The *business plan* is your map to starting your business – and achieving success. It answers the questions before your investors, financiers, partners, or employees ask them.

You need to do some things in a particular order when you're developing your business plan. Some steps are prerequisites for answering other questions. For example, if someone asks you about your advertising budget, you can't really answer until you know what your *overheads* – you general business costs – are, what kind of food budget you're developing, what kind of sales you're forecasting, and so on. Feel free to look around and read whatever interests you, but when you actually put pen to paper, remember that you need to follow some steps in order.

# *Don't Fly Blind: Understanding Why a Business Plan Matters*

A business plan explains in a very detailed way what you envisage your business being. You clearly explain your concept and why it's viable and outline your budget. You're anticipating where you'll spend money (expenses), forecasting how much you expect to take in (sales), and estimating when the money will be coming in and going out (cash flow). Your business plan helps you in several ways:

✔ It starts you analysing your restaurant in very detailed manner. This process can help you avoid some problems altogether.

✔ It helps you answer questions that many people involved in your restaurant will ask.

✔ It helps you identify and define the goal of your business, the customers you're hoping to serve, and your ideas for getting there.

✔ It provides a tool for potential investors to evaluate your business, your philosophy, your operating know-how, and your market.

✔ It provides a mechanism for figuring out how much money you realistically need to get started and to keep going until the business can sustain itself.

✔ It creates a tool for you to use and update regularly in your daily operations to get you on track and keep you there.

✔ It helps you decide whether your proposed business is likely to face problems from the beginning.

The more detailed your plan is, the better off you are in the long run. Do as much planning as possible and save yourself some time and money. But even with a business plan in hand, you're going to forget something. Assume the worst in your expense projections and be conservative in your sales forecast to account for this eventuality.

Business plans vary from organisation to organisation. A plan can be a relatively simple document, or it can be a book. Don't overwhelm yourself at the beginning: Start with a simple one-page outline and flesh it out as you go. Not every business plan is an extremely detailed document, but we suggest you put in as much work as possible – to the point that creating the plan makes you think about even the smallest details, such as 'How much does this teaspoon cost?' or 'Should I choose silver, stainless steel, or plastic?'

As a general rule, the more detailed you business plan gets, the more questions you find need answering. Including the details gives you great ideas for your to-do list and helps you realise the points you still need to ponder and research before you get your answers together.

# Laying Out a Business Plan

Here is the basic outline of most restaurant business plans.

✔ **Cover page and table of contents:** The cover page identifies your plan. Use it to differentiate your plan from those of other restaurants or companies that your potential investors may be looking at. The table of contents provides them with a map for inspecting your plan. You may also want to include an *executive summary,* a brief couple of paragraphs explaining what the plan's about.

✔ **Management team:** This section provides information about you, your management team, and any other key employees. Detail the experience, expertise, and strengths of your team in this section. Place this section at the front of your plan if your team is a strong selling point; otherwise, it's usually better placed later in the document.

✔ **Definition of your business concept:** Chapter 3 goes into detail about choosing your concept and theme. Take a look at the section ' Expressing the concept and theme', later in this chapter, for details in communicating that theme in your business plan.

✔ **Your menu:** Include a copy of your menu. For details on developing, formatting, and working out a cost for your menu, check out Chapter 9.

✔ **Market analysis and plan:** Here, you show the world how your business is different from other restaurants. You identify the market for your restaurant and discuss how you'll do it fresher, faster, with more buzz, and how that means 'better' from your diner's point of view. Check out Chapter 4 for details on understanding your market and Chapter 16 for putting your marketing plan together.

✔ **Clientele demographics:** Discuss who your customers will be. Confirm that you have sufficient numbers to draw from in your market to make your business a success. Also detail why your concept and marketing plan will appeal to them. For more on winning and keeping your clientele, check out Chapters 16, 19, and 20.

✔ **Financials:** With this section, you're trying to communicate how much money you need, what you're going to spend it on, and how you're going to build upon it. Financial analysis is an important step, even if you're not looking to borrow money from anyone. You need to set up realistic timing for money going out and coming in.

Depending on your plan, you may break up your finances into a couple of different categories, maybe *assumptions* (details about what you're basing your forecasts on) in one section and *forecasts* in another. You need to be the judge of what works for your business. But make sure that you include a few basic elements:

- Forecasted sales
- Forecasted cash flow
- Forecasted expenses
- A break-even analysis
- An income statement
- Balance sheet

In this section, and this chapter, we provide you with the basics on writing a business plan – including the finances – in general, and the restaurant-specific issues you need to account for. But whole books have been written on the subject. So if you want even more information, we suggest that you check out *Business Plans For Dummies* by Paul Tiffany, Steven D Peterson, and Colin Barrow, published by Wiley.

A quick example of all the variations: Some business plans also include *confidentiality agreements* that the reader signs and returns at the time he receives your plan. Others include technology plans, which detail computer systems, security systems, and other key electronics info.

## Expressing the concept and theme

Most restaurants have a theme and a concept. They're really two sides of the same coin. The *theme* is the common thread, idea, or image that binds your restaurant together. The *concept* is the entire package, including your menu, price point, décor, and atmosphere. When someone tells you about a new restaurant in town, the person usually describes the establishment's theme and concept: the new *family-style seafood restaurant* or the new *Chinese buffet*. Definitely take a look at Chapter 3 for great tips on identifying and expressing your theme and concept.

This section of your business plan is where you get to relate your vision of the business to the reader. It's the qualitative, or descriptive, component, as opposed to the quantitative, financial portion that lays out the numbers. Here, you describe *what* you're going to do, not *how* you're going to do it.

Consider your audience when you're developing this section of your plan. Usually you write business plans for potential investors, a banker, and other financiers. But you may also use this section in other business documents down the road, such as your mission statement or employee manuals. The better you can communicate your vision of your restaurant to another person, the more likely you are to get the money you need to get started, and to keep your focus on your goals so that you can stay in business.

In the restaurant world, people sometimes use the word *concept* instead of the word *restaurant.* It's just sort of understood that you're talking about a restaurant, so you don't need to say it. For example, they may describe Pizza Express as a pizza concept or Café Rouge as a casual dining concept. This convention is used most often when discussing chains of restaurants.

## Creating your menu now

You need to develop your menu to match your concept, attract your desired clientele, and beat the competition. You can't do much in the way of predicting what you need to buy in terms of equipment, table settings, and so on until you know your menu. You definitely can't predict how many chocolate tarts you're going to sell unless you know that chocolate tart is on your menu.

You also need to work out what your *menu mix* (how many of each dish you're likely to sell in a given time period, like a shift, a week, or a month) will be so that you can work out how many people you need to do what jobs. If everything on your menu is fried, you may not need to budget for a grill cook. Figuring your menu mix also makes it much easier to work out your forecasted *bill average,* or the average amount an individual diner spends during a meal period, which you need in order to forecast your sales. Are you sensing a pattern here? For help on getting your menu together and forecasting your menu mix, check out Chapter 9.

You may also choose to include your projected menu mix in your business plan. We recommend that you do, because it shows potential investors that you've really done your homework. They can see that you're basing your numbers – like bill averages and revenue projections – on calculated assumptions rather than random guesses. Include your menu mix for a month so that they can see what you're expecting to sell over a good chunk of time. Include your menu mix as supporting detail for your forecasted sales.

## Describing your clientele

As you develop your plan, you must decide who your customers are. Who are you trying to appeal to? Who do you want eating in your restaurant every shift? You must know this information before you can even identify your audience or your competition, and in Chapter 4 we provide you with suggestions and resources to help you accomplish this task.

When you're ready to compose your business plan, put together a few concise paragraphs that describe your clientele. Include information about their income level, dining frequency, and where they currently dine. Make sure to include information highlighting why they're likely to come to your restaurant.

You could contract with a demographic research company to put together reports for the geographic areas near your proposed restaurant, like within a 1-mile, 2-mile, or 5-mile radius. Include copies of these reports in your business plan. Check out Chapter 4 for details on working with a demographics research company.

## Laying out your market analysis

Your business plan must include a thorough *market analysis.* A market analysis identifies and describes the market you wish to compete in and your competitors in the market. Include specific information about your competitors that's relevant to your business plan. You can include things like their proximity to your location, their hours of operation, and any special draws that you believe contribute to their success. If you're able to get any kind of sales information for your competitors, include that info as well.

Your competition doesn't have to be next door. It could be down the street, in the next neighbourhood, or across town. Your *direct competitors* are those who are offering the same kind of food, the same style of service, and similar prices. Your *indirect competitors* are those who don't have the same concept or theme you do, but they're vying for the same customers you are. For example, say that you want to open a Thai restaurant. Right next door is a fish and chip shop. If you're both going for a lunch crowd, you're competing with each other. A diner is going to eat lunch only once a day, probably. Who is she going to choose? Check out Chapter 4 for all the details on researching the marketplace.

# The Bottom Line: Focusing on Finances

Financial data helps you create a plan for making your business a reality, entices investors to take a chance on your venture, and can help you manage your business after you're up and running. In particular you'll continually project sales and expenses throughout the life of your restaurant. Stay at least six months ahead in your planning, but you can also devise long-term plans that cover one to five years. Plus, you'll use reports like the income statement, balance sheet, and cash flow analysis on a regular basis (with your real-life numbers, of course) to evaluate your business and its success.

We introduce these financial tools in this section, and give you details about using them in the restaurant business. But to get a detailed picture on how to set them up and how to use them, check out the latest edition of *Understanding Business Accounting For Dummies* (by John A Tracy and Colin Barrow; Wiley).

Ultimately, your business plan comes down to the numbers. Your business plan must show that you can come up with the sales to fund the expenses you plan to incur. If you can't, you should rework your concept. If you're looking for investors in your business, they'll pay particular attention to this section no matter who they are. Whether an investor is your uncle or a canny property developer, both of them will probably spend some time here to decide whether your restaurant is a good place to invest their hard-earned cash. (For tips on getting financing, take a look at Chapter 6.)

To be thorough, you want to show three sets of numbers for each _forecast_ (prediction of what you'll spend or take in):

- ✔ A low-end, sort of worst-case scenario
- ✔ The best-case scenario that shows what'll happen if all the pieces of your puzzle fall exactly into place and the restaurant gods are smiling on you
- ✔ A mid-range set of numbers that show what happens if some things go your way and others don't

Take the calendar into account when you're forecasting your sales and expenses. February is the shortest month, with the fewest operating days. The months of January, March, May, July, August, October, and December each have 31 days. But if you're not open on Mondays, for example, look at the calendar for the years you're forecasting and make adjustments to your projections. In the example used to create all the figures in this chapter, March had the most operating days in the six-month period we were forecasting, and its sales _and_ expenses are a little higher.

In the restaurant business, expect the worst and hope for the best to avoid at least some disappointments by anticipating and avoiding disasters.

## Forecasting sales

Start your foray into the world of financial forecasting with sales. If you don't know how much you'll be taking in, you don't know how much you can spend. Forecast your sales before you forecast your expenses.

You have to develop some assumptions for estimating what your sales will be. Maybe you choose to estimate it based on your different _profit_ centres (separate areas in the restaurant that take in money, like the dining room, bar, take out, and so on). Maybe you actually estimate how many guests you'll have at different time periods and estimate what each guest will spend. Or you can use some combination of both methods. Eventually, you'll have to do all of the above, but maybe you only use part of it in your actual plan.

In Figure 5-1, we start with a simple example. We work how many guests we'll have during a meal period, also known as the number of *covers,* and multiply that by the *bill average* (which we abbreviate as B/A in the figure), or the average amount that each guest spends in the restaurant. We're assuming that we have a 40-seat restaurant with a casual dining atmosphere.

Don't let the term *bill average* fool you. The term may sound like it means the average for the entire bill, no matter how many people are sitting at the table and paying on the same bill. It's an industry standard to use this term to describe the per-person average spent in the restaurant.

Here's one way to forecast your sales:

1. **Work out how many seats you have in your restaurant.**

   In the example used in Figure 5-1, the restaurant has 40 seats.

2. **Work out how many guests will actually be in those seats for each meal period.**

   Depending on your business levels, every seat in the restaurant may be occupied multiple times. So take that fact into account when you decide how many covers you anticipate during each meal period.

3. **Try to estimate what each guest will spend during each meal period.**

   Your menu prices, your clientele, and your concept affect this number. Diners usually spend more money at dinner because prices are higher (usually because portions are larger), they have more time to spend, and they're more likely to drink alcohol in the evening. So they may have a bottle of wine at dinner instead of a glass of sparkling water. They may choose a starter, and a main course at dinner, whereas they may order only a main course at lunch.

These steps offer a very basic representation of how you start the forecasting process. Before you include your forecast in your business plan, you actually need to do some additional estimating to account for how your business levels will ebb and flow over the months. If you're a holiday-based business that's open only four months each year, you want your business plan to reflect that schedule. If you're attached to a shopping centre and hope to get most of your sales -in the months leading up to Christmas and New Year's Day, your business plan should show that goal.

**Cover Counts and Bill Average**

**Food**

| Lunch | Mon | Tues | Wed | Thurs | Fri | Sat | Averages |
|---|---|---|---|---|---|---|---|
| Covers | 40 | 40 | 40 | 50 | 60 | 70 | 50 |
| B/A | £10 | £10 | £10 | £12 | £15 | £18 | £12.50 |

| Dinner | | | | | | | |
|---|---|---|---|---|---|---|---|
| Covers | 50 | 50 | 50 | 60 | 75 | 80 | 60 |
| B/A | £20 | £20 | £20 | £25 | £35 | £35 | £25.83 |

| **Total:** | **£1,400** | **£1,400** | **£1,400** | **£2,100** | **£3,525** | **£4,060** | **£2,314** |
|---|---|---|---|---|---|---|---|

**Beverage**

| Lunch | Mon | Tues | Wed | Thurs | Fri | Sat | Averages |
|---|---|---|---|---|---|---|---|
| Covers | 40 | 40 | 40 | 50 | 60 | 70 | 50 |
| B/A | £3 | £3 | £3 | £5 | £6 | £6 | £4.33 |

| Dinner | | | | | | | |
|---|---|---|---|---|---|---|---|
| Covers | 50 | 50 | 50 | 60 | 75 | 80 | 60 |
| B/A | £6 | £6 | £6 | £8 | £9 | £12 | £7.83 |

| **Total:** | **£420** | **£420** | **£420** | **£730** | **£1,035** | **£1,380** | **£734** |
|---|---|---|---|---|---|---|---|
| **TOTALS:** | **£1,820** | **£1,820** | **£1,820** | **£2,830** | **£4,560** | **£5,440** | **£3,048** |

| | |
|---|---|
| **Average daily food sales:** | **£2,314** |
| **Average daily drinks sales:** | **£734** |
| **Average daily sales:** | **£3,048** |
| | |
| **Total weekly food sales:** | **£13,885** |
| **Total weekly drinks sales:** | **£4,405** |
| **Total weekly sales:** | **£18,290** |
| | |
| **Annual food sales:** | **£722,020** |
| **Annual drinks sales:** | **£229,060** |

**Figure 5-1:**
Developing a sales forecast.

## *Forecasting expenses*

Even before you open the doors, your restaurant incurs expenses – time is money. Even if you're not paying rent, you've bought the fridge, stove, pens, papers, computers, and so on. You sink money into your business before you realise a single pound in *income* – notice we did not say *profit*. That's way down the line.

You shelled out money when you bought this book. Save the receipt to claim it back on your taxes. Consider buying at least two copies: one in your office to loan out and one at home as a backup.

In some ways, forecasting your expenses is very different from running your business. When you're forecasting, you anticipate every possible thing you'll need to spend money on; when you're running your business, you should be looking at every opportunity to control the cost.

We know that we're repeating ourselves, but the more detailed you can be in preparing your forecasts, the better off you'll be in the long run. Figure 5-2 is a broad list for just about everything you could possibly need for your restaurant. Use it to start thinking about what expense categories you should forecast for your business. You may even find a few things that you hadn't thought about before.

Figure 5-2 is actually the restaurant chart of accounts for an income statement (see the 'Estimating profits' section later in this chapter). The numbers in the column to the left correspond with the account codes used in your *general ledger,* the master set of books that tracks all the financial transactions in your restaurant. Use whatever number system works for you, as long as you're consistent throughout your system.

When you forecast expenses, include *everything* – from produce to salaries to advertising expenses. We provide a scaled-back version in Figure 5-3. If we were to show you a full year of an expense forecast with every category, it would take up way too much space in this book. Besides, you can really get a good picture of the process by using this snapshot. The next couple of sections give you the details on what we summarise in Figure 5-3.

Include at least a full year forecast of expenses in your business plan. Make sure to include three possible scenarios: best case, worst case, and most likely to make your plan complete.

**Income Statement Accounts**

| | | | | |
|---|---|---|---|---|
| 3000 | **SALES** | | 4500 | **MARKETING** |
| 3010 | Food | | 4510 | Selling & Promotion |
| 3020 | Liquor | | 4520 | Advertising |
| 3030 | Beer | | 4530 | Public Relations |
| 3040 | Wine | | 4540 | Research |
| | | | 4545 | Complimentary Food & Beverages |
| 4000 | **COST OF SALES** | | 4550 | Discounted Food & Beverages |
| 4001 | Food: | | | |
| 4002 | Meat | | 4600 | **UTILITIES** |
| 4003 | Seafood | | 4610 | Electrical |
| 4004 | Poultry | | 4620 | Gas |
| 4005 | Produce | | 4630 | Water |
| 4006 | Bakery | | 4640 | Rubbish Removal |
| 4007 | Dairy | | | |
| 4008 | Larder & Dry Goods | | 4700 | **GENERAL & ADMINISTRATIVE** |
| 4009 | Non-alcoholic Drinks | | 4705 | Office Supplies |
| 4020 | Liquor | | 4710 | Postage & Delivery |
| 4030 | Bar Consumables | | 4715 | Telephone / Communications |
| 4040 | Beer | | 4720 | Payroll Processing |
| 4050 | Wine | | 4725 | Insurance - General |
| 4060 | Paper (QSR) | | 4730 | Dues & Subscriptions |
| | | | 4735 | Travel Expenses |
| 4100 | **SALARIES & WAGES** | | 4740 | Credit Card Discounts |
| 4110 | Management | | 4745 | Bad Debts |
| 4120 | Dining Room | | 4750 | Cash (Over) / Short |
| 4130 | Bar | | 4755 | Bank Deposit Services |
| 4140 | Kitchen | | 4760 | Bank Charges |
| 4150 | Dishroom | | 4765 | Accounting Services |
| 4160 | Office | | 4770 | Legal & Professional |
| | | | 4775 | Security / Alarm |
| 4200 | **EMPLOYEE BENEFITS** | | 4780 | Training |
| 4210 | Payroll Taxes | | 4785 | Miscellaneous |
| 4220 | Worker's Compensation Insurance | | | |
| 4230 | Group Insurance | | 4800 | **REPAIRS & MAINTENANCE** |
| 4240 | Management Meals | | 4810 | Maintenance Contracts |
| 4250 | Employee Meals | | 4820 | R&M - Equipment |
| 4260 | Awards & Prizes | | 4830 | R&M - Building |
| 4270 | Employee Parties & Sports Activities | | 4840 | Grounds Maintenance |
| | | | 4850 | Parking Lot |
| 4300 | **DIRECT OPERATING EXPENSES** | | | |
| 4305 | Car & Van Expense | | 5000 | **OCCUPANCY COSTS** |
| 4310 | Uniforms | | 5010 | Rent |
| 4315 | Laundry & Dry Cleaning | | 5020 | Equipment Rental |
| 4320 | Linen | | 5030 | Property Taxes |
| 4325 | Tableware | | 5050 | Insurance-Property |
| 4330 | Silverware | | 5060 | Other Rates |
| 4335 | Kitchen Utensils | | | |
| 4340 | Paper Supplies | | | |
| 4345 | Bar Supplies | | 6000 | **DEPRECIATION & AMORTIZATION** |
| 4350 | Restaurant Supplies | | 6010 | Buildings |
| 4355 | Cleaning Supplies | | 6020 | Furniture, Fixtures & Equipment |
| 4360 | Contract Cleaning | | 6030 | Amortization of Leasehold Improvements |
| 4365 | Menu & Wine List | | | |
| 4370 | Pest Control | | 7000 | **OTHER (INCOME) EXPENSE** |
| 4375 | Flowers & Decorations | | 7010 | Vending Commissions |
| 4380 | Licences | | 7020 | Telephone Commissions |
| 4385 | Banquet & Event Expenses | | 7030 | Waste Sales |
| 4390 | Other Operating Expenses | | 7040 | Interest Expense |
| | | | 7050 | Officers Salaries & Expenses |
| 4400 | **MUSIC & ENTERTAINMENT** | | 7060 | Corporate Office Expenses |
| 4410 | Musicians & Entertainers | | | |
| 4420 | Cable TV/Wire Services | | 8000 | **INCOME TAXES** |
| 4430 | Royalties to PRS & PPL | | 8010 | VAT |

**Figure 5-2:**
Chart of restaurant income and expense accounts.

**Q1 AND Q2 FY'08**

| | JAN £ | FEB £ | MAR £ | APR £ | MAY £ | JUN £ | TOTAL £ | TOTAL % |
|---|---|---|---|---|---|---|---|---|
| **CONTROLLABLE EXPENSES** | | | | | | | | |
| **Cost of sales** | | | | | | | | |
| Food cost | 17,355 | 16,661 | 18,743 | 18,049 | 18,049 | 18,049 | 106,907 | 30.00% |
| Drink cost | 4,588 | 4,404 | 4,955 | 4,771 | 4,771 | 4,771 | 28,259 | 25.00% |
| **Total COGS** | **£21,943** | **£21,065** | **£23,698** | **£22,820** | **£22,820** | **£22,820** | **£ 135,166** | **55.00%** |
| | | | | | | | | |
| **Payroll** | | | | | | | | |
| Salaries | 7,620 | 7,315 | 8,230 | 7,925 | 7,925 | 7,925 | 46,939 | 10.00% |
| Hourly wages | 11,430 | 10,973 | 12,344 | 11,887 | 11,887 | 11,887 | 70,409 | 15.00% |
| Benefits | 6,096 | 5,852 | 6,584 | 6,340 | 6,340 | 6,340 | 37,551 | 8.00% |
| **Total payroll** | **£25,146** | **£24,140** | **£27,158** | **£26,152** | **£26,152** | **£26,152** | **£154,899** | **33.00%** |
| | | | | | | | | |
| **Other controllable expenses** | | | | | | | | |
| Direct operating expenses | 1,905 | 1,829 | 2,057 | 1,981 | 1,981 | 1,981 | 11,735 | 2.50% |
| Music & entertaining | 381 | 366 | 411 | 396 | 396 | 396 | 2,347 | 0.50% |
| Marketing | 3,810 | 3,658 | 4,115 | 3,962 | 3,962 | 3,962 | 23,470 | 5.00% |
| Energy & utilities | 1,524 | 1,463 | 1,646 | 1,585 | 1,585 | 1,585 | 9,388 | 2.00% |
| General & administrative | 2,477 | 2,377 | 2,675 | 2,576 | 2,576 | 2,576 | 15,255 | 3.25% |
| Repairs & maintenance | 762 | 732 | 823 | 792 | 792 | 792 | 4,694 | 1.00% |
| **TOTAL CONTROLLABLE EXPENSES** | **£10,859** | **£10,424** | **£11,727** | **£11,293** | **£11,293** | **£11,293** | **£66,888** | **14.25%** |
| | | | | | | | | |
| **NON-CONTROLLABLE EXPENSES** | | | | | | | | |
| Rent | 5,334 | 5,121 | 5,761 | 5,547 | 5,547 | 5,547 | 32,857 | 7.00% |
| Property taxes | 1,143 | 1,097 | 1,234 | 1,189 | 1,189 | 1,189 | 7,041 | 1.50% |
| Lease expenses | 533 | 512 | 576 | 555 | 555 | 555 | 3,286 | 0.70% |
| FF&E reserve | 1,524 | 1,463 | 1,646 | 1,585 | 1,585 | 1,585 | 9,388 | 2.00% |
| Insurance | 1,524 | 1,463 | 1,646 | 1,585 | 1,585 | 1,585 | 9,388 | 2.00% |
| **TOTAL OTHER EXPENSES** | **£10,058** | **£9,656** | **£10,863** | **£10,461** | **£10,461** | **£10,461** | **£61,960** | **13.20%** |
| DEPRECIATION | 991 | 951 | 1,070 | 1,030 | 1,030 | 1,030 | 6,102 | 1.30% |
| INTEREST | 762 | 732 | 823 | 792 | 792 | 792 | 4,693 | 1.00% |
| **TOTAL INTEREST AND DEPRECIATION** | **£1,753** | **£1,683** | **£1,893** | **£1,822** | **£1,822** | **£1,822** | **£10,795** | **2.30%** |

**Figure 5-3:**
Sample six-month expense forecast.

## Controllable expenses

*Controllable expenses* are expenses that you can change for the better by running your business well. At the same time, these expenses can quickly get out of hand. Here are the categories of controllable expenses:

- **Cost of sales:** This category includes your food and drink costs. It represents your outlay for raw materials and reflects what you spend to buy the ingredients that go into your menu items. As the price of your ingredients fluctuates, your expense line will, too. If you're buying ice cream and dairy prices are high, your ice cream prices will be high.

  If you sell anything else, like T-shirts or custom-labelled sauce, the expense you incur by buying them to sell to your customers goes in this expense line.

- **Payroll:** This summary category includes salaries and wages for both salaried and hourly employees. It also includes other costs associated with employees, such as benefits, taxes, and national insurance.

  The more sales you generate, the more hours your employees work, the more you pay them, and the more you pay in taxes and some benefits. Take those facts into account when you're forecasting your expenses.

Salaries may not seem like a controllable expense, because you pay a manager the same amount each period, whether she's at the restaurant 10 hours or 110 hours. But ultimately, if your sales can't support the expense of another manager, you can't hire one. Co-author Mike took on an additional responsibility of running the wine side of his restaurant to save money on hiring a *sommelier,* or wine expert. Although his budget might support the extra salary now, he's found that he really doesn't need a sommelier, thus saving himself thousands of dollars each year in this category.

✔ **Other controllable expenses:** This category includes the following:

- **Direct operating expenses:** Here's where you account for incidental expenses, like uniforms, table linen, tableware, paper supply, cleaning supplies, and so on, that you must incur for your business. They're the result of your processes and are required to some extent, for every business.

- **Music and entertainment:** Include the costs for a live musician, satellite TV, your sound system and your music licences.

- **Marketing expenses:** You can control how much you spend, but most restaurants spend something on ad campaigns, PR, and research (trends, competitive analysis, and industry knowledge).

- **Energy and utilities:** These are controllable because everyone can turn off lights that aren't needed and fix leaky taps.

- **General and administrative:** This category includes office supplies, postage, phones, dues, and subscriptions. Account for professional fees, such as solicitors' fees, here. Credit card fees that you pay as a business owner and banking fees also go here.

- **Repairs and maintenance:** This category includes upkeep of your property and your equipment.

### Non-controllable expenses

Some non-controllable expenses are *fixed expenses* (or expenses whose amounts don't change). Some may be *variable expenses* (or expenses whose amounts change). The items in this list can get confusing, especially when you're just starting out. Get a copy of *Understanding Business Accounting For Dummies*, and keep it handy as you work through the first few months of your real restaurant reporting. Here are the details of the summaries we made in this section.

✔ **Occupancy costs:** This expense includes your rent (or mortgage), equipment rental, rates, insurance on the building and its contents, and personal property taxes. This number may be a constant flat rate, such as in the case of your rent payment, or it may fluctuate depending on your sales. Also think about any assessment for grounds maintenance or *common area maintenance* when you're filling out this section. Common area maintenance includes the upkeep of things like landscaping. Common area maintenance also applies to tenants in shopping centres or multi-tenant buildings for the upkeep of the lobby, public toilets, and keeping the communal outside areas clean.

✔ **Depreciation:** Basically, this is the accounting process of booking the expense of a capital purchase over a period of time known as its *useful life.* Depreciation is usually taken care of by accountants, so seek help from your accountant in figuring out your depreciation schedules.

✔ **Interest expenses:** Include any charges you will sustain for long-term debts or notes that you plan to take out. If you make payments to investors, it can show up here. These costs could be variable or constant, depending on what you set up with your investors. For example, some investors may want to be paid back in equal payments over five years, while some want a percentage back each year, with a *balloon payment,* a payment that includes the remainder of the principal in one lump sum, on the fifth year. See Chapter 6 for tips on finding financing and working out payment arrangements.

Figure 5-3 contains an FF&E Reserve line. FF&E stands for furniture, fixtures, and equipment. You can put money aside in an FF&E account in preparation for replacing these items. Your FF&E reserve account isn't a separate bank account; it's part of your operating bank account, but from an accounting perspective, this money is separate.

## *Breaking even*

After you forecast all your expenses, run a *break-even analysis,* like the one in Figure 5-4. A break-even point is the point where your revenues equal your expenses. The break-even analysis helps you determine that point, or how much you need to sell to cover your expenses before you make even £1 in profit. This step is critical. If you can't possibly get the revenue to support your projected expenses, you must adjust your expenses.

In Figure 5-4, we add most of our projected monthly expenses from Figure 5-1 to create the Monthly Expenses line. We pull out the cost we pay for food and drink (lumped together as Cost of Goods Sold or COGS) and show it on our graph as Monthly COGS. We add them together to get our Monthly Expenses + COGS so we can see what our minimum revenue must be to cover our costs.

We recommend splitting your expenses into these two categories, so that you can see how and where your cost control measures are helping you. So if you negotiate a better lease, it will show a dramatic improvement in your Monthly Expenses line, but will have less of an impact overall. If you negotiate a volume buying agreement for your food, you'll see a dramatic improvement in your Monthly COGS line, but less of a change in the overall numbers. Having this information cut into smaller pieces helps us manage our businesses more effectively. Ultimately, if you want to just provide the combined total of your monthly expenses and COGS to show your ultimate break-even point, you can do that. Use whatever method works for you. The important thing is to know how much revenue you need to cover your costs.

| | | | | | | |
|---|---|---|---|---|---|---|
| MONTHLY EXPENSES + COGS | £69,758 | £66,968 | £75,339 | £72,548 | £72,548 | £72,548 |
| REQUIRED REVENUE | £69,758 | £66,968 | £75,339 | £72,548 | £72,548 | £72,548 |
| MONTHLY EXPENSES | £47,816 | £45,903 | £51,641 | £49,728 | £49,728 | £49,728 |
| MONTHLY COGS | £21,943 | £21,065 | £23,698 | £22,820 | £22,820 | £22,820 |

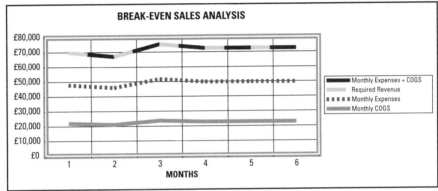

**Figure 5-4:**
Break-even
analysis.

# Estimating profits

In a nutshell, you estimate your profit by taking your sales and subtracting your expenses. The remainder is your profit. In the real world, it's not quite that simple, but it follows the same principle. Figure 5-5 shows you a sample income statement. We use the same summary categories that we've worked with throughout the chapter, so if you need additional explanation on what detailed accounts are included in the summary categories, check out the preceding sections and look at Figures 5-1 and 5-3.

Basically, we take our forecasted sales, or revenue, and subtract all of our expenses (controllable, noncontrollable, and depreciation and interest) to come up with our final net profit/loss figures.

This figure is a key indicator for many investors. Many consider the net profit/loss figure the bottom line. Of course, you must prove all your other assumptions are correct, but many people start with this number.

| Q1 AND Q2 FY'08 | JAN | FEB | MAR | APR | MAY | JUN | TOTAL | TOTAL |
|---|---|---|---|---|---|---|---|---|
| REVENUES | $ | $ | $ | $ | $ | $ | $ | % |
| Food sales | 57,850 | 55,536 | 62,478 | 60,164 | 60,164 | 60,164 | 356,356 | 75.92% |
| Drink sales | 18,350 | 17,616 | 19,818 | 19,084 | 19,084 | 19,084 | 113,036 | 24.08% |
| Other income | 0 | 0 | 0 | 0 | 0 | 0 | 0 | 0.00% |
| TOTAL REVENUE | £ 76,200 | £73,152 | £82,296 | £79,248 | £79,248 | £79,248 | £469,392 | 100.00% |
| | | | | | | | | |
| EXPENSES | | | | | | | | |
| Food cost | 17,355 | 16,661 | 18,743 | 18,049 | 18,049 | 18,049 | 106,907 | 30.00% |
| Drink cost | 4,588 | 4,404 | 4,955 | 4,771 | 4,771 | 4,771 | 28,259 | 25.00% |
| Total COGS | £21,943 | £21,065 | £23,698 | £22,820 | £22,820 | £22,820 | £135,166 | 55.00% |
| | | | | | | | | |
| Payroll | | | | | | | | |
| Salaries | 7,620 | 7,315 | 8,230 | 7,925 | 7,925 | 7,925 | 46,939 | 10.00% |
| Hourly wages | 11,430 | 10,973 | 12,344 | 11,887 | 11,887 | 11,887 | 70,409 | 15.00% |
| Benefits | 6,096 | 5,852 | 6,584 | 6,340 | 6,340 | 6,340 | 37,551 | 8.00% |
| Total payroll | £25,146 | £24,140 | £27,158 | £26,152 | £26,152 | £26,152 | £154,899 | 33.00% |
| | | | | | | | | |
| Operating expenses | | | | | | | | |
| Direct operating expenses | 1,905 | 1,829 | 2,057 | 1,981 | 1,981 | 1,981 | 11,735 | 2.50% |
| Music & entertaining | 381 | 366 | 411 | 396 | 396 | 396 | 2,347 | 0.50% |
| Marketing | 3,810 | 3,658 | 4,115 | 3,962 | 3,962 | 3,962 | 23,470 | 5.00% |
| Energy & utilites | 1,524 | 1,463 | 1,646 | 1,585 | 1,585 | 1,585 | 9,388 | 2.00% |
| General & administrative | 2,477 | 2,377 | 2,675 | 2,576 | 2,576 | 2,576 | 15,255 | 3.25% |
| Repairs & maintenance | 762 | 732 | 823 | 792 | 792 | 792 | 4,694 | 1.00% |
| Total operating Expenses | £10,859 | £10,424 | £11,727 | £11,293 | £11,293 | £11,293 | £66,888 | 14.25% |
| | | | | | | | | |
| GROSS OPERATING PROFIT | £18,253 | £17,523 | £19,713 | £18,983 | £18,983 | £18,983 | £112,438 | 23.95% |
| | | | | | | | | |
| OTHER EXPENSES | | | | | | | | |
| Rent | 5,334 | 5,121 | 5,761 | 5,547 | 5,547 | 5,547 | 32,857 | 7.00% |
| Property taxes | 1,143 | 1,097 | 1,234 | 1,189 | 1,189 | 1,189 | 7,041 | 1.50% |
| Lease expenses | 533 | 512 | 576 | 555 | 555 | 555 | 3,286 | 0.70% |
| FF&E reserve | 1,524 | 1,463 | 1,646 | 1,585 | 1,585 | 1,585 | 9,388 | 2.00% |
| Insurance | 1,524 | 1,463 | 1,646 | 1,585 | 1,585 | 1,585 | 9,388 | 2.00% |
| TOTAL OTHER EXPENSES | £10,058 | £9,656 | £10,863 | £10,461 | £10,461 | £10,461 | £61,960 | 13.20% |
| | | | | | | | | |
| ADJUSTED PROFIT | £8,195 | £7,867 | £8,850 | £8,522 | £8,522 | £8,522 | £50,479 | 10.75% |
| | | | | | | | | |
| Interest | 762 | 732 | 823 | 792 | 792 | 792 | 4,693 | 1.00% |
| Depreciation | 991 | 951 | 1,070 | 1,030 | 1,030 | 1,030 | 6,102 | 1.30% |
| | | | | | | | | |
| NET PROFIT/LOSS | £6,442 | £6,184 | £6,957 | £6,700 | £6,700 | £6,700 | £39,684 | 8.45% |

**Figure 5-5:**
Income
statement.

# Projecting cash flow

Your *cash flow projection* maps out when your sales are coming in and when your payments are going out. It shows you how, over time, your business should be able to keep itself afloat. Take a look at Figure 5-6 for an example.

Buying in bulk hurts your short-term cash flow but helps you in the long run. But don't sit on the inventory too long, or you miss the opportunity to use the cash on another money-making opportunity. Check out Chapter 20 for details on managing your cash flow.

**Q1 AND Q2 FY'08**

| | JAN £ | FEB £ | MAR £ | APR £ | MAY £ | JUN £ | TOTAL £ |
|---|---|---|---|---|---|---|---|
| **CASH RECEIPTS** | | | | | | | |
| Food sales | 57,850 | 55,536 | 62,478 | 60,164 | 60,164 | 60,164 | 356,356 |
| Drink sales | 18,350 | 17,616 | 19,818 | 19,084 | 19,084 | 19,084 | 113,036 |
| Sales receivables | 0 | 0 | 0 | 0 | 0 | 0 | |
| **TOTAL CASH RECEIPTS** | **£76,200** | **£73,152** | **£82,296** | **£79,248** | **£79,248** | **£79,248** | **£469,392** |
| | | | | | | | |
| **CASH DISBURSEMENTS** | | | | | | | |
| Cost of sales, food | 17,355 | 16,661 | 18,743 | 18,049 | 18,049 | 18,049 | 106,907 |
| Cost of sales, drink | 4,588 | 4,404 | 4,955 | 4,771 | 4,771 | 4,771 | 28,259 |
| **TOTAL COST OF SALES** | **£21,943** | **£21,065** | **£23,698** | **£22,820** | **£22,820** | **£22,820** | **£135,166** |
| | | | | | | | |
| **CONTROLLABLE EXPENSES** | | | | | | | |
| | | | | | | | |
| **Payroll** | | | | | | | |
| Salaries | 7,620 | 7,315 | 8,230 | 7,925 | 7,925 | 7,925 | 46,939 |
| Hourly wages | 11,430 | 10,973 | 12,344 | 11,887 | 11,887 | 11,887 | 70,409 |
| Benefits | 6,096 | 5,852 | 6,584 | 6,340 | 6,340 | 6,340 | 37,551 |
| **TOTAL PAYROLL** | **£25,146** | **£24,140** | **£27,158** | **£26,152** | **£26,152** | **£26,152** | **£154,899** |
| | | | | | | | |
| **Operating expenses** | | | | | | | |
| Direct operating expenses | 1,905 | 1,829 | 2,057 | 1,981 | 1,981 | 1,981 | 11,735 |
| Music & entertaining | 381 | 366 | 411 | 396 | 396 | 396 | 2,347 |
| Marketing | 3,810 | 3,658 | 4,115 | 3,962 | 3,962 | 3,962 | 23,470 |
| Energy & utilities | 1,524 | 1,463 | 1,646 | 1,585 | 1,585 | 1,585 | 9,388 |
| General & administrative | 2,477 | 2,377 | 2,675 | 2,576 | 2,576 | 2,576 | 15,255 |
| Repairs & maintenance | 762 | 732 | 823 | 792 | 792 | 792 | 4,694 |
| **TOTAL OPERATING EXPENSES** | **£10,859** | **£10,424** | **£11,727** | **£11,293** | **£11,293** | **£11,293** | **£66,888** |
| | | | | | | | |
| **OTHER EXPENSES** | | | | | | | |
| Rent | 5,334 | 5,121 | 5,761 | 5,547 | 5,547 | 5,547 | 32,857 |
| Property taxes | 1,143 | 1,097 | 1,234 | 1,189 | 1,189 | 1,189 | 7,041 |
| Lease expenses | 533 | 512 | 576 | 555 | 555 | 555 | 3,286 |
| FF&E reserve | 1,524 | 1,463 | 1,646 | 1,585 | 1,585 | 1,585 | 9,388 |
| Insurance | 1,524 | 1,463 | 1,646 | 1,585 | 1,585 | 1,585 | 9,388 |
| **TOTAL OTHER EXPENSES** | **£10,058** | **£9,656** | **£10,863** | **£10,461** | **£10,461** | **£10,461** | **£61,960** |
| | | | | | | | |
| Interest | 762 | 732 | 823 | 792 | 792 | 792 | 4,694 |
| Other deductions | 0 | 0 | 0 | 0 | 0 | 0 | |
| | | | | | | | |
| **TOTAL CASH DISBURSEMENTS** | **£68,767** | **£66,017** | **£74,269** | **£71,518** | **£71,518** | **£71,518** | **£423,607** |
| | | | | | | | |
| **CASH FLOW FROM OPERATIONS** | | | | | | | |
| Cash receipts | 76,200 | 73,152 | 82,296 | 79,248 | 79,248 | 79,248 | 469,392 |
| LESS: cash disbursements | 68,767 | 66,017 | 74,269 | 71,518 | 71,518 | 71,518 | 423,607 |
| **NET FROM OPERATIONS** | **£7,433** | **£7,135** | **£8,027** | **£7,730** | **£7,730** | **£7,730** | **£45,785** |
| **CASH ON HAND** | | | | | | | |
| OPENING BALANCE | 0 | 6,433 | 10,568 | 14,595 | 17,325 | 19,055 | |
| PLUS: New loan (debt) | 0 | 0 | 0 | 0 | 0 | 0 | |
| PLUS: New investment | 0 | 0 | 0 | 0 | 0 | 0 | |
| PLUS: Sale of fixed assets | 0 | 0 | 0 | 0 | 0 | 0 | |
| PLUS: Net from operations | 7,433 | 7,135 | 8,027 | 7,730 | 7,730 | 7,730 | |
| **TOTAL CASH AVAILABLE** | **£7,433** | **£13,568** | **£18,595** | **£22,325** | **£25,055** | **£26,785** | |
| | | | | | | | |
| LESS: Debt reduction | 1,000 | 1,000 | 1,000 | 1,000 | 1,000 | 1,000 | |
| LESS: New fixed assets | 0 | 0 | 0 | 0 | 0 | 0 | |
| LESS: Profit distributions | 0 | 2,000 | 3,000 | 4,000 | 5,000 | 5,000 | |
| **TOTAL CASH PAID OUT** | **£1,000** | **£3,000** | **£4,000** | **£5,000** | **£6,000** | **£6,000** | |
| | | | | | | | |
| **ENDING CASH POSITION** | **£6,433** | **£10,568** | **£14,595** | **£17,325** | **£19,055** | **£20,785** | **£20,785** |

**Figure 5-6:**
Sample of cash flow projections for six months.

Keep the flexibility to cover some unforeseen expenses. Managing your cash flow is managing your sales and expense projections in a timeline. For example, why are you getting a lobster order on Monday when you know you're not going to sell them until Thursday, Friday, and Saturday? Your money is sitting in the fridge for days waiting to be recouped.

## Creating a balance sheet

A *balance sheet,* shown in Figure 5-7, is a summary or snapshot of your business on a given date, usually at the end of an accounting period. It summarises the money you have (assets) compared to the money you owe (liabilities). One of the ways an owner or manager can utilise the information on the balance sheet to help evaluate the efficiency of the restaurant is to measure the number of turns on inventory for the accounting period. The inventory pound amount for the period is stated on the Balance Sheet in Assets. This figure is divided by revenues to arrive at a ratio that will tell you how efficiently you use your money. Every industry has an average number of turns they're trying to achieve. In the restaurant business, you want to get around four turns a month. Otherwise you are tying up more cash than you need.

| Assets | | | | Liabilities and Capital | | |
|---|---|---|---|---|---|---|
| **Current Assets:** | | | | **Current Liabilities:** | | |
| Cash | | £0 | | Accounts Payable | £0 | |
| Accounts Receivable | £0 | | | Sales Taxes Payable | 0 | |
| Less: Reserve for Bad Debts | 0 | 0 | | Payroll Taxes Payable | 0 | |
| Merchandise Inventory | | 0 | | Accrued Wages Payable | 0 | |
| Prepaid Expenses | | 0 | | Unearned Revenues | 0 | |
| Notes Receivable | | 0 | | Short-Term Notes Payable | 0 | |
| **Total Current Assets** | | | £0 | Short-Term Bank Loan Payable | 0 | |
| | | | | **Total Current Liabilities** | | £0 |
| **Fixed Assets:** | | | | | | |
| Vehicles | 0 | | | **Long-Term Liabilities:** | | |
| Less: Accumulated Depreciation | 0 | 0 | | Long-Term Notes Payable | 0 | |
| | | | | Mortgage Payable | 0 | |
| Furniture and Fixtures | 0 | | | **Total Long-Term Liabilities** | | 0 |
| Less: Accumulated Depreciation | 0 | 0 | | | | |
| | | | | **Total Liabilities** | | 0 |
| Equipment | 0 | | | | | |
| Less: Accumulated Depreciation | 0 | 0 | | | | |
| | | | | **Capital:** | | |
| Buildings | 0 | | | Owner's Equity | 0 | |
| Less: Accumulated Depreciation | 0 | 0 | | Net Profit | 0 | |
| | | | | **Total Capital** | | 0 |
| Land | | 0 | | | | |
| **Total Fixed Assets** | | | 0 | **Total Liabilities and Capital** | | £0 |
| **Other Assets:** | | | | | | |
| Goodwill | | 0 | | | | |
| **Total Other Assets** | | | 0 | | | |
| **Total Assets** | | | £0 | | | |

**Figure 5-7:** Sample balance sheet.

Basically, balance sheets are designed to show that your assets (cash in hand, receivables, and inventory) balance out your liabilities (your upcoming payments and debts) and *owners' equity* (includes the amount you initially invested and anything you've earned and then reinvested in the business).

# Chapter 6

# Show Me the Money! Finding Financing

*In This Chapter*

▶ Determining how much money you need

▶ Figuring out how much you can contribute

▶ Turning to investors

▶ Asking a bank for a loan

▶ Working with your landlord and suppliers

*F*inding the money to start a restaurant is one of the toughest hurdles for any budding restaurateur. You can have dreams of a popular restaurant, featuring great food and bustling with happy diners, but you need money to make it a reality. How much you need varies with how large your dreams are, the size of your own savings, and how many investors you can sway with your business plan (see Chapter 5 for the details on creating a business plan). In this chapter, we help you work out how much money you need and how much money you already *have,* and we give you tips on getting more. Finally, we give you some the inside track on clever ways to free up some cash at start-up.

## Knowing How Much Money You Need

Most people, including the experts, find it hard to start the process of figuring out how much money they need to run a restaurant. Every restaurant concept is unique. Your costs vary with your location, your building costs, the china you pick out, and a thousand other factors. Use Figure 6-1 and the expense worksheets in Chapter 5 to help you work out how much money you need.

# *Calculating start-up costs*

Many of the things that you need for your business are one-time only purchases. Items such as tables for your dining room, racks for your glasses, and shelves for dry storage usually fall under this category. Unfortunately, you have to buy them before the cash starts rolling in, so you need to plan for these expenses when you're finding your financing. Figure 6-1 can help you get started. Make lists of all the items you need and then consolidate your list on this worksheet. So under the furniture category, include the cost of your tables, chairs, barstools, seating for the bar, your host podium, equipping toilets, artwork, vases on your tables, your office desk, and so on.

| Start-up Costs | | |
|---|---|---|
| | Range of Costs | Final Projection |
| Deposits – utilities, landlord, and so on | | |
| Building and design costs (Chapters 10 and 11) | | |
| Furniture and decor (Chapter 10) | | |
| Signage (Chapter 10) | | |
| Fixtures and equipment (Chapter 11) | | |
| Licences and permits (Chapter 8) | | |
| Professional, legal, and consulting fees (Chapter 8) | | |
| Initial advertising and PR (Chapter 16) | | |
| Starting inventory of goods and supplies (Chapters 14 and 15) | | |
| Salaries until doors open (Chapter 2) | | |
| Operating reserve (this chapter) | | |
| Other | | |
| **Total One-Time Start-up Costs** | | |

**Figure 6-1:**
One-time
start-up
costs
worksheet.

We include chapter references in Figure 6-1 for where to find more information about each category of start-up expense. But remember, because all of these costs are directly related to your particular concept, location, schedule, day you hire the first manager and dishwasher, and so on, we can't give you specific advice on how much you will (or even should) spend. You have to research costs for your particular needs.

## Opening with operating reserve

You probably won't be surprised to discover that you don't stop needing money the day you open your doors. When you're planning for the amount of money you need to get started, plan to include at least three months' worth of operating expenses. This cushion helps you stay open until your business level picks up. You'll have some sales early on, but you can't expect to hit your stride until a few months into the process. Take a look at the figures showing expense forecast and cash flow projections in Chapter 5 to help determine what your monthly operating expenses will be. Chapter 5 also gives advice on forecasting your expenses and sales.

# Looking at How You Can Contribute

As frightening as it may sound, you have to contribute a significant amount of your own money to your new venture. If you don't believe in your restaurant (and put your money where your mouth is), no one else will. Using your own money does have its benefits, such as keeping complete control of your business. You don't have to share control with investors (see the section 'Working with Investors,' later in this chapter). You can also skip the paperwork involved in getting a loan (see the section 'Getting a Loan,' later in this chapter).

Using your own money to finance your restaurant does have a downside: You have no guarantee of success, so you could lose all your savings, your credit rating (if you get behind on payments), and your home (if you've borrowed against it). You want to be able to feed yourself even if your restaurant doesn't succeed, so make sure that you don't compromise your future (or your family's future). Make sure that anyone who depends on you financially (such as your spouse, significant other, or children) understands the risks involved if you decide to sink your life savings into this kind of a venture.

People can contribute to their own restaurants in several common ways:

✔ **Use savings:** People use their general savings, retirement savings, and their children's university funds, and they cash in savings bonds. They also pilfer their other rainy day accounts, and sell other investments to get money for their restaurants.

If you do decide to use savings, discuss this with your family as any reckless spending of joint funds can lead to strife – and possible financial difficulty for the family.

✔ **Get a home equity loan or line of credit:** Okay, technically speaking, this isn't their money; it's a bank's money. But should the restaurant go belly up, the loan taker is still *personally* responsible for paying back 100 per cent of this loan.

Think very carefully before going down this route. Taking out a loan of this type can jeopardise your family home. Explore other avenues of finance first.

✔ **Use credit cards:** Credit cards can be good for short-term financing options because the funds are ready when you need them. They can even help you order supplies, décor, and other items online. Plus if you shop for competitive perks, you can find low rates (usually only in the short term), get cash back on your purchases, earn bonus points, and get consolidated billing.

But rather than using credit cards to cover a wine order or pay for cash on delivery (COD) deliveries, save them for true emergencies. For example, say one winter, a storm contributes to a broken water main that floods the basements of your restaurant. You would have to pay for the cost of pumping out the water, and would also suffer further financial losses resulting from flood damage to the heating units and the subsequent freezing from loss of heat. Settling claims with your insurance company for these types of losses often takes several weeks or longer. You'll probably need to pay for the plumbers and other service technicians you might need and then get reimbursed later. Make sure that you have enough credit available on your cards to handle these emergencies.

Don't bite off more than you can chew on your credit cards. Pay the balance off as soon as possible to avoid paying high interest rates or worse.

Even if you don't borrow a penny from anyone else, we highly recommend that you write a business plan. A business plan is essential when searching for investors, but it's also a great tool for other reasons. Your business plan can save you a lot of your own money, help your restaurant make money faster, and hopefully, spare you a few headaches. See Chapter 5 for details.

# Working with Investors

Most people can't completely fund their own restaurants, so they need to look for outside investors. Investors can include partners (both silent and not-so-silent), people looking for a new investment, your friends and family, or a combination of all of these people. We cover these scenarios in the following sections. (And check out Chapter 8 for the legal details on setting up your business as a partnership or corporation.)

### Having a partner

A *partner* is usually an informed investor. Typically, a partner is more involved in the business than a typical investor, also called a *silent* or *limited partner.*

### Tallying up the types of partners

Some partners don't actually invest cash. Instead, they may invest their expertise. Normally, you select your partners because they bring something to the team that you're lacking. It could be money, bookkeeping abilities, or culinary prowess. Whatever the situation, each partner should bring something valuable to the party, or that person shouldn't get a seat at your table.

Bringing in a partner is always a strategic move. Here's a list of good reasons to bring in a partner or two:

- ✔ **They bring capital.** This is the most common reason to bring in a partner: You need the money.

- ✔ **They bring other financial services.** Sometimes, you can barter a percentage of your business for other services that you need accomplished. Get creative, but don't give too much away. For example, you probably don't want to give free meals for life to the accountant who prepared your tax return once. Think about people who have these skills if you don't:

  - Accounting

  - Business acumen

  - Financial planning

  - Fundraising

- ✔ **They bring a particular restaurant expertise.** Maybe they've spent time in the business doing something that you have zero experience with. Teaming up can help to increase your chances of success. Look for these skills in a potential partner:

  - Culinary abilities

  - Efficiency expertise

  - Front of house expertise

  - Local restaurant knowledge

  - Marketing skills

  - Operations skills

✔ **They bring reputation or name recognition.** Maybe your partner doesn't lend cash or involvement in the day-to-day operations of the business. But he brings a reputation and is available to consult as needed. For example, you may decide to bring in a big-name chef to consult on your menu and advise you on various aspects of your back-of-the-house operations (see Chapter 13 for more information on hiring a chef and other employees). Or perhaps you team up with a local wine expert who comes in to oversee changes in your wine list.

### Making the relationship work

You have heard the adage 'Too many cooks spoil the broth.' The more partners you have, the more different ideas you'll have about where the restaurant should be going and how it should get there.

Someone should have the final say in your restaurant. The best-case scenario is if one person makes the decisions. If you need to have a committee meeting to take care of minor decisions, such as what type of bread to serve, you'll end up wasting a lot of time. Don't think, 'We'll just come to a decision. We're united. No big deal.' Think again, because it usually doesn't work that way. One person doesn't have to make every minor decision; in fact, different people can take charge of different areas in the restaurant. But you must have a clear hierarchy, and the ability to make a final decision should rest with a single person.

You should settle decision-making issues before you present your first business plan, seek the first pound of financing, or even think about opening the doors. If all the partners can't come to an agreement about this point, you shouldn't go into business together. In fact, if you can't come to an agreement at this point, it's fairly unlikely that you ever will.

## Seeking other outside investors

If you're considering going to outside investors, complete your business plan and factor in the one-time only start-up costs we outline in Figure 6-1. Before you have the first conversation with the first potential investor, you want to know how much you're going to need from your investors, and be able to tell them how soon they'll get a return on their investment and how much it will be. And of course, make sure that you have your business plan in tow (see Chapter 5 for the details).

People who invest in a restaurant may think they have a say in what goes on. Even those silent partners can become not-so-silent if they spend time in the restaurant. 'Why did you get those curtains? They don't go with the chairs.' People may say that they don't want to get involved until things don't go as well, as quickly as you hope. Don't give them a valid reason to comment. Run your business right from the beginning.

Investors have friends; hopefully, they'll encourage them to come to the restaurant. If your investors are paying for their own meals, it's even better. Some investors expect to eat in the restaurant for free as one of the perks of 'ownership.' Consider offering discounted meals for investors if you think they're appropriate for your business. Make sure to write down the full terms of repaying your investors, including any perks like free or discounted meals, so that everyone knows what to expect.

## Asking family and friends to chip in

You've probably heard all the warnings about being careful about borrowing money from friends. Borrowing from friends puts both the borrower and the lender in tough situations. You don't want to lose your life savings or your relationships with friends and family. Instead, rely on them for emotional support and encouragement.

If you do decide to borrow from friends and family, treat them with the same terms you'd treat your other investors, including a signed contract with deadlines for repaying the loan.

## Compensating your investors

No one buys into the risky proposition of starting a restaurant without significant opportunity for a return on that investment. How you structure your compensation deals is important to the long-term success of your operation and the short-term success of your drive to raise money. You have to strike a balance between compensating investors fairly without burdening the business with high salaries, free meals, and unrealistic payment plans. The following sections explain a few typical compensation plans.

There's no right or wrong way to structure a compensation plan. Some investors don't want an open-ended deal. They're looking for a short-term investment. Others may want to stay involved in the business so they can say that they have a restaurant. No matter how you set it up, work with your solicitor to draft the document that stipulates the terms of each agreement. Make sure that the solicitor who draws up the agreement isn't also an investor in your business – it's a conflict of interest.

The sooner you pay back your investors, the faster you can reap the benefits of your hard work.

### Earning your percentage

Suppose you have a partner who brings money to the operation; you, on the other hand, bring a little money but a lot of experience. In fact, you're the one who runs the restaurant day in and day out, and you draw a salary from the business. Assuming that the business goes well, the investor will get a return on his investment. Depending on how you structure the partnership agreement, you can gradually gain a larger equity stake in the business over time (meaning you earn a bigger share of the business), which, you hope, will then eventually pay you a larger return on your share of the investment. Or you could forgo the growing equity and get a return on your hard work through profit sharing. In this scenario, you won't build a larger share of the business unless you invest more cash, but you do get a chance to share in the profits of the business as soon as there are any.

### Paying them back with interest

In this scenario, an investor provides you with an initial investment amount, with the assumption that you'll eventually return the stake plus interest. The timing for each – repayment of initial stake and interest payments – varies. You can find as many repayment scenarios as you can find investors. Each investor probably has certain things that appeal to him more than others. Suppose that you borrow £10,000 from an investor. In one scenario, you can pay him 10 per cent annually (£1,000 each year) for each of four years *and* return the principal (the £10,000 you borrowed) on the fourth year, for a total of £14,000 over four years. Or you can pay him back another way, say over three years. Maybe you pay him £4,000 the first year, £4,000 the second year, and finally £5,000 the third year, for a total of £13,000 over three years.

### Revving up performance-based percentages

If you pay someone back based on how the restaurant performs, this person is considered more of a limited partner. She's hoping for you to do well, so you pay her more money as a return, while she maintains a percentage of your business. Suppose that she invests £10,000 in your company, and that's 10 per cent of the value of your business. For every £10,000 of profit you make, she gets £1,000. You could add a buyout clause to her compensation plan, so in addition to getting her principal back, she gets a lump sum cash bonus. You continue to pay her dividends until you buy her out.

# Getting a Loan

Because the restaurant business is so risky, many banks won't loan money to one that's just starting out. If they do, they usually require the owner to personally guarantee the loan, meaning that the owner is personally responsible for repaying the loan, no matter how the restaurant does financially. In this section, we give you some tips on how to make yourself look like the best possible financial risk for a bank and then give you some tips on getting some help from the government if you qualify.

## Visiting your local bank

For most start-up restaurants, getting a bank loan is probably not an option. Even if you have a great reputation and working relationship with your bank, most banks look strictly at the numbers. You're better off looking for individual investors.

On the other hand, if you have a bakery and want to expand your business to include a café, you may have a shot at getting a loan from a bank. If you can show that you have collateral and a proven track record for success, and are looking to expand an already-successful business, you may qualify for a loan. The bank may require a co-signer or ask you for collateral, such as your other business, your house, or anything that minimises the bank's risk of losing its money.

Either way, the bank looks at some of your financial and business records to decide whether you get a loan. The bank will probably ask for the following info:

- ✓ **Proof of your ability to repay the loan:** Use your business plan to get this point across. For details on creating your own business plan, check out Chapter 5.

- ✓ **Your personal credit history:** The bank runs your personal credit report and assigns you a credit rating.

- ✓ **Equity:** Equity usually takes the form of your investment in the company. It's sort of like a down payment on a house.

- ✓ **Collateral:** This is any asset that you can use as security, like your house, your car, and certain kinds of investments such as a boat or jewellery, if you default on your loan.

- ✓ **Experience:** Here's where your industry-specific experience pays off. To leave the best impression, make sure that your business plan includes details of your experience in the business and managing in the business.

For more info, check out *Starting a Business For Dummies,* by Colin Barrow, published by Wiley.

# Finding Government and Business Organisation Assistance

A number of organisations exist in Britain to help small businesses develop. Don't be afraid – or too proud – to ask for help! A couple of the best resources are Business Link, a UK governmental body, and the Federation of Small Businesses, an umbrella organisation set up by business people to help, and lobby on behalf of, small business owners.

## Business Link

Contact Business Link (www.businesslink.gov.uk), a government organisation geared up to help small businesses. You will find good, practical, well-tested advice about choosing the right finance and finding a grant to suit your business. Business Link can also offer advice on setting up premises, sales and marketing, and taxes.

## The Federation of Small Businesses

The Federation of Small Businesses (www.fsb.org.uk) is the leading organisation for these types of business in the UK and campaigns on their behalf to improve the financial and economic environment in which they operate. Alongside this influential lobbying, FSB members also enjoy a unique protection and benefits package providing instant access to legal and professional advice and support.

## The British Chamber of Commerce

You can also get support from the British Chamber of Commerce (www.britishchambers.org.uk), the national face of Britain's network of accredited Chambers of Commerce. This organisation campaigns to reduce burdens on business and create a more favourable business environment.

## Business Debtline

Ideally you have the necessary accountancy skills, or can call on people who do, from the beginning of your venture. But there may be worrying times when some good, practical advice from experts helps enormously. The psychological boost of just talking to someone who deals with financial problems is quite energising. Business Debtline (0800 1976062) is a national telephone service that offers free, confidential and independent advice to small businesses on tackling cashflow problems.

## *Other helpful contacts*

A number of other organisations exist to provide you with more general business information and advice. The most useful include:

- **Companies House (`www.companies-house.gov.uk`):** Companies House is responsible for:

  - Examining and storing company information under the Companies Act and related legislation

  - Filing information on a company directors' register

  - Finding information on a company

  - Incorporating and dissolving limited companies

  - Making all this information available to the public.

- **Her Majesty's Revenue and Customs (`www.hmrc.gov.uk`):** HMRC is responsible for collecting the bulk of tax revenue. Visit the Web site for:

  - An employer pack

  - Help with National Insurance

  - Corporation Tax information

  - Information on starting a new business

  - Help with how to register a new business for VAT

  - Day-to-day payroll advice

  - PAYE and other business information

- **The British Hospitality Association (`www.bha.org.uk`):** The British Hospitality Association is the national trade association for the hospitality industry and represents over 9,000 hotels, 11,000 restaurants and 19,000 contract catering units. It promotes and protects the interests of its members by being heard at local, national and international levels, influencing industry decision makers, helping to shape policy and minimising the burden of new legislation.

- **The VAT Helpline (0845 010 9000):** For help on all aspects of Value Added Tax.

# Considering Other Ways to Increase Your Liquidity

When most people think of getting financing together, they usually think of borrowing money, liquidating accounts, and maybe even looking down the back of the sofa for loose change. But you can make the money you have go further if you know where to look and who to ask, in the form of deferred rent and extended credit terms. Check out the next few sections for details.

## Securing landlord investments

One of the biggest expenses in your budget is your rent or mortgage. Negotiate the best deal you can to keep ongoing expenses as low as you can, and perhaps to even help with start-up costs. Look for a landlord who is pro-business. Hopefully, he's looking for you to renew your lease after the initial term ends. And maybe he even works to make it easier for you to make money. Ultimately, your success increases the value of his property.

### Negotiating start-up savings

Many landlords give breaks on rent during the start-up phase of your operation. For example, if you need to *build out* the space, meaning demolish the existing space and construct a new space, and you're investing £50,000 to do it, maybe your landlord will give you three months of free rent. Check out Chapter 7 for details on finding and leasing your space.

Maybe you can take it to the next level. For example, you can propose that if you open up by a certain day, your landlord gives you another two months rent-free. A busy, successful restaurant benefits a landlord's other properties – if he has any. Perhaps the landlord also owns the space next door, down the street, or maybe just the rest of the building. Ultimately, a building's landlord doesn't want any of his space to be vacant. He makes money only when the space is leased. An operating business (especially a new restaurant) is much more attractive to a prospective tenant than an empty space or a shop with a closed sign and painted windows. An operating business shows neighbourhood vitality. If you're just coming in, the landlord wants to get you in and up and running. The sooner you're making money, the sooner he is.

### Negotiating your long-term lease

Consider making your landlord a partner. We don't mean that he should manage your bar or take over your ordering. But see whether you can work out a rent based on a percentage of the profits. (For more information on partnerships, see the 'Working with Investors' section, earlier in this chapter.) So if you're not doing well, you're not getting destroyed with a huge payment. But if your concept is going like a train, you're bringing him along for the ride and stuffing his pockets. Another option is to try to negotiate a rent schedule that allows lower monthly payments in the early stages, with annual increases built into the term of the lease.

If you have a five-year lease and you're expecting to make infrastructure changes to things like the heating and cooling units, electrical systems, plumbing and so on, make sure that you get some kind of a reduction in your rent. If you walk away, you can't take the plumbing with you, so you're really paying for an improvement to someone else's building.

Landlords are looking for long-term investments and if the tenant has no track record, the landlord may ask for a rent deposit of a year in advance or a bank guarantee. However, the tenant (that's you) may ask for a rent free period if money is being spent on the property (for example for re-wiring, re-decorating, or new plumbing). The best lease is a full-repairing and insuring one with five year rent reviews, the rent only increasing, not decreasing. The amount of rent increase can be calculated on profits, or a comparable method of calculation such as the turnover. Securing a break clause is advisable. This is a walk-away sum should the lease be broken. You should also include a sub-let clause. The shorter the lease, the less security there is for the restaurant and the less its borrowing power. A longer lease can be used as security against a loan as well as providing a sense of security. Ask a tax advisor about setting off a large rent deposit against taxes, because after start-up a period of non-profit making needs to be taken into account. Get the rent right, as this is key to a successful restaurant. Always take professional advice when dealing with a lease.

Be the best tenant you can be. If you're not paying your rent on time, you can't expect your landlord to go out of his way to work with you. And if you're not paying your rent at all, you have bigger issues than dealing with your landlord.

## *Relying on suppliers' credit*

Your vendors and suppliers can be a source of credit. They're not exactly giving you a loan, but they can defer the payment of your bills, which is sometimes even better. Basically, your supplier approves you for extended payment terms, like *net 30* or *net 45 days* (paying within 30 or 45 days). Then you can use your cash for other things in the short term. New restaurants may have a tough time qualifying for extended credit terms, but you may be able to qualify for smaller purchases. Check out Chapter 14 for more on dealing with suppliers.

Suppliers can offer you some equipment at no charge if you buy other products from them. So, for example, they may give you a dishwasher or espresso machine as long as you buy your soap and coffee from them. Such an agreement isn't exactly a loan, but if you need the equipment, it can help reduce your start-up costs.

# Chapter 7

## Choosing a Location

. . . . . . . . . . . . . . . . . . . . . . . . . . . . . . . . . . . . . . . . . . . . . . . . . . . .

. . . . . . . . . . . . . . . . . . . . . . . . . . . . . . . . . . . . . . . . . . . . . . . . . . . .

*Y*ou've heard it countless times before: The cardinal rule in estate agency is location, location, location. But finding the perfect location is much easier said than done. Part of the reason is that what works for some concepts definitely won't work for others.

The key in choosing a location is finding a spot that makes it easy for *your* targeted or desired clientele to reach *your* restaurant on a *regular* basis. It may be a restaurant in a busy shopping area. It may be a gastropub in the country. It may be a lunch-only restaurant near the station. There is no right answer that fits every concept or area. Use the suggestions in this chapter to decide on the best spot for your restaurant.

# Looking at the Local Property Market

Everything starts with the local estate agents' market. Here are a few ways to find potential locations:

✔ **Work with a commercial estate agent:** Finding one who knows the restaurant market is preferable.

✔ **Comb areas you think match your requirements:** You need to think about your concept and wished-for *footfall* (the number of people who pass by either on foot or by transport). Look for locations that interest you even if it's not obvious that they're up for sale or lease. And check out the 'Paying attention to footfall' section later in this chapter.

✔ **Check in with your local chamber of commerce:** It's a good source of information.

✔ **Get info from your local governing bodies:** Consult local and district councils, and any other agencies that dole out licences and are likely to know of new development opportunities.

Most people look at the estate agents' market and potential locations in one of two ways.

✔ **A sure thing:** They start a restaurant in an already hip, trendy area of town, and hope to make some profit. Locations where people are often mingling provide a built-in customer base. But they come at a price – a hefty amount of money to get the space. (See the 'Looking at other businesses in the area' section later in the chapter for related info.)

✔ **The ground floor:** Some people choose to be pioneers and hit a part of town before it becomes a great area for restaurants. Choosing to be one of the developers of the area means paying less in rent than in established areas. But it also means not having the built-in potential customer base of lots of footfall nearby (which can translate into increased marketing costs). Just keep in mind that with the greatest potential for profit comes the greatest possibility of failure. Your estate agent should be able to help you find up-and-coming locations.

If you choose to establish your restaurant in an area before it becomes fashionable, you may not realise your business potential for a couple of years. Make sure that you have enough cash to sustain the wait – few people have unending money supplies. Your overhead will be heavier while you wait for business levels to improve and sustain you.

The direction you take depends on your concept, business plan, and the specifics of each space.

# Examining Location Specifics

No two locations are identical. What works for some restaurants definitely doesn't work for others.

Research the history of your proposed space, building, and neighbourhood. Find out what was there before and what has succeeded and failed. Try to work out why businesses in the area either made it or didn't survive. Here are a few ways to get started on your research:

✔ **Ask landlords for info.** Even if landlords can get you only the names of the previous tenants, you at least have a starting point for your research.

✔ **Visit the library.** The resources at your library can be helpful if the space you're interested in has been around for a long time.

The librarian can point you in the right direction as well as giving you Web site addresses. Visit local government Web sites (they're usually more up-to-date than printed booklets or other publications) to find out about new housing or businesses in the area. Have a good look at the demographics of the area, and the types of business already well established there.

✓ **Talk to past to lessees and owners.** If you can talk with the past lessees, you can get invaluable information on their problems and solutions for the space, saving yourself some trial and error down the road.

✓ **Talk to the planning department.** Consider talking to your local council planning application department for information on renovations that have been made, when they were made, and so on. All renovations, additions, and many minor construction projects require permits that must be granted by this department. They keep a copy of all plans and permits on file.

✓ **Chat with the neighbours.** They're always a source of information, but take whatever info you get with a grain of salt. They may have accurate observations but inaccurate conclusions.

✓ **Contact your local restaurant association, if one exists.** If the space you're considering used to be a restaurant, the association may have insights to share about why it is no longer used for that purpose.

You may not be in the market for a truly unique location, but here's a list of things to look for that benefit most restaurants:

✓ **Easy access:** Think about your restaurant from the guests' perspective. If they have to drive past your restaurant, turn left at the next light, and then backtrack to get to you, they may not bother. Often when people eat out, their first consideration is convenience. Make it as convenient as possible for them to get to you.

✓ **A high-profile location:** Corner plots are desirable because people can see you from two streets instead of one. You'll get more exposure, instead of being buried in the middle of the block. Say that your restaurant is close to the shopping centre. If possible, you want to be out in front of, rather than behind, the shopping centre because that's where the most exposure is. If you can get the front corner of a large car park, right on the street, so much the better.

✓ **Availability of parking:** Unless you're in an urban area that benefits primarily from foot traffic or public transport, abundant, well-lit parking is a must.

## *Paying attention to traffic*

*Traffic* doesn't just mean cars. It means potential customers passing by your restaurant. Traffic includes walking people, biking people, people in taxis, people on public transport, people driving by – any means people use to travel near your business.

Watch the traffic near your proposed location and make judgments about how well the people fit the profile of your proposed clientele (see Chapter 4 for more on targeting the right customers). If you have a concept nailed down and a great flow of traffic but the traffic is not your desired clientele, you'll have a tough time succeeding. For example, lorry drivers want a good hearty meal that's good value. If you're trying to sell them small, expensive portions, forget it. Here are some thoughts to ponder to get you started:

✔ Where are these people going? Are they going to or from work, shopping, visiting a nearby museum or theatre, going to school? Are these the people you're targeting? Are they likely to come in?

Sometimes, putting a sign in a proposed location works better than placing a restaurant there. For example, being located along a busy commuting thoroughfare isn't a guarantee of success. People may see you but not want to give up their spot in traffic or return later to your restaurant if they'll have to fight the same traffic again.

✔ Do your proposed operating hours match the traffic flow? If you open at 5 p.m. in a business district, you may have already missed the traffic flow that existed from 9 a.m. to 5 p.m. But in a suburb, opening at 5 p.m. may be ideal – people start returning from work around that time.

Visit your proposed location many different times, at different times of day and on different days of the week, to get a feel for the traffic flow. Make notes about the volume and type of traffic you see. Look for patterns to help you evaluate the location.

Commercial demographic company reports can help you identify demographics, average car traffic, and so on. Start with your local chamber of commerce, but then look for companies that specialise in segmenting the population into different demographic groups. Two examples are Cartogen (www.cartogen. co.uk) and The Market Segmentation Company (www.marketsegmentation. co.uk), who offer cost-effective reports on the UK area you are looking at and the customer lifestyle.

## *Knowing which locations to avoid*

In a perfect world, people come to your restaurant for your restaurant's sake. If it's good, they come back; if it's not, they don't come back. But in the real world, outside factors affect your business more than you may realise. Your best bet is to pinpoint and avoid things that may keep customers away from your restaurant. For starters, avoid locations that feature

✔ **Businesses that your customers or others may find unsavoury.** They may feel uncomfortable and may stop coming altogether.

✔ **Permanent building areas.** You don't want heavy machinery and trucks going through during dining hours. Also, guests may have trouble getting to you through the construction mess. If the construction is short-term or pervasive throughout your area, you may not be able to avoid it.

Spend the necessary time talking to the people at your local council's transport planning department. They can tell you what their long-term plans (one-, three-, and five-year time frames) are regarding road projects in the areas you're considering. Surviving and/or recovering from an extended road construction project can be difficult, or impossible. Many of your potential customers will choose other routes to their destinations and never even find out that you exist, and the ones who know about you won't want to deal with the hassle.

✔ **Remote or hard-to-find addresses.** Don't locate your restaurant in a remote or hard-to-get-to location. In a very few cases, remoteness can be a draw, such as in the highest-grade fine dining, where you're going after exclusivity. In most cases, though, people want convenience to some degree. They consider the efficiency of their time when making dining and drinking choices. Another consideration is that people are less likely these days to venture far from home when drinking.

✔ **Other counter-productive features.** For example, if you're targeting a business clientele, don't locate your restaurant near a large school where teenagers go out for lunch. They may discourage other patrons from coming in. Depending on your concept, however, teens may be your ideal audience – they do have considerable disposable income these days.

Ultimately, let your own conscience be your guide when it comes to avoiding certain situations and neighbours. Remember who you want to attract to your business and how they see the world and your restaurant.

## Looking at other businesses in the area

Your neighbours affect your business, and vice versa. Businesses such as theatres, cinemas, and shopping centres go hand in hand with restaurants. Attractions such as a scenic river walk in a city centre area, a sea view, or wildlife are great restaurant hooks.

Look for businesses that feed off restaurants. Think about the relationship between the remora and the shark. The shark attacks and claims its prize. The remora, attached to the shark, sustains its life off the successes of the shark by eating the leftovers. Restaurants and their neighbours are similar to the remora and the shark. Think about the number of chain restaurants located close to shopping centres, tourist attractions, and so on. Many restaurants, chains and independents alike, locate themselves near a busy office building, office park, or business district, hoping to capture a booming breakfast, lunch, and dinner business. Putting a restaurant in such a location is a completely calculated move, designed to capitalise on already-present traffic.

Also consider how your particular restaurant fits in with the current restaurant mix. If you want to open a Mexican café, but two other Mexican concepts are established in the same area, do you want to be the third? You may be successful if the other two are both highly commercialised versions of Mexican cuisine and yours is truly authentic *and* your clientele can appreciate the difference. But if you're offering more of the same, think about choosing a different location. There is a big exception, though. In larger city areas, common cuisines can make up large city streets that become areas known for different cuisines, such as Soho (Chinese) or Little Turkey in London.

## Considering security

Security is a key concern for any business owner. Restaurants have a decent amount of cash on hand, despite the prevalent use of credit cards, and they can make a tough-to-resist target for thieves. Therefore, you must evaluate a potential location for security. Keep the following advice in mind:

- Avoid blind interior and exterior corners. Blind corners, like blind driveways, are corners that can't be seen from the normal flow of traffic.

- Stay away from buildings with poorly lit stairwells and hallways.

- In today's security-aware climate, consider potential terrorist targets in your location selection. If you're planning to be located near a courthouse, a power plant, or a government building, consider the possibility that you may have to temporarily close your doors during erroneous bomb threats, evacuations, and the like.

- Avoid natural disaster areas (particularly flood plains) when possible. If you're in an area where floods, for example, are prevalent, simply try to find the safest location possible.

In addition, make sure that your new location includes these safety features:

- Working locks and alarms on exterior doors or other secure areas

- Working security system with cameras

- Safe access to and from the rubbish area

- Plenty of food storage in secured areas

- Well-lit exterior and parking area

- A working safe

All of the things in these lists can be remedied with time and money.

# *Factoring In Cost Considerations*

The primary cost of your location is your rent (or mortgage). For the most part, the restaurant owner isn't also the building owner. Buying the building is typically too expensive for a new restaurateur, so unless you're very established and successful, you'll probably have a landlord. Ultimately, a building's landlord doesn't want to keep the space vacant. He makes money only when the space is leased. Unless his is a highly sought-after area, he should be motivated to help you get up and running. Check out Chapter 6 for more information about negotiating with your landlord.

Here's a quick list of questions that should affect your decision to lease a particular space:

- ✔ **Is your landlord pro-business?** Is he making it easy for you to make money? Your success increases the value of his property. You want to sign with someone who is looking for you to be there in the years beyond your initial lease.

- ✔ **Is your landlord willing to adjust your rent on a short-term basis?** Look for a landlord who's willing to give you some months of free rent – known as *rent abatement* – especially while you're setting up. It's not uncommon to ask for and get a 90-day abatement so that you can keep expenses down during your pre-opening period. Other tenants may depend on your being open because a closed space is an eyesore. If the rent is based on sales, the landlord wants to get you up and running as soon as possible. But keep in mind that it's also not uncommon for your landlord to give you nothing at all.

- ✔ **Is your landlord willing to foot some of the bill for building costs?** This situation is less common, but you can still ask. Landlords are more likely to give you free rent rather than money out of their pocket. In some cases, you can get landlords to give you *x* amount of pounds per square metre toward the tenant improvements. One key factor in getting contributions is the state of the local commercial leasing market. If things are soft, and space is sitting vacant for extended periods you can be more aggressive in negotiating.

- ✔ **Is your landlord willing to help pay for required upgrades to the HVAC (heating, ventilation, and air conditioning system) and/or electrical systems as needed?** Sometimes when you get into a space, unforeseen complications occur that have more to do with the landlord's building than with your restaurant. Find out what the landlord's policy is on these kinds of upgrades before they happen.

If you're looking at a space that wasn't previously a restaurant, fitting it to accommodate the kitchen, dining room, and so on will be very expensive. Have an experienced restaurant builder look at the space and help you understand all the ramifications of building before you sign the lease. Ducts and plumbing don't just appear – they require hard work and money.

Depending on the age and configuration of the space you're considering, you may not be able to make the modifications necessary for a restaurant. Maybe the infrastructure of the building can't support the configuration, or perhaps the building's a historic landmark, and the modifications necessary aren't within the charter. Check to see if the building is listed and if there are restrictions. You don't want to get locked into a lease and then discover that you can't install a range hood in your kitchen. You still owe five years' rent. Don't go bankrupt before you make any money.

If you decide to lease a space, consider talking with the other tenants about their experiences with the landlord. You'll get info that's not in the public domain, shall we say, about the history of the space, and you can probably find out some details about why the previous tenant left. You're guaranteed to get a different perspective from the one the landlord gave you.

In addition, get the true story regarding the planning situation of your space from the your local planning office. Maybe plans don't allow for an outdoor café, but your business plan and concept demand one. On the other hand, the council may try to promote outdoor eating in specific areas and provide financial incentives to develop restaurants that offer it.

# Chapter 8

# Paying Attention to the Legalities

. . . . . . . . . . . . . . . . . . . . . . . . . . . . . . . . . . . . . . . . . . . . . . . . .

## In This Chapter

▶ Figuring out who can help you with legal affairs

▶ Choosing the best legal setup for your restaurant

▶ Obtaining licences

▶ Putting together your insurance plan

. . . . . . . . . . . . . . . . . . . . . . . . . . . . . . . . . . . . . . . . . . . . . . . . .

More than any other topic in this book, legal issues vary within the British Isles and from concept to concept. You need to know about the specific laws in your area so that you stay out of legal trouble that could result in fines, loss of your licences or, even worse, prison. Laws dictate some details of your business that may surprise you. For example, laws dictate the number of hours your business can be open, whether you can serve diners on your terrace, and whether children are allowed on your premises.

To help sort through these complex issues, just about every restaurant needs the assistance of outside professionals, including a good solicitor, a thorough accountant, and a reputable insurance agent. These business-canny pros can help you navigate the legal necessities that are part of every small business and those that are unique to the wonderful world of the restaurant business.

In this chapter, we get you thinking about the legal realities of the business. We tell you exactly who you need to help you. Then we go over details concerning how to set up your business, what you need to know about local laws and licenses, and the types of insurance you need to be thinking about.

## Identifying the Help You Need

Professionals you turn to for assistance should have experience in the business. If you get a 'deal' from someone without restaurant experience, you may actually lose money in the not-so-long run. If your solicitor doesn't know how to get all the licences you need, you may be in trouble. And if your accountant doesn't depreciate your furniture correctly, you may not have the money to buy the new stuff when the old has to be replaced.

Find people with verifiable, positive references in the industry, and ask for a client list or a list of other restaurateurs they're working with. If they're not currently working with any, consider finding someone else. Call a few clients and get their impressions of the expert's service. Don't be shy; you can save yourself time and money by weeding out problems before they start.

Look for people who can understand your concept and goals. Because each restaurant is unique, make sure that they understand you and your vision. Bring them into your space or show them your plans. Be sure that they understand what you're trying to achieve so that they can help you get there.

The people you hire must be objective and able to have the hard conversations with you. Hire people who can tell you that you're spending too much money or the manager you really like has his hand in the booze store cupboard. You hire experts because they bring you knowledge that you don't have, and their input can ultimately benefit your business (even if what they're saying is hard to take). Don't let your ego get in the way of the success of your business. If two people in the room always agree, one of them is unnecessary.

Our advice is to contact experts with experience in the industry for specific advice in

- ✔ How to set up your business
- ✔ How to get the right insurance for your business
- ✔ How to get the necessary permits and licenses to do the business you want to do

## Cross-examining solicitors

Solicitors can expedite your paperwork through the maze of bureaucracy and advise you as to what's necessary to do things the right way. They can be very helpful to the new restaurateur, especially when you're setting up your business. They can do the following:

- ✔ Recommend and file the appropriate paperwork to set your business up as a business, partnership, or sole proprietorship.
- ✔ Draw up partnership agreements and any other agreements.
- ✔ Review contracts, like your lease and your vendor agreements.
- ✔ Do the hard work of filing proper paperwork for permits and other licenses. For more help, see the section ' Getting licences,' later in this chapter.

Depending on the size of your operation, you also may eventually need a few different lawyers, such as a labour lawyer, intellectual property lawyer, tax lawyer, and divorce lawyer, er, we mean, general business lawyer.

Your lawyer may also have contacts, clients, or colleagues looking for a good investment. She may be willing to pass along your name to interested parties.

## Auditing accountants

If you're brand new to running a restaurant, an accountant should be one of the first people you speak to. In the early stages, before you even open your doors, an accountant can walk you through the financial planning aspects of creating your business plan. He can explain complex financial stuff like depreciation, debt reduction, and raising capital. He can work with your lawyer to show you tax advantages to setting up your business in one way or another. Using a qualified accountant to guide you can help you avoid paying for a lawyer to get you out of trouble later. After you're up and running, he can help with preparing the monthly books and reports, preparing taxes, and conducting internal audits and reviews.

If your landlord bases your rent on the sales that you generate, you probably need to hire an accountant to review your books and make a statement to your landlord. See more about negotiating your lease in Chapters 6 and 7.

## Ensuring your insurance agent

Insurance coverage is important in any business. You need liability insurance, property insurance, and workers' insurance. Your insurance agent should be able to walk you through the basics of balancing deductible amounts, giving you the appropriate amount of coverage with reasonable payments that protect your business without putting you in the poorhouse. See the section 'Buying the Insurance You Need', later in this chapter, for more details.

# Setting Up Shop on Legal Grounds

Your solicitor and your accountant can help you decide how to set up your business. You have a number of options from going it alone to setting up a partnership to incorporating your business. Your decision determines how your company is taxed, how you earn an income from the business, what your obligations are if your business fails, and many other expensive decisions. In the following sections, we discuss some of the most common options.

Even if you're the only investor or are involved in a partnership, you still may want to form a business. Without the legal protection of forming your business, your creditors can come after you if your business goes under. They can lay claim to your home, cars, savings, and anything else of value.

## Going it alone: Sole proprietorships

A *sole proprietorship* is owned by one single person – in this case, you. Your solicitor registers your business as a proprietorship by completing a simple form. You keep everything that you make, and you personally owe everything that you spend.

## Teaming up: Partnerships

A *partnership* is similar to a sole proprietorship, but you're adding extra people to the mix. You share all the profits and all the risk. No two partnerships are the same, but the partners should spell out the details, in writing, with a solicitor, before they begin. Each partner should consider hiring separate solicitors to make sure that the agreement is all present and correct. (Check out Chapter 6 for info on finding financing through partners.) Shop around for a solicitor's company-forming package deal. Solicitors who specialise in restaurant set-ups offer a package deal incorporating the lease, details on forming a company, business partner advice, accountancy tips, the low-down on laws regarding staffing, and legislation on hygiene.

Make sure that your agreement includes details about all of these concerns:

- **Responsibilities and hierarchy:** Sort out who's responsible for what tasks or areas of the restaurant, who makes which decisions, and who reports to whom.

- **Ownership stakes:** Whether a partner is contributing money, time, or both, she's making an investment in the company. In return for that investment, she owns part of the business. Spell out the details of your arrangement clearly, so that no one is confused.

- **Pay rates and profits:** Make sure that everyone knows how you plan to divide profits. Spell out who gets a salary and when it starts. Often, as you're building a business, the owners take a small salary (or sometimes no salary) until the business has the money to spare. Resolve all financial issues clearly and to the satisfaction of all parties involved.

- **Ultimate decision-making authority:** When humans work together for any length of time (usually no more than 15 minutes), disagreements pop up. Having more decision makers can mean that making decisions becomes more complicated, so clarify how your decisions will ultimately get made. Your first line of defence is to discuss, persuade, and then compromise. But the occasion will arise that requires one person's opinion to win the day. Write it down before you start.

✔ **Exit options:** You never want to think about this possibility before you start, but your partnership will probably end at some point. Make sure that you have an exit strategy outlined in your agreement. Usually, one partner can buy the other out, either in a lump sum payment or over time.

✔ **Death contingencies:** Definitely not a fun one to think about, but you need to consider it. Have a clear plan for handling this situation.

## Almost teaming up: Limited partnerships

*Limited partners* are more like investors in the business than actual partners. They limit their liability legally because they aren't involved in the operation. Say that your friend, John Brown, wants to invest in your restaurant. He doesn't want to be involved in the day-to-day, but he thinks you're a canny businessperson and wants a piece of the action. He gives you £25,000, and he owns a corresponding percentage of your business. You draw up an agreement that specifies what he gets as a *return on investment* (or ROI) and when he gets it. Maybe he gets a percentage of profits paid quarterly or annually. Fast-forward five years: Things have been going well for several years, but the worst-case scenario occurs, and your business folds. John Brown doesn't get his money back, but he also doesn't incur any debts as a result of your business folding. Creditors may take your house, but Joe's is safe and sound. That security for the investor is the beauty of limited partnerships.

As with any partnership agreement, have your solicitor draw up a document with the specific language detailing the terms of your agreement with any limited partners.

## Playing it safe: The business entity

Creating a business that owns your restaurant, offers you some protection if your restaurant goes under. Your solicitor can set up your business for you, and you can be the only shareholder in your business and still own it completely. But creating a businesses also has some significant tax implications. Definitely discuss your options with your solicitor and accountant for the pros and cons of your specific situation.

Creating a business doesn't remove all your responsibility in the event that your business fails. As a new restaurant owner, many lenders require you to personally guarantee loans, which means that even if your business fails, you're still responsible for the debt. Weigh the options. We know of many people who have lost both their businesses and their personal credit ratings when their businesses fell apart. And don't plan to use your business as a shield if you have less than honourable intentions. If you run out on your rent or creditors, you develop a negative reputation that will follow you throughout your career.

# Knowing Your Law

Laws govern just about everything about any business. The restaurant business is no different. Most laws related to this industry are governed and enforced by local and national government agencies. Your local council health and safety department determines the many specific health regulations you must follow to continue to serve diners in your area. Your local planning department determines what steps you must take to make your restaurant safe to be occupied by people. And who knows who handles alcohol licences in your area? (Well, actually, we show you how to find out who handles them in your area, so don't worry.) Rules and regulations exist governing the following:

- When you must close and when you can open
- How big you can make your signage and where you can post it
- The process for applying for required permits
- Where you can have your outdoor seating
- Details about building codes that you must follow
- How you can sell alcohol

There have been quite radical changes in the law in the past few years in the UK regarding any business that serves alcohol to customers.The following licensing arrangements are now essential:

- All premises undertaking licensable activities must have a licence.
- A designated premises supervisor must be named on the premises license.
- Anyone who authorises the sale of alcohol must hold a personal licence.

All businesses must, of course, be licensed. England, Scotland, Wales and Northern Ireland each have their own licensing laws. A *licence* is a legal document issued by -your local council giving you permission to do a very specific thing. For example, in the case of the restaurant business, you need a licence to serve alcohol. If you serve alcohol without one, you can be shut down, fined, or even go to prison if you continue to flout the law.

Within those boundaries each local authority draws up their own documentation on licensing which reflects its locale and may differ from a neighbouring one. Although all of the necessary regulations covered in this chapter may at first appear daunting, local authorities are very keen to help you along the way.

# *Making the joint legal: obtaining a premises licence*

A premises licence can be granted either for a one-off event or indefinitely, as in the case of opening a new restaurant. Applicants have to submit a plan of their building and an operating schedule. The premises licence also covers the provision of entertainment facilities, such as:

- Dancing (for example, a dance floor)
- Entertainment of a similar description (for example live bands, or a comedy club)
- Making music (for example, a karaoke machine)

When applying for a licence you should make an appointment to talk to your local licensing officer. You will be given an application form to fill out. Get this right, as it will smooth the way in obtaining your licence. Premises licences last indefinitely and do not need to be renewed.

Do not make promises you can't keep on you application form (for example, that you will arrange taxis for customers) It is a criminal offence not to adhere to your conditions of licence, so get it right and go over the form with your licensing officer.

The Licensing Authority form covers:

- Who the applicants are
- Your operating schedule (when you wish to start)
- Description of the premises, its type, general layout and location
- What licensable activities you intend carrying out on the premises (live or recorded music, for example)
- Late night refreshment
- Supply of alcohol
- Public opening hours

✔ The steps you will undertake to promote the four licensing objectives, namely

- Prevention of crime and disorder

- Public safety

- Prevention of public nuisance

- Protection of children from harm

When you apply for a premises licence, you must send the completed application form and fee (which varies depending on the ratable value of your premises) to the council, and send copies of the application form to the responsible authorities (the police, fire authority, and certain council services). You must include a plan of the premises and an operating schedule describing the proposed activities. You must also advertise the application in the local press, and on notices displayed at the premises for a period of 28 consecutive days. Interested parties such as neighbours, other businesses, can see the application on the local authority's Web site.

The responsible authorities and *interested parties* (people living or working in the vicinity of the premises) have the right to make *representations*. That is, they can comment or raise objections. The authority will grant a licence if no-one makes any representations. If someone does make representations, the application will be determined by the Licensing Committee.

## Getting personal: Perusing personal licences

Anyone who allows the sale of alcohol needs a *personal licence* from their local authority. Once issued, a personal licence is valid for ten years. There are various duties on holders of personal licences, and the licence may be forfeited if the holder is convicted of certain offences. Personal licences currently cost £37.

The Designated Premises Supervisor (DPS) is the point of contact for the licensing authorities, the police, and fire services, and must hold a personal licence. in the DPS is in charge of the daily control of the business and is also responsible for the supply of alcohol, but can give authority to staff for sales. If a member of staff commits an offence under the Licensing Act, the DPS may be held responsible.

To get a personal licence, you must:

✔ Be over 18

✔ Have no relevant criminal convictions as detailed in the Licensing Act 2003

✔ Possess an approved licensing qualification

✔ Pay the required fee

Someone with a personal licence can hold up to 50 *temporary or occasional events* a year at other premises that are not licenced. Temporary or occasional events are classed as small events where less than 500 people are likely to attend and the event lasts for less than 72 hours.

## Getting stuck in to registering food premises

Food business operators – that'll be you – must register all the establishments they use by law. *Establishments* includes premises used for the storage, production, sale or distribution of food. Registration enables local authorities to keep an up-to-date list of food premises in their area so they can plan inspections and target advice and enforcement resources. The frequency of inspections will depend on the type of business.

Registration is free and you can't refuse if you want to be legit. You must register your establishment 28 days before it is brought into use, and you must notify the council if there are any major changes to the business or if the establishment closes.

## Playing along with music licences

You must have a licence from the Performing Rights Society (PRS) if you play recorded music in your restaurant. The PRS distributes payments to composers and publishers.Check out the details and how to apply on the society's Web site: www.prs.co.uk.

You also need a licence from Phonographic Performance Limited (PPL), which also collects performance royalties on behalf of over 3,000 record companies and 30,000 performers. It was set up in 1934 by the recording industry to grant licences for the playing or broadcasting of sound recordings such as CDs, tapes and records in public. If you do not take out a licence, you are infringing copyright. Check out www.ppluk.com for more details.

## No smoking? Not joking

From July 1 2007 smoking in any enclosed public space such as a pub, restaurant or office in England is illegal. Businesses face fines of up to £2,500 if they break this law. Wales and Northern Ireland took the pledge in April 2007, Scotland in April 2006 and with Ireland led the way in 2004.

The ban includes smoking tobacco, anything that contains tobacco, or any other smoking substance. It includes manufactured cigarettes, hand-rolled cigarettes, pipes, and cigars. Other provisions of the law include:

- In the legislation wording an *enclosed space* is one with a ceiling or roof.
- Tents or marquees are also classified as enclosed premises.
- Structures located outside premises may be designated as smoking areas as long as 50% or less of the structure is covered by walls or windows.
- Vehicles used by companies must be smoke-free if more than one person is present.
- The local authority is responsible for enforcing the smoke-free regulations.
- All premises and vehicles must have no smoking signs. They must meet the requirements set out in the legislation.
- Failure to display no-smoking signs may result in a fixed penalty notice of £50 or a fine not exceeding £1,000.

For more information on smoking legislation in Britain consult the Web site of the Office of Public Sector Information: www.opsi.gov.uk

Work with your solicitor, bookkeeper, or other support personnel to create a system for alerting you when licences need to be renewed and processing any applications and fees required to get and stay current.

Make licences a priority. By doing so, you're not just trying to keep yourself out of trouble; you're truly making sure that everybody's going to be safe in your restaurant. Go above and beyond to assure that your customers and employees are safe and sound.

## *Paying attention to building regulations*

Before you can begin building or remodelling your new space, you need to get the appropriate building permits. Check with your builder, your local authority, and your solicitor to make sure that you have the appropriate paperwork in hand before starting work.

After you finish construction, your local planning department will inspect your premises before giving you permission to start trading.

Be nice to your inspectors, but don't be too nice. It's absolutely no use, not a good idea, and, in fact, detrimental to your business to attempt to bribe or influence any inspectors. Be friendly and agreeable but always professional.

The planning permit shows that:

- ✔ You've followed all building regulations. You haven't knocked down load-bearing walls, for example.

- ✔ Your facility conforms to current safety requirements, which include things like having the right electrical systems and wiring and making sure that you don't have any asbestos or lead paint around.

- ✔ Any modifications that you've made to your space are sufficient and appropriate for your new use of the space. Typically, you must submit copies of your plans with your application for the inspector to review.

- ✔ Your building is safe to occupy.

## Notification of accidents

Employers must notify the Environmental Health Office of any fatality, major injury, accident, disease or dangerous occurence on their premises under the Reporting of Injuries, Diseases and Dangerous Occurences Regulations 1995. For further information see www.riddor.gov.uk.

## Finding out about fire certification

Some types of food businesses require a Fire Certificate. Consult your local planning authority or Fire Prevention Officer to find out whether you need one. According to the Regulatory Reform (Fire Safety) Order 2005, achieving fire safety is often a matter of common sense. In more complicated premises, more expert help may be needed.

To see if your premises complies with the new legislation, an online self-assessment form is available. This will give you information on signage and fire extinguishers and other vital facts. You'll find the necessary forms at www.fire.gov.uk/Workplace+safety/WhatTheLawRequires/.

## Taking up trademarks

As you build your business, you build your reputation. Customers come to understand your style of service, menu, and quality standards, and they have an expectation when they step in the door. If you're successful, they associate all the terrific things about your restaurant with its name and its atmosphere. The last thing you want someone to do is to sabotage your hard work by stealing your name and using it to open a restaurant.

Plan ahead and trademark your name, logo, tag lines, and so on. Get the proper paperwork to protect your intellectual property in the UK or internationally.

A solicitor can help you navigate through this confusing landscape. But to get started, legalise your restaurant by giving it the status of a business. Refer to the section 'Playing it safe: The business entity' earlier in this chapter. Then check with the government office that deals with trademarks, the Intellectual Property Office (www.ipo.gov.uk) to determine the protection you can obtain for your name, logo, and so on. Before applying to register a trade mark, carry out a full search of the UK trade mark records, to identify any prior conflicting registered rights which may block your path. After you have registered your trade mark, you have exclusive rights in it, as well as the right to prevent the use of a confusingly similar mark in certain circumstances.

A UK trademark registration is valid for 10 years, but it may be renewed indefinitely for 10 year periods on payment of a renewal fee. Intellectual property (IP) law is a complex area. There may be strategic and financial reasons why applying for IP rights may not be commercially advantageous. You should consider seeking professional advice, for instance from a patent agent or trademark lawyer, before deciding how to proceed.

Don't assume that because your future mark isn't listed that someone hasn't applied for it. The only way to be completely sure is to file your own application and get it approved.

After you're registered, you must protect your marks or risk abandoning them. Get your solicitor to help you establish a strategy for maintaining your rights.

# Buying the Insurance You Need

The law requires you to obtain certain insurance, but other forms of insurance are optional. The amount of coverage you carry and the *deductible* (which is the amount you're required to pay before your insurance kicks in) you choose affects the amount of your *premiums* (the amount you pay for your insurance).

Talk with your insurance agent to find the best, most appropriate coverage for your business. Here's a list of common business insurance coverage:

  ✓ **Property:** Property insurance protects your property in the event of damage. Many policies cover only specific damages. You may want to consider other coverage, like earthquake, flood, wind, and hail insurance, if those natural disasters are likely in your area.

✔ **General liability:** Liability insurance protects you in case someone sues you for something. For example, someone may file a lawsuit if he falls on the pavement outside your restaurant or claims that he became ill after eating in your restaurant.

Check your lease for any required minimums for liability insurance. Your agent may have additional recommendations for how much liability insurance you should carry, based on the assets of your business.

✔ **Vehicle liability:** Vehicle liability insurance covers any lawsuits that arise from an employee, including you, driving a company vehicle. Automobile liability may be covered in your general policy, but you may have to get a separate *rider,* or additional coverage, added to a larger policy.

✔ **Workers' insurance:** Employer's liability insurance is compulsory under UK law. It covers damages arising from injury or illness to your employees whilst working for you. A whole package, offered by insurance companies, includes this as well as covering contents, business interruption, public liability and legal expenses. But it doesn't compensate you for things such as sick pay, damage to equipment, fines or loss of reputation. Speak to your insurance company for advice.

✔ **Unemployment insurance:** This insurance pays your out-of-work, ex-employees until they find another job.

Consider protecting yourself with life insurance and long-term disability insurance, as well. If you're killed or injured in an accident, you or your heirs may need to pay someone to run your business. Having this kind of insurance can help mitigate the extra expenses.

And consider these additions (*riders*) to your policy:

✔ **Specific peril:** This policy addition covers flood, earthquake, or other weather-related perils.

✔ **Employment practices liability:** This addition protects you against wrongful termination cases, sexual harassment suits, and so on.

✔ **Loss of business income:** This insurance enables you to recoup income if you lose sales through one of the covered causes.

✔ **Food contamination and spoilage:** This policy covers your losses if something like a thunderstorm knocks out the electricity that powers your fridges or freezers and results in large-scale food spoilage or contamination.

These additional policies may seem attractive, but the premiums required are often much more expensive than standard insurance. Think of it like insuring your jewellery: You can add the jewellery rider to your homeowner's policy, but the cost of the insurance can be close to the cost of replacing that jewellery. Consider what you're saving and gaining by adding the coverage. Your insurance agent can help you weigh the pros and cons of additional coverage.

# Part III
# Preparing to Open the Doors

'...and once word gets around that this is the best fish restaurant in town...'

## *In this part . . .*

We cover all the tasks you need to take care of to make your idea a reality. In this part, you can find information, tips, and tricks on planning your menu; setting up your drinks list; designing your exterior, dining room, bar, and kitchen; negotiating with suppliers; setting up your office (including all the electronics); and implementing a marketing campaign.

# Chapter 9

# Composing a Menu

. . . . . . . . . . . . . . . . . . . . . . . . . . . . . . . . . . . . . . . . . . .

## In This Chapter

▶ Looking at your concept, diners, and kitchen for inspiration

▶ Getting your chef involved

▶ Determining how much to charge

▶ Thinking about how often to change your menu

▶ Getting the hang of basic menu design

▶ Being a creative menu writer

. . . . . . . . . . . . . . . . . . . . . . . . . . . . . . . . . . . . . . . . . . .

The menu is the epicentre of your restaurant. *Everything* revolves around it: the ingredients you order every day, how you design your kitchen, which equipment you purchase, how you organise and train your staff, who your chef is, what selections are on your wine list, even the name of the restaurant. If the idea behind the menu wasn't the inspiration for your restaurant in the first place, then you must focus on it now. Creating your menu should be fun.

As important as the menu is, flexibility should be a consideration in almost every choice made for it. Ultimately, your diners make the final decisions about what's on your menu based on their consistent choosing of some items and avoidance of others. In this chapter, we go over what you need to know to plan your restaurant's menu, from deciding on core items, to determining its layout, to deciding how often to change it.

## Making Some Initial Decisions

Your menu should match your restaurant's *concept* (or theme) and atmosphere, your guest's expectations, and your kitchen's capacity to pull it all off. Discard any dishes that don't. After you have a general idea of what you want to put on the menu, you must decide what makes the final cut. In this section, we get you started with your menu planning by tailoring your menu to your restaurant, your clientele, and your kitchen.

The basic premise 'quantity doesn't necessarily equal quality' applies. Some of the most acclaimed restaurants in the world have modest-sized menus. Other concepts are based upon the diversity of their menus. Success or failure doesn't depend upon the size of a menu in general. How well the size of your menu works within your overall operation determines your level of success.

The first thing you need to do is get together a core group of menu items that you think you want to serve. The number of menu items you begin with depends on the approximate number you envision ending up with.

As a general rule, start with three times more items than you need. You can get a good core menu from this group, plus have some backup items ready when you need to revise.

## Matching your menu to your concept

Do all your menu choices match the feel of the restaurant? Just because coq au vin is your favourite dish, having it on your Thai restaurant menu doesn't make sense. All right, maybe that example is too obvious, but you want guests to have a consistent experience the entire time they're in your restaurant. If your menu is inconsistent, now's the time to sort that out. Here are a few questions to get you thinking along a matching line:

- ✔ **Is your restaurant an ethnically themed restaurant?** If so, do all the dishes on the menu come from the culture or country that you're showcasing?

- ✔ **Is your restaurant themed?** For example, if you want to become known as the old-school Italian restaurant in your neighbourhood, you may have decorated accordingly. Does your proposed menu match that theme, with spaghetti bolognese lasagne, mozzarella with avocado, tomato and basil, and the like?

- ✔ **What kind of atmosphere do you want to achieve?** Are you located just off the High Street? You may consider having a menu conducive to the activities going on around you. For instance, consider getting to grips with your takeaway menu so people can grab snacks and bottled water and get back on the road. But, if you have white tablecloths and candles, you will want to skip the bottled-water display and offer a wine list to diners when they're seated.

- ✔ **What are your opening hours?** If you're open at 9 a.m., people will probably expect some breakfast items. They'll be surprised to see roast beef with all the trimmings on the menu.

- ✔ **Are you a bar that serves food or a food place that serves drinks**? This question doesn't have a right or wrong answer, but it's one that you should answer. And when we say *drinks,* we don't mean only those that contain alcohol; drinks can be smoothies, coffee, and or anything else. If you're a bar, and your goal is to sell drinks, you'll likely have a limited menu, with some snacks and some salty things, which make people – you guessed it – thirsty. You get the idea.

## Thinking about whom you want to feed

Think about your restaurant from the diner's point of view. What would they expect and demand? How can you delight and surprise them? How can you keep them coming back for more? Map your menu to your clientele and their needs. See Chapter 4 for info on figuring out your customers, and take a look at a few questions to get you started:

- ✔ **Are you looking to capture the lunch crowd?** Because lunch diners often take a break from work to go to restaurants, they have less time to linger. Be sensitive to their need for speed and efficiency. If you want to to be known for offering a quick, good lunch, offer items that can get them in and out in 30 to 40 minutes. They'll appreciate the consideration and may make you their regular place for their lunch hour.

- ✔ **Do you want to focus having a takeaway restaurant?** Takeaway customers want convenience: easy menus, easy ordering, and easy collection. Consider combining – creating a single menu item that actually includes several menu items. For example your roast-beef-sandwich combo includes a small salad and a drink. That way, they can order a whole meal with a single item. If you're planning on doing a lot of takeaway business, have food that is portable and *holds* (stays fresh after it's cooked).

- ✔ **Are you starting a family-type business?** Busy families turn to restaurants to give parents a cooking break. They want familiar, easy-to-eat items for their fussy, pint-sized offspring. If you're targeting families, offer a few child-friendly items or maybe a separate menu.

- ✔ **Do you want to be a destination restaurant?** People love to feel special, especially during a celebration in their honour. If you pride yourself on being a celebration or destination restaurant, make sure the customer-service touches complement your fantastic menu. Offer personalised menus for the guest of honour. Create a special dessert for celebrations. Give the party a behind-the-scenes tour of the restaurant. Do a follow-up call with them afterward. Find whatever works for your restaurant.

- ✔ **Is your food familiar to guests?** Consider how familiar the food is when determining the final menu. If you're going for eclectic (taking influences from many different sources or styles of cuisine) or *haute cuisine* (by which we mean fine dining)– you probably want fewer items on the menu than you would if you were starting a diner or family restaurant. People will probably take longer with a menu full of items they're not familiar with.

# Tapping into the links between your kitchen and menu

The size of your kitchen, its layout, the size of your fridges and freezers, and your dry-storage capacity all affect your menu. If you want to serve only from-scratch items, you need lots of refrigerated space to store it. If you need to have 15 different kinds of ovens to produce the items on your menu, you have to decide whether you have the space (or budget) to accommodate them. Answer these questions early in your menu development process and save yourself hassle later on:

- **How big will your dining room be?** The size of your dining room dictates how much room there is for the kitchen and related storage space. Too much area dedicated to the dining room may severely limit what the kitchen can produce. You have to consider space for fixtures, equipment, storage, and staff access to tables, but keep in mind that too much space in the kitchen could reduce seating from the dining room and curtail revenue potential. In general, restaurants use between 15 and 25 per cent of their total space for kitchen space. The perfect balance depends upon what you do with the space in each. Take a look at Chapters 10 and 11 for dining room and kitchen layout and design tips.

- **Does your menu have a number of different cooking techniques?** Assuming that you have several different *stations* (areas to prepare food, like the grill and the fryer) in your kitchen, you want to have dishes with a number of prepping techniques so that you maintain a balance of the number of dishes coming out of one station at a single time.

Finding a 57-burner cooker or managing that many grill chefs in the kitchen at one time is difficult. Give the grill chef something to do. As they say, too many chefs spoil the grill, er, we mean, broth. For more on the different stations in a restaurant kitchen, have a look at Chapter 11. As with many things in this book, this is not an absolute rule. If your concept centres around a particular preparation technique, don't feel like you *must* diversify. A well-known restaurant concept fries chicken all day and all night. You can't argue with success!

- **Do your menu items have a consistent preparation time?** You want most items to be prepared in about the same amount of time. That way, all items are cooked at about the same time and come out at about the same time. Or if you have inconsistent preparation times, you can find ways to partly cook items so that some of the work is done early, and the dish is finished when it's cooked or plated.

- **Does your menu reflect a synergy between ingredients?** Or more simply, do the items on your menu work well together? And represent your stock? For example, unless you're known for the variety of seafood you have available, you may want to just keep one variety of clams on the menu and use them for pasta dishes and seafood salads as well as seafood stew. For more on managing your stock, check out Chapter 14.

# Cutting Your Chef (If You Have One) In on the Action

Assuming that you're opening a restaurant that requires a chef, you may choose to hire her before designing the menu. Or you may opt to hire a chef later and determine the appropriate candidate based upon her expertise in light of the menu. If you're the chef, even better. Either way, the chef will run the show and must be completely in step with how you want the menu to work. Take every step to ensure that this happens. (For information on deciding whether you need a chef, check out Chapter 13.)

Employing your chef before you begin the menu-development process has several advantages and disadvantages. First, the good news:

✔ You can get a feel for her food style and creativity early in the process and ensure that your styles and philosophies mesh.

✔ If you're not a hands-on foodie, a chef's input isn't only valuable but also essential in the early stages of menu planning. Nothing is quite as disappointing to a diner as trying a new restaurant only to discover by taste that the menu creator has spent more time reading food magazines or watching cookery programmes than she's spent in the kitchen.

Hiring your chef before you develop your menu has its downside:

✔ The sooner you hire her, the sooner you have to pay her. Depending on your budget, (and her salary), you can quickly spend a lot of money before you even open the doors.

✔ The more people involved in planning the menu, the less control you have over the final product. If you're a control freak, developing a menu with a team of people may be a problem for you.

Ultimately, your name is on the door, so win the war if not each and every battle.

Test runs of all recipes with the chef are essential. You can do this in a test kitchen, your home, or in the restaurant if you already have possession and the fixtures are in place. These very important sessions should occur as early in the process as possible. During testing, you'll probably decide to tweak some recipes or scrap ideas. An accidental discovery has also been known to occur.

Test runs are an excellent time to get a good sense of how you and the chef will work together. They're not true reflections of reality because you don't have the stress involved with guests waiting in the dining room. But you do get a good idea of your chef's food philosophy, creativity, cleanliness, management style, and efficient work processes (or lack thereof). And you get a sense of how a chef deals with feedback, both positive and negative. These important attributes don't show up on a CV, so pay attention.

Your chef will be instrumental in standardising your recipes and creating production manuals for the kitchen staff to use each day to prepare dishes that recur on the menu. These manuals help train new staff and ensure that all staff members are making the dishes the same way, every time. The manuals establish the consistency that is essential to building and maintaining a clientele. These are particularly useful if you choose to change your menu less often (quarterly, for example). If you have a more dynamic menu, you'll need a much more experienced chef who can develop recipes and training materials, for both kitchen and front of the house (FOH) employees, like waiting staff, quickly. For details on training employees, see Chapter 13.

Don't give your chef carte blanche to buy a case of truffles to run a pasta special next month unless you know the specific reason. Know what she's ordering and why. In most cases, you want consistency over creativity, so make sure that you and your chef are singing from the same hymn sheet when it comes to food costs and ordering procedures.

# Working Out How Much to Charge

You can follow several different strategies when pricing a menu. No matter where you start, you'll end up with the old-fashioned, tried and tested process of trial and error. Books, such as this one, can give you basic strategies, but ultimately, if your customers won't pay what you charge, then you have a problem. Conversely, if they'll pay more than what you charge, you're missing an opportunity.

Several components determine menu price points, including consumer demographics, competition, and accepted standards. In the following sections, we help you fix your price points and get focused on food costs and how they affect your menu prices. We even show you how to keep your menu priced to compete even when some of your costs don't cooperate.

## Deciding on your menu price points

*Price points* are ranges of prices for types of menu items. For example, on your lunch menu, your sandwich price points may be between £3.50 and £6.50, and your salad price points may fall between £7.50 and £10.50. Using price points to determine your menu pricing is particularly useful (and darn near necessary) if you're entering a highly competitive market. For example, if you're opening a steakhouse in an area with several successful steakhouses, you have to pay diligent attention to the prices charged by your competitors for what diners perceive to be like products. If you're charging more for your product, you must establish a point of difference (in quality, atmosphere, service, and so on) to justify the price.

A consumer will pay more for quality food, but exactly how much more is a question that only the consumer can answer.

Determining your price points isn't an exact science, but asking yourself a few key questions may help you get started:

- ✔ **What type of clientele are you trying to attract?** Suppose that you want to be a family restaurant that serves lunch and dinner six to seven days a week. Create an atmosphere through your pricing that encourages people to eat there on a weeknight and bring the family for sustenance. If you've done your research and determined that you can't sell a main course that costs more than £10.00, stick with that plan even if it means you can't serve your personal favourite, beef fillet.

- ✔ **What are your competitors' price points?** Think about the £1 menu war waged by fast-food restaurants. Most have a £1 or 99p menu, but each restaurant varies the items on the list based on what it can sell at that price without losing money.

- ✔ **What price points are in tune with the atmosphere you offer?** If you're opening a cheaper type of restaurant with bar service, you'll be hard-pressed to have many £10 items. When people pay £15 for a main course, they usually expect to sit down at a table with a tablecloth or in smarter surroundings. They may also expect to be able to order a drink from the bar or a glass of wine. If your restaurant offers neither, you probably want to lower your price points.

- ✔ **To get those price points right, what cheaper ingredients can you offer?** Can you use less-expensive cuts of meat to produce wonderful flavours through braising, and offer a fantastic beef casserole for £9? Because a casserole has a much lower food cost than your favourite beef fillet, you have a much higher profit margin. You make more money and have a great beef dish on the menu.

## *Looking at food cost percentage*

Your *food cost percentage* is the cost of all the ingredients used to make a dish (your *food cost* for that dish) divided by the menu price. It's a benchmark used to help control costs and gauge profits.

Restaurants take in money when diners choose items from the menu and pay for them. This is your *only* source of revenue. So your menu prices have to cover the cost of the food you're serving, the wages of your employees, your rent and utilities, and most importantly, your profit. So when you're running a restaurant, you set a target food cost percentage to cover all your costs of doing business.

Most restaurants target food cost percentage somewhere between 20 and 40 per cent, but your choice will depend on a number of factors, including your actual overhead costs (like rent and utilities) and accepted pricing standards for your type of restaurant. To work out your menu price of a particular item by using your food cost percentage, follow these steps (and see 'Creating dishes and recipes and then costing them', later in the chapter, for more details):

1. **Find the food cost of the menu item.**

   Factor in all the raw ingredients costs associated with creating a dish, including any 'freebies' like bread (if this it is complimentary in your restaurant), to create your food cost.

2. **Divide the cost by your food cost percentage goal.**

   If you want to run a 30-per cent food cost, any dish that costs you £3.75 in ingredients, will cost the customer £12.50. (£3.75 divided by 30 = £12.50).

So at various food cost percentages, your prices would look like this:

| *Percentage* | *Food Cost* | *Menu Price* |
|---|---|---|
| 20 | £3.75 | £18.75 |
| 25 | £3.75 | £15.00 |
| 30 | £3.75 | £12.50 |
| 35 | £3.75 | £10.75 |
| 40 | £3.75 | £9.50 |
| 45 | £3.75 | £8.50 |
| 50 | £3.75 | £7.50 |

If you get your calculator out to check our figures, you may notice that some of these percentages aren't exact. For example, a 40 per cent food cost is actually £9.38, but that price would be, well, just weird to see on a menu. Ideally, you want to round up and end in 25 pence increments (like £12.50, £10.75, and so on), or to an exact pound figure (like£15.00) or just shy of full pound increments (like£12.95). There's no set rule, but you want your guests to be able to roughly add the prices in their heads.

At first glance, it may seem like you're making a whopping profit on each dish. In our 30-per cent food cost example, you net £8.75 for each person ordering the dish. But before you book your next South African safari, don't forget all the overheads required to run the restaurant. You have wages to pay – including the manager waiting staff), the kitchen porter, the prep chefs, the head chef, the suppliers . . . the list is almost endless. And that doesn't even begin to cover the utilities, rent, linen service, flowers, décor, cleaning service, and so on. And what happens when the guest doesn't get the dish he ordered or a waiter drops a plate full of food? Guess who eats that food cost? You do. You get the point: Running a restaurant isn't cheap.

Food cost is only one part of the equation. Ultimately, the lower the food cost you can run, the better off you are. That way, you'll have more left over for the other percentages, like, staffing, overheads and the like.

Don't take the 'lower the better' guideline as an absolute rule. Your food cost percentage is definitely affected by the kind of food you serve and your atmosphere, because they're key indicators of what prices your clientele will expect to pay. If they expect shaved truffles in their risotto – these little nuggets of gold are so expensive – you'll be unlikely to make a decent percentage from them. Stay flexible! The other side of this issue is that in your drive to maintain low food costs, don't sacrifice your quality. Doing so will backfire on you eventually. As people see your quality deteriorate, they'll stop coming. Stay true to your standards, but run an efficient business.

## Creating dishes and recipes and then costing them

Go through each recipe and determine its food cost and food cost percentage. Determine if those numbers meet your goals for the restaurant. If they do, keep them. If they don't, ditch them. If you still want to keep them, see whether you can adjust portion sizes and ingredients to bring the costs in line with your goals for the restaurant.

In this first scenario, you pick some recipes, test them (check out 'Cutting Your Chef (If You Have One) in on the Action' earlier in this chapter), create standardised recipes, and then cost your menu. So if you're serving pasta with marinara sauce, follow these steps:

1. **Work out the cost of a serving of pasta.**

   If you're going to serve 225 g portion of pasta for each serving, it costs you approximately 50 pence.

2. **Add the cost of a single serving of marinara sauce.**

   If you make your sauce from scratch, it'll cost you approximately 85 pence. So, you're up to £1.35 per serving.

3. **Add the cost of a sprinkle of Parmesan cheese.**

   If you use 50g of Parmesan cheese on each serving, add 25 pence. Now, you're looking at £1.60 per serving.

4. **If you garnish the plate with a little fresh chopped parsley, include it in the food cost.**

A little sprinkle of parsley costs around 10 pence, so your current total is £1.70 for this dish.

5. **Add in the costs of any complimentary items that each customer enjoys to the food cost for each entrée.**

   So if you serve chips and sauces or bread and butter to each visitor to your restaurant without charging for it, include that in your food cost. In this example, you may serve bread and butter to each guest, so add 50 pence or more to the food cost depending on the quality of the bread. Also, add an additional 5 to 10 per cent of your current total (£2.20) to cover things like foil, plastic wrap salt, pepper, and sugar packets, bringing your grand total for the food cost of this dish to £2.42.

This process is for costing a recipe. It tells you how much money you spend for the raw materials to put a dish on a plate and serve it to a guest. Determining the complete food cost percentage picture for your restaurant requires you to look further at your inventory to determine the extent of wasted food (which occurs when food spoils, is dropped, or is overportioned, meaning, for example, cutting a 300 g fillet steak instead of the 225 g portion specified on the menu). You also need to consider factors such as poorly cooked food that must be cooked again or losses from theft. For details on gauging your restaurant's food cost percentage, check out Chapter 20.

## *Dealing with price fluctuations*

There are no guarantees in the restaurant business. The price you pay for your products is no exception. Even if you negotiated the best possible pricing with your suppliers, some products vary in price almost every time you order them. This variation can wreak havoc with your precisely laid-out food cost percentages and menu pricing. But never fear, because we have some strategies for dealing with these situations on your menu:

   ✔ **Put 'market price' on the menu instead of the actual price.** This strategy is acceptable for things such as seafood, unusual items like truffles, or seasonal or specialty produce (such as Valhrona chocolate or trompettes de mort mushrooms) that can have very large price swings (multiple pounds per kilo). Normally, you inform your staff of the daily market price, and they pass it on to your diners.

   ✔ **Establish a cost factor based on fluctuating prices.** So if you know that pork tenderloin is £7 per kilo during the holiday season but £8 per kilo the rest of the year, cost your menu as if tenderloin costs £10 per kilo year-round and price your item to fall within your margins. When tenderloin is cheaper, you make more, but you can still keep it available year-round. Items that experience massive price swings, like lobster, aren't good choices for this strategy. You could be cheating yourself out of revenue (and profits) because the highs are too high for your clientele but the lows are just right.

✔ **Print your menu daily.** This is a great choice if you have the capability to do it on site and you have many items with prices that fluctuate. Printing your menu daily is much easier than having waiting staff rattle off the prices of 15 fish main courses at each table.

✔ **Work with price changes.** Maybe the most common strategy for handling price changes is just dealing with it. This strategy is particularly effective when the price increase is only temporary (expected to last only a couple weeks) or it affects smaller components of your menu. For example, maybe a light freeze occurred in the citrus-growing countries, and the immediate crop of lemons was damaged. As a result, for a week or two, your lemon costs double. You probably don't want to change your menu prices to account for the difference; the costs will return to normal soon.

## *Mixing your menu*

Not all dishes will come out to a perfect food cost percentage; some will have a higher percentage, and others will be lower. Make sure that you sell the right amount of each, called a *menu mix,* to maintain your overall food cost percentage goals. Some dishes will be loss leaders, to borrow a supermarket analogy.

Look at Table 9-1 for an example of how this works. You may set a food cost percentage goal for the restaurant of 27 per cent and achieve it with an overall food cost percentage of 26.8 per cent. But notice that you don't set the price for each and every main course at an exact 27 per cent food cost. Instead, you adjust your prices (price some a little higher and some a little lower) to achieve your overall goal. If you sell 20 steaks for £15 each at a 35 per cent food cost, 40 orders of pasta with marinara for £9 at 25 per cent food cost, and so on, you'll end up with a food cost well under your goal. To figure your overall food cost, take your total cost from all items sold and divide it by the total revenue from the items sold. For the details on creating a detailed menu mix analysis, see Chapter 20.

| Table 9-1 | | | | Sample Menu Mix Analysis | | |
|---|---|---|---|---|---|---|
| *Item* | *Number Sold* | *Menu Price* | *Food Cost* | *Total Revenue (Number Sold × Price)* | *Total Cost (Number Sold × Food Cost)* | *Food Cost %* |
| Angus rib-eye steak | 20 | £15 | £5 | £300 | £100 | 35% |

*(continued)*

| Table 9-1 *(continued)* | | | | | | |
| --- | --- | --- | --- | --- | --- | --- |
| Item | Number Sold | Menu Price | Food Cost | Total Revenue (Number Sold × Price) | Total Cost (Number Sold × Food Cost) | Food Cost % |
| Pasta | 40 | £11 | £2.75 | £440 | £110 | 25% |
| Salmon | 15 | £13 | £2.50 | £195 | £37.50 | 22% |
| Chicken | 30 | £12 | £3 | £360 | £90 | 25% |
| Total | | | | £1,295 | £337.50 | 26.1% |

Don't be afraid to include some dishes that are trendy or local, and that don't fit the food cost percentage mould. Experimenting is a good thing. But remember: Your menu as a whole should be priced so that the overall cost of the items you actually sell balances out to achieve desired food cost percentage. So the 25 per centers and the 40 per centers should balance out.

# Deciding When to Change Your Menu

Even franchises change their menus, in large part because of an increasingly canny dining public. With more people going out to dinner more often, the question isn't *if* you're going to change your menu but *when*.

## Staying flexible when you first open

Give your menu a chance to work. After a change or new opening, allow at least a couple of weeks or maybe a month to let people get familiar with your offerings, try out several different things, and establish favourites. Watch for trends at different times of the day and different meal periods. If your starters are selling better at lunch than at dinner, try to work out why.

Don't get locked into a *tiered menu pricing system* (one that requires all starters to be £*x,* all main courses to be £*y,* and so on) with no room for change. If your starters are really working well but no one is interested in ordering the crab-stuffed mushrooms, you may want to consider dropping the price by a pound or so. Be open to that possibility. Ultimately, diners determine what works and what doesn't based on their willingness to buy menu items.

# *Reassessing your menu later on*

Ultimately, when you change your menu, you're trying to capture that new prospective diner and keep him coming to your restaurant while keeping your signature dishes that made you successful to begin with. Here are a few reasons you may want to change your menu:

- **Keep up with rising (or falling) trends and competition in dining out:** Being at the forefront of the 'wraps' trend was terrific, but if you're still tied to it, that's not so good. If the bistro down the street is packing them in and your bistro is empty, work out why. Look at your competitor's menu and analyse what it's doing right and wrong. You can capitalise on its mistakes and improve on its successes.

- **Take the seasonal approach to food:** You may want to take advantage of the seasonal produce and other items. Or if you live in an area that sees dramatic climate changes, you may want to consider embracing the way dining habits change with the seasons. So in July you may include a gazpacho (a light, fresh, cold veggie soup) on your menu but replace it with beef stew in October. Seasonality dramatically affects top-end restaurants, but it's less important if you don't promise fresh items to your diners.

- **Go up a level with your dishes:** You have always wanted to stick with the tried and tested. But you can still try new items. If the name of your restaurant is Thai Garden, don't put lasagne on the menu just because you read an Italian cookbook this week. Instead, consider adding a different kind of Thai fish dish to the menu. You can also make these changes to showcase trendy, new, popular ingredients, or celebrate holidays or local activities.

Very seldom do you ever want to change the entire menu. In fact, we can't think of a single time when you'd change it all at once. Changing an entire menu isn't effective. Your regular patrons walked in your door for a reason. They probably developed favourites and may not come back if they can't get them. Plus, changing an entire menu isn't efficient; many hidden costs are associated with changing your menu including testing and tasting new recipes, reprinting the menu, retraining your staff (both kitchen and floor), and drastically changing your ordering system.

# *Paying attention to specials*

There are three big reasons to run specials:

- **To showcase limited availability and truly special dishes:** Maybe you can order Canadian lobster, which is available only a few months each year and want to offer it to your customers.

✔ **To create efficiency with ingredients in your larder by reducing waste from perishable items going off before they're sold.** Specials can turn these ingredients around at a discounted price if you sell them before they perish.

Never use specials as the last stop before throwing them out. If you're concerned that a perishable may have already perished, toss it. Don't risk making someone sick and ruining your reputation just to save a pound or two. When in doubt, throw it out!

✔ **To promote your favourite, high-margin items:** You can offer items at a discount, hoping to increase customer counts and increase profits. You can even create a regular weekly schedule for specials (Thursday is fish day, for example) so diners know what to expect and put you on their calendar.

One added benefit of changing the menu is your staff will be excited by the change. Consider giving your chefs or culinary team an opportunity to create items when you plan on offering specials or doing a menu revision. They get a chance to be creative, which usually increases morale. (For more on motivating employees, check out Chapter 17.)

## Laying Out Your Menu

Designing the menu on paper can be fun and challenging. You must balance the artistic creativity of various menu selections with easily understood information for the diner in the design. The decisions you make here also depend on those you made elsewhere. Today, with simple software available, you can create new and attractive menus quite easily, every day, even every meal. But be careful. You don't want to change the menu *style* day to day. Your customers will note the change, which takes away from the familiarity you hope they develop.

If you don't want to invest in software specifically for menu development, consider using Microsoft Word or Microsoft Publisher. Both have a decent selection of templates, fonts, and graphics that add a professional touch to your printed menus, without costing much, and both are fairly easy to use. If you need help getting started, check out the latest version of *Word For Dummies,* by Dan Gookin, or *Office XP For Dummies,* by Wallace Wang (both published by Wiley).

After you know what to put on the menu, you must put pen to paper (or fingers to keyboard). Whenever possible, keep your menu printing options open. If you have the means and expertise on staff to print your menus yourself, do it. You'll probably save money, be able to fix errors and price fluctuations immediately, and make changes on *your* schedule, not the printer's.

If you're new to the business or you don't consider yourself a desktop publishing wiz, you may want to hire a firm to design your menu for you. If you had an outside company design a company logo or signage, ask whether it provides menu services as well. At a minimum, it may be able to help you with layout and possibly set up a template so you can still maintain some independence to print your menu daily. Also check with other restaurant owners for suggestions for menu design companies. But even if you hire someone to design the menu, you need the information in the following sections to get that company started and make final decisions on the design.

## Choosing your main menu options

Most restaurants use a main menu and a supporting cast (like table tents – see the section 'Table tents and specials boards' later in the chapter — beer and wine lists and takeaway menus for some). As you develop your menu, consider which format best serves your diners' needs, matches the feel of your restaurant, and adequately showcases the items on your menu. An outdoor cafe, for example, might choose a one page menu because the cafe offers a few simple items that diners are familiar with. A family-style restaurant might pick the multipage menu to show that it has something for everyone. And a Chinese takeout place may opt for set menus to quickly move diners through the ordering process.

### One-page menus

A one-page menu can be one- or two-sided and has become commonplace in restaurants of every size, shape, and service level. These menus contain all the restaurant's offerings from starters and salads to main courses, desserts, and drinks. They can offer several advantages:

- ✔ **Flexibility:** One-page menus can be easily revised or updated without generating huge amounts of paper or going to a professional printer.

- ✔ **Simplicity:** They provide the guests with a simple and quick tool to guide them through the meal. Diners appreciate uncluttered menus that are straightforward and make their selection process smooth.

- ✔ **Quicker orders:** A menu that's easy and quick for the customer to read cuts down on her scrutiny time, which means you may be able to turn over the table more quickly. If you can seat more customers during a given dinner shift, you can make more money in the same amount of time for about the same overhead.

Quick turnovers are ideal (even essential) for just about any restaurant, with two notable exceptions: high-end-casual and fine-dining restaurants. If you don't encourage three course meals or offer an extensive wine list, you make your money on the number of people you bring through the door each and every meal period.

If you want to make sure a guest *doesn't* come back, make him feel rushed, as if he's not welcome to linger as long as he wants. Making diners feel rushed or hurried is usually not a good idea. Your goal is to make it easy for them to get in and get out, without making them feel like you *want* them to get in and get out. A well-designed menu can help you strike this delicate balance. (For more on building a clientele, check out Chapter 19.)

Consider the complexity of your food when you choose your menu format. Although a one-page menu can prove advantageous for many restaurants, it does have a few downsides:

- ✔ **Space:** It reduces the space that you may use to explain a particular dish to your customer. We've had customers say, 'I had no idea that the Beef curry and coconut milk with basil would be garlicky.'

- ✔ **Lack of variety:** A limited number of offerings may turn off some diners who choose restaurants because of the variety they offer. If you limit yourself to one page, you probably won't draw in those diners.

### Multi-page menus

A multi-page menu consists of – you guessed it – more than one page. For example, it may include a page for starters, soups, and salads; another page for house specialties and main courses; and a third for desserts. This format offers the following advantages:

- ✔ **Details:** A longer format or multi-page menu offers your guest a more detailed look inside your menu. You can list key ingredients and cooking methods if they aren't apparent in the name of the dish itself.

- ✔ **Space and time:** Multi-pagers can also provide a conversational ice-breaker at a table or just enough literary substance for an on-time diner waiting for a late guest.

But every yin has its yang, and multipage menus have some drawbacks:

- ✔ **Intimidation factor:** Some customers complain of the intimidation factor of a big menu. 'There are just too many choices, I can't decide!'

- ✔ **Production problems:** Although you can print multipagers yourself, doing so is also multi-difficult. You must take special care to ensure all the old pages are replaced by all the new pages. Embarrassing customer moment number 343: 'Why is the dessert page between starters and main courses?' Also, the difficulty in producing and maintaining these menus will probably decrease your flexibility and increase costs in revising the menu.

### A central fast-food menu

You may recognise the central or queuing menu from the usual type of fast-food restaurant. Any restaurant that has a single menu posted in a central location has one central menu. Usually, the person who takes your order takes your money. Your diners order, pay for their meals, and then receive their meals.

This style of menu may be the way to go, thanks to the following advantages:

✔ **Ease of setup and maintenance:** You set the menu up once. When you change it, you change it once. No printing, no wiping down food spills.

✔ **Quick ordering:** People read the menu while they stand in line to order and then make quick selections when their turn comes up.

But the central-type menu doesn't work for everyone; here's why:

✔ **Limited space to explain menu items:** Because you're probably just starting out, your customers may need a little more guidance and explanation of menu items.

✔ **Doesn't match the atmosphere:** Unless you're running a quick-service restaurant of some kind, this style of menu may be off-putting to diners. As with just about everything we mention in this book, make sure that your menu decisions are consistent with the feel of your restaurant.

Although many very successful chains and franchises have adopted this style of menu, don't make the mistake of taking your imitation of it too far. They may be able to get away with central-type menus, sometimes showcasing just new items, but you probably won't. They rely on brand identity, the diners' familiarity with their menu offerings, and longevity of their product lines to lead diners to their menu selection.

## Considering additional presentations

Most restaurants don't rely on a single kind of menu to address the needs of every diner. They often add to the dining experience with other formats. Take a look at the following sections, and decide if your restaurant could benefit from employing these hard workers of the restaurant world.

### Table tents and specials boards

Table tents, those folded cards placed on tables, and specials boards serve the same purpose using slightly different formats. A table tent becomes part of the table decor and is typically multisided, offering everything from an advertisement of special events to drink specials to chef specials to, in rare cases, the entire menu. You may even consider it a one-pager in its crudest form.

Specials boards are large chalk, marker, or electronic boards used to display specials. They sometimes morph into being the entire menu. Place them in a prominent spot where customers can view them with ease. You may want the waiters to bring the board to the table and explain it there (or just leave it!). Specials boards are handy because they're easy to change, but as a rule the simpler the better. Make the information large and clear enough that people can easily read it with just a few items, so the board's appearance is not overwhelming.

### Takeaway /delivery menus

Takeaway menus are particularly handy because customers can take them with them, you can hand them out, and so on. Many people collect them, so they have them on hand when making decisions on where to have a quick bite to eat or order a takeaway. Takeaway menus are great marketing items. Always have your address, phone number, times of opening and fax number on them. If diners can place orders at your Web site, include that address as well.

If you have items on your regular menu that aren't available to take away, do not, we repeat, do *not* put them on your takeaway menu. Most people assume that they can call in an order and come in to pick it up, or have it delivered, when they see the item on a takeaway menu. If they choose a selection from your menu that can't be taken out, they get grumpy. You've now taken a perfect opportunity for a sale and blown it by frustrating your diner.

# Selling the Hot Spots

You can have the best food in the area, the most knowledgeable staff, and the best wines, but if diners don't order the high-margin items on your menu, you're missing a huge revenue opportunity. In this section, we show you how to lay out your menu and describe the items on it the most effective way.

## Menu engineering

Menu engineering is the strategy of laying out your menu to encourage diners to order the food you want them to buy, usually your highest-margin items. The location of an item on the menu, highlighting, graphics, and formatting all have an effect on your customers and the choices they make.

Think about going to a supermarket. Their shelves are like a menu. They put the things they want to sell you in the most accessible, most visible location, usually at the ends of aisles or at eye level on the shelves. Menus are very similar. The first place the diner looks on your menu is the middle of the upper half of the menu. Check out Figure 9-1 to see this in action.

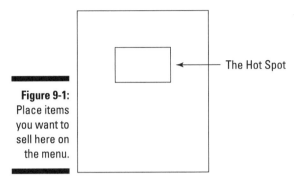

The Hot Spot

**Figure 9-1:**
Place items
you want to
sell here on
the menu.

TIP

Understand the 'power of three.' If you have something you want people to buy, put two similar items on either side of it. Price one higher and one lower. They'll go for the middle-priced one all night long. For example, if you have three sizes of the same cut of steak, your menu may look like this:

| Small Rib-eye (225g) | £9.95 |
|---|---|
| Medium Rib-eye (300g) | £10.95 |
| Large Rib-eye (375g) | £12.95 |

You're practically guaranteed to sell more Medium Rib-eyes than either the Small or Large

## *Menu language that sells*

A few choice words can improve the perceived value of your menu items, which means you can charge more money and have more money in your pocket. When coming up with your own menu descriptions, think about these questions:

- **What's in the dish?** Great ingredients make for great descriptions. Are there any items that stand out or are hard to find? Does a dish contain seasonal items that you should highlight?

- **How is it prepared?** Many attractive menu items start with the preparation method. Words like braised, seared, pan-fried, oven roasted, wood-fired, and *poached* lend another level of prestige to a dish that increases a diner's perception of the value of it.

- **Why is it special, different, or unique?** Is your beef Scotch and well aged? Are your eggs organic? Is your bread *baked in-house each morning?* Is your produce *locally grown* or *organic?*

- ✔ **Where do the ingredients come from?** Scottish Aberdeen Angus beef and rack of Welsh lamb mean something to people.

- ✔ **Do all the foods in a dish share a theme?** Maybe you include an autumn root vegetable soup, an Asian chicken salad, or Mexican chillies on your menu. Use common themes (seasonal, ethnic, geographic, and so on) to describe and name menu items.

- ✔ **Can you be more specific?** You may be serving *pasta,* but what kind of pasta? Say if it's tortellini, fettucine, or rigatoni. And that sauce you're serving with your fish is wonderful, but be more descriptive – mussels and cream, beurre blanc with dill or Mediterranean tomato and olive, for example. Getting down to specifics has the dual advantage of providing more information and enhancing the diner's perception of the dish.

Be creative. Anything that makes £1.50 in food cost sound like £20 will work to your advantage. As an example, we once offered herb crusted Scottish organic griddled salmon fillet with a crayfish sauce and Boulangère potatoes. It cost about £4 in food cost and sold on the menu for £24, making that a 17 per cent food cost. If we'd called it baked salmon with a seafood sauce and sliced potatoes, we couldn't have charged the same price. By using descriptive language and attractive cooking techniques, we sold more than 20 each night.

Never, ever mistake creative menu writing for misleading the diner or outright lying. If you're cooking pizzas on a standard conveyer oven, don't menu them as *wood-fired pizzas.* Or if you deep-fry your prawns, don't say they're panfried. Diners will know the difference and feel cheated. Not only will you lose customers, but you could also be subject to legal action, including heavy fines for misrepresentation or fraud.

# Chapter 10

# Setting Up the Front of the House

*T*he *front of the house* (or FOH) is restaurant-speak for any place the diner can be. The FOH includes the dining room, bar, toilets, banquet rooms, entrance, exterior, and so on. These areas set the mood, set your guests' expectations, and set you apart from your competition. Spend some quality time developing the environment and atmosphere that you want your diners to experience. The front of the house is your face to the world. Show them your best.

In this chapter, we help you work out what you want from your restaurant design and decide whether you need help. Then we take you through a tour of the inside and outside of your restaurant to help you decide what needs work. Finally, we go over two things you may not think of as part of the FOH but which are essential to creating a good impression on your clients: your waiting stations and your reservations systems (if you choose to have one).

Because the bar is a key part of some restaurants and nonexistent in others, we separate the details about bars and put them all together in Chapter 12. If you're planning on incorporating a bar into your concept or opening a bar without a restaurant take a look at Chapter 12.

## Digging into Design

Not everyone needs to worry about design. If your margins are low to begin with, and your concept doesn't require a particular atmosphere, don't spend a lot on your restaurant's design. For example, if you specialise in takeaway food, focus on speed and efficiency in your kitchen *and* in the front of the house. Maybe your FOH just consists of a few chairs with or without tables, so people can sit while waiting for you to finish their orders.

But the design and décor often impact the success of your restaurant. They provide a basis for diners to form initial expectations about your concept and the experience it'll provide. You have two missions: Provide a design and décor that accurately convey what you want your concept to be, and then live up to those goals. If you're going to charge £20 for a main course, your customers expect a stylish design and expensive décor, and if you have expensive décor, you're customers won't be surprised to find £20 entrées on your menu.

Throwing money at the design doesn't make it good. Anything you do must fit with your concept. When thinking about design, make sure it's

- ✔ **Flexible:** Make sure that the design is flexible and can be updated. If you're adding a wall to separate a dining room, consider making it a movable (or *removable*) wall to keep your options open.

- ✔ **Comprehensive:** Be sure that your designer covers all the basics including furniture, floor tiles, the ceiling, and ceramics. Small touches can make a huge impact.

- ✔ **Suitable:** Confirm that the design will fit in with your dinnerware, glassware, silverware, and your menu. For example, if you're serving Chinese food, you don't want a Moroccan motif. Also, make sure that your chosen design works both inside and out.

- ✔ **Practical:** Make sure that the designer considers all the front of the house spaces and the flow between them before implementing the design.

## *Identifying pros who can help*

If you're interested in creating a particular atmosphere or maintaining a theme throughout, a good interior designer, architect, and/or contractor can help you accomplish your goals. We say *can* because, depending on the state of the existing space, your budget, and your concept, you may want to perform many of the functions these pros provide on your own (or skip them entirely). But whether your restaurant is upmarket, fine dining, casual, or quick service, these professionals can help you make choices to deliver a consistent experience throughout your establishment.

If you're taking over an existing successful restaurant, consider whether you want to change the look at all. If the design is working, consider how the décor benefits the atmosphere and decide whether your changes are improvements or may negatively affect your diners' expectations. Change is good, but too much of a good thing can be bad.

Anytime you deal with consultants or other contract workers, get the *detailed* terms of your agreement in writing. Always have a schedule for finishing work, with a financial penalty if the work is not completed on time. Every day contractors' schedules lag is a day that you're not open, not bringing in revenue, and not turning a profit. Be fair with them, but don't let them run the show. You're the customer, and your business is affected by how well they run theirs.

Be prepared to be the mediator if you're working with more than one of the people in the following sections. They may all have different priorities, but you should have the final say.

### Drawing out the designers

Look for a designer who can implement your vision – someone who can hear your thoughts and turn them into the restaurant of your dreams. Give the designer a budget and your vision and see what she can come up with. Or have several designers compete with each other by asking them to present sketches and bid on the job before you make a selection.

Make sure that the designer coordinates her work with any architects and contractors; the last thing you want is the beautiful fireplace to billow smoke into the dining room because the new flue didn't make it to the contractor's to-do list.

Here are a few tips on finding a designer:

- ✔ Contact the British Interior Design Association (www.bida.org) or other organisations for members in your area.

- ✔ Check out pictures of restaurants in trade magazines. Search for designs you like. Often the designer is listed, but you can contact the restaurant or the magazine for details if the designer isn't listed.

Don't end your search with trade magazines. Consumer magazines, such as *The Restaurant Magazine,* your local entertainment magazine, and so on, all do stories on restaurants, usually with pictures of their interiors and exteriors. Architectural trade magazines can also be good choices.

- ✔ Look in the phone book for designers in your area. Many take out large ads that give you information about the services they offer.

- ✔ Contact the British Hospitality Association(www.bha.org.uk) for further information on sourcing a good designer.

### Coming up with contractors

Basically, *contractors* carry out construction work at your site. A good general contractor can spot practical flaws in the design and suggest ways around them. If your designer wants to remove a wall, your contractor should know whether it's load bearing and be able to suggest an alternative, such as adding support columns. If your contractor has restaurant experience, he'll be a huge asset to the process. Contractors should be familiar with all building and fire regulations and maybe even health and safety regulations related to building issues, such as electrical requirements to maintain refrigeration temperatures. Doors to walk-in fridges are constantly being opened, so maintaining food at a constant temperature is of paramount importance.

### Accessing architects

An architect is like the interior designer, but he deals in the structure of your space rather than the accessories. Many design firms have architects on staff and vice versa. Usually, you just select a single firm, and that firm provides both types of resources as you need them.

Architects are essential if you're putting a restaurant or other commercial space in what used to be a house or other non-traditional space. They can help you reinforce the floors to hold commercial equipment, widen stairs if necessary (for traffic flow and safety reasons), and make sure that your toilets comply with regulations as well as being aesthetically pleasing.

If you're located in a historic area, an architect familiar with your neighbourhood can help assure that your design is consistent with integrity of the neighbourhood. Pre-emptively plan your design with the neighbourhood in mind. If you don't, you could get tied up in bureaucratic meetings and other red tape and end up where you should have started: with a harmonious design. An architect will also be able to help with local planning processes.

## Finding out about potential pros

These professionals are only as good as the projects they complete on time, on budget, and to the agreed-upon specifications. Check references, look at completed projects, and talk with satisfied clients. Here are a few ideas:

- ✔ If you go into a restaurant and love the atmosphere, ask the manager or owner whether he'd recommend the designer. If the design is great but you find out that the designer is habitually late or a bit unreliable, you may want to keep looking. But always take this advice with a grain of salt. You don't want to be too cynical, but consider the manager's motivation for helping you if you're going to be a competitor.

- ✔ The Internet can help you make your first steps toward finding an architect, designer, or a contractor. Using Web sites may be more helpful as a way to rule out certain businesses rather than a way to actually choose a designer. Use Web sites to compile a list of a few firms you'd like to interview and collect bids from. Look at Web sites of restaurants similar to your concept. If they have pictures of the interior and exterior of the restaurant, use them to virtually visit their restaurant. If you like what you see, ask who the designer is.

Never base your decision entirely on what you see on the Internet. Anyone can design a site with flashy graphics and a fake client list. Check the references and confirm with clients who had projects similar to yours.

✔ Check your potential contract employees out with your local Chamber of Commerce or other organisations. Doing so seems like a small thing, but it can make a huge difference. If you find out that they left the last three clients high and dry with no completed design, think twice before signing on the dotted line.

✔ If a contractor claims to be a member of a particular organisation, check it out. Professional trade organizations often have a code of conduct for members.

# Thinking Outside the Box – the Exterior

The exterior sets the tone for the interior and atmosphere. The exterior of your restaurant is your first impression to the public. Depending on what it looks like, potential diners may never make it through the front doors. Take your exterior seriously, or you risk failure before you start.

Here are a few points to think about regarding your exterior:

✔ **Announce the concept with appropriate logos and signage:** Think about what works for your concept. Do you need signs that people can see (and read) from miles away? Are you located in an urban area with lots of foot traffic and in need of eye level signage?

One of our (Heather and Andy's) favourite Mexican restaurants announces its presence to the world with a huge neon red pepper on the roof. (As a toddler, our daughter couldn't pronounce its name, and the whole family still calls it the Pepper restaurant in her honour.)

On the other extreme, Gordon Ramsay, a world-class fine-dining restaurant on London's Royal Hospital Road has minimal signage – only the chef's signature on the exterior. This signage matches the owner's goals, the restaurant's atmosphere, and the diners' expectations. It contributes to the exclusivity and understated elegance that the restaurant consistently achieves.

✔ **Fit in:** When designing the exterior of the restaurant, be sensitive to the neighbourhood. If the neighbourhood is full of restored Victorian and remodelled stone and brick terraced houses, don't panel your exterior with galvanized tin, wagon wheels and a life-sized sculpture of an Angus bull just because you're using a Texas barbecue concept. Besides being out of place, you'll need planning permission for this kind of exterior – and others that may fail to receive permission.

✔ **Consider how guests will enter and exit your restaurant:** If you have tables near your entrances and exits, make sure that diners sitting there are comfortable. Britain's variable climate may require you to install a second set of doors at the main entrance to keep the wind chill to a minimum. Set out floor mats to prevent slips and falls during rainy or snowy weather.

✔ **Decide how much of the outdoors you want indoors, and vice versa:** Outside noise from traffic and weather affects your atmosphere. Do you want to be able to open windows (or even move walls) on sunny spring days? If you have outdoor seating, is it an extension of the inside, or a completely different space? Maybe your outside dining is more casual, with all-weather furniture, awnings, and logoed umbrellas.

If you're planning outdoor seating, check to see whether you need planning permission from your local planning department within the local council. (Check out Chapter 8 for more info on permission and licences.) Questions that arise include whether the proposed use is suitable for the area; whether any external alterations or additions are in character with your building; whether there is an increase in noise or disturbance will be an issue; whether there is any visual effect on the landscape, such as tree felling or hedgerow removal.

✔ **Keep it clean:** As smoking in public places is now banned, more diners smoke outdoors, usually right outside a restaurant. If you keep ashtrays handy, make sure that you maintain them as needed. Pick up any rubbish in your parking area or landscaping. Find out whether regulations in your area require a certain cleaning schedule.

✔ **Decide how delivery and service people will enter the restaurant:** Do you have a separate service entrance or are deliveries coming through the front door? If it's separate, is it a secured entrance with a bell or maybe a video camera? Who has the key? Make sure that you control this entrance for security purposes.

If you share any common areas with your neighbours, make sure that they also maintain their responsibilities. Even if it's not your property, it's close to you and reflects on you and the neighbourhood. Choose your neighbours wisely. For more on choosing the right spot for your restaurant, check out Chapter 7.

# Laying Out the Interior

Your diners spend their most important time inside the restaurant. They relax and wait for a table in your bar. They read a menu and enjoy a meal in your dining room. They freshen up in your toilets. Each area performs a different function, but they all must work together to deliver the same consistent experience.

How will your bar and restaurant affect each other? Will your bar be a service for your restaurant diners, or do you plan on doing independent bar business? The clientele can be very different for each, so consider creating a barrier, either a fixed barrier (like a wall) or a movable barrier such as plants (if you want to keep them separate.

## Allowing space for the flow

The flow of service in your establishment has a lot to do with the design and layout. The term *flow of service* means keeping service going at the pace and schedule that you've determined fits your concept. It's keeping guests flowing in and out of the restaurant at the right pace and continually producing food to flow out to the dining room quickly and harmoniously from the kitchen. Consider these points:

- Think about how your food flows into the dining room and how the dirty dishes flow out. Sometimes a side space for the dirty stuff lends itself to a better atmosphere for diners.

- Determine the paths diners will take to get to their seats, your bar, the toilets, and so on. Make sure the paths are clear and easy to navigate. Minimise tight areas that would cause guests to squeeze through or require them to move chairs or other furniture to move freely around the restaurant.

- If you offer food prepared or finished beside diners' tables (like making crêpes Suzette or flambéing a main course leave adequate floor space for it in your layout and logistical planning. If you need to move a trolley around the dining room to present cheeses to diners, you need plenty of aisle space to manoeuvre your trolley, plus space to stand next to it and prepare the dish. And if you have low ceilings, you may want to rethink your idea about serving flambéed dishes. Safety first!

## Building your floor plan

Check out Figures 10-1 and 10-2 for layout ideas. In both examples, the dining rooms, kitchen, and toilets are equally sized. But the key differences can improve traffic flow and layout.

- Tough-to-seat tables are usually located near doors or heavily trafficked paths. We've marked these tables with an X in Figures 10-1 and 10-2. The placement of the front door and the host desk in one corner, rather than in the middle of the front wall, cuts down on the number of 'bad' tables around the host desk. This layout helps cut down on traffic moving from the front door through the dining room to tables.

✔ Positioning the bar along a wall rather than in the middle of the restaurant cuts down on traffic around the bar. Check out the partition between the bar and the dining room in Figure 10-1 for extra traffic-flow control.

✔ Locate the service entrance in the kitchen rather than in the dining room. At some point you'll get an untimely delivery during the middle of the lunch rush. Running it through the dining room isn't an option. Plus, you can save some wear and tear to your dining room carpets if you accept all deliveries through a back entrance, should your property on these crowded islands allow for such a luxury.

✔ Place toilets in a corner so you don't lose space on both sides of them. And avoid placing tables near them when possible. Seating people in these tables is tough because people line up outside, making the guests seated nearby uncomfortable. Also, whenever possible, make more space in the women's room than in the men's room. You won't be sorry.

Arrange your tables so that you can easily create and take apart larger tables. Booths are nice, but you can't really move them around. For flexibility's sake, use mostly tables rather than booths.

## Creating space to wait

Hopefully, your restaurant will be so successful that you'll have more diners than tables at some time each day. Consider these ideas when you're deciding how much space to create for waiting:

✔ Where are people going to wait to be seated? Decide how much space you're going to allot to a waiting area, and bar. Decide what you want them to do while they're waiting. Should they admire your décor (or other interesting stuff to look at) or get a drink or nibble? Should they have menus and wine lists to read? Will you offer waiter drinks service (service by a server at tables next to the bar), or will customers get their own drinks from the bar? If video games fit your concept, do you offer them as a way to pass the time? How do you ensure that people are comfortable and that the thermostat is set at the right temperature?

✔ Where do people store their stuff? Are you located near or in public transport (like an airport, train station, and so on) with a travelling clientele who may have luggage? In Britain it rains a lot so people need to hang coats and weather gear close by. Are you going to devote space to a cloakroom?

✔ Do you want guests hanging around? Are you planning on being a take-away place, or do you want a restaurant where people want to come early, relax, and take in the atmosphere?

✔ Who will seat your diners? If you need a host stand, leave space for it and all the equipment involved, including menus, telephones, pagers, a computer, a reservation book, pencils, mints, toothpicks, and whatever else is essential for your operation. See the section 'Setting Up A Reservation System,' later in this chapter, for tips on getting all the necessities together.

If you don't have a host stand, diners usually take this as a sign that they will have to seat themselves if no staff member is around. A centralised menu (see Chapter 9 for details) and a cashier may be other clues. Many restaurants simply have a sign that says, 'Please wait to be seated,' which means that diners don't have to guess about what to do.

**Figure 10-1:**
Example of good dining flow.

**Figure 10-2:**
Example of bad dining flow.

Nothing says *uncomfortable* from a customer's perspective like walking in the door to a restaurant and not knowing what to do. Make sure that the host stand is visible to all guests entering, even when the restaurant is very busy. By doing so, you keep your guests moving and the cash register ringing. Whatever your decision, make sure that it's obvious what the customers should do, either wait to be seated or seat themselves.

# Keeping Service Support Close

*Staff support* is basically anything the staff need to do their job and to provide the best possible guest service. Depending on your concept, you'll probably need at least one service station, often at the bar, and a few POS (or *point of sale*, meaning computers to order food and drinks) stations in your restaurant. The secret to good use of space in this area of the restaurant is efficiency. Keep everything you need to complete a task close at hand. Keep coffee cups and teaspoons near the coffee pot, glasses near the ice bucket, and so on.

For the following reasons, don't be tempted to combine your POS and your service station:

- ✔ Your POS is electrical, and you want to avoid spilling ice water, tea, sticky sodas, and so on, on its components and backup supplies, such as printer ribbons and paper refills.

- ✔ You don't want staff waiting to ring up orders getting in the way of other staff trying to get drinks to tables.

- ✔ You run the risk of waiters congregating, hanging around, talking, and not playing their part to the full.

You want to keep service, and bodies, moving and flowing, not getting in each other's way. If you have to combine these stations, make sure that there's some sort of physical barrier, such as a partition, to divide the space and minimise the congestion.

## Service station

The service station is the supply area for the FOH staff. They make and pour their non-alcoholic drinks here and may clean and restock the dining room tables from here. The service station should contain anything that staff needs to do their job. Here's the short list of things that you should include in your service station:

## Keeping your kitchen in mind when you design

A newish trend in restaurants is for kitchens to be partially or fully open to public view. As a result, kitchens now need to be a more important part of the interior design of the restaurant, meaning that more interior designers are more involved with restaurant kitchen design. But in most cases, their decisions are secondary to those of the kitchen designer, who's charged with creating an efficient, workable kitchen. A kitchen, no matter how open, isn't technically part of the front of the house, but the design matters here more than ever.

- Coffee station, including the machine, cafetieres, coffee, filters, teaspoons, and cups.
- Fridge, stocked with milk, cream, and butter.
- Soft drinks station, including glassware, ice bucket with cover and scoop, and straws.
- Hot tea supply, including tea bags, lemons, teaspoons, cups, and saucers.
- Wine buckets.
- Breadbaskets.
- Extra table linen, including napkins, tablecloths, and a few bar towels.
- Clean china, silverware, and glassware (usually not barware).
- Rubbish bin.
- Oil and vinegar cruets, a pepper mill, and any other condiments that *float* (meaning items that aren't on the tables but a guest might need on occasion).

Depending on the size and layout of your restaurant, you may need additional, or *satellite,* service stations. A satellite service station is usually smaller than the main station and contains less stuff. For example, your main service station may have the coffee machine, while a satellite station may have only a warmer to keep already brewed coffee warm. It also probably won't have a fridge or plumbing. Satellites are designed to keep a few essentials at the ready but not take the place of the main station.

No restaurant rule says that you can have only one service station, though. If you have the space, budget, and a logistical challenge, a second (or third) full service station may help you solve it. If your staff have to use stairs to get from your kitchen to your diners, an extra station on the dining floor might really help. Or if you do an equal amount of indoor and outdoor dining, you might consider a second station close to your terrace, or even a rolling portable station that you can bring inside when you close your terrace.

## POS station

Your POS (point of sale) system is the computerised system for ordering food and drinks. The system may consist of individual computers, or it may be a network of terminals connected together to a single computer in the office. At a minimum, each terminal allows a staff member to enter food orders, which are automatically sent and printed at the stations that prepare the items and to the *expediter* (the person in charge of the kitchen on a given night – check out Chapter 11 for details). Drink orders are automatically sent to the bar. Staff members also prepare and finalise bills to present to diners in these stations.

If you are a small business and don't go down the electronic route, make sure that you keep your paperwork up to date, particularly with regard to ordering, and where your stock is going. A simple order pad is in order too!

If your budget allows it, we recommend having one POS terminal for every three staff members on the floor per shift.

Your POS supply list is a little longer than you might think:

- ✔ **Backup ink cartridges:** Keep at least one ink cartridge in the POS station.

- ✔ **Bill folders:** A bill folder is the plastic or 'pleather' holder that you present a guest's bill in. You can usually get these from your credit card companies. Make sure that you have enough extras for staff members to keep their working tickets in. The folders really help them stay organised.

- ✔ **Credit card imprinter:** Computerised credit card systems occasionally die, so it's good to keep these dinosaurs (and their corresponding paperwork) on hand for emergencies. Keep a list of the credit card companies handy as well, so you can call for a verification of charges. Staff members can get an authorisation code from the credit card companies and manually write it on the paperwork in case of a dispute later on.

- ✔ **Credit card machine:** Often this is just a swipe pad connected to the terminal. But if your system requires a separate machine, make sure to allot space for it.

- ✔ **Extra paper for the printer:** Store extra rolls of paper nearby for mid-shift changes.

- ✔ **Manual backup checks:** Computers are great – when they work. Don't get caught, however; keep a supply of manual bills (with multiple carbons) on hand for emergencies. Match up the carbons at the end of the night to account for any tickets that may have become 'lost' without being paid for.

- ✔ **Operation manuals for the POS and the printer:** Manuals are extremely helpful for new employees and veterans alike.

> ✔ **POS terminal:** This is the actual screen that servers use to process orders.
>
> ✔ **Printers:** A printer is attached to the system to print credit card receipts and copies of bills to present to diners.

If your staff handwrite orders and don't use a computerised system for ordering, you can disregard this supply list. Instead, you need only bill holders, bills, and a central cashier. Make sure that you set up some kind of inventory and accounting of your bill numbers so that guest bills don't disappear. This loophole can be a slow leak of revenue that adds up quickly.

Computers are great tools for keeping track of bills, money, and so on. If you're intimidated by the thought of computers, check with other restaurant owners in your area to find a reputable hospitality software salesperson. She can demonstrate how a computerised system can benefit even small operations. (And check out Chapter 15 for more on the technical details of POS systems.)

## Table settings

Think of the table settings as little self-service mini service stations. They're made up of all the stuff your diners will need to make it comfortably through a meal. As with most things in this business, what shows up at your tables is based on your concept. There's no right or wrong answer. We've seen it all, ranging from a single linen napkin on the simple side of the spectrum to a heap of individual butter containers, a roll of paper towels, and a galvanised bucket full of silverware on the other. You want to provide guests with the tools and condiments they need without encroaching too much on the eating area.

The tabletop is an extension of your concept. If you're a fine-dining establishment (with prices to match), your diners expect good linens, heavy silverware, and great glassware waiting when they arrive. If you're a family restaurant, they expect to find the familiar sweetening selection and probably ketchup, salt, and pepper. Latin-themed and Japanese places often include their preferred pepper sauce and soy sauce selections, respectively, on the table.

# Setting Up a Reservation System

Often, a diner's first direct communication with a member of your staff is via telephone. The diner may be calling about menu offerings or business hours, and will probably ask about reservations. Make the most of this opportunity by training anyone who answers the phone in basic phone etiquette and spend some time educating them on your reservation policy.

You can't stress enough that anyone answering the phone must be friendly, informative, and helpful. If people are treated with any kind of negative attitude, a harried voice, or lack of respect, they will not appreciate it. The Gordon Ramsay restaurant empire – currently standing at nine in Britain plus two pubs – has a centralised phone line for all of its restaurants, and two or three people do nothing else but answer the phones, answer questions, and take reservations. Spending this kind of time on customers pays off. This empire also has a must-have online reservation service in common with many restaurants.

Decide whether you want to take reservations. More than just about anything else we cover in this book, this is a personal choice. There is no right or wrong answer to this question. Many places take only customers with reservations (sometimes months in advance), and others don't take any reservations at all – ever. If you take reservations and people stand you up, you lose revenue. At many exclusive restaurants, diners provide a deposit via a credit card to reserve the table. If the diners don't show up, their credit card is charged a standard amount.

If you decide to take reservations, you must do it well. You probably won't get a second chance with customers if you disappoint them. People expect their table to be waiting when they get there if they've made a reservation.

Here's a quick list of the basic supplies you'll need to get your system started:

- Clipboard and wait list
- Pens and pencils
- Phones
- Podium – if you have the space, otherwise the bar might do
- Reservation book

You can add convenience to your system with a few technological advances:

- **Computer:** Keep track of reservations and estimate waiting times. People may argue with your manager, but they won't argue with a computer. Many computerised reservation systems are available, for example e-restaurant 3.0 (`www.kernow-software.co.uk`) and orbital (`www.epos systems.co.uk`). These systems compute your available tables and the current numbers of guests booked in for each time slot, prevent over-booking, offer internet reservations, and even remind customers of their reservation by text message.

- **Online reservation system:** Some third-party systems, like `www.open table.co.uk`, process reservations for you and integrate their system with yours. You usually pay a fee for this service, so read the small print.

- **Pagers:** These personal, hand-held devices alert customers when their tables are ready but haven't as yet caught on in Britain.

If you don't take reservations, have the overflow space to keep customers there while they're waiting. If not, people probably won't stick around, at least not until you've established yourself. Check out the section 'Creating space to wait,' earlier in this chapter, for tips on allocating this space.

Here are some tips for taking reservations:

- ✔ Reserve at least one table for special guests. You never know when one of your financiers, the bank managers, the restaurant critic you've been dying to impress, or Jude Law and his latest squeeze may stop in for a quick bite.

- ✔ Get a phone number when you take the reservation. Confirm the reservation with your diners the day before. Doing so is a great way to add a personal touch to their experience *and* protect against revenue loss from diners who made other plans.

- ✔ Make sure that you have enough phone lines. If customers are calling your restaurant and the line is constantly busy, they will give up. If your manager is on the line talking to the to the accountant, the chef's ordering on another, and one of your waitresses is talking to a boyfriend, how many other lines do you have to take a phone call? Consider getting an intercom system on your phones to ease the flow of inter-restaurant communication. Also, limit personal phone calls on restaurant phones to emergencies only.

- ✔ Consider getting voice mail or a message machine. Make the most of your message by giving directions, your hours, seasonal promotions, and the reservation number if it's different from the main number.

## Talking toilets

Toilets in smart restaurants and hotels used to be a place to rest and refresh. Nowadays, people usually get in and get out. Decide whether you want employees to share the toilets used by your diners. Also decide whether you want your toilets open to the public or reserved for customers and staff. Keeping the toilets solely for guests can be difficult because you risk alienating potential customers.

If you have public telephones, locate them near the toilets. Diners expect to see them here.

If you are building a new restaurant you must comply with regulations on disabled access and toilets. This, however, is not necessary if you are taking over an existing business, particularly where the layout does not give you the space to convert an area into a disabled toilet, or to provide a ramp for disabled access. Always check with your local planning officer when taking over a property for renovation to make sure you are within the law on any building matter. You can read the Disability Act 2005 at www.opsi.gov.uk.

## Providing public facilities

Toilets are an extension of the front of the house. You must give just as much attention to maintaining these areas as you do to your dining room. Make appropriate supplies available, including (at a minimum) toilet paper, paper towels, soap, hot and cold running water, and plenty of rubbish bins. If you have the space, install nappy-changing areas in both the women's *and* men's room because fathers share the responsibilities these days.

Conduct regular toilet checks to confirm that your facilities are clean, tidy, and in proper working order. If you want a constant presence in the toilets, and your restaurant is a genuine fine dining establishment, consider employing an attendant. Guests might appreciate the extra service and amenities. An attendant usually offers cologne, hairspray, and a nice selection of hand lotion. But customers may resent the feeling that they need to leave a tip. Decide what's best for your concept and clientele.

Whatever choice you make about maintaining your toilets, make sure, at a minimum, that you have a schedule for checking it, a staff member assigned to do it and good follow-up.

Decide whether you have room for a lounge area. If you're drawing in families, a couch in your toilet is a nice feature for nursing mothers or older children waiting for parents to finish with younger siblings.

A full-length mirror is a nice addition to the toilets, especially if formal attire is standard at your place. Diners can confirm that all's well before returning to their table.

## Earmarking areas for employees

Providing separate toilets for your staff is a good idea. You can post staff notes and reminders on doors where everyone will see them at some time or another. You'll need to stock the basics in the employee toilets, including soap, paper towels, and toilet paper. Make sure hot and cold running water are available at all times.

At a minimum, you must post a sign stating something like this: 'Employees must wash hands before returning to work.' Depending on your staff, consider getting a multilingual sign in the appropriate languages. If your employees share a toilet with guests, the sign must go in that toilet. With a separate facility, you can add additional information, like the proper hand-washing technique diagram in Chapter 18. And you may want to include a friendly reminder that you won't tolerate any food or drink in the area.

If you take the next step and add a locker room to the employee facilities, keep the following things in mind:

- ✔ The locker room is not a place to hang out. Employees should change into or out of their uniform and move along.

- ✔ The locker room is a self-policing area. Make sure that the staff know that the condition of the room is up to them. They have to clean it themselves.

- ✔ You can't post cameras or conduct locker searches. Employees legally have an expectation of privacy when using these facilities.

- ✔ Food and drink aren't allowed in the locker room. If you don't implement this policy from the outset, the locker room will become packed full of dirty dishes and glassware. The next thing you know, it's packed full of pests (of the four-legged variety).

- ✔ Recommend that employees put dirty uniforms in the laundry hamper as soon as they take them off and then immediately place tomorrow's clean uniform in their locker. This system prevents employees from rushing when they report for work and keeps the dirty laundry from soiling the clean.

# Chapter 11

# Setting Up the Back of the House

. . . . . . . . . . . . . . . . . . . . . . . . . . . . . . . . . . . . . . . . . . . .

*In This Chapter*

▶ Deciding how your menu affects your kitchen

▶ Designing your kitchen

▶ Starting with an existing kitchen

▶ Buying and leasing equipment

. . . . . . . . . . . . . . . . . . . . . . . . . . . . . . . . . . . . . . . . . . . .

Setting up the back of the house is even more important than setting up your dining room. The *back of the house,* or BOH, is any area of your restaurant that a guest can't normally see. If the dining room is the face of the restaurant, the kitchen is the heart. And how it works greatly affects the finished product that guests do see, including how long it takes their food to get to the table and what condition the food is in when it gets there. In this chapter, we reveal the first thing you need to consider when creating the back of the house – your menu and how it affects your kitchen. Then we cover the basics of layout, give you some tips on designing from scratch and dealing with an existing kitchen, and offer ideas on the kitchen equipment you need.

## Planning a Kitchen with the Menu in Mind

Which came first, the menu or the kitchen? It's difficult to say, because you can't have one that works without the other. And you can't be successful without both. Your menu and kitchen should be in perfect harmony or at least on the same page of the same book. Whether you're designing your kitchen from scratch or working with an existing kitchen, you need to work out how your kitchen will run based on the menu you're serving in order to set it up right. (See Chapter 9 for more on composing your menu.)

Look at your menu item by item and determine what equipment you'll need to prepare it, store it, and serve it, from beginning to end. (The 'Reviewing the basic kitchen stations' and 'Taking control of your prep' sections later in the chapter can help.) Make a list like the example in Table 11-1 of menu items and the related equipment and stations you need to prepare those items.

| Table 11-1 | Equipment and Stations Needed in Kitchen | |
|---|---|---|
| *Menu Item* | *Station/Area* | *Purpose* |
| Fresh oysters | Walk-in fridge | Store oysters until ready to shuck and serve |
| | Reach-in fridge | Store a few pre-shucked orders |
| | Prep area | Prepare garnish, shuck oysters, garnish plate and place oysters on the plate |
| | At the pass | Check plate, send out the order |
| Fried calamari | Freezer | Defrost in refrigerator and then store in refrigerator |
| | Prep area | Cut calamari to desired size, if necessary |
| | Fryer | Fry calamari to order |
| | At the pass | Check plate, garnish dish, send out the order |
| Chicken Caesar salad | Walk-in cooler | Store lettuce, dressing, and cold plates |
| | Prep area | Tear lettuce, prepare dressing |
| | Dry storage | Store canned anchovies |
| | Grill | Grill chicken breast |
| | Prep area | Finish salad to order |
| | At the pass | Check plate, garnish dish, send out order |

After you make your list, take a look at the forecasted menu mix analysis that you created in your business plan. Your *menu mix analysis,* sometimes shortened to *menu mix,* is a report, or in the case of a forecast, a prediction, of what menu items sell in what quantities. Among other things, it tells you how many orders of Oysters, Fried Calamari, and Chicken Caesar Salad you sell in a given shift. (Check out Chapter 20 for tips on creating a menu mix analysis if you don't have one.) Determine which stations will be doing most of the work by looking at how many items in a shift will be coming out of each of them. Make sure that busy stations have enough under counter fridge space, counter space, and so on. Share these spaces with less-often used stations. Look for other ways to improve efficiency based on your menu.

# Laying Out Your Kitchen

As you design your brand-new kitchen or refurbish your existing one, a single word must be in the top of your mind: flow. How are things going to flow? Imagine your meal from delivery of product to delivery of the dishes to your guests. Picture the wine delivery person carrying a case of wine. Can he pass the dish area without falling, getting wet, and disturbing the kitchen porters washing up? Take a look at Figure 11-1 for an example of a kitchen layout with good flow.

Here are some ideas that can help you make sure that your kitchen design is going with the flow:

✔ Determine which stations are getting the heaviest (and the lightest) workload based on your menu.

✔ Make sure that you have enough) refrigeration in the right spots (close to their specific stations) to keep your product at a safe temperature until use. In Figure 11-1, the pastry station (left side) has a three-door fridge; it's dedicated to products that might otherwise suffer from the constant in and out of the main fridges, and it's isolated from the heat of the hot line. *Fish files* (under-counter refrigeration drawers) are a space-saving way to bring refrigeration to the hot line while conserving space and avoiding the space problems common with fridges.

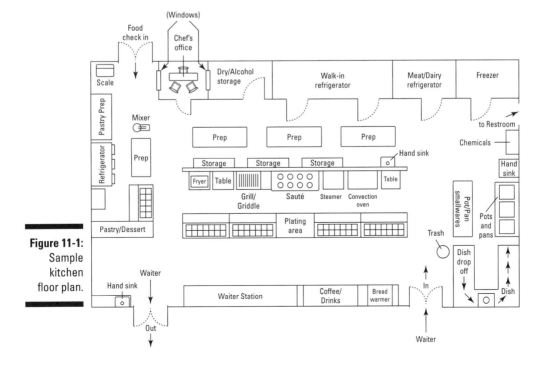

**Figure 11-1:** Sample kitchen floor plan.

✔ Keep your prep area close enough to the line to quickly restock it when needed. Notice in Figure 11-1 that the prep area is located between the main walk-in coolers (produce and meat/dairy) where food flows to the prep tables and then to the line.

✔ Ensure that your staff can efficiently get dirty plates, pots, and pans off the line and to the dish area. Waiters flow in the 'in' door and stop at the dish area. The pot-and-pan shelf is located at the end of the right side of the line for the line cooks to place pans needing a wash.

✔ Keep the dish and prep workers out of each other's paths during busy shifts. The dish area is separate from the prep area in Figure 11-1.

✔ Keep the path to the ice machine clear so that bartenders and waiting staff have easy access to refill ice buckets during peak times. The ice machine in our example could be located along the front wall of the kitchen near the service station, with easy access for anyone who needs it.

✔ The waiting staff should be able to get dirty dishes into the dirty dish area without falling and without hindering someone else's workflow. Our dirty dish area is the first stop on the way into the kitchen, with an extended table so waiters won't block the door or anyone else trying to come in.

✔ Menu items should flow down the line and to the expo with ease and efficiency. The plating area in Figure 11-1 is located in the middle of the line, so plates come in from sides and through the plating area, for a check with the pass and then out the door.

Work cleverly, not harder than you have to. You and your employees will be on your feet many, many hours each day. Save as many steps as possible by designing an efficient layout. Get expert help if you need it; experts are available who deal specifically with flow and efficiency. Other ways to put experience on your side include:

✔ **Turning to a broad-line equipment supplier who carries many types and brands of equipment for free design help.** The Catering Equipment Distributors Association (www.ceda.co.uk) regulates codes of good practice amongst its membership and offers after-sales maintenance and service. Many suppliers throw in 'free' design help.

Nothing is actually 'free'. You'll pay for the design help through equipment prices that can be a little higher. See the section 'Acquiring Your Kitchen Equipment,' later in this chapter. Price the equipment from several sources and check into the cost of a kitchen design consultant to see which way you may come out ahead.

✔ **Hiring an experienced general contractor who is familiar with outfitting restaurants and has excellent restaurant references.** Not every contractor understands the needs and motivation of a restaurant. The ones who do are invaluable. They can help you get your -extractor hoods working; make sure that you have enough power outlets for your blenders, mixers, food processors, and so on; and keep the plumbing flowing in your favour.

Each of your power outlets should be on a dedicated circuit with a minimum of 20 amps of power. Many restaurant-grade appliances use up most of that allotment, and if you try to plug in two on the same circuit, you'll trip the breaker.

✔ **Reviewing your kitchen plans, especially the finishing details, with other restaurateurs.** They probably have experience with a variety of setups and can help steer you in the right direction

## Reviewing the basic kitchen stations

A *station* is an area of the kitchen designed to accommodate a particular cooking technique. So foods that are fried, like chips, onion rings, and fried mushrooms, are prepared at the fryer station. Items that are grilled, like steaks, grilled veggies, and grilled chicken are prepared at the grill station.

A station is defined by the way the food is prepared, not by the kind of food prepared there. The station refers to the main equipment, such as a grill, and the setup and organisation of the supplies and products that the cook needs to finish preparing menu items. In the case of a grill, the supplies and products could include the food to be grilled, brushes to clean the grill, side dishes to complete the grill menu item, knives, spatulas, tongs, plateware, and sauces to complete the presentations. Some foods have a variety of cooking techniques. Depending on your menu, a scallop could be grilled, broiled, smoked, steamed, or sautéed. So several stations could prepare scallops.

The *line* is the area of the kitchen where food is prepared, placed on a plate, garnished, and then sent out to the guest. The line is made up of all the stations in the kitchen. When a station receives an order to *fire* an item (cook a dish immediately), it means that a guest has ordered, the waiter has placed the order with the kitchen, and the kitchen should begin preparing the item.

### Grill

The restaurant chargrill is just a bigger version of the outdoor barbecue grill you might have in your garden. A chargrill is distinguished from equipment like an overhead grill or oven by the direction of the heat – the heat comes from under the food being cooked. (An oven's heat surrounds food, while an overhead grill's heat comes from above, surprisingly enough.)

You can find two basic versions: a *chargrill* and an *overhead grill.* Depending on your menu, you may have one type of grill or both. If you cook a lot of steaks and want to serve them with nice little checkerboard grill marks, go for the chargrill. If you cook grilled ham and cheese, consider an overhead grill. If you have room for both, you can be more flexible with your menu offerings. A salamander grill has the heat coming from above and is a real bonus in the kitchen for grilling and gratinating dishes.

At the grill station, you need the following:

- Grill (surprise!)
- Under-counter fridge for your main course items (like salmon, kebabs, chicken, and steaks for a chargrill, or bacon, tomatoes, mushrooms, and so on for an overhead one)
- Seasonings (salt, pepper, signature spice blends, and so on)
- Grill brush
- Oil wipe (to wipe the grill and keep it from sticking)
- Water bottle (to squirt down flames)

### Sauté

During busy times, several cooks work this station, preparing everything from pasta to poached fish, from sauces to sautéed spinach. If it's cooked in a sauté pan, it's cooked here. Sauté cooks usually use a multiburner cooker to prepare multiple dishes at a time. Sautéed items (like pasta dishes, sauced starters and sometimes the veggie of the day) are usually popular and high-volume items, so you need people who can keep up with the pace for the entire shift.

### Fryer

The fryer is an extremely versatile station. You can use multiple fryers in a single station to finish dishes and supply other stations with a continuous stream of *parcooked* (partially cooked) product to stay ahead during busy times. Look for pressure fryers with lids or quick recovery fryers to speed up frying time if you're planning on doing lots of fried food. Always opt for a fryer with a working – and calibrated (accurate) – thermostat so that you can monitor the temperature and frying times on your menu items to get a consistent-quality product.

Other things that might be part of the fry stations include the fry baskets (for easy retrieval of items), plateware, sauces, a skimmer for removing errant fries, a small under-counter fridge and freezer, and anything else your chef needs to get the job done.

### Oven

The oven station can consist of any variety of ovens:

- **Combination oven:** If your budget allows, you can combine your oven and a steamer by using a combination oven. These freestanding cabinet-style ovens combine dry heat and moist heat, convection or conventional cooking, plus the ability to act as a stand-alone steamer. These machines, although rather frightening to the uninitiated due to their complex electronic devices, offer a highly consistent type of cooking and are highly recommended. They have multiple shelves and, once conquered, are good for any sized restaurant kitchen.

✔ **Convection oven:** This type of oven uses a fan to circulate heat for quicker, more even cooking.

✔ **Conveyer oven:** The perfect choice for sandwiches and pizzas, the conveyor oven is usually an infrared heat source, heating food from both above and below. You control the cooking time by adjusting the belt speed and the temperature, and by where you place the food on the conveyor belt.

✔ **Rotary oven:** This large piece of equipment (the size of a small room) holds five to seven large trays that turn like a Ferris wheel. It may work for you if you're doing house-made bread, pastries, and desserts.

Your menu and your concept determine what type of oven you need in your restaurant. If you're a pizza restaurant, the majority of your menu items will probably come out of the oven. You need a different oven from the Chinese take-away place down the street. Tailor your choice of oven to your menu needs.

### Pastry

The pastry station is typically reserved for dessert items. If your concept doesn't call for a pastry chef or even a pastry station, you can use one of the prepping stations. Your waiting staff can be in charge of *plating* their own desserts (putting them on a plate for service) in a station in the kitchen.

### Bain marie hot cupboard

The *bain marie* is basically a huge *chafing*, or warming, dish that holds items that have been previously cooked and keeps hot foods hot until they're ordered. It is located on the line. Large and small metal pans fit into various configurations to make up the compartments of the bain Marie. For example, if you're a family restaurant or café, your line may consist of a steam table full of vegetables, roasted potatoes, braised meats, fried chicken, and so on, all completely cooked but held at the right temperature until a diner orders them. In this sort of concept, your prep area is where dishes are prepared, and then the main course items are plated on the line.

### The pass

The pass is a station that ensures that all the stations on the line are working in harmony. The person at the pass, usually the head chef, ensures that all dishes going to the dining room are up to par with your restaurant standards, including presentation, portion sizes, temperature, within the specified time for an order to be prepared, and so on. The pass is the last quality-control check before a dish leaves the kitchen. Complete this station with a spindle (a metal stake to 'stab' completed tickets), a highlighter, pen or pencils, a wet and a dry towel (for cleaning up plates), and any garnishes the pass might use.

Chefs in all sections often taste dishes before the pass to confirm consistent seasoning and must do so according to health regulations (this means taste-testing with a clean spoon, which must be sent to the dirty dish area immediately after use – no double dipping!). An experienced chef can take the proper steps to protect you and your customers from breaches of hygiene practices.

The pass, and the chef at it, is the communication funnel. He protects the individual stations from things they don't need to know about, like waiters complaining about a missing main course that should've been sent, side dish requests, and special orders. He sets the priorities for everyone working the line and serves as the kitchen's link to the dining room. If the chef working at the pass doesn't know everything that's going on in the restaurant, he isn't in control. Without good info flow, a kitchen can crash and burn at 7 p.m. and still feel the effects at 9 p.m.

### Specialty equipment

Your concept may depend on a station or piece of equipment that we don't mention. If you're a casual Indian restaurant, you may need a tandoori oven. If you specialise in wood-fired pizza, you need a wood-burning stove or oven to create those menu delights. And believe it or not, the microwave isn't just for heating up cold coffee. Restaurants, especially large casual chains, have taken advantage of this tool, paired with the power of food science, to ensure quick ticket times and consistent products.

*Your* menu will determine what equipment *you* need. Purchase, lease, and lay out your restaurant accordingly.

## Taking control of your prep

You may have noticed that your average restaurant can get a pasta dish to your table faster than you can boil water at home. We assure you that no witches and wizards are hiding behind the curtain. The masters of the culinary world, whether on TV or at your local deli, rely on the time-honoured tradition of *prep* (short for preparation) to make quick work of orders as they come into the kitchen.

In fact, most members of the kitchen staff have done some time as a prep cook in their restaurant career. It's an invaluable place to watch and learn if you're interested in pursuing a career in the culinary arts. And in some of the more prestigious kitchens in the world, working prep is an initiation into the culture that is their restaurant. Whether you've painstakingly created 30 kilos of pommes Parisienne (little potato footballs), only to see the executive chef turn them into mashed potatoes before your eyes, or you've spent eight hours meticulously separating 300 quail breasts, prep can be a rite of passage.

More commonly, though, prep is just a means to an end – getting a product ready to go so that you can get finished dishes to the table as efficiently as possible. Most prep is done at off-peak times. If you do a busy lunch and dinner business, your prep staff will probably be working early, say, 6 a.m. to 2 p.m., to get the basics done before the lunch rush starts around 11:30. If you're a busy breakfast place, the prep staff may be in even earlier, maybe 2 a.m., and stay until 10 a.m. Consider a few pieces of equipment as you put together your prep area game plan. Read on for the specifics.

### *Refrigeration*

Most restaurants have at least one walk-in refrigerator or cold room (familiarly referred to as the *walk-in*) that's the size of a small, medium, or large room. Many stations have their own small fridges under the prepping counter (see the section 'Laying Out Your Kitchen,' earlier in this chapter) to store prepped food that's finished at the station.

Refrigerators, like at home, hold anything perishable, from produce to butter to prepared sauces. All raw food, such as eggs or marinating meat, goes in the walk-in cold room or fridge. Anything wet, like sauce or soup goes in a cooler. Any food that isn't tinned dried, or frozen (from fresh fish to fungi) goes in a fridge. Even if you might not refrigerate it in your home (apples, for example), you'll probably refrigerate it here. Your restaurant's concept (and your suppliers' delivery schedule) dictates how many and what size cold rooms or fridges you need. If you're opening a place that deals mostly with tinned or pre-packaged foods, you may need only a small walk-in and a fridge. If you depend on daily shipments of perishables, you may not need much refrigerated walk-in storage and can get buy with a single walk-in cold room. If you're part of a franchise that delivers frozen products on a regular schedule, maybe you can get by with a freezer and a couple of small fridges for the line and a smaller walk-in to thaw frozen products or store thawed products. Take a look at Table 11-1 to help you assess your need for refrigeration and other restaurant equipment.

### *Freezers*

A freezer is simply a place to keep frozen foods. Freezers range in size from large rooms to smaller chest freezers, ideal for ice cream at a dessert station or backup ice in a service bar. Your concept and menu dictate what size freezer you need. If you pride yourself on serving fresh seafood, you may need only a small freezer area to store things such as chips and ice cream. If you buy a lot of your food already prepared, a freezer may be an ideal way to save labour and still get a high-quality, consistent product.

When you're figuring out your freezer requirements, don't try to figure in your ice needs with it. Invest in a separate ice machine. You can get freestanding units that produce enough ice to keep up with a very busy restaurant, like the ones in hotel vending areas.

### Prep tables

The rows of stainless steel tables known as *prep tables* are essential to a smooth prep shift. You need plenty of work surface and sinks for several members of your staff to prepare multiple items at once in a sanitary environment. For example, in one area, Jennie may be washing lettuce for salads. At the same time, James may be slicing and weighing tuna steaks. You don't want these two to get in each other's way. If any of the fish bits get near the lettuce, you create a huge food safety issue (see Chapter 18).

Depending on your volume, you may need separate workspaces for two to eight people to work independently. Consider your prep schedule and par levels when determining how many prep tables you need. Par levels are the goal levels you set for each item on your prep list for a given day based on the amount you forecast using for that day. For each shift, you count your food on hand and then prep to your par level. For example, if the par level for mushroom soup on Tuesdays is 15 litres and you have only 3 litres on hand, you'll prep 12 litres that day.

Make sure that the prep tables are at the right prep height, usually a minimum of 36 inches, to ensure comfortable standing while prepping. And leave plenty of space for rubbish bins around your prep tables. Prep generates lots of rubbish, including tins, cartons, and vegetable remnants. You may also wish to be eco-friendly and separate your rubbish to recycle it, in which case you'll need more bins.

### Dry storage

Dry storage is the commercial version of your larder, a walk-in storeroom that holds all your dry goods. Any food item that's tinned or bottled (such as tinned tomatoes, olive oil, and tomato paste), dried (beans or pasta), or shelf-stable (vinegar or spices) can be stored here. You can also keep other consumables here, like paper napkins or candles.

Dry storage can be an organiser's dream or nightmare. Keep your dry storage organised to quickly know what you need to order and stay a step ahead at inventory time. Whenever possible, locate your storage area as close to your delivery door as possible. It saves time and energy and hopefully will be out of the way of the majority of your prep.

Consider creating a cage in your dry storage area if you keep expensive non-perishables on hand. A *cage* is simply a locked cabinet that can hold your saffron, truffles, caviar, or other expensive items securely. For more on managing inventory and purchasing, check out Chapter 14.

### Tilt bratt pan

A *tilt bratt pan* is a huge freestanding pan. It has a handy feature that lets you tilt the pan (either by means of a manual crank or electric switch) to pour your finished sauce, soup, rice, or whatever into your storage container. You can use it for sautéing, searing, or braising large quantities of foods that don't fit into a conventional pan suitable for use on a range top. For example, you can sear 12 pork loins or 50 chicken breasts at one time, braise 20 osso buco at a time, or poach 100 eggs at a time. It's an indispensable tool for high-volume restaurants that prepare just about anything from scratch in bulk. Tilt bratt pans range in size from around 30 litres to 120 litres capacity.

If possible, situate your tilt pan near a grated floor drain to quickly dispose of used liquid, overflows, and spills. If you're opening a new restaurant or remodelling an existing one, build in drains where you need them now. Doing that job later is costly; you not only have to pay additional construction costs, but you actually have to shut down your business for at least a few days. Drains are also handy for easy cleaning of big pieces of equipment. Just clean them out and dump the rinse water onto the floor and down the drain.

### Boiling pan

A boiling pan (can be as small as 5 gallons or as big as a hot tub. These specialised pieces of equipment use the even heating of superheated steam to evenly cook soups and sauces in volume. A crank system (similar to a tilting bratt pan, explained in the preceding section) allows the contents to be carefully poured into smaller containers for storage. The even heating of a boiling pan is unmatched for preparing things like stocks, long simmered sauces like bordelaise, and chilli for you and 500 of your closest friends. Locate your kettle near a grated floor drain for quick cleanup of spills.

### Smoker

A smoker is a piece of equipment designed to do a specialised job. A cold smoker uses indirect heat to impart smoky aromas and flavours to the food, thanks to the fragrant wood that fires it. Cold smoking doesn't cook the food; it simply adds the flavour to create items such as smoked salmon or smoky cheeses, including some provolones and cheddars. A hot smoker uses direct heat – a smoke box with fragrant woods – to cook and smoke simultaneously. Barbecued items are often cooked in a hot smoker.

Most restaurants don't have a smoker and if they do, it tends to be a small smoker for specialist foods like venison, as most ingredients can be sourced already smoked.

### Mats

Commercial restaurant floors are usually concrete or quarry tile. Standing on these hard surfaces for several hours a day causes stress on knees, leg muscles, and feet. General work processes can make floors wet and greasy. Invest in some well-designed kitchen mats to alleviate fatigue and eliminate slippery floors. Place mats in prep areas, on the line, behind the bar and host podium, and anywhere else people stand for long periods of time.

## Researching the right gear

There are many kitchen equipment items on the market to research and if you are new to cooking commercially, it is a good idea to seek advice from those who have been in the game for a while. You may be tempted at the onset to buy equipment that doesn't suit your business or be led to believe that it is essential by a pushy salesperson.

There are pass through ovens, for example, which are invaluable in a large, busy kitchen, the doors on either side of the ovens, situated in an island, means that food is accessible on both sides of the island for chefs. But they may be overkill – and expensive – if you're a small outfit.

If you are looking to open a small restaurant you may need only the basics if you have an uncomplicated menu. But do make sure you have the best knives – your very best friends in the kitchen – as they will last a lifetime.

If your restaurant is a large one do a lot of research beforehand – and once you have decided on what kind of a menu you will be offering – before buying. You may need industrial-sized equipment such as some of the mentioned equipment above. But you can buy smaller items like pasta boilers with automatic basket lifts, multi-cookers for vegetables, pasta and rice, vegetable washers and dryers, vegetable prep cutters and dough rollers to suit most sizes of kitchens.

# Working with an Existing Kitchen

Congratulations! You've found a site, and it already has a kitchen. A big piece of your business plan, including start-up costs and equipment is probably based on not needing to invest in a kitchen, because there's one in your space already. But many times, modifying an existing kitchen is more expensive than building a new one. After you figure in the costs of demolition and disposal, running gas lines, and updating the plumbing, ventilation, and fire suppression systems, you could really eat into your budget.

Plumbing is extremely important. Before leasing, have it all checked out, especially the sewage main. Kitchens produce a lot of grease and food matter that can clog pipes. We recommend a thorough jet cleaning of all pipes before you open. Nothing kills appetites like backed-up toilets!

Ask yourself these questions before you sign on the dotted line:

- **Is the kitchen right for you and your menu?** Does it have the space to accommodate your food? Can you work with the layout to get the flow you need for your menu?

- **Does the existing equipment work?** Can you use it? Just because the equipment is there doesn't mean it's not held together by duct tape and coat hangers. Have it inspected by a certified restaurant service pro. If you find that the equipment isn't in top shape and can't be upgraded at the landlord's expense, exclude it from the deal and buy your own.

✔ **Does the heating, ventilation, and air conditioning (HVAC) system work?** A working HVAC system is a necessary asset; one that doesn't work is a liability.

✔ **Do the wiring and the gas systems meet current building regulations?** Be wary that in some instances the previous owner may have received exemption from regulations through a grandfather clause, but now you may have to make major updates to fit in with current regulations at your expense. Check with your local authority.

✔ **What's the sale price of the kitchen?** If the owner is charging a lot for used equipment, you may be better off starting over with your own.

If you choose to include the equipment in your deal, stipulate in writing that the equipment must be in good working order.

An existing kitchen that has a good flow relative to your concept can save you tens of thousands of pounds. But don't get caught up in the fact that a space already has a kitchen and then alter your concept to match. If you've done the work and created a concept you believe in (and have the numbers to back up your plan), fit the kitchen to your concept – not the other way around.

Going into an existing operation can be a little off-putting at first. You may be expecting something that's as clean as the pristine television kitchen. But look at the space with an eye for storage, immovable equipment like plumbing, the line, and so on. You can't move them, so make sure you can work with them. Don't worry if the kitchen is dirty. Floors can be cleaned, grease removed, and equipment repainted. Don't let the level of dirt and grime affect your decision. Look for floor drains to make floor cleaning easy.

## Accepting the things you can't change

Suppose that you find the perfect space with one tiny problem: The kitchen is downstairs, and the dining room is upstairs. In the restaurant business if there's an obstacle, there's always an answer. With some creativity, time, and money, you can usually make it work. The most common obstacles that you'll find and need to address in existing restaurants are the following:

✔ **Stairs:** If you're going to make a two-level situation work, you are advised to install skid-resistant stair liners and paint the edges highly visible colours to help keep people from falling. Consider installing dumb waiters (very small service lifts designed for transporting trays of food and drink – not people – between floors). A lift may be another solution.

✔ **Distance from dining room to the kitchen:** If the dining room is too far away from the kitchen, you may have trouble keeping food hot until it gets to the table. Perhaps you can set up satellite food stations, such as a soup station, close to the dining room to keep soup from cooling off on the way to the table.

If servers are regularly too far from the kitchen, they're not available quickly to answer questions from the kitchen or relay guest requests to the kitchen, delaying guest service times. Some places use headset microphones, hand-held-style ordering systems, or even vibrating pagers to assist in long-distance communication. The physical distance between the dining room and the kitchen can add miles to any shift, so consider adding a food runner to help lighten the load, if your budget permits.

✔ **Structural inconveniences:** Is a column located in a place where you want a refrigerator? You have to find a less convenient spot for your refrigerator. Is a load-bearing wall blocking your view of part of the dining room? If you can't easily see your diners, make an extra pass through in that part of the dining room to make sure that guests are being properly attended to. Usually, removing these kinds of structural elements isn't economically feasible, so you have to be creative and work around them.

With a little ingenuity, these structural inconveniences can become intriguing parts of your interior space. One Portsmouth restaurant opened in a large, old bank. The attractive, solid old safe could not be easily demolished, so the owners decided to make it a feature, and stored wine in it.

## Changing the things you can't accept

In some cases, you have to make modifications to your kitchen to make it workable for your concept. If your concept is based on rotisserie meats, for example, your kitchen must accommodate a rotisserie oven. If you're a wood-fired pizza place, you have to have a wood-fired oven and the appropriate vent work and floor supports to go with it. If you can't add those things *necessary* for your concept, you have the wrong space.

The special features required for your concept don't need to already be present in your space, but you must be able to add them. Check with your contractor, kitchen design consultant, and landlord for advice (and for permission) on the cost and schedule for the modifications you must make to the space to stay true to your concept. If the modifications are too expensive for your budget, find a new space.

You may have to work with your existing plumbing because changing it is usually cost prohibitive, but you can usually add power where you need it. For example, bringing power in through a drop ceiling with hanging GFCIs (ground fault circuit interrupters) on a retractable pulley can solve the problem, if you're trying to run equipment at a location away from a standard wall outlet. Check with your electrical contractor to make sure you're working within the health and safety regulations.

Look at an equipment solution to infrastructure problems. For example, if your water heater is in the basement and it's having a tough time keeping up through antiquated plumbing, you can buy a dishwasher with a *condenser*, which reuses the hot water to save the cost of heating the water, and save wear and tear on your hot water heater. Or you can add a water preheater to an existing dishwasher. A *preheater* is a reserved source of hot water to make sure your machine is always running at the right temperature – important if you're using a heat-based (rather than chemical-based) sanitising system.

Consider adding a reverse osmosis water system to your operation. It extends the life of your plumbing and increases the efficiency of your chemicals. Plus you can cook with and serve tasteless, purified water.

## Power cleaning

If you start with existing equipment, get it the cleanest it will ever be again. Then establish a regimen to maintain that level of cleanliness, always. See Chapter 18 for more information on keeping things clean.

### Getting started

Here are some suggestions on this part of the cleaning job:

- Remove anything that's removable, including smallwares (small equipment items like soup bowls, tongs, and spatulas), plates, mixers, pans, tables, and shelving units that the previous owner may have left. Decide whether these items are worth keeping or should be replaced, and clean and disinfect each item before putting it into use. As you're cleaning the removables, check for any in need of repair.

- As you're removing items, watch for evidence of vermin (usually along the walls). The signs may include faeces or shredded paper. Ask a pest controller to check inside the walls, particularly in dish and high-moisture areas – the most likely homes for creepy crawlies. Get a jump-start on pests immediately or you'll lose out.

- Pay particular attention to cleaning the underside of tables, often overlooked in the cleaning process.

- Check out anything with silicone seals – a possible bacteria breeding ground. Decide whether you can clean the silicone or should reapply it.

- Look at the corners and *coping* (waterproof moulding that gradually curves to meet the wall from the floor) to see whether they're sealed to the wall and check for bugs, vermin droppings, and so on.

✔ Check all gaskets along coolers and ice machines. Gaskets are tough to clean but inexpensive to replace.

✔ Check for lime scale buildup in plumbing, particularly in the dish area. Lime scale, if left unchecked, can ruin expensive dishwashers.

✔ After you take out all the removables, contract with a reputable cleaning company to power wash and disinfect the entire kitchen, walls, and floors. A reputable company knows to avoid the equipment and electric outlets and gadgets. But walk the space with the cleaners to reinforce where you don't want water and make sure they understand your expectations.

### *Putting it back together*

After you clean the floors and walls, you need to do the following:

✔ Reinstall, replace, and reset the tables, smallwares, and equipment according to the flow.

✔ Break the kitchen into stations appropriate to your concept.

✔ Reinstall equipment where it makes sense for your operation.

✔ Start to envision production. Walk through the experience of creating a dish from start to finish. Try to set things up so that cooks have to move as little as possible and can avoid a lot of bending and stooping. Most people are right-handed, so place reach-in fridges with that fact in mind. You won't be 100 percent right about your setup right from the start, but the closer you can get the first time, the better off you are.

✔ Now is a great time to set the standard for cleanliness and organisation. Take pictures of perfectly setup stations, well-organised storage areas, a clean dish area, and so on. Refer to the pictures a week later and a month later as a gauge of how you're doing.

✔ Integrate a pest control management system and set up contracted or internal cleaning procedures.

# *Acquiring Your Kitchen Equipment*

Finding equipment is usually via the Yellow Pages, online and in dedicated catering shops. Whether the products are new or used, you'll probably source them from these places. If you're not located in a major city, going to a major supplier may be worth the trip, just for the money you can save and for the used equipment, but bring your bartering hat – and do your homework.

Know what equipment you need for your operation. Use Table 11-1 and Figure 11-1 to create a list of the equipment you need to produce the menu you've chosen. Know what it costs new and used. Shop around. Check out equipment Web sites, national companies, local companies, and restaurant equipment auctions. Talk to other people in the business about their good experiences and bad ones. Get names of good companies to work with from them. If they can introduce you to someone specific, you'll be a step ahead. Be canny. Know when you're getting a good deal and when you're not.

Building a big kitchen is a huge expense. Consider hiring a consultant to advise you about purchasing equipment. Here's what a consultant can do:

- ✔ **Review your concept plan and assist in choosing equipment for your concept.** Together, you create a list of the equipment you need, including the quantities of each item, and whether it should be new or used.

- ✔ **Develop a sourcing action plan for those pieces of equipment.** The sourcing action plan includes using resources (online, network, and trade shops) to figure out several sources for each piece of equipment, developing a process for evaluating the different options (manufactures, distributors, used equipment dealers, and so on) for each piece of equipment, and creating a schedule for acquiring the equipment.

- ✔ **Solicit bids for new equipment.** Your consultant should also help you evaluate the bids when they come in.

- ✔ **Facilitate purchase of used equipment, including negotiating the purchase price, conducting inspections, clarifying guarantees, and scheduling delivery.**

In a restaurant situation, the simpler the equipment, the better. For example, skip the equipment that boasts internal sensors. They're virtually useless and just another part that can break. Check oven knobs to see how robust they are, and how easy they are to clean. If it's fiddly, you're storing up trouble for you and you staff.

## Looking at leasing

Finding financing for equipment is tough until you're an established high-volume restaurant. But feel free to check with your bank if you need a piece of equipment you really want to purchase.

Leasing equipment has certain advantages. You pay for equipment only for the time you use it. When your lease is up, you get a brand-spanking-new piece of equipment with all the latest gadgets by signing a new lease. And when a piece of equipment breaks, it's not your responsibility to fix it.

Things shouldn't change between the time you talk to your salesperson and the billing department sends you a bill, but sometimes they do. Spell out all the financial details in the agreement so you're not surprised when the bill arrives. Get it in writing and check your invoices.

Here are a few items, in particular, that we suggest you lease:

- ✔ **Ice machines and refrigerators:** Both units have relatively short lives. Their motors and condensers work very hard and burn out. They're expensive upfront, and there's virtually no market for used ones. It's better to roll the price over in a lease format for a time, so that when your machine is about to die, your lease will be up, and you'll move on to a new unit.

- ✔ **Dishwashing machines:** This equipment is the restaurant version of your home dishwasher. It's very expensive upfront and usually can be leased through your chemical supplier. Some chemical suppliers give you the machine if you buy your products from them.

- ✔ **Coffeemakers:** Coffee companies often give you the machine if you buy the coffee from them. You may pay a little more for the product, but this option gives you flexibility and more positive cash flow. Plus if there's a breakthrough technology, you can usually upgrade quickly.

- ✔ **Linens:** Lease, don't buy, all your linens, including entry floor mats, uniforms, towels, tablecloths, and napkins. Usually you pay a single bill to have them delivered, stocked, and laundered.

Depending on your volume of purchasing, large food suppliers such as Brake offer pro-active IT solutions for easy ordering with them.

## *Buying – used versus new*

Wheeling and dealing with used equipment can be a lot of fun, but it's no different from buying a car. Be ready, willing, and able to tell the salesperson no and walk out of the shop. It's no secret to him or to you (because you've read this book) that you can get the same thing two doors down. Expect to pay between 40 and 60 per cent less for used equipment.

When buying restaurant equipment, negotiating is acceptable and expected. For example, say, 'I'll buy this oven and grill if you throw in the stainless steel table.' You may walk out with a mixer and food processor instead, but you probably need them anyway.

With used equipment, get some kind of a guarantee in writing. It may not be an extended warranty, but you need some assurance that it's going to run for a while. When you buy used equipment, you trade off extended warranties and factory support in favour of a lower price. The only way that used equipment benefits you is by saving you money. If you don't save money buying used equipment, you might as well have bought new equipment in the first place.

Don't worry about missing knobs and handles. You can usually add them. Focus on the all-important questions: Does it work? Will it work tomorrow? Is there a guarantee that it will work a week from now?

Don't buy very specialised pieces of equipment used, such as a combination oven (a combination steamer and convection oven) or a conveyer oven. You benefit from a warranty and complete information on the ideal cleaning and maintenance regimen that comes with a new oven. But you can buy many pieces of equipment used, like those in the list below, and sleep soundly:

- **Gas ranges:** These appliances are excellent candidates for buying used. Unless you derive some sort of personal satisfaction from it, don't go for the copper-clad import from Lyon when plenty of sound products are available that don't command the price. The biggest consideration when buying a gas range is how much heat it puts out.

- **Ovens:** Gas ovens, like gas ranges, are okay to buy used. But be cautious of purchasing used electrical ovens because so many things can go wrong with them, including problems with the sensors and temperature controls.

- **Fryers:** Buy fryers used, but get a guarantee that the thermostat works. Calibrate the thermostat to make sure that the temperature is actually correct. If you don't know how to change the oil, when to change the oil, how to clean it, and so on, get the information from your salesperson. If you can get a manual with the equipment, even better.

- **Grills:** Grills are usually okay to buy used, especially the gas variety. But do a detailed visual inspection of wood and gas grills because, over time, the guts eventually burn out. The heat warps and distorts the grill's inner workings. Make sure the grill surface is flat. If the grates are removable, inspect them to make sure that the surface is level.

- **Smallwares:** You can buy almost all used smallwares (like tongs, salt and pepper shakers, and soup cups) with confidence.

# Chapter 12

# Setting Up a Bar and Drinks List

. . . . . . . . . . . . . . . . . . . . . . . . . . . . . . . . . . . . . . . . . . . . . . . . . . . . . . . .

. . . . . . . . . . . . . . . . . . . . . . . . . . . . . . . . . . . . . . . . . . . . . . . . . . . . . . . .

*W*hether you're looking to open your town's new favourite bar where regulars become permanent fixtures, the 'in' club with the best music and drink specials, or an elegant wine bar attached to a chic new restaurant with an up and coming chef, this chapter is for you. In it, we cover everything you need to think about when opening your bar – from equipment and supplies to attracting customers.

But don't be so quick to skip past here if your establishment doesn't have an actual wooden bar with stools and all. If you're planning on serving alcohol, you'll want to stick around because we also help you set up a drinks programme, including working out what you need based on your restaurant concept, tips on stocking, pricing, and selling beer, wine, and alcohol, and important information on serving alcohol responsibly. Bear in mind that cocktails are up and coming, and you may wish to have a slice of this lucrative action by offering them to your customers. The information in this chapter gives you the low-down.

## Setting Up Your Bar

Your bar must match your concept. If you have a bar and restaurant together, the themes should be connected. One successful chain of Australian steakhouses consists of what are basically bars that happen to have restaurants built around them. Some diners come in and have to wait for a table just long enough to sit at the bar and have a drink. Most other successful restaurants have only a service bar, with no stools or counter, that's accessible only to the waiting staff.

Before buying any bar equipment, think about your goals. Decide if you want your bar to be the primary source of income for your business or assist the restaurant's takings. This exercise helps you determine how much space to dedicate to your bar, your dining room, and all the other front-of-the-house areas. (Chapter 10 covers laying out the front of the house.)

Form and function go hand in hand when setting up a successful bar business. If you have a freestanding bar, spend time considering both factors in your design. The following sections focus on the specifics.

## Selecting equipment

Decide where you want the basic structures of your bar to be. After you set these items up, they'll stay put for quite awhile. The basic bar equipment list looks something like this:

- **Bar:** Decide where to put the actual bar.

- **Bar stools:** Choose the number of stools you need based on the length of your bar. Each stool should have about 2 feet (60 centimetres) of dedicated bar space (So if your bar is 12 feet (3.75 metres) long, you'll need 6 stools).

- **Payment system:** Tie your bar payment system into your main system. The bar should have a separate cash drawer and computer terminal (if you're using a computerised system). If you plan to serve food at the bar, the bartenders need access to any food ordering system you use. If you plan to use a computerised system, your service bar will also need a printer to print out the restaurant's bar orders as they come in.

- **Pour options:** Weigh your options for metering, pouring, or strictly controlling the amount of alcohol in each drink. Systems range from pour tops added to control the speed the liquor flows, to full computerised systems that dispense the measured amount of alcohol at the touch of a button and keep track of the number of drinks made from each bottle.

Strict guidelines regarding measurement of alcohol are of prime importance. Make sure your staff know how to measure all alcoholic drinks (including wines by the glass).

- Now that smoking is banned from public places, make sure your customers adhere to the law or you could be fined.

- **Refrigeration:** Your fridge should be large enough to hold your inventory of white and rosé wines, your backup bottled beer supply, and any other supplies your bar uses regularly that must be kept cold.

- **Wells:** Each area where a bartender works needs a well or dedicated drink space for stocking and prepping drinks. The well holds ice (with a dedicated ice scoop), well brands of the basic alcoholic drinks (vodka, gin, whisky and rum), a garnish station, and a soda gun.

✔ **Hand sinks with soap and:** Hand sinks are small sinks reserved for washing hands only. Stock the sink with antibacterial soap, paper towels, and hand disinfectant.

✔ **Beer taps:** The kegs can be in the bar or in the cellar, with lines run to the bar, depending on your setup.

✔ **Reach-ins:** Reach-in fridges (usually shortened to *reach-ins*) are the restaurant equivalent of a small under counter fridge found in small kitchens. Choose under counter or tabletop high fridges or both. Look for the best setup for your operation.

✔ **Soda system:** The bar usually shares your restaurant's soda system (for soda water, tonic, cola, lemonade and other soft drinks), with 'guns' in the drinks prepping area.

✔ **Glass racks for hanging glassware:** Installing glass racks above the counters in the bar saves valuable counter space.

Here's a list of smaller, but important bar equipment if you are choosing to do cocktails in particular, some of the items to suit all bars. You probably need some of the items but don't buy them until you have sorted out your drinks list. You can set it up in multiple ways and change it, as you need to:

✔ **Spirit measure and shot glasses:** Use these to measure alcohol for mixed drinks.

✔ **Cocktail shakers:** Use these items to shake cocktails such as martinis.

✔ **Cocktail strainers:** These gadgets strain ice from shaken drinks that are served without ice.

✔ **Garnish holder:** This item holds lime wedges and lemon twists.

✔ **Bar spoons:** These long-stemmed items are essential for stirring drinks.

✔ **Floor mats:** Industrial-grade rubber mats cushion achy knees and soothe aching feet. These mats are typically grids of small circles that connect at the edges and can be thoroughly hosed down daily or between shifts.

✔ **Corkscrews:** Depending on your level of wine service, determine whether you need industrial wine openers for quickly opening bottles.

✔ **Bottle openers:** If you do a booming beer business, get the ones with a built-in bottle cap holder.

✔ **Blender:** This small appliance is sometimes called a barman's least favourite friend – it's for all those drinks like daiquiris and frozen margaritas that typically take longer to make than a standard cocktail.

✔ **Knives:** You need these utensils to cut the garnishes.

✔ **Cutting board:** Here's where you cut the garnishes.

✔ **Glass-washing equipment:** For sanity's sake, get a glasswasher. You will not only save time but you will have very clean, hygienic glassware. Make sure, however, that the cloths you polish the glasses with are spotless and changed often.

✔ **Containers with colour-coded tops:** Keep a supply of bloody Mary mix, orange juice, and the like in your bar fridge for easy access and to keep contents fresh.

✔ **Drink recipes:** Your collection may take the form of a folder, recipe-card box, or even a computerised database of drinks. It may be a comprehensive list of every cocktail known to mankind or just a quick reference to your house specialties. Make sure that staff manning the bar know how to make these cocktails or, if not, get them trained up to do them properly. Guessing just isn't good enough.

✔ **Ice buckets:** Ice containers must be used *for ice only.* If anything else gets in these buckets, they must be cleaned and disinfected before using them for ice.

If you plan to use a lot of ice, or if your ice machine is a long way from your bar, get rolling ice buckets or bins for restocking the ice. The wheels save strain on the staff because they won't need to wrestle the bins through the dining room. Use bins that are small enough that people can pick them up without back strain.

Most UK restaurants place cappuccino/espresso machines behind the bar. When employing staff, make it clear that their duties include making coffee and make sure they know how to operate these machines. All staff should be trained *baristas*, makers of top cappuccinos, lattes and other types of fashionable coffees. Expectations are high, and customers expect a really good cup of coffee, so don't let them down. The profit margins in coffee offer one route to success.

## Looking at your supplies

A *supply* is anything you stock and restock on a fairly regular basis. *Consumables,* such as napkins, straws, and garnishes, are supplies. So are *hard goods,* such as glassware, that are used, cleaned, and restocked. (Beer, wine, and spirits are supplies, and we cover each later in the chapter. And Chapter 14 gives you the lowdown on purchasing and management.) Your supply list will vary, but here's a general all-purpose list:

✔ **Glassware:** You need an assortment, from beer glasses to wine glasses to coffee drink glasses, depending on your concept.

✔ **Drink menus:** You may have an entire list of different cocktails or just a list of spirits that you carry. Be creative, but informative.

✔ **Soaps, cleaners, and sterilisers**: Get the right cleaning supplies for your equipment. Check with your manufacturer for details.

# Setting up a service bar

The service bar is the bar that *services* the restaurant dining room. When waiters order a glass of wine or a cocktail, they pick it up at the service bar. You can set up a service bar in many different ways, but your service bar must ideally be separate from the main bar from the guest's perspective. They may see this open area as the perfect place to stand and order their own drinks, causing congestion for the waiting staff. Make it easy for your staff to get in and get out without interrupting the customers. Here are a few of the most common options:

✔ **Separate drinks area at the main bar:** This design is the easiest from a setup perspective, because the bartender can access the same beer taps, and less often used alcoholic drinks, without moving too much. But it gets complicated from a customer's perspective if it's not obviously marked. The absence of bar stools isn't enough to distinguish it from the main bar. You could put a 'service point only' sign to distinguish it from the customer area.

✔ **Separate window behind the main bar:** Bartenders still have easy access to the full bar, and customers can't get to it, but depending on the layout of your place (such as if your bar is situated against an exterior wall), this configuration may not be possible.

✔ **Freestanding unit not attached to the main bar:** This option is great if your main bar and dining room are on different floors or if the main bar is far away from the dining room. Easy access for waiters to the bar usually means more drink sales and more money. The downside is that you probably won't have everything here that you have in the full bar, so bartenders may have to go between the two to make certain drinks.

The service bar needs the same basic equipment and supplies as the main bar. You may not keep every brand of vodka there, but you need the common ones. You may not have a full cordial selection, but develop a system for quickly serving drinks that require them. You will get to know your customers' preferences and be able to stock the bar accordingly, putting the less popular drinks at the main bar.

✔ **Garnishes:** Examples include maraschino cherries, lemon slices, lemon twists, celery, lime wedges, lime twists and olives.

✔ **Paper goods:** You may need things such as straws, stir sticks, coasters, drinks and dinner napkins.

✔ **Towels, bar cloths, and sponges:** Keep a supply of these items handy to wipe up sticky drinks, overflowing beer taps, and spills.

✔ **Sterilising spray:** Use this to regularly sterilise your surfaces but keep it away from glasses, ice and other areas, as the spray must not be consumed.

✔ **Menus:** Any food available in the bar should be on a menu there. If you have the same menu, keep a supply of dining room menus in the bar. If a limited menu is available in the bar, create a separate menu.

✔ **Requisition forms:** Employees use these forms to request more supplies.

✔ **Food-specific supplies:** If you serve food in your bar, you need other supplies, including silverware, plates, salt and pepper, and condiments.

Don't use glasses to scoop ice – ever, never, not under any circumstances. If your glass chips or breaks in the ice bin, you have to pour hot water in it to melt all the ice (*burn* it, in industry speak), remove the broken glass, and clean and sterilise it. Then you have to restock the ice.

 If you do have your logo on glasses or other items such as attractive salt and pepper pots, they may go 'walking' as they are considered a trophy by some diners. Even if you don't have your logo on covetable items, they too may disappear so make sure your designed tableware isn't too small to be nicked. Have your staff keep on eye on your tableware and remove items after the main course (diners won't need the salt and pepper then) which may help keep down theft.

# Keeping Your Bar Clean

Your bar should be just as clean as, if not cleaner than, any other area in the restaurant. Here, your patrons get an upfront, intimate look at the sinks, shelves, counters, and cabinets. If they see dripping, sticky bottles and a mildewed fridge, how long do you think they'll keep coming back? Develop a cleaning and sterilising system immediately, before you open your bar. Your bar is subject to health inspections just like any part of your restaurant. We cover cleanliness in detail in Chapter 18, but here are a few bar-specifics points to consider.

✔ Don't allow any eating behind the bar. Bits of food can get mixed in with supplies and equipment.

✔ Don't allow drinking behind the bar by the staff. It looks bad for a start. Allow bar staff to have a break and to have a drink then.

✔ Bar staff and other staff who use the bar should wash their hands often. They shouldn't be mixing drinks and touching the ice scoop without washing their hands. In addition, after a bartender touches his own mouth or nose, he should wash his hands.

✔ Bar staff must use utensils – not their hands – to stir drinks.

✔ Bar staff should never, ever stick their hands in dirty glasses. It may seem efficient to pick up four glasses at a time by placing your fingers inside them, then clamping your fingers together, but each time you do it, it's like sticking your fingers in someone's mouth.

✔ Create a rotation system for garnishes and mixes, especially during slow times. Just because you have lime wedges left over from the weekend, it doesn't mean they're still useable for Wednesday night cocktail specials. Rotation is often more of a problem in the bar than in the kitchen, because kitchen staff members are usually beaten over the head with the info from Day 1. Bar staff aren't. Check your perishables and make sure you're practicing FIFO (first in, first out).

# Drawing Crowds

Creative bar owners bring in the crowds in a variety of ways. Whether it's music, games, or drink specials, behind every busy bar is a reason why people come. Maintain flexibility in your design so that you can reconfigure your space easily as your bar business changes. In this section, we give you some pointers on what you may want to use to both draw and entertain the masses.

## Promotions

*Promotions* are events you use to attract customers – and make more money. Your job is to find a balance between getting people in the door and actually profiting from this increased traffic. If a promotion doesn't make money, it's not successful, no matter how many people you get in the door. Planning and analysis are key: Use the same process for forecasting expenses and sales we show you in Chapter 5 to outline the best, worst, and most likely scenarios for each promotion. And then follow up to determine the actual outcome.

Promotions are only limited by your imagination (and all applicable laws, of course). Put yourself in your potential customer's shoes to work out what will draw them in. Here are a few creative promotions we've heard of, which we include to spark your creativity. We don't recommend that you do or do not use them: Think about what works for the clientele you're going after, what fits with licensing laws, and what's profitable for your business.

- ✔ **Sponsor an amateur football team:** You get advertising space on the team shirts or in the league programmes, and the players, and their friends and family become part of the greater bar family. This approach works with other sporting events (like golf outings) and leagues, too.

- ✔ **Take part in radio station promotions:** Partner a local station to broadcast from your bar. Give away free stuff like shirts, merchandise, and event tickets to improve your chances of drawing a crowd.

- ✔ **Create a bar event schedule:** For example, you can make Monday football night, Tuesday karaoke night, Wednesday mud wrestling night (we're only joking!), and Thursday £2 draught beer night.

Successful bars advertise. Take a look at Chapter 16 for the full details.

# Entertainment

Keep your sports ear to the ground and the other tuned to the local music scene. There are sports to watch, games to play, music to hear, and songs to sing. If you're looking for entertainment for your bar, start here.

If you're running a bar inside a restaurant, think carefully before adding entertainment. If the bar crowd gets rowdy, it can affect your restaurant patrons. Owners of stand-alone bars can be a bit more creative and/or edgy with entertainment options.

## Turn on the TV

Sports bars or pubs are common in many parts of the country. Many have satellite packages that let customers watch many types of sport, such as football, golf, and rugby. You need to pay a fee to display the programming for commercial use. Check with your satellite company about the regulations in your area. You will certainly need an entertainment licence. Ask your local authority how to obtain one or see the section 'Turning up the music' regarding music and dancing.

## Playing games

Gambling is strictly regulated so check with your local authority for further details if you are keen to add gaming machines to your bar or restaurant.

Gambling of any sort is not permitted unless the premises are properly licensed. If you don't have the right licence and you have gambling machines, you are breaking the law

## Turning up the music

Adding music to your bar isn't always easy. You can get started with a jukebox. If you're looking to have dancing on the premises, consider hiring a DJ. DJs usually have their own collection of music they bring with them and play at your bar. You pay them a fee for their services. The fee can be a flat rate, a percentage of sales, or a percentage of the cover charge, if applicable.

You will need an entertainment licence for dancing under the Public Entertainments (Licensing Act 2003) Act. You will also need PPL (Phonographic Performance Ltd) and PRS (Performing Right Society) licences. These cover CD, tape or record playing and the rights of composers, songwriters and music publishers. Check out the Performing Right Society Web site at www.mcps-prs-alliance.co.uk, and the Phonographic Performance Ltd Web site at www.ppluk.com.

*Karaoke* allows your customers to get up on stage and sing along with recorded music. If you're interested in starting a karaoke night, consider renting a machine, or hiring a service to run your programme to see how it goes. A commercial-quality system starts at around £300.

If you want to move beyond recorded music do some research at other bars and restaurants in your area and get to know the local music scene. Live music is a great way to bring in customers. Many local bands have their own followings and bring their fans with them. Expect to pay from £100 for a solo artist or small band in for a weekend night. Some charge a flat fee, and others charge a percentage of sales and boost their income on the night by selling their CDs. Usually, the bigger the band, in number of members and in popularity, the more you pay. Talk to other bar and pub owners to find out acceptable rates.

Check out www.functioncentral.co.uk, a Web site with a nationwide database of performers, from soloists to swing bands.

## Bar staff

Bar staff can bring in customers. Attractive female bartenders bring in men. (Attractive male bartenders bring in women who bring in men. But looks are only one way your bartenders can bring in customers.

Knowledgeable bar staff can also be a draw. They should be well versed in beer, wine, and spirits, with an emphasis on your specialty drinks. But don't stop with drinks. Educate your bartenders about your food as well. Even if they don't know the full menu, bartenders should know your specialties. If your bartender knows your signature dish, the special cheeseboard, or the secrets of where you source the best fish, they can build a regular bar clientele and encourage them to bring in friends for meals in the dining room.

# Providing Liquid Refreshment

The term *alcoholic list* generally applies to restaurants that serve alcoholic drinks. Nonalcoholic drinks are usually priced and found listed with your food products. Sourcing your non-alcoholic drinks such as tea and coffee may be from different companies, as you will be trying to source the best quality and price for your restaurant.

Use the same creative drive in your drinks list that exists in developing your menu. (Check out Chapter 9 for help.) Before you can think about what to put on the list, you must understand your concept and your clientele. Then make choices on what to include on your drink lists based on these factors. If your interior design and menu are taking some risks, your drinks list needs to stand out, too. If you're running a family restaurant offering traditional fare, plan a drinks list to match.

Decide how to focus your list. Are you going to offer sought-after vodka, gins, and scotch, or does a basic well (the least expensive brands of basic liquors) do it? Watch your competition. Where's your point of difference from the place down the street? Maybe being familiar (or edgy) is your point of difference. Will you be offering all types of alcoholic drinks or just going for the beer and wine and not whisky, gin, brandy and vodka and others?

Don't try to take on too many choices from the beginning. It's not a good idea to reduce the number of your choices, especially alcoholic drinks, after your restaurant opens; it's much better to start smaller when you first open and add to your list later. If you serve 15 different regional bottled beers when you first open but later reduce that list to 2 regional beers to create inventory efficiency, you risk disappointing customers.

# *Becoming Beer Brainy*

Many restaurants get by with a very limited beer menu. Unless you want to be known for your beer selection, you may be able to limit your beer choices to a few internationally well-known and regional beers), Most beer drinkers probably can find something to satisfy them from that list. But your concept may require you to dig a little deeper. If you're a Belgian brasserie, you probably have to have a Belgian beer, or three, on your list.

You can approach pricing bottles and cans of beer much like you do wine. But when you're working with pricing a pint of draught beer, put your calculator away. You'd need to work out the number of millilitres per keg and the number of millilitres per pour and hope that your keg system is working perfectly. If your gas isn't working properly, you could be wasting lots of beer. Keg systems require maintenance, incur lots of spillage and waste, and give you good profits.

Because beer is so readily available and people know what you paid for it, price it according to market norms – and don't charge too much. You can't charge £3 for a bottle of lager and sell very many (unless you run the concessions at a professional sports venue). People will rebel. But also keep in mind that lowering your prices can harm your credibility. From a customer's perspective, lowering your prices is considered a retreat or a sign of desperation. Bumping up your prices a bit is much easier.

If you're going down the better, local beer route, have a number of premium beers to choose from and be knowledgeable about them. You can charge more for these types of beer as they will appeal to the connoisseurs, those more interested in a really top notch beer than the usual fizzy, dull stuff.

You may be interested in looking at the Cask Marque, an independent accreditation scheme set up to acknowledge excellence with cask ales. Look into this system and find out about the wide choice of quality cask beers available and how to choose them. Take a look at www.cask-marque.co.uk for more details.

# Getting With It about Wine

As with most other facets of your restaurant, your wine list choices depend heavily on your concept because it affects customers' expectations for both your list and the food you serve. But whether you're a family-style restaurant or a fine dining establishment, you can use a wine list to your advantage.

## Creating your list

Having a good rapport with wine reps helps your restaurant. When stocking difficulties emerge with certain labels and vintages, the reps can make sure that you know about them and help steer you towards other quality wines. Wine companies will also store wine for you if you have limited space.

### Customer expectations

Many customers know what they want in a wine; others are always open to experimenting and trying something new. A popular strategy for developing a wine list over time is to give your diners familiar choices to start with and then expand your offerings to include similar yet less familiar choices as you go along. You can introduce them to new wines and let them explore the unfamiliar ones by the glass.

Anything that makes your customers happy (and keeps them spending money) is a good choice for your wine list. If a customer comes in once or twice a week and wants a particular wine on the menu, give it to her.

Your customers may interpret your use of 'supermarket wines' (wines that are extremely familiar and inexpensive) as the cheap end of the market. But, depending on your concept, your clientele may expect these wines. Make sure that you make this type of wine a deliberate choice, not just an easy choice.

### Menu offerings

The ability to match your wine list to your menu is key to running a good restaurant wine list. Co-author Michael frequents a restaurant run by a husband and wife team. She does the wine list, which includes only 10 or 12 wines that go perfectly with the menu. She focuses on what's on the menu and pairs accordingly.

If you're just getting started or want to update your list but don't know where to begin, consider having your wine salespeople taste some recipes and help you pair your offerings with their wines. Wine reps love to give their input. Just know that they'll design the list around their own portfolio exclusively.

### Length of list and quality level of selections

A wine list doesn't have to be long, eclectic, or familiar to be good. And a good wine doesn't have to be serious; it just has to be a wine that someone enjoys. Find a balance between the eclectic and familiar stand bys. Don't get too esoteric or you risk intimidating guests with your offerings.

If people don't recognize the types of wine you're serving, make sure that your staff knows them, can explain them in detail, and brings the diner a sample. Also, if pronunciation may be intimidating, give each wine a number on the menu so guests can order by number instead of avoiding the unfamiliar because they're afraid to look foolish.

Or, you could add simple wording to your wine list for easy accessibility such as 'wines under 14 per cent alcohol,' 'wines under £20,' or 'light-bodied, 'medium-bodied,' 'full-bodied. Or simply group your wines according to whites and reds and how 'mellow,' 'spicy,' 'dry,' 'sweet' they represent.

When serving wines, staff should present the bottle to the customer before opening it. If the wrong bottle is opened and the customer says he doesn't want it, you're left with an unsaleable bottle of wine unless you can sell it by the glass or shift it otherwise.

Measurements such as 125 millilitres, 175 millilitres and multiples thereof must be displayed or be written up in menus or wine lists to comply with the law. Your spirits measures and prices should also displayed.

The 'supermarket wines' or wines that everyone knows, are definitely on the way out in restaurants because many diners can work out what you paid for the bottle, so justifying the price you need to charge to make your margins is tough. But have no fear; plenty of other excellent wines are available at reasonable prices. Work with your wine rep to find wines that fit with your menu items and that you can buy at a low price and meet your margin.

## Pricing your wine

Determining your selling price for wines by the bottle is relatively easy. You simply decide on the factor you want to multiply the cost by. For example, you could pick a factor of two to three times what you paid for it. This system is really just another way to look at food cost. Here you're multiplying, with food cost you're dividing. The more expensive the wine is, the lower the factor that you might multiply by. So, if you buy the wine from your supplier for £5, you might charge £15 (multiplied the cost of the wine by 3). But if you paid £50 for a bottle of wine, you'll probably charge closer to £100 than £150 per bottle. Your percentage is lower, but your profit is higher.

Fifty pounds worth of stock does you no good on the shelf. Don't be tempted to overprice your wine – you could price yourself out of a sale. With wine, don't worry about keeping the percentage that you make off your list low. Move wine through your restaurant to keep money flowing rather than tying it up in storage.

Pricing your wines by the glass is tougher, but you can do it. First decide on the size of your pour, usually either 175 millilitres or 250 millilitres. A standard wine bottle is 750 millilitres, so you get four plus 175-millilitre glasses or three 250-millilitre glasses from each. Then decide on the factor you want to multiply by, usually around three times the initial cost. Check out Table 12-1 for what this might look like.

Please note that Table 12-1 gives you the prices for different sized glasses of wine at the lower end of the price range. When you are selling higher class wine, reduce the percentage from between 2½ and 3 times the cost. The norm is to drop your margins as you go up in price per bottle. Otherwise you will not shift the wine unless you have a wine preservation system such as the Presorvac wine-by-the-glass saver or multiple bottle professional systems. See storage below for other solutions.

Please also note that the cost per bottle excludes VAT.

| Table 12-1 | Wine-by-the-Glass Pricing at 3½ Times Cost | | | |
| --- | --- | --- | --- | --- |
| *Cost per Bottle* | *Bottle Sale Price* | *125 ml Price* | *175 ml Price* | *250 ml Price* |
| £4 | £14 | £2.80 | £3.50 | £4.60 |
| £6 | £21 | £4.20 | £5.25 | £7.00 |

This difference in the price you pay versus the price you charge may seem huge. But don't forget that you have to cover all your costs, including waste, if the rest of the bottle isn't sold before it goes off. Take a look at Chapter 9 for details on what expenses you need to cover with your food and beverage prices.

Or, you may choose to calculate pricing in another way, for example based on a desired gross profit, as Table 12-2 shows you.

| Table 12-2 | Standard Multipliers for Different Gross Profits |
|---|---|
| *Desired Gross Profit* | *Multipliers* |
| 45% | x 2.14 |
| 50% | x 2.35 |
| 55% | x 2.61 |
| 60% | x 2.94 |
| 65% | x 3.36 |
| 70% | x 3.92 |

Whichever method you choose to use, round up the prices so that they don't look clumsy. Your staff will also need to be able to calculate the prices in their heads, and work out the change easily.

## *Storing your wine*

Storage is a huge issue for wine. Wine's biggest enemies are air, temperature, humidity, and light. Most wine cellars are below ground, because the temperature underground is constant and cool. Caring for wine is relatively easy in your restaurant.

Take your cue from these wine cellars and guard your wine against these forces by picking a cool, dry, and dark location for your stock. And store the bottles on their sides or upside down while they're in their cases. This prevents the corks from drying out and letting air seep in. If your investment in your wine list is sizable, you may want to invest in your own climate-controlled wine cellar.

Wine storage: as wine dislikes wildly fluctuating temperatures, vibration or warmth, red wine should be stored between 14° C and 16° C and whites between 10° C and 12° C.

Beyond the bottle storage concerns, many restaurateurs worry about storing and preserving open bottles on their by-the-glass list. If you have an extensive by-the-glass list, consider investing in a wine preservation system. These systems evacuate the air in a bottle, replacing it usually with nitrogen, and then seal the bottle until you open it again. The price for a basic system starts at around £1,000 for a four-bottle system and goes up, depending on what gadgets you want and how many bottles you need to preserve. If you don't have that kind of budget, consider using a product designed for home use, like VacuVin brand products. These products remove the air from your bottle of wine and seal it until the next time you open it, preserving the quality of the wine for up to two weeks.

If you can't afford a wine preservation system, a really competent staff member can be an ally, especially if she works almost every day. She can keep an eye on open bottles, steer bar patrons toward those selections, and help avoid waste. She should also know when to ditch a bottle that's been open too long.

Watch out for the urge to overstock. Allocate your valuable bar space to stuff that moves. You can probably skip Benedictine and sloe gin, no matter what your wine and spirits rep says. And resist the sales pitch that promises free bottles of stuff you don't use. If the free bottle is only a dust collector, how does that help you?

You can't *marry*, or *consolidate*, bottles of alcohol. Doing so is illegal. You may think that you're being efficient by adding your half bottle of well vodka from the south well, to the bottle of well vodka from the north well and then stocking a fresh bottle in the south well. But you can't. Basically, the government is trying to protect consumers from fraud – bar staff putting cheap vodka in a high-end bottle and charging more. So no bottle-combining.

## *Measures and pricing*

Your *measure,* or how much alcohol you pour into each cocktail, is important. It determines what the finished drink costs you, how much you can charge, and how much profit you make on each drink.

A typical serving of alcohol in a mixed drink is 25 millilitres for whisky, gin or vodka, for example, and 50 millilitres for port, vermouth and liqueurs. If you pour 25 millilitres per drink, you'll get 30 shots from each 750-millilitre bottle. If you pour 50 millilitres, you'll get 15 shots from each bottle. So if you pay £15 for a bottle of whisky, for example, those same shots will cost you 50 pence and £1, respectively. Add in another 50–70 pence

When calculating your drinks costs, take into consideration rent, rates, staffing, and all of the costs involved as well as all of the ingredient costs for each type of drink. You must aim for at least 67 per cent to make a decent percentage profit. If you go down below 60 per cent you're in trouble.

Soft drinks make up the profit margins. It is perfectly possible to make a 200 per cent profit on the post mix, or gun dispenser but, if you go for more expensive bottled tonics, coke and sodas, your profit will be down if you don't take these into consideration when calculating the final sale price.

Stocktake on a weekly basis to make sure you are getting your return and to check that no theft is occurring or free drinks are being taken.

When giving out free drinks be sure to put it on the till as a 'complimentary' otherwise you will lose track of the transaction.

You charge more than the drink costs you to make because you have to account for *buybacks* (buying the occasional drink for regular diners or for guests spending lots of money in your establishment), overpouring, spillage, breakage, employee drinks, the occasional unscrupulous bartender – and don't forget profit.

Make sure that if you are charging higher prices for drinks if you're a trendy restaurant or bar, the customer is getting value for money. Don't use cheaper 'house' brands but offer premium brands. Keep up to speed if you're a trend-setter and set the pace! Also, serve good mixes with these premium brands, not gun soda or tonic. Source top of the range ones and your customers will thank you for it.

You determine the price you need to charge your customers to hit the margins you've set based on the pricing you get from your suppliers. But remember to take your overheads into account as mentioned earlier. Even if the percentages you make from each drink are equal, the profit you make from top quality spirits, Champagnes, wines and liqueurs, are much higher, so encourage your staff to learn their l brands (liquor distributor sales reps can help train them) and to recommend the more profitable, higher quality ones to your diners.

# *Serving Alcohol Responsibly*

If you serve alcohol to the public, you need to be aware of the risks you're taking and take steps to minimise them. Get up to speed from your local authority for specific guidelines on what you can and can't do. Take their recommendations and stated penalties seriously. Check out Chapter 8 for information on how to obtain your alcohol licence. Here are a few tips that can help you and your staff keep your customers safe:

- ✔ Keep the phone numbers of several taxi services handy.
- ✔ Offer an incentive for designated drivers by offering them free nonalcoholic drinks all night long.
- ✔ Check with your insurance company for recommendations they may have on ways to lower your liability.
- ✔ Be vigilant about potential problems. For example, don't assume that you can give people darts and alcohol and expect nobody to ever get hurt.
- ✔ Decide whether you need to hire bouncers. If you have a rowdy crowd, bouncers can help deter dangerous behaviour.

Be careful when hiring and screening bouncers. They can be the catalyst, instead of the deterrent, for violence. Conduct thorough background checks on them to discover any arrests, criminal convictions, or even complaints filed against them. You can be sued if your overly aggressive bouncer decides he needs to punch someone to keep him in line.

✔ Make sure you have an ID process in place to deter under-age drinking and those banned from premises.

Bear also in mind your staff. A recent case in which a restaurant manager gave a staff member a drink after a shift, which resulted in an accident, also resulted in the manager being sued by the staff member.

Keep an eye on the age of your clientele if you are selling alcohol. Current legislation regarding age and alcohol states the following:

✔ **Children under 14:** Can go into a pub with a children's certificate, but must be with an adult and stay in the garden or family room.

✔ **Children under 16:** Can go into a restaurant where alcohol is served and at the licensee's discretion may consume (but not purchase) alcohol bought by a parent or guardian as long as it is with a meal.

✔ **16-17 year olds**: May purchase beer, port, cider, or perry in an eating area on licensed premises (in Scotland this applies to wine too) as long as it is with a meal.

✔ **Adults**: May not buy or attempt to buy alcohol for consumption in a bar by a person under the age of eighteen. The maximum fine is £1,000.

No matter what advice they receive, some owners insist on walking the line between what's legal and what they think they can get away with. Our advice: Toe the line. If you're open when you're not supposed to be, you could risk your business. If you consistently have underage drinkers on your premises, you'll eventually get caught. You could be fined or lose your licence.

Sometimes a manager just needs to be able to recognise potentially hazardous situations before they become problems. When you mix people and their emotions with alcohol, problems can escalate. Watch for the people who've had too much to drink. Be aware of conflict building up on your premises. Preventing problems before they happen is more an art than a science.

Your bartender should be the authority figure. He has the responsibility to keep everything in the bar running smoothly and safely. No matter what gender (or size) your bartenders are, they should have control over the clientele. At one time or another, someone will challenge their authority.

# Chapter 13

# Employing and Training Your Staff

A chain is only as strong as its weakest link. You've heard this idea related to business a million times. Choose a good team and train them the right way to maximise your chances of success. Whether you're starting a new restaurant from scratch or revitalising an existing one, the information in this chapter can improve your staff development today.

## Finding the Right People

Before you can work out who you need to help you operate your restaurant, you need to fully develop your concept (see Chapter 3) and menu (which we cover in Chapter 9). Then put on your operations cap and think about what jobs you need to fill. If you're a fast-food restaurant, you don't need a member of staff to help people find a table or take reservations, but you will need some cashiers to take orders and others to clear up If you're an upmarket restaurant, you need people to greet customers, give them menus and seat them; you'll also need waiters, bar staff, and kitchen staff – but no cashiers. Use our suggestions in Table 13-1 (and the descriptions throughout this section) to determine the employees you need based upon your concept.

Different jobs in the restaurant world require different personalities. For example, a quick order cook doesn't need an outgoing personality: You don't want him to be so chatty that he can't focus on what he's doing. And a timid, unhospitable person in front of house greeting guests will alienate customers. You need people to be friendly when they interact with guests, but focused on productivity where you need production. And you probably need a drill sergeant to make sure it all gets done.

| Table 13-1 | Employees Needed for Each Shift |
|---|---|
| *Type of Restaurant* | *Positions to Fill* |
| Casual/family style | Managers<br>Waiting staff<br>Kitchen porters<br>Cooks<br>Cashiers |
| Fast food with a centralised menu | Cashiers/order takers<br>Kitchen staff<br>Kitchen porters |
| Fine dining | Managers<br>Waiting staff<br>Kitchen porters<br>Chefs (several with different grades such as head chef, chefs de partie, sous chefs)<br>Sommelier or wine waiter<br>Bar staff |
| Bar and grill | Managers<br>Waiting staff<br>Kitchen staff<br>Head chef and other chefs (several with different specialties)<br>Bar staff |

In the following sections, we give you an overview of what to look for in potential employees. We break up the information by position, detailing the scope of the responsibilities for each one. We even include a sample organisational chart, Figure 13-1, to show you how everyone fits together.

Create your own formal job descriptions for each position, preferably before you hire the people to fill them. The process of creating job descriptions can help you immensely during the hiring process by clarifying who you need for your operation and defining their responsibilities. (Chapter 2 discusses when in your restaurant opening timeline you should develop job descriptions.)

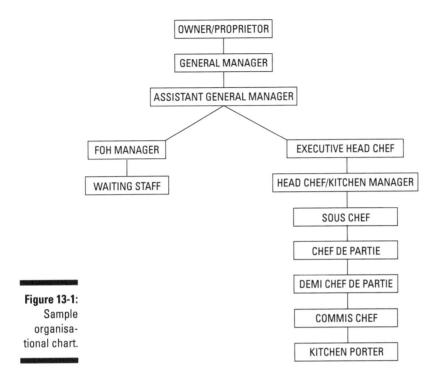

**Figure 13-1:**
Sample
organisa-
tional chart.

## *Managing your quest for managers*

Managers set the tone for the rest of the staff. So hire the best people for the job. They affect how smoothly your operation runs, how your staff control the chaos and treat the customers, and how much money you'll ultimately make. In the following sections, we let you know about some key things to watch for when selecting the best people for your management team.

Hiring a recruitment agency to help you look for restaurant managers and chefs can be a smart move. Recruiters usually charge you, the employer, anywhere from 10 to 25 per cent of the new employee's salary for their services, but they can really cut down the length of your search and improve the quality of your candidates. The agency's recruits will work for a probationary period and, on completion of the time, the agency will invoice the company for their percentage. You should like the staff you hire, at least on some level. You're together for at least 12 hours a day, so need to get along.

Cross-training management team members is a good idea. Your manager, for example, may not need to know how to run or staff the kitchen, or expedite orders coming from the kitchen, but in most cases, the more cross-trained your managers are in each position, the better. You gain more flexibility, you respond rapidly to changes in business levels, and you're better equipped to deal with the inevitable holidays, sick days, late arrivals, and simply not calling you or turning up that your staff will take at the most inopportune times.

### General manager

In any business, a *general manager* (GM) must have a grasp of all facets of the operation. You can employ a GM, but many owners choose to serve as the GM. They may or may not use the title, but they perform the duties, and save an extra salary. If you've never waited on tables, known what to do with coats, or made a salad or a cocktail, get yourself a quick education. If you don't, the employees in those areas will dictate the business. That may be okay, but think about this: If your chef says he has five chefs but needs eight, how are you going to know if he's on target or asking for more than he needs? He's asking you to increase your labour costs by 60 per cent for a single shift. You need to know enough to make an informed decision. Otherwise, your productivity goes down, your labour costs go up, and your profits go out of the window.

The GM is ultimately responsible for the staff's knowledge and commitment. He must lead by example. He must be able to do financial forecasts, budget objectives, and all the other numbers. Control of the restaurant is important as a means of maximising profit and maintaining cash flow.

The GM represents the restaurant not just while he's in the restaurant but out in the community as well. If he goes out and gets drunk down the street, sleeps with a competitor's wife, has a dispute with local councillors, and runs someone over on his way home from the restaurant, it's not good community relations, to put it mildly.

### Assistant general manager

The *assistant general manager,* or AGM, is the heir-apparent to the GM, or next in line. (See the preceding section for details on traits of a good GM.) The AGM should be aspiring to be a GM, trying to do the job before he gets the job. The GM delegates responsibilities to the AGM to prepare for an eventual promotion. The AGM either knows or is learning how to be the GM. As the owner, you may be attending to the GM's responsibilities without the title, and your GM may be acting as an AGM.

The titles matter less than the responsibilities. You need someone to be in charge and someone right behind him serving as a backup, the next in line, and learning all the ropes.

## *Chef*

If you are running a restaurant you need chefs. If you're running a fast food place you need competent food handlers and a kitchen manager. Base your search for a chef on your concept. Anticipate your volume of business, the technical difficulty of your menu, and whether you want the chef to be part of your public relations machine. Then narrow down your hunt. You can categorise chefs by their specialised cuisines or the types of operations that they have experience in.

A chef brings creativity, expertise, and leadership to your kitchen. Be aware that many people call themselves chefs when they really don't know which end of a knife to hold. The title has been diluted, with young chefs taking on jobs as head chefs way before they are ready to as they won't have had the necessary experience to run a tight, effective ship. A true chef will have a proven track record for the following:

✔ Managing, training, teaching, and developing a staff

✔ Developing a menu

✔ Running efficient, profitable, and clean kitchen operations

✔ Demonstrating specific knowledge of service, wine, and spirits and how to apply them to your concept

If you don't need or want someone else to be that involved, consider hiring a kitchen manager (KM) instead of a chef. (See the KM description in the 'Staffing the kitchen' section.)

Use quality chef recruiters to find a quality chef. Newspaper ads have limited success, but they may work if you're located in a large metropolitan area. Your choices may be more limited if you're in a smaller market. With a typical newspaper ad, your response isn't very targeted. You'll get resumes from every joker with an apron in your market. A recruiter can scour the country quickly for candidates that match your concept and budget, checking references and saving you time.

A good chef understands his diner's wishes.. He is current with food trends. He has the adaptability, creativity, and passion to see an opportunity where others may not bother with 'difficult' diners.

Stereotypically, chefs are notorious for boozing, yelling, and the like. Your chef is a manager, just like any other restaurant manager. He should conduct himself in the same way you expect every other manager to behave. The restaurant is a tamer environment than it was 15 years ago, and that kind of behaviour is no longer tolerated. Make sure that your chef understands this!

# Staffing the kitchen

We list these positions in order from most essential (kitchen porters) to less essential (the commis chef or KM). Someone must be in charge of the kitchen, but it may be a single manager in charge of every restaurant employee or a head chef but few restaurants can survive for long without a kitchen porter.

### Kitchen porter

The kitchen porter job involves very physical labour. Boots and an apron, preferably waterproof, are the standard uniform. In addition to washing dishes, kitchen porters are also often asked to prep vegetables and fetch and carry goods, as well as wash up and clean the kitchen and other storage spaces, including the bins.

Kitchen porters are the serfs of the restaurant world. But most experienced chefs and managers agree that they're among the most important people in the building. They deserve respect. The most amazing food in the world will do you no good if you don't have a clean plate to put it on or a clean fork to eat it with. Obviously, in a small restaurant there may only be a couple of members of staff, both taking turns to wash up as it is economically unviable to hire another staff member.

Many cooks and chefs start out in the washing up area. If they have the desire, kitchen porters can and do move from dishwasher to commis chef to chef de partie to sous chef. Promotion from within your organisation is an ideal way to sell an employee on working in the washing up area. Motivating someone to dig his elbows deep in discarded food is tough. Promotion can be the carrot dangling out in front of the employee. If you're able to hang on to your kitchen porter and move him up the ranks, you and he will both have a great story to tell.

When you're looking to hire kitchen porters, start here:

- ✔ **Word of mouth:** If you have a good employee who recommends a friend or relative for a dishwashing position, definitely consider that person.

- ✔ **Newspaper ads:** For entry-level positions in your restaurant, newspaper ads generally get a good response from qualified candidates.

After you get some candidates in the door, make sure they have the following traits before hiring them:

- ✔ **Good work history (if they have a history):** Don't discount applicants just because this is their first job, but if they've been fired from their last five washing up jobs, you may not want to give them the sixth.

✔ **Punctuality:** If applicants are late for the job interview, it could be a sign of things to come. You definitely want a kitchen porter you can count on to show up on time.

✔ **Organisational skills:** Keeping the dish and washing up area neat and organised is important in order to keep dirty dishes flowing in and clean ones flowing out. Make sure the person you hire is up to the task.

✔ **Necessary physical attributes:** Kitchen porters must be able to stand for long periods of time. They have to be able to lift heavy loads, like stacks of plates or full rubbish bags. They should also be fairly dexterous and not clumsy. They should be able to carry a tray of glasses through a busy kitchen without getting in someone else's way.

### Commis chef

*Prep* is short for preparing, or making preparation. It's the root system of the kitchen. Your commis chefs are the prepping chefs, the unsung heroes of the kitchen, the ones who do the daily grind work. Commis chefs touch every part of your menu and kitchen, whether they're cutting steaks off the side of beef; washing salads; making soups, prepping vegetables, or making pizza dough Commis chefs prepare your kitchen for the shift to come.

Many people believe that prep is the most important part of the cooking. If it's not done right, nothing can fix it. Take soups, for example. Soups aren't cooked to order. They're prepared early in the morning so flavours are melded by the time the soup is served at lunch or dinner. When a diner orders a piping hot bowl, the waiter serves up a ladleful and goes on her way. If the soup isn't prepared right in the prep stage, you can't do much to change this after it's ordered.

In other cases, your commis chef start the process, and your chef de partie finishes it. For example, your commis chefs peel and devein prawns for salad but don't assemble the final product.

Commis chefs should have a working knowledge of the storerooms and larder fridges so they know where to find product. They know where to find all the ingredients they need for whatever they're making. They also need to know how to operate many kinds of equipment – an ice cream maker, food processor, tilt skillet, fryer, or even the grill. They could be roasting peppers and then frying noodles for a garnish – all within the same shift.

Look for the following traits and characteristics in a good commis chef:

✔ Punctuality and dependability

✔ Ability to take direction, criticism, and instruction well

✔ Organisational skills

✔ Ability to complete tedious, repetitive tasks over a long period of time

✔ Ability to read a recipe and apply basic maths skills

✔ A real desire to be in the business (an applicant in it just for the money could be gone next week, searching for that extra £2 per hour)

✔ Ability to stand for long period of times and lift and move cases of food with relative ease

Experience in other restaurants is always a plus. If applicants don't have experience but seem like they could be good employees, consider them as candidates for the kitchen porter position.

### Chef de partie

A chef de partie is assigned to a station (the section of the kitchen where food is finished, or cooked when ordered). Literally, 'head of a team,' this is a managerial step up. In a small restaurant a chef de partie may be in charge of just one chef, or several in a large one. Duties could include sauces, meat and fish and hot starters, plus the staff meal.

Chefs de partie should have some kitchen experience before working on stations. Many people start in prep and work up to the position. Depending on your concept, you can start inexperienced chefs de partie on a cold station, like the pantry or pastry, and then cross-train them on other stations as their abilities and interests develop. Usually, these cold stations have a more limited menu than the hot stations and require fewer skills to run. Typically, the sauté cook needs the greatest amount of kitchen experience because this station has the greatest volume of dishes passing through and requires the most expertise.

The key traits of a successful chef de partie are:

✔ **Punctuality:** As with any employee in the restaurant, chefs de partie need to show up on time.

✔ **Willingness to learn:** From what goes into the menu items to plate presentation, a chef de partie is always learning. Whether he's getting to know his station or learning to run the one next to him, successful cooks are those who are consistently learning.

✔ **Previous experience:** Chefs de partie need to have some experience before they start on stations. Decide which particular station they're suited to by comparing their past experience with your needs and concept.

✔ **Positive attitude:** Because busy times in a restaurant are so hectic, you need chefs who can keep their cool and go with the flow. You also need employees who can follow instructions and follow the directions of their head chef or sous chef, especially during shifts.

Cross-training is ideal for this type of chef. During slow business levels, it's good to have cross-trained employees. If one chef can work a station that consists of the oven and the fryer, plus he knows his way around the pantry, you have the flexibility to send some of your other staff home early. You save money but maintain your full menu and service levels.

But beware: You must have the agreement of the staff member you are sending home when business is slack. They can refuse if they want the full amount paid to them during the shift.

### Sous chef

The *sous chef* (*sous* is pronounced *sue,* French for *under*) is the kitchen's second in command. He's usually in charge when the chef isn't around. The sous chef is sort of the executive chef in training, but he may still train the underlings. A sous chef is in the process of learning ordering, inventory management, and food costing. Also, the sous chef is probably trying to pick up on the creativity of the chef, understanding his style of cooking and food philosophy. Some chefs use them as assistants. But other sous chefs are actually running the kitchen, and sometimes several sous chefs work in a single kitchen.

### Kitchen manager

A kitchen manager, or KM, knows the nuts and bolts of running the kitchen machine. He may do the ordering and manage the staff, but he may not have advanced culinary training. KMs must be good at maintaining consistency. A good KM knows the standards and can follow production manuals, but he doesn't have to be creative or focused on technique. He can teach the staff the basics. He should be very production-focused and efficient.

## Filling the front of the house

The *front of the house* (FOH) is restaurant-speak for any area of the restaurant where a diner can be. (For more details, check out Chapter 10.) FOH employees have regular contact with your diners.

### Host

Many UK restaurants don't have hosts, but the role is a growing part of the upmarket and chain restaurant concept. You may call them *hosts* or *hostesses, greeters, seaters, reservations desks,* or a host (pun intended) of other names. Whatever name you use, the basic function is the same. These staff members greet your diners, show them to their tables, and start their meal and experience on the right foot. They're also the last face that guests see on their way out of your restaurant. You want them to thank everyone and send diners off with a good final impression.

In many instances hosts double up as waiting or wine staff when they are not required at the front desk. Many managers deal with this job too when no specific host or hostess is employed.

Look for composed, friendly, and organised people to fill these positions. They're essential to your success. This is one of the most difficult jobs in a busy restaurant. The nicest person in the world won't appear nice to prospective diners if she can't control the phones, deal with the customer who hated his soup, get the complaining waiter in Station 4 back on track, and deal with the smoke coming out of the kitchen, all while maintaining her composure. And if your host isn't taking down the correct time, number of people, and names for the reservation, it can be a disaster. Enough chaos will develop in the restaurant; you don't need a host staff contributing to it.

You don't need a beauty queen or Adonis to serve as your host, but she or he does need to capture the mood of the restaurant. Hip, trendy restaurants should have hip, trendy greeters. And communication skills are a must. Knowing when to communicate with the manager or the kitchen can keep the shift running smoothly. Effective communication with the diners means going beyond friendly; it's understanding what you have to say to make this person happy but not becoming over-familiar or talking too much with customers, thereby neglecting others.

### Cloakroom service

Staffed cloakroom areas are relatively rare in British restaurants, but are increasing in popularity in upmarket restaurants. Overseas visitors, in particular, are often accustomed to being able to check in their coats and belongings. Checking in coats and other belongings is often a function of the host staff. On busy nights, you may employ a designated coat-check person. This staff should be organised and methodical in how they take the coats, label the coats, and so on. The success of the cloakroom is determined by the equipment that you give your staff. If you have the right tools (like hanger tags, as well as labels for accessories such as hats, umbrellas, bags, and so on), you should have a smooth operation.

If you don't have a good cloakroom system, you *will* have problems that involve claims against your establishment for missing or damaged goods. You'll probably find yourself settling these claims in the spirit of goodwill, at a not insignificant cost. Copy whatever successful system local good-quality chain restaurants or s upmarket restaurants use. These establishments have risk management people in their organisations who have worked it out for you. Be sure to put a notice up indicating that the management takes no responsibility for items left in the cloakroom or on the premises.

The cloakroom, if it is a proper room, is a good place to put a closed-circuit television (CCTV) camera. Theft does occur so having the eye in the sky as a backup is a help. It can also vindicate an accused employee who's innocent.

### Cashier

You may need a cashier if you have a fast food restaurant or a mix of delicatessen and café, for example.

Cashiers should be honest, organised, and friendly and know exactly what is on sale, how much it costs, and the details of any discounts or other offers.

### Waiter

Waiters are salespeople. They're the most direct connection between your diner's wallet and you. They should be friendly and able to relate to people. Successful waiters are able to make judgment calls about what kind of customer they're waiting on and what their diners' expectations are. They should be able to read their diners and react accordingly. They should know when to chat people up or leave them alone. Is the couple that's been married for 40 years simply quiet but otherwise happy? Are they involved in an intense, private conversation? Or maybe the group is out to celebrate and want the waiter to entertain them. Make sure that you and your waiting staff know the difference between intrusive, over-friendly behaviour and looking after your customers in a professional manner.

Waiters should be able to smile no matter what happens. Coauthor Mike tells them, 'Pretend this is a stage and you're entertaining these people. Don't let them see your problems. Don't let them even know you have any. They're supposed to have a good time, so let them.'

### Bar staff

Your bar staff should have an extensive knowledge of making cocktails, especially those that are associated with your concept. If you have a Mexican restaurant, your bar staff need to know how to make many kinds of margaritas, for example. They should also be likeable and friendly with guests. (We cover good traits for bar staff in more detail in Chapter 12.)

Don't jump to hire a person just out of bartending classes. Bartending is a skill that you learn from hands-on experience.

The *bartender* makes the drinks for the waiters, helps other bar staff, and assists in prep work. The service bartender usually doesn't have much contact with guests. A bartender may use a bar back during busy shifts.

If possible, don't require a diner to pay his bar bill when moving from the bar to the dining room for dinner. Just add his bar tab to his dinner bill. Making diners pay two bills usually annoys them.

# Staffing office functions

The office is the nerve centre of your restaurant, where all the information in the restaurant gets tied together. Your point of sale (POS) system, payroll records, and telephone systems are usually housed here (see Chapter 15). Staffing the office can be as complicated as staffing any other part of the restaurant. Depending on the size of your operation, different people will wear different hats. In fact, until you can support the expense of hiring people, you may be wearing all the hats! Marketing, reservations, and accounting may all be handled by the same person. You, as the manager, need to know how your office runs, inside and out. If not, people will rob you blind. If you think the bartender can do it by giving away free drinks, just wait until the office does it.

Office staff should be honest because they provide the checks and balances for both the physical cash that moves through your restaurant – counting *banks* (usually cash drawers set up to give change at the bar and cashier station) and *drops* (cash deposits ready to go to the bank) and monitoring FOH cash handling – and the financial records. You may hire an outside accountant to come in to audit monthly, quarterly, or annually, or more often if you feel it's necessary.

### Accounting

Your accountant may have no idea of what the business does, but she is responsible for checking numbers. The best bookkeepers can understand the numbers and give you advice on how they apply to your business's past performance and future needs. If you're new to the restaurant business, you need someone with this type of experience. Find an accountant who does the books for other restaurants. Contact the British Hospitality Association (www.bha.org.uk) for relevant publications. If you have your accountant set up your books according to industry standards, comparing your operation to others will be easier. See Chapter 8 for more info on accountants.

### Payroll

Larger restaurants often employ an outside company to manage the payroll. The manager is usually in charge of sending the information required (such as hours worked, pay scales, and employees' bank details). This needs to be double-checked by the manager to ensure all is present and correct. If there are any discrepancies, the manager or person he has given the job to, will sort it out.

For details on planning for payroll, be sure to visit Chapter 15.

### Marketing

Someone in your organisation should be in charge of this important function, even if you get help from an outside source. In some cases, a general manager or owner serves as the liaison between an outside marketing consultant and the restaurant or may choose to perform the duties himself. If you delegate this job to someone else in your organisation, pick someone who knows the operation and the concept behind the restaurant. If this employee doesn't know your business thoroughly when she starts, she has to get to know it quickly. If you hire someone without an interest in how the lamb is getting to the table with its special Armenian mint, what are the chances this person will have an interest in the long-term success of your business? Your marketing person should understand your passion and the nuances of your concept. Take a look at Chapter 16 for details on marketing and promoting your business.

### Technical experts

You can hire outside people or outside firms to maintain your computerised POS system, but you need someone in your operation to watch over them. Even if you sign up for a 24-hour support team available to you with your newly purchased system, you need someone on your staff to be the liaison with them. You need someone who can handle the situation. This person may not have specialised training to handle the systems, but if he has an aptitude and an interest in helping out, you'll be a step ahead.

# Interviewing the Candidates

When employing someone, do your best to make a sound decision based on the facts and your gut instinct. But don't be hard on yourself if it doesn't work out. In the restaurant business, lack of experience isn't always a good reason to not hire someone. The only way people really learn a job is to do it. If you think someone has the right attitude, give him a try. If it works, let it keep working. If it doesn't work, cut your losses right away. Consider including a probation period, usually 60 to 90 days, for new staff. That way if someone really isn't working out, you can get rid of him quickly with very little trouble later.

Consult the law regarding probationary periods and unemployment laws. One useful Web site is `www.direct.gov.uk`. If you've never managed a business (or even if you have) do seek advice regarding employment laws from your solicitor who will be able to put you in touch with a specialist employment solicitor. This may only be necessary if you have a large staff to employ.

You should also check out *Small Business Employment Law For Dummies* by Liz Barclay (Wiley).

We recommend at least two interviews for most positions with at least two different people in your company. Use the first as a screening interview to get a feel for how the person fits into your organisation. Many second or third interviews involve, cooking dishes, for example, to gauge standards and cooking practices.

## Placing an ad and sifting through CVs

When you're looking to employ people to staff your new restaurant, start by placing an ad in the newspaper. Newspaper ads advertising new restaurant jobs get a *huge* response. The industry is full of people looking to change jobs. If you're the newest restaurant on the block, waiters assume you'll be busy, so you'll get swamped with applicants who jump from one opening to the next. Organising your recruitment process to account for this volume of response is important to stay afloat in the sea of 'people persons' and dependable, hardworking people who wonder if they can have Friday and Saturday off.

If you see obvious errors or red flags on a CV or application, don't bother to interview the applicant. If someone says she's an expert on French wine but she misspells *Burgundy,* it's probably a red flag. Or if she's worked three months at each of her last ten jobs, skip her.

## Round 1: The meet and greet

Use this round for screening out people whom you *definitely won't employ.* Keep your questions short. Have the applicants fill out applications, get their background information and get a feel for how they answer questions. You won't have a lot of people whom you definitely extend an immediate offer to, at this point – save that for Round 2. Here's a quick list of good Round 1 questions:

- ✔ What's your employment background?
- ✔ Why do you want to work here?
- ✔ What are your strengths? Your weaknesses?
- ✔ Why did you leave your last position?
- ✔ What do you think is the most important aspect of the job you're applying for?
- ✔ Why are you equipped to succeed in this position?
- ✔ Are you looking for a career or a job?

You could do worse than check out *Answering Tough Interview Questions For Dummies*, by Rob Yeung (Wiley) for further ideas.

Cull it down to the few applicants you'd like to find out more about. For FOH positions, put yourself in the guest's position. Do you want this person talking to you? Is she engaging? Is her voice nice to listen to? For BOH positions, does an applicant present herself as eager to learn? Is she modest, or very impressed with herself? Beware the hotshots in the kitchen; they're often resistant to training specific to your concept. Good candidates are attentive, willing to learn, and physically capable of doing the job.

# *Round 2: Comparison shopping*

Make a list of the available positions, and add spaces for the number of people you need in each position. During Round 2, build a roster of candidates to fill the available slots. Use paper, a chalkboard, a dry-erase board, or whatever works for you. By the end of Round 2, you start to build a roster of your first, second, and third picks for each position.

The goal of the second round of preopening interviews is to ask the hard questions and get to the core of who the applicant is, in 15 minutes or less. Let the applicants know the good, the bad, and the ugly of the available position. Assess whether this discussion should continue to the next phase. Scare off the weak. Find out why they want to work at your restaurant – and it better be for reasons other than because you're looking for staff.

Get specific with the applicants' past background, job-related skills, techniques, and specific knowledge. Field their questions. Discuss pay rates, as appropriate. By the end of this round of interviews, you should start to feel comfortable making offers of employment.

When making your final hiring decisions, make sure that all applicants

- ✔ Have the applicable specific experience you're looking for.
- ✔ Meet the criteria you've established for the position they're applying for.
- ✔ Are available to work the number of hours you need them.
- ✔ Have a solid work history (unless for entry-level positions).
- ✔ Have a positive attitude, desire to learn, and enthusiasm for your restaurant.
- ✔ Mesh with your philosophy, company culture, and work style.

Never ask candidates about their religion, marital status, sexual orientation, age, gender, race, political affiliation, national origin, disability, or if they have children. Answers to these questions could be construed as a reason that someone didn't get a job and set you up for legal action. Go to the Equal Opportunities Commission for more details (www.eoc.org.uk). Make sure that everyone in a position to hire on your behalf understands these rules. You're liable for their actions if they're on your payroll.

## Forms for new staff

After you pick your staff, they'll need to complete some basic government forms. Give them their employee manual, and have them sign for it. Also have them complete any helpful forms, like emergency contact information, at this time.

✔ **Attendance record:** This allows you to quickly document any attendance discrepancies, calculate holidays, and the like.

✔ **Emergency contact card:** This card is handy in case the unexpected happens in your restaurant. If you have to take an employee to the hospital, you'll be glad you have the name of a close friend or family member to call.

Keep a file on each employee, in which you retain all of these forms, along with the person's initial job application and/or resume. Doing so isn't just a good business practice; it's essential in case of a government audit.

# Employing Foreign Nationals

You need to know if a prospective employee is allowed to work in the UK, and whether they have the correct work permit or visa allowing them the right to work.

### Accession state workers

If prospective employees are from one of the new European Union member, or 'accession', states they may need to register with the Home Office under the Worker Registration Scheme within one month of starting a job. The countries affected are:

✔ Poland

✔ Lithuania

✔ Estonia

✔ Latvia

✔ Slovenia

✔ Slovakia

✔ Hungary

✔ The Czech Republic

✔ Bulgaria

✔ Romania

Workers from Bulgaria and Romania are restricted in the sorts of work they can do.

However, employees don't need to register to work in the UK if they are

✔ Self-employed

✔ From Cyprus or Malta

As an agency or temporary worker an employee needs to register to work within a month of starting work.

## Students

International students may not need permission to work in Britain when they are studying but can only work 20 hours a week If their home country is in the European Economic Area (EEA), or they are a Swiss national, they can work without restrictions on the type or amount of work they do.

If the employee from the EU has a blue registration card, he has full access to work in the UK. A yellow card – for students – indicates that the student can work no more than 20 hours a week. Check out www. employingmigrantworkers.org.uk or www.direct.gov.uk for full details.

Otherwise, any potential overseas student employee should check the visa stamp in his passport. If it says 'prohibited' he can't work in the UK. If it grants him leave to enter or remain in the UK as a student, he can work here provided he:

✔ Doesn't work more than 20 hours a week during term time, unless the employment is part of his studies or is an internship

✔ Doesn't engage in business, is not self-employed and doesn't provide services as a professional sportsperson or entertainer

✔ Doesn't take a permanent full-time position

## Seeking proof of nationality

If a possible employee is from an EEA country,he will need to show a prospective employer his passport, national identity card or Home Office Residence Permit.

Employers can face unlimited fines if they employ illegal workers, so they need to make sure that no one they employ is working in the UK illegally. However, to protectyourselfs against discrimination laws you should treat all job applicants equally. Even UK nationals should be asked to provide proof of their nationality.

If they don't have a passport or haven't access to it. Other combinations of documents are allowed as proof of identification.Go to www. employingmigrantworkers.org.uk for details on how to stay within the law on employment for non-British workers.

### Work permits

A number of schemes and programmes exist for people who want to work in the UK. If they are not from an EEA country or Switzerland, they're likely to need a work permit to work here.

There are six separate groups for ordinary work permit applications:

- Business and commercial
- Training and work experience
- Sportspeople and entertainers
- Student internships
- General agreement on trade in services (GATS)
- Hospitality and food processing (sector-based schemes)

# Training Your Staff

Assume that, when you hire your staff, they have no preconceived knowledge about your business. The more information you give them about the way your business runs, your expectations, your concept, your menu, and so on, the better they'll be as employees. Training is expensive. It uses up money to teach employees about your business. It uses up money printing out manuals. It uses up manager time in putting all the materials together. But think about how much a poorly trained employee can cost you in terms of wasted products and supplies, broken equipment, and lost customers.

Make sure you take a look at Chapter 2 for details on when to conduct specific training sessions during your opening schedule. There's excellent information in that chapter about how to hold mock service sessions and dry runs (serving food in a real-life setting to a few of your closest hundred friends) to make sure your staff is ready for opening day.

# The employee manual: Identifying your company policies

An employee manual is your chance on paper to spell out for your employees what you expect of them in terms of performance, behaviour, communication, appearance, and so on. You need to make sure everybody gets one, so every employee is on the same level. Get each employee to sign and date the manual, acknowledging that they've read it and have been given a copy for their personal records. If their signature is their statement that they've read, understood, and agreed to abide by the contents, give them a chance to read it thoroughly before signing. You'll eat it in court if you don't. Be sure to tell them that they should keep it and refer to it as necessary. Any changes that you make to the manual need to be handled the same way. The changes must be given to all employees and signed for. The following list contains some standard items that make an appearance in many employee manuals:

- Welcome letter
- Mission statement
- Company history
- Orientation period
- Communication policies
- Performance and job standards
- Code of ethics
- Confidentiality policies
- Emergency procedures
- Drug and alcohol policies
- Antiharassment policies
- Customer-service programme
- Problem-solving procedures
- Safety issues
- Training meetings
- Performance evaluations
- Performance rewards
- Food-safety procedures
- Other policies such as meals on duty, breaks and the like

Use the manual to get your new staff excited about your restaurant. It's an opportunity to show your employees that they all contribute to the big picture and explain to them why they're important. Show them what safeguards are put in place to make sure the big-picture things happen.

The employee manual serves as documented proof of your policies. You can easily tell a waiter to remove his earring if you have it written in black and white that earrings aren't permitted. You have a consistent way to handle situations. If you have employees' signatures on file saying that they've received and read the manual, you have some protection if they take you to an employment tribunal for terminating them based on something clearly spelled out in the manual.

No one employee manual suits every operation. Each is as different as the operation you run and the goals you set. If you're new to the business, don't let your GM write the manual because he has restaurant experience and you don't. This is one of those things you can't delegate: If he leaves in six months, you want the manual to reflect *you* and *your* philosophies. It's also an item that you may wish to have an expert employment solicitor review before it gets issued to any employee. The money spent here will be minimal compared to the potential damages paid later. (And make sure that the GM reads and signs for his copy.)

## *Operations manuals: Understanding specific job functions*

An operations manual helps you train employees to perform specific duties for each position, from kitchen porter and head chef to manager, . Thoroughly explain each position, including duties, standards, and objectives. Tell them what they're here to do, how to do it, when to do it, your quality standards, and so on.

The more detailed you can be, the more successful your training will be. Outline in black and white what you want them to do. You may feel like you have to spend a lot of time putting your operations manuals together, but you'll more than make up for it by not having to take time to re-explain how to do things, when to do things, and so on. With the details written down for employees, their training time shrinks and they're up and running much more quickly.

Here are some examples of what should be included in the job-specific operations manuals:

- **Waiting staff:** Your waiting staff operations manual includes standards of service, timing (when to order which food, when to clear plates, and the like), product knowledge, opening and closing procedures, side work expectations such as printing off menus, prepping butter to go with bread baskets, kitchen interaction parameters, and cash handling procedures.

✔ **Bar staff:** The bartender operations manual includes standards of service, standardised pours, product knowledge, inventory procedures, cash handling procedures, guest interaction parameters, opening and closing procedures, and responsible alcohol service guidelines.

✔ **Chefs:** The chef operations manual contains station opening and closing procedures, standardised recipes for the station, prep amounts based on volume, station-specific proper food handling procedures, and the kitchen cleaning responsibilities chart. Each station may have its own manual with station specific info.

✔ **Managers:** This operations manual includes the master opening and closing procedures for the whole restaurant, instructions on using the POS software, overall daily cash handling and reporting procedures, instructions for dealing with employees, and instructions for dealing with guests. The manager operations manual should include everyone else's info and then some. Managers should know, how to wait on tables, how to light the pilots on the ovens, and how to change the paper in the POS printer.

Cross-training is important. Kitchen staff should be able to deputise for a staff member when off sick or on holidays, for example. If you notice someone who's trying to learn more – a kitchen porter who wants to learn how to make pastry, for example – never discourage his efforts. Consider allowing him time during his regular workday to assist or learn the ropes. Not only will you be encouraging his interests, but you'll also have a possible substitute in case someone can't make it in one day or leaves.

## Certification-based training

Your local authority offers training such as HACCP (Hazard Analysis and Critical Control Point) food safety training, which complement in-house training programmes. Often, authorities sponsor these training sessions at little or no charge. Encourage your staff to attend whenever possible. The info is valuable to every food-service professional. You will also find information regarding a safe alcohol service at your local authority as well as training courses with Alcohol Concern (www.alcoholconcern.org.uk) and other organisations.

## Ongoing training

Don't think that, because someone's training period is over, he's trained. Training is an ongoing process. Keep products fresh in your employees' minds. Include training on current specials, new wines, or whatever else your staff needs every single shift. Hold weekly position-specific meetings and monthly all-employee meetings to go over important information with the staff. Regularly scheduled meetings keep lines of communication open and prevent misunderstandings. See Chapter 17 for more info on the subject.

# Chapter 14

# Buying and Managing Supplies

· · · · · · · · · · · · · · · · · · · · · · · · · · · · · · · · · · · · · · · · · · · · ·

*In This Chapter*

▶ Getting control of purchasing

▶ Picking the right suppliers

▶ Working with prices, quality, and service

▶ Developing a solid stock system

· · · · · · · · · · · · · · · · · · · · · · · · · · · · · · · · · · · · · · · · · · · · ·

*A* wise man once said, 'You make more money buying than selling.' That adage is true in any business, particularly a competitive one like a restaurant. Purchasing, or buying, takes vigilance and enthusiasm. You must be diligent in your research, knowledgeable about what works for your concept, current on the latest food trends and production techniques, and confident in your volume of goods purchased. Good purchasing decisions result in positive bottom lines.

In this chapter, we take you through purchasing from start to finish. We show you how to work out what you need to buy and who you need to buy it from. From an stock management viewpoint, you need to develop a system for confirming that you got what you ordered, it's stored in its appropriate location, and it stays there until you're ready to use it in your restaurant.

## Getting Started in the Stock Room

Before you order that first supply, you have to understand your concept (see Chapter 3), your menu (see Chapter 9), the amount of time you have to devote to preparing your menu items, and the number of people available to produce them. If you have lots of time and people, you can start with less-refined products (like whole chicken instead of boneless, skinless breasts).

But even after you have decided on your menu, the purchasing work has only begun. You know that you'll need some specific things, such as a particular brand of pasta or a certain type of wine. But for the most part, you'll probably know only that you need olive oil; you may not know which particular brand of oil or case size to get.

So how do you work out what you need to order? Start by researching products you don't know: Go out to eat. Try new things. Read the industry magazines (see Chapter 22 for a list of resources). Any information you can get helps you make better decisions.

*Purchasing* entails buying anything you need for your restaurant: food, drink, equipment, paper goods, tables, silverware, and everything else. After you purchase the basic equipment for your restaurant start-up, you spend the majority of your purchasing time buying food and drink. If yours is like most restaurants, you spend not only lots of time but also lots of money buying these types of supplies. So we focus our examples in this chapter on food and drink purchasing. But you can definitely apply these same principles and tips to purchasing just about anything else you need for your restaurant.

## Making your lists

Make a list of all the food and drink supplies you're going to need according to your menu. Organise the list by category, as we've done in our example in Table 14-1. You need to have this list in hand before you start locating and interviewing suppliers. (Although our example deals exclusively with food and drink items, you can use this approach for every purchase, including bar equipment, paper goods, and linen.)

Your list should contain all the items you need to be able to offer customers the full menu and contents on the drinks list. Make a column for those perishables such as fish, meat, or dairy produce that you may be ordering on a daily or weekly basis.

The categories in the table are organised the same way that most suppliers specialise. You might have a meat guy, a seafood guy, and a *wholesale supplier* (a large supplier who carries a variety of goods across many product lines, like a cash-and-carry). The list in Table 14-1 is by no means comprehensive. Your list will be based on your menu.

Be specific with your final list. Don't just write 'fillet of beef.' Instead, write 'Scotch beef fillet, trimmed, 21 day aged', if that's your specification. If you just say ' beef fillet', the supplier could give you a price for a lesser quality piece of beef fillet that looks great from a price perspective but that may not be the right quality match for your concept.

Deciding on your menu, your recipes, and desired end results before you draw up your list is a real plus when you're not sure about the exact product you want. You can then turn to your supplier for guidance. For, example, tell him that you need chicken breasts but want to taste all of his company's different chicken breast options before deciding. You can try 2, 10, or 20 products side by side (have them cooked first!) and discern why something works for your application and why it's the best choice for your restaurant.

| Table 14-1 | Sample Supplies List | | |
|---|---|---|---|
| *Item* | *Category* | *Unit* | *Projected Weekly Volume* |
| Bread, French roll, 40g | Baked goods | Case, 144 | |
| Bread, roll, herb garlic, 40 g | Baked goods | Case, 144 | |
| Ciabatta loaves | Baked goods | Each | |
| Bread, wheat, French roll, 40 g | Baked goods | Case, 144 | |
| Butter, unsalted, 250g | Dairy | Case, 36. | |
| Butter, salted, 250g | Dairy | Case, 24 | |
| Cheese, Parmesan | Dairy | Case, 3kg | |
| Cheese, Blue, | Dairy | Case, 10kg. | |
| Cheese, Cheddar, shredded | Dairy | Case, 7kg. | |
| Cheese, Stilton | Dairy | Case, 3kg | |
| Cheese, local | Dairy | Case, 2kg | |
| Cheese, mozzarella, fresh | Dairy | 2 kg | |
| Cream, double | Dairy | 4 litres | |
| Cream, single | Dairy | 6 litres | |

# Considering prep time as a factor

Convenience foods are popular, and there's no shortage of the restaurant versions of these foods. You can definitely save yourself time and money by using them, but consider all the factors to make sure that they're economical for your business. Think about going into a supermarket and buying a ready-made meal. You may be able to microwave it in 7 minutes, but you pay £4 to £6. But you could've made the same meal for £2 in about 20 to 30 minutes. What you gain in convenience, you pay for in price. Determine whether you have an army of prep people skilled enough to create the items on your menu completely from scratch. Not all restaurants can do it, and it's very costly.

Don't have your prep team spend time on menial tasks that have little impact on your quality or profit. Throw your labour hours at the greatest product cost savings, and order the rest, when possible. For example, suppose that one person, who makes £7 per hour, takes four hours to cut all the potatoes for the 15 kilograms of thinly sliced potatoes you need every day. By doing it yourself, you save £1 per pound on the cost of whole potatoes versus packaged frozen chips. It cost you £28 in labour (4 hours × £7 per hour) to make up £15 (£15 pounds × £1) in food cost – at the end of the day, you're losing money. Not too efficient, eh? However, if that same person spent that same time prepping the 15 kilograms of marinated lamb and vegetables on skewers you could save money and make a good profit.

Before you make a final decision to put convenience food items on your menu, taste them and determine whether they fit your concept. Decide how close the quality of the commercial product is to the scratch version and whether the savings in labour are worth any sacrifice in quality. Ultimately, if your diners don't like it or it tastes like it came out of a box, they won't come back.

Here are a few examples of products that are available to make your prepping labour pounds go further:

- ✔ **Sauce bases, such as demi-glace, pesto, and so on:** You purchase the base and add a few other ingredients to finish them as you need them.

- ✔ **Meats that are cut, portioned, and individually sealed:** These products are more expensive, but you have little waste and spoilage. Use them if you don't go through a lot of meat or don't have the skill to cut it yourself but want to keep some meat options on your menu. On the other hand, if your staff have good butchery skills, suggest buying in carcasses and using all cuts of meats to transform into casseroles, slow roasts, pâtés, terrines and other dishes which are currently tremendously popular – and cost-effective.

- ✔ **Baked goods, including breads, pastries, and other desserts:** Many good products are available prepackaged these days. Work with your suppliers to see what may work for your restaurant. Consider partnering with a local bakery to get locally known breads, pastries, and desserts. Make sure, however, that you are buying quality, not quantity just for the sake of saving money. You may end up shooting yourself in the foot instead as customers don't return.

# Finding and Interviewing Potential Suppliers

Now that you know what you need, find out what's available from different suppliers, both locally and via truck or van delivery. But keep in mind that there's a fine line between working with your sales rep in a partnership that benefits you both, known as *consultative selling,* and letting the sales rep run your show, known as *getting taken for a ride.* As often as possible, work out what you need before the sales rep tells you what you need. They won't tell you about their competitors, so don't use them as your only research source.

## Finding suppliers

The best way to find potential suppliers is to talk to other restaurateurs whom you respect. Doing so saves you hours of looking in phone books, doing online research, and going to food shows. When you talk to other restaurateurs, you're talking to people who have made a conscious decision to go with one supplier over another. Find out why. Ask them who else they considered and who else is out there.

For example, seek out a restaurant that is doing the type of seafood you want to do or a restaurant that has fresh, tasty products all the time and ask the owners which supplier they use. Usually, other restaurants are willing to pass along this information. Ask them why they purchase from Monsters in the Deep Seafood rather than London's Finest Seafood supplying Buckingham Palace.

This process works in all categories, from cleaning supplies to specialty foods. Make a list of supplies you need and next to each item write the name of the suppliers the competition is using for each category. Start with no fewer than three suppliers in each category for the interviewing stage.

## Interviewing suppliers

With your list of potential purveyors in hand, pick up the phone, call each supplier, and get a *sales rep* (salesperson) assigned to you. Set up times to interview each one. Have the meeting at your restaurant if possible. You may also choose to tour the supplier's facility to observe the sanitation level, the size of the operation, and how its warehousing systems work.

### Engaging in your first conversation

When you talk to suppliers on the phone, tell them who you are and describe your situation. Let them know if you're new ownership, new management, or a brand-new restaurant. Maybe you have an existing restaurant and want to interview potential alternate purveyors.

Get the supplier's sales rep *and* her boss into your restaurant for the meeting. That way, your salesperson has a clear understanding of your objectives, and her boss gets the same info firsthand from you. Often, the real power in negotiating prices doesn't lie with the sales rep. Usually her boss or boss's boss gives the thumbs up or down on special requests. If they know that you're professional and organised, with concise needs and wants, the whole process goes much more smoothly, and you can cut out much of the game playing before getting to the real pricing.

### *Conducting your first meeting*

Be concise in the meeting. Your goal is to educate the supplier about your concept, your specific needs (and limitations as you see them), your concerns, and what you expect from a supplier. Show them your kitchen, your equipment, your delivery area – basically the whole operation – so you can make them aware of all the logistics.

When you have that initial meeting, bring copies of your supply list (the whole list), divided by categories (see Table 14-1 for a sample list). Suppliers may surprise you with a more broad-based inventory than you were expecting. Co-author Andrew worked with a dairy supplier who noticed that he was using a lot of imported olive oil and specialty goods. Two years earlier, the dairy supplier had quietly amassed an inventory of these items and was selling them at a significantly reduced cost compared to the local specialty suppliers. This chance meeting became an exclusive purchasing arrangement for dairy and select specialty products at a big savings over the previous supplier.

Keep in mind that suppliers are salespeople – they're coming to sell you products, whether it be food or equipment. The more you buy, the more they make. Don't ever lose that thought as you could end up with items that are surplus to your requirements. You can always order more items at a later date but you may not be able to return those five chafing dishes you were coerced into buying.

Go through the list item by item with each supplier, starting with the supplier's specialty. Explain what you're looking for in terms of flavour, performance, packaging, and cut, and provide an estimate of how much you'll need in a given week. The supplier may interject and say things like 'We don't supply that, but we do have this kind instead' or 'Ours is in a 10 kilogram case, not a 5 kilogram case'. Your response should be a version of 'I understand. My decision is simple. I'll give my business to the company that can service the needs on this list. I'm going to spend money, and this is what I'll spend it on. If you want my money, get what's on this list done for me. If you don't want my money, I'll find someone who does'.

It's becoming increasingly common for large restaurants, chain ones in particular, to enter into *primary* (or *preferred*) *supplier agreements* with their vendors. In these contracts, a restaurant agrees to purchase selected items from one vendor in exchange for fixed prices, volume-based rebates, and the efficiency of having a minimal number of vendors. If you fall into the chain category make it clear that you're looking to establish primary supplier agreements and that you're going to buy a certain group of items from one company. If a supplier walks away understanding that they get all or none of a group of items, you'll be amazed to see what a supplier can make happen in terms of prices, discounts, delivery, and special orders.

Don't assume that a company can't bring something in for you packaged a certain way. Sometimes a supplier really can't, for lots of reasons. But maybe the only thing a supplier needs to do to get all your business is bring in a couple additional products, take a loss of a couple pence on the pound, or split a case of a product that comes only in a quantity that's more than you need. Then the supplier has to make a decision whether your volume of business is worth the additional inventory, reduced margins, and increased customer support. Not all restaurants qualify for these types of deals, but all restaurateurs need to understand that these volume-based incentives exist and that in most cases you get only the discounts, pricing structures, delivery schedules, and products that you *ask* for.

If suppliers aren't interested in getting your business, they aren't going to be interested in servicing your business. Make it clear to them that you want them to understand your restaurant and how you want it to work. You're setting up an ongoing relationship, not just buying produce on a regular basis. The best suppliers understand their clients' business and bring them ideas, new products, and opportunities in the market place that can benefit their business. They must understand your goals, business, costs, order and delivery requirements, and where you want to position yourself in the market place. If they can understand your business and maintain and increase your quality, while maintaining or decreasing your costs or your labour, then you're likely to buy that product from them.

### Giving them a chance to respond

At the end of each meeting with all those suppliers you have initially selected, send them on their way with your list, an understanding of your objectives, and an understanding of your desire to have a purchasing program with a supplier in this category. Remind him that the supplier who can meet most of your needs will get the lion's share of your business. Give the supplier a definite time interval to get back to you. Make it clear that you're interviewing several suppliers in your category, and mention the competitors by name. Let the supplier know that you're willing to engage in a preferred provider agreement with his company, provided that he comes back with the best possible price guaranteed for one year based on your expected volume. This step shows the supplier that you know what you're doing and you're confident in your research.

Request your sales rep's office and mobile, numbers. Ask for her boss's office and mobile numbers, too, but make sure that the sales rep is aware that you've asked for the boss's contact info. Taking this step gives her the courtesy of not being caught off-guard if you call her boss, and keeps the pressure on because she knows that you may call.

# Comparing Prices, Quality, and Service

After your suppliers get back to you with their prices on the stuff you're interested in, evaluate their bid. Their response should include more than just their pricing strategy. It should specify their terms of service, delivery schedule, credit terms, ordering process, any extras you've asked for, applicable bulk discounts, and so on. If the agreement is to be *contractual* (agreed upon by a written contract with specific order volume or a specific time period), you need to get your lawyer involved to review the contract. This may only apply to large restaurants, as smaller ones may not need to go to such lengths.

Now's the time to iron out any logistical details as well. If you need your product before 8 a.m. every day, you need to tell the supplier that and make sure that the commitment is in writing. If you need net 90-day payment terms (90 days to pay the bill), you both should agree to that upfront. You're building relationships and goodwill with your suppliers, but not completely relying on the them. You both should be comfortable with the relationship, but the supplier shouldn't get too comfortable.

How fast you pay can often dictate what your prices are.

## Considering the size of suppliers

Working with a large supplier has a major upside. Because large suppliers buy in bulk, they get better pricing than smaller companies and can pass those discounts along to you. They usually carry more categories of stuff, and within those categories, they often have many choices. They probably carry thirty brands of mayonnaise, while a smaller company may have only five.

Larger suppliers often have additional bonuses and incentives for agreeing to sign with them for a particular volume. They may be able to schedule daily deliveries if you need it because they have a larger trucking fleet than the little guys.

Larger suppliers can also provide you with other perks, such as electronics equipment or complimentary tickets to events. Some companies frown on accepting these gifts, which can be considered kickbacks and could give employees and other suppliers the impression that improprieties are occurring. So carefully weigh the options before accepting any gifts, other than preferred pricing. And if your chef is getting freebies, make sure that you're still getting the best possible pricing.

The big downside when working with major suppliers is that you're one of many customers. They take your money but won't go out of business without it. They may be less likely to give you a generous pricing program unless you can give them a guaranteed volume. They can be a bit less reliable with their deliveries, invoicing, and the like. As with any large company, considerable red tape is usually involved, and often what you and your rep discuss doesn't make it to the accounting department. A problem can take weeks to get straightened out. And major suppliers have been known to bully a customer here or there, especially when it comes to a verbal agreement. Get all agreements in writing.

Small suppliers often offer excellent service. They have to, or they'll be out of business quickly. With a small supplier, you *are* his business. Small suppliers will often go above and beyond to make sure that you're happy and satisfied with your service. You can often build business relationships that last decades.

## Getting what you ask for the way you ask for it

After you set up your purchasing plan, you buy things a certain way for a good reason, maybe several good reasons. If the products you order aren't the products you receive, you have a problem. If you get bone-in chicken breasts priced at the boneless, skinless price, you're not only paying more for the product, but you'll throw good money after bad spending extra on labour to debone the chicken. If you get a great price on litres of gin but receive it only in smaller quantities, you may not be getting a deal at all.

These kinds of problems happen regularly. The situation is compounded when the person who does the ordering doesn't do the receiving. Purchase order to the rescue! A *purchase order,* or PO, is a form that the purchaser fills out and leaves for the person who receives the order. Check out Figure 14-1 for a sample purchase order. The receiver compares the stock he receives, the PO, and the invoice and looks for things that don't match. That way, if you know that you got the wrong chicken, you can fix it before someone starts cooking and serving it.

If you're signing for a product, you have to know what you're signing for. You can't just order things, think that you got a great price, and assume that everyone along the line will perform flawlessly and the whole process will run smoothly without a hitch. More often than not, mistakes are caused by honest human error, either on the ordering end or at the supplier's location.

When trouble occurs, how do you resolve it? Your first call should be to your sales rep. For example, suppose that the supplier's delivery driver doesn't bring you everything you ordered on a certain day. Call your sales rep. If the rep wants to keep your business, the supplier will resolve the problem for you. If suppliers promise to deliver in a certain way by a certain time, they should resolve any problems for you, delivering it themselves, if necessary.

Date _____ Company Name _____     Order No. _____
Account No. _____ [Your account with the supplier] _____     Page ____ of _____
Salesperson _____

To: _____ [Supplier Company Name] _____
Fax Number: _____
Email: _____

**Please send the following:**

**Deliver Via:** _____ [Your transportation requirements] _____

**Deliver By:** _____ [Date and time you need it] _____

**Special Instructions:** _____
_____
_____

| Quantity | Size of Unit | Item | Unit Price | Extended Price |
|---|---|---|---|---|
|  |  |  |  |  |
|  |  |  |  |  |
|  |  |  |  |  |
|  |  |  |  |  |
|  |  |  |  |  |

Page Total    _____
Order Total    _____

Receiving Supervisor: Please complete the following information:

Rec'd by _____    Condition of order _____
Date rec'd _____    Other info _____

**Figure 14-1:**
Sample
purchase
order.

# Understanding how to negotiate pricing

Pricing figures prominently on both sides of the equation – buying and selling. Your goal is to get products that match your concept and meet or exceed your customers' expectations at the lowest price possible. Then you work to sell your menu items at a price that matches your guests' expectations, covers all your costs, and leaves you a nice tidy profit.

You may have ten types of baguettes to choose from. One is cheaper than the other, but which one matches your quality standards?

Minimise your physical inventory, but maximise the way you use what you get. If you bring in beef fillet for your menu, think about where else you can use it. Can you bring the fillets in whole, so you get a better price, and then use the scraps for beef bourguignon, a stir fry, or salad? This type of purchasing helps you get more utility for the same product, increasing your volume and decreasing your cost.

The only thing that matters to a supplier is how much you buy from him, not your total purchases combined from all your suppliers. Use volume buying whenever possible. One company co-author Andrew worked with thought that it was doing a good job by calling around to get the best price on a particular cheese. The company was buying 80 different cheeses from 8 different suppliers, diluting the power of its quality-cheese-buying. Take your menu and narrow it down to a core group of cheeses that you need. Do you need eight varieties of blue cheese? Maybe the three varieties that one supplier has will do, and while you're at it, cut down that list of cheddars to four, Parmesan to two, and so on, all from the same seller. You're beefing up your volume with a particular buyer to get better pricing.

If you can't take control of the market with volume buying, take control of your menu to take control of the market. If one company sells grated cheddar cheese, one sells block cheddar cheese, and another sells sliced cheddar cheese, why store three different varieties of the same cheese and hope that the respective menu items sell? Instead, bring in the core item, the block cheese, and then slice or grate it according to your needs, as part of the prep. You're buying more cheese from one person, driving costs down, and fulfilling the needs of your menu.

# Building an Efficient Stock System

Your stock sheet is a record of supplies you have on hand at any given time. It's an investment, and you get no return on that investment until that product sells. You want as little money as possible tied up in stock but still want to be able to efficiently run your business. You do need to have an adequate supply of product on hand, but keep backup stock on hand for a purpose, such as having enough key ingredients if an order is missed or you experience an unexpected upsurge in business. Not having a key menu ingredient can be bad for business. People understand that you may occasionally run out of a menu item when you're dealing with fresh products, like seafood. But if you're consistently out of tuna for your salade Niçoise, they'll start to go elsewhere.

Inventory is also a warehouse of your cash flow. Excess stock ties up money that you can't use for other necessities until the products sell. Not managing the balance between cash flow and stock is the failing of many a restaurant. In a competitive business such as a restaurant, you want your money where it can work for you, not tied up in the tins of passata tomato sauce that you got for half price and that are now taking up space in the storeroom.

Salespeople love to come up with incentives for you to buy in bulk, but examine the offer closely. For example, they may say, 'If you buy 100 cases of water today, you'll save ₤2 a case'. Take a look at that deal. If you buy 100 cases of bottled water at ₤20 per case, you've invested ₤2,000 in bottled water. Suppose that it takes you two months to sell this water, but you're on net 15-day terms with your vendor. In the meantime, at your margin of 50 per cent (which means half the price to your customer goes to cover what you actually paid for the water) on bottled water, it will take you a month to break even on the investment and two months to realise your profit, all to save ₤200. For two weeks, you're in the red on that investment, meaning that you paid more than you made. If this is a pattern in your purchasing system, your money is tied up in stock. Meanwhile, you have payroll to meet, a lease to pay, and repairs to the toilet that backed up during the Saturday night rush.

## Managing the stock sheets

There's no *one* way to manage and track your stock. Many systems exist for tracking stock. Some are high tech (such as scanner guns and bar codes that automatically update the system), and some are low tech (monthly hand counting your stock items). Some systems are fully integrated, tracking products from the time they're delivered, through the preparation process, to the time they make it to the customer. Other systems can automatically count down your inventory as you use products. If you're missing a single tin, it shows up. The systems work well if you're planning on having an exceptionally stable menu. If you're planning any kind of a change, systems that are completely automated can be more work than they're worth.

### Establishing your levels: Keeping enough product on hand

Most restaurants resort to the tried-and-trusted process of manual counts for inventory purposes. In most cases, food is counted on a shift-by-shift basis. Use *daily stock sheets,* (itemised lists of the amount of prepped stock you need to have to enough product on hand until your next prep period), like the one in Figure 14-2, to count your food and set up your prep schedule. For example, in the kitchen you might set a level for the amount of tins of passata tomato sauce to have on hand or the number of steaks ready to grill. In the waiting station, you set a level for the number of lemons to cut for drinks. The bar keeps a level for everything from lemons to coffee.

Build a functional stock sheet system by analysing your recipe ingredients and historical or projected sales of an item. For example, if an ingredient is in your number-one selling item, you'll use a lot of that item, so you need to have a lot of them on hand. If you're Pizza Express, you'll need more pizza fillings than salad ingredients. That information becomes the basis for your *ordering sheet,* an itemised list of the amount of stock you need to have to keep you up and running between orders.

This stock plan doesn't work for some things that you purchase in *economic order quantities,* which refers to things that are packaged so that you have to buy more than you immediately need to get a reasonable price for them. For example, restaurants don't typically place an order for one 2 kilogram bag of sugar, which may last only a couple days and cost more per kilo. Instead, restaurants buy a 25 kilogram bag of sugar, which is enough to last through the month and cheaper per pound than the 2 kilogram bag. Economic order quantities are usually nonperishable staples that you buy in bulk because the products aren't available in many different sizes.

**Daily Stock Sheet**

DATE  January 24, 2008   DAY OF WEEK  Thursday

POSITION  Prep

| Menu Item/ Product | Amount on Hand | Par Levels | | Amount to Prep | Shelf Life | Container | Comments |
|---|---|---|---|---|---|---|---|
| | | Mon - Wed | Thu - Sat | | | | |
| Mackerel | 12 kg | 4 kg | 8 kg | 12 kg | 3 days | Plastic tray | Gut and clean. |
| Mushroom Soup | 10 L | 10 L | 15 L | 25 L | 2 days | 5 L containers | Prep for the weekend. |
| Beef Wellington | 6 | 10 | 15 | 20 | 2 days | Plastic trays | Make Madeira sauce for this dish. |
| | | | | | | | |
| | | | | | | | |
| | | | | | | | |

**Figure 14-2:** Sample daily stock sheet.

Keeping stock levels and doing *shift counts* (counting your products before or after every shift) help you stay on top of your inventory. Don't wait until the end of the month to find out that you're missing supplies. Alternatively, many restaurateurs find that doing a weekly stock check, usually on a Sunday evening when supplies are low, is an excellent way of keeping tabs on stock – and checking whether items have gone walkies or been over-ordered.

## Counting your stock

As part of your monthly income statement (which you can read all about in Chapter 5), you count your stock. Or do it weekly to really get on top of perishables in particular. Even if you have an accountant prepare your reports, you must provide the stock count to the accountant. This count is a full and complete account of all supplies in your restaurant. Any items that are restocked or replaced on a regular basis are supplies, while things that are part of your restaurant for a long time, like tables and chairs, are called equipment. Don't include equipment on your stock sheets. You're reconciling your assets on hand (your stock) against the liability of the invoices (the bills you've paid or must pay).

Use a spreadsheet program like Excel to help you calculate the value of your stock. Do a physical count of the products you have on hand and then multiply that by the price you paid for them. This figure gives you the value for each item on your stock. Add up the values you paid for everything you still have on hand (from lettuce to alcohol), and you have your total value of stock. This number will be listed as an asset on your monthly income statements. Check out Table 14-2 for an example. (We use just the dairy section of Table 14-1 to show you how it works.)

| Table 14-2 | Sample Monthly Stock Sheet | | | |
|---|---|---|---|---|
| *Item* | *Unit* | *Unit Price* | *On Hand* | *Value* |
| Butter, unsalted × 40 | Case, 40 × 250g. | £12.99 | 20 | £6.49 |
| Fresh double cream × 6.81 litres | 2.27 litres | £3.15 | 4.54 litres | £6.30 |
| Fresh whipped cream × 2.27 litres | 2.27 litres | £4.21 | 2.27 litres | £4.21 |
| Greek yoghurt × 200 grams | 200 g | 53p | 5 | £2.65 |
| Cheese, Cheddar × 5 kilograms | 5 kg | £35.55 | 2.5 kg | £17.77 |
| Stilton halves, 4 kilograms each | 4 kg | £28 | 1 kg | £7 |
| Eggs, × 5 dozen tray | 5 doz tray | £4.88 | 2 ½ dozen | £2.44 |
| Cheese, mozzarella, fresh mini balls | 2 kg | £10.98 | 1 kg | £5.49 |
| Cheese, Parmesan, × 5 kilograms | 5 kg | £42.95 | 1 kg | £9.49 |
| Cream, sour, 2 kilograms | 2 kg. | £3.99 | 1 kg | £1.99 |
| Total value of stock | | | | £63.83 |

You can keep track of your gross margins by the method shown in Table 14-3.

| Table 14-3 | Typical Gross Margin Report | |
|---|---|---|
| *Gross margin report* | | |
| *Period* | *Week ending 9/12/07* | |
| | *Food* | *Drink* |
| Net sales | 8000 | 8000 |
| Opening stock | | 6100.13 |
| Purchases | 3007 | 2780 |
| Closing stock | | 5700 |

| Gross margin report | | |
| --- | --- | --- |
| *Period* | *Week ending 9/12/07* | |
| Gross consumption | 4993 | 3180.13 |
| Petty cash | | |
| Transfers stock into bar | | |
| Transfers from kitchen into bar | | |
| Sub total | | |
| Transfer stock out to restaurant | | |
| Sub total | 50 | 5 |
| Staff drinks | | |
| Wine and food tasting | | |
| Credit note | | |
| Sub total | | |
| Net consumption | 4943 | 3165.13 |
| Gross profit | 3057 | 4834.87 |
| Gross profit% | 61.79% | 60.44% |

## Using requisition sheets

*Requisition sheets* are kind of like POs, but they can be less formal as your business dictates. Any form that you use to track requests for supplies can be a requisition sheet. Your manager or bartender can use a copy of the wine list to request a new stock of wine. Your sous chef can use a stock sheet to request more olive oil. Or maybe you actually create a separate form that people who need stuff fill out and give to whoever buys for the restaurant. Whatever system you use, make sure that it's a written system, understood by everyone involved. It's tough to keep track of who needs what if you carry 50 wines by the glass or 15 different kinds of cheese. A written system provides an excellent way to communicate requests and start a paper trail for your supplies.

Requisition sheets also provide one more check to make sure that products are staying on the shelves until they're sold – and not walking out the door or being misplaced. If your chef needs a 5 kilogram block of cheddar but the person in charge just got one in the day before, a requisitions sheet can help start the search for the product.

# *Preventing theft*

Maybe preventing theft is too lofty a goal. Controlling theft or managing theft may be a better way to put it. In the restaurant business, theft has always been a problem and will continue to be. Employees aren't the only ones guilty of theft; customers, delivery people, and neighbours may also be on the take. Robbery also falls into the theft category. Deterrence is as important as actually catching the thieves. Here are ideas that can help with both.

- ✔ **Put a lock on the door:** This suggestion sounds simple, but if you want to keep people out of something, lock it up. You can lock up fridges, freezers, storerooms, have separate cages for very expensive items, offices, bar wells, alcohol storage, and just about anything else. Locks don't keep out thieves, but they keep honest people honest. If you don't give people the opportunity to steal, most people won't. If people want to steal, they'll work out a way, but locks are your first line of defence.

- ✔ **Give keys to as few people as possible:** The fewer people with keys, the easier to find out what's going wrong. And in this case, keys are a deterrent to the few people who do have keys – they know that it's usually not hard to work out what happened.

- ✔ **Install security cameras, but move them often:** Cameras (even dummy cameras) can be a deterrent to theft. If people think that they're being watched, they tend to behave better. If you leave the camera in the same place too long, though, the camera becomes part of the environment. People forget it's there and don't continue to stay on their toes. Consider camouflaging cameras by hiding them in a plant or behind alcohol.

  Don't install cameras, hidden or otherwise, in bathrooms or staff locker rooms. You could open yourself up to serious legal trouble.

- ✔ **Install a security system:** Use motion detectors and integrate your system with local emergency organisations, such as the fire and police departments. Consult an expert in commercial, preferably restaurant, security before you buy a system.

- ✔ **Make cash handlers accountable:** Develop a system of checks and balances for waiters, barmen, and cashiers to be accountable for accurate checkouts. Employees who accept cash must be accountable for their sales, cash, checks, charge receipts, coupons, and any other things you accept as legal tender. At the end of the shift your POS (point of sale) system should generate a report telling you of each member of waiting staff's transactions.

- ✔ **Change cash drawers in the middle of a shift:** Remove the working cash drawer and replace it with another one. Make it an expected part of the practice. Don't do it only if you're trying to find a problem, or it's a lose-lose proposition. You're giving a thief a clear warning or you alienate the honest person. If you do it on a regular but unscheduled basis (at least as far as your staff is concerned), you can deter thieves.

✔ **Stay visible and in the know:** Personal involvement is the best defence. Know the people you deal with and let them know that you're around. Having good, professional relationships with your employees will help you find things out via gossip. If employees feel like part of the restaurant family, they'll have no trouble turning someone in. If you treat them badly, they'll feel like you get what you deserve.

## *Keeping breakage under control*

How many times have you sat in a restaurant and heard the wonderful tinkling sound of breaking glass? Have you sat close to a busy kitchen door and heard the thudding and clanking of the dish area? Whether it's Wally the Waiter or Kevin the Under-enthuse Kitchen Porter, all that noise costs someone money. You spend a lot of time finding china, glassware, cutlery, and cooking utensils (and an equal amount of money), so it's important to preserve them as long as possible. Whether it's one glass or a handcrafted Limoges plate, the effect is the same: a pain in your wallet.

Accidents will happen. But the root of breakage is disorganisation. If your waiting staff are organised, your food is coming out of the kitchen on time, and your dish area is tidy, you're much less likely to sustain breakage than if everything is chaos. Breakage is an expense that you probably can't eliminate, but you can take steps to control it:

✔ Keep your dirty dish area organised and as clear as possible. Keep the dishes from piling up.

✔ You'd be amazed if you realise the amount of cutlery that gets thrown away in restaurants. Busy servers scraping plates at the washing up area inadvertently drop a fork, knife, or spoon in the rubbish. They may not even know they did it, so the chances that they'll go diving down a bin to retrieve it are small.

✔ Try motivating the kitchen porters and waiting staff to be careful with the cutlery by giving them a monetary award for every piece of silverware they extract from the rubbish.

✔ Use the right racks and shelving for your glasses and stemware as they're washed and stored. Make sure that the dishwashers work properly and that you use the proper detergents and other cleaning agents. If not, you'll have to hand wash them, and there's no quicker way to break glasses than to handle them in bulk by hand.

✔ Organise your washing up area so that plates, china, cutlery, and so on are neatly stacked coming in and going out.

✔ Use rubber mats in the washing up area and storerooms where glass items, from stemware to alcohol, are stored. A simple thing can go a long way in getting more punch for your pound.

✔ Employ quality staff and then train and communicate with them. Educate them about your values. Reward them for following the rules.

Assess what hard goods you're buying on a regular basis. Some things are more prone to breakage. Make adjustments if necessary. If the breakage is too much, you can change your china and glassware. If you're serving soft drinks in highball glasses but going through a ton of glasses, you can raise the sift drink price by 50 pence or thereabouts and serve them in a sturdier glass.

## Reducing waste

Waste costs money, plain and simple. Waste occurs in many places: perishable food, equipment, labour, and so on. Spend some time analysing your operation. Identify areas where waste occurs.

The easiest way to reduce waste is to be organised and vigilant. When you're visible, your employees are less likely to leave the water running, steal something, or forget FIFO (first in, first out; see Chapter 18 for details). Train your trainers to have your eyes for waste. Financially motivating your employees about the importance of controlling expenses benefits you immediately and forever.

Here are a few key ways to reduce waste:

✔ **Keep your equipment usage in check.** Close the refrigeration doors. Don't open windows when the air conditioning is on and it's 30° C outside. Turn off unused burners on your ranges on a slow night. Turn off lights in storerooms and walk-in fridges when no one's working in them. Fix leaky taps as soon as you can.

✔ **Keep tabs on use of office supplies.** Sticky notes, pens, paper, and menus add up. Don't let your employees stock their home phone areas and offices with your office supplies, which are the most stolen items in a restaurant. They're small and aren't usually tracked.

✔ **Ration your linens.** Chefs can use enough towels to scrub down the QE II in a given day. Once it's dirty, every towel has to go out to the cleaners at your expense. Many kitchens ration their towels. Each kitchen or bar employee gets, say, two towels to last him or her the whole day. Also, clean up floor spills with dirty linen, not clean linen. Doing so may seem disgusting at first, but it's much more efficient to clean up a bucket of iced water with dirty linen and then clean the floor with a mop than to do the same exercise with fresh-from-the-package linen.

Shortsightedness can be a huge waste. If you buy cheap china, you'll have to replace it all much sooner, at a greater expense, than if you buy decent stuff to begin with. If you buy cheap pots and pans and kitchen utensils, they won't last two shifts in a busy restaurant. But don't waste money on buying items that are more expensive than what you need in your particular situation, either. Don't buy cookware just because it has some famous chef's name on it. Be realistic about what your needs are and buy with an eye for longevity. If you're a 200-cover restaurant focused on getting people quickly through your doors, leave the copper cookware for the TV blokes. Buy what you need to get the job done. Buying too cheaply or too exotically is a waste of money.

Waste can be as simple as serving food portions that are too big. If your specification is 125g of fresh vegetables on the plate, don't give diners 250 grams. If you've done your homework and studied your food costs, put your knowledge into practice.

## Eliminating spoilage

Most people have opened their fridge at one time or another and found a science project. It could be a pint of strawberries wearing a mohair sweater, rotting bagged salad, or pork chops bought on sale that smell a little funky. In the restaurant world, however, you'll find a tray of strawberries, a case of lettuce, and maybe the whole pig. The volume is greater in a restaurant, and the impact on your wallet is, too.

The good news is that spoilage can be prevented. Begin with an attitude that spoilage is unacceptable. Don't buy a case of shredded lettuce to serve the week after next, because it won't last that long. It doesn't matter if you got a good deal on it or your sales rep gave you two tickets to a cinema premiere. The fact is that you're not going to use that lettuce before it goes bad. So whatever you paid for it is wasted money. But if you do get a good deal from your supplier, use the product to make creamy lettuce soup and either put it on a special or freeze it.

Order the amount of any item that you'll use well within its shelf life. For example, you may need to order berries twice a week and fresh tuna three to four times (or more) each week.

After you establish your stock levels and are organised about your ordering amounts, be vigilant and visible. The chef, the owner, or the any of the junior chefs should be in the fridges and storage areas looking at products several times a day. Fresh products are preferable to frozen ones, but fresh is more prone to spoilage. If you are running an upmarket restaurant or gastropub, there is no question of offering frozen food. Only good quality fresh food will do.

Equip yourself with the means to properly store, handle, and extend the shelf life of foods. Invest in proper stackable food storage containers to store and hold food properly. See your equipment food rep to purchase them. Make sure that refrigerated items are covered labelled, and dated. (Look at Chapter 18 for details and tips on setting up a safe kitchen, rotating product, and establishing an effective hygiene system.) Vacuum sealing, individually frozen or ready-to-cook portioned food items, and advancements in shelf-stable technology are improving food safety and eliminating the risk of spoilage. (Chapter 18 has details on reducing the risk of foodborne illness.)

Spoilage can happen before the product even enters your refrigerator doors. If it's happening outside, you have to investigate. Did the delivery person handle it wrongly, leaving your case of lettuce on the pavement for an hour while he delivered to another restaurant? Were your litres of cream mishandled from the depot? After you find the cause, correct the problem. And make the person responsible for the mistake accountable for his or her actions.

Spoilage from the supplier is more likely for restaurants that don't order in case quantities. Some suppliers (certainly not all) seize opportunities to palm off less-than-fresh produce on opened cases. But don't ask for full cases if you don't need them. Order what quantities you need, but demand first class, totally fresh products when you do.

Believe it or not, beer and wine are perishable. If they're not stored at a consistent proper temperature, the perishing process speeds up. If you buy 20 cases of wine and your storage area temperature is fluctuating, you better be going through your stock quickly, or the wine quality will be affected.

# Chapter 15

# Running Your Office

## In This Chapter

▶ Organising your communications systems

▶ Stocking up on basic office equipment

▶ Getting ready for payroll

▶ Keeping your records safe

*Y*our office is an important part of your restaurant. More often than not, however, restaurateurs give very little thought to the setup and location of office space. But much of the important management of the business takes place in this space, so set it up right to maximise your productivity, keep a close proximity to your diners and staff members, and protect your vital data.

## Deciding Where to Put Your Office

Your office size and location, along with the number of offices you have, are a direct result of the size of your operation. Most restaurants have a main office that's relegated to the least valuable storage space and serves as a shared office for all managers. (Sometimes a chef or kitchen manager gets a desk in the dry storage area, the kitchen area where you store dry goods and tinned goods so they can be closer to the kitchen and closer to their staff.)

You'll likely be stuck with an existing office or have little choice of where to locate your office. But if you have the luxury of deciding where to put it, determine who will be using office space before you decide its final location. If your managers (rather than just an office staff) are using the office, it should be as centrally located as possible to give equal access to the various departments. You want to be as accessible to your staff as possible.

If your office is next to the kitchen, consider having lots of windows looking into the kitchen so that you can still see what's going on there while you're in the office. You can add adjustable blinds for occasional privacy.

If you have the space, and if you have a large staff, put all managers in the same office. If you have no other choice, all the better. Each manager can benefit from knowing what's going on in other departments. The chef can hear how you buy advertising, which can impact how he buys produce. Listening to simple phone conversations conveys your purchasing philosophy, your employee treatment, and so on, which should be consistent throughout all the business.

Some people separate managers' office space due to personality conflicts or animosity. If your chef and general manager, or your general manager and controller, don't get along and don't want to work near each other, your problems are larger than the seating area. Separating them is just putting a tiny plaster on a gaping wound.

# Creating a Communications Hub

The office is the central place through which all internal (managers and staff) and external (customers and suppliers) restaurant communications flow. And, in the restaurant world, open lines of communication are key (despite the example of many screaming chefs and temperamental managers).

## Counting on your computer

For most restaurateurs, computers have become essential for administrative and management tasks. Computers mean efficiency in all areas – ordering, tracking sales, financial analysis, menu planning, communications with customers, staffing, you name it.

You may find laptops more useful than standard desktop computers. They save space and are easily portable if you want to work in the bar or the storeroom, for example. But, the computers can get lost, stolen, or damaged if you move them around, so take proper steps to protect your equipment.

In addition to the actual equipment, also known as *hardware,* you'll need the following items to get your computer systems running smoothly:

✔ **Software:** You need a variety of programs, including software programs that protect your computers from outside attack (including firewalls and other security software), total your sales and sales tax received and owed, track your waiting staff's sales and declared tips, and reconcile credit card receipts. You also definitely need the following software:

  • A word processing application, such as Microsoft Word (for creating menus, business correspondence, and so on)

- • A spreadsheet application, such as Microsoft Excel (for tracking inventory, ordering, and working out daily food counts)

- • An accounting application, such as QuickBooks (for tracking your accounts, writing checks, and managing receivables)

✔ **Printer(s):** You need to print out all the reports, spreadsheets, menus, letters, checks, and so on.

✔ **UPS:** This is an uninterruptible power supply, which helps keep your computer's data intact in case of a power cut. Most also have surge protectors built in to protect your system in the event of a power surge.

## Picking up the phone

Get with a reputable, phone company or advisor to help you pick the right system for you. But consider these issues to make sure that you get the features you need without paying for the ones you don't.

✔ **Number of lines:** Think about your volume, both personal and professional (especially during peak hours). If your buyer and your Accounts Payable person are using two of the lines and you have three lines, you're left with one line for taking reservations. Maybe you just need a single line with call waiting. Or instead maybe you need several phone lines, each one dedicated to something different: reservations, orders, general business, and so on.

Factor in extra phone lines for Internet, fax machine, and credit card modems. Think about losing five potential dinner reservations because you ran an American Express card during a hectic lunch or faxed an order to your supplier (see the 'Using e-mail and online services' section, later in the chapter).

✔ **Personal call policy:** Set a policy on your staff making personal calls and make it consistent. Detail it in your employee manual so everyone knows the expectation. This issue affects both the number of lines you have and the location of phones.

✔ **Number and placement of phones:** Maybe you want one at the bar by the booking system, two in the office, and one in the kitchen. Decide how convenient you want the phones. But remember that more convenience means more use – and abuse.

✔ **Long-distance access:** Requiring some type of code to dial long distance adds another level of protection against high long-distance bills.

✔ **Fax:** You definitely need a fax machine, with a dedicated line. Use your fax machine to accept orders, receive contracts, and even send out your menu to diners who call and request it. Menus can, of course, be emailed or downloaded if you have a website.

✔ **Voice mail:** Generally, you need voice mail boxes for anyone who has business-related contact with the outside world if you have a sizeable restaurant. These employees include your buyer (if you have a specific person doing the job), public relations staff (ditto), accountant, and anyone who places orders or supervises staff members.

✔ **Conference call capability:** If you need to place conference calls from your restaurant, consider investing in a system that has a speaker phone and allows you to tie in callers from multiple lines at a time. Again, this is for a larger type of business.

✔ **Intercom:** An intercom system is a great addition to a busy restaurant. For example, a staff member such as a manager can page the office or kitchen without leaving the restaurant and doesn't risk missing an incoming diner.

Adjust the speaker volumes for business levels. What's way too loud for a quiet afternoon may be inaudible for a busy Saturday night. And keep the microphones on the office phones on at all times. Nothing is more frustrating than responding to the intercom and not being heard on the other end.

✔ **On-hold recording:** Do you want holding music, a general message, or specific promotions? If you want the ability to change the message on a regular basis, make sure you know that before you buy your system.

✔ **Toll-free-numbers:** If you're a destination restaurant with people coming from far and wide, a toll-free number may be a good idea. If you're a small restaurant, skip the expense.

Don't get more phone lines than you can answer professionally and promptly. You don't want to make potential customers angry with long holding times and lost or unanswered calls.

Call BT or other large communications companies to ask about business rates before you select a system. They offer different rates for different kinds of systems, and the price difference may affect your buying decision. There are many systems to choose from and they include online services, faxes and other systems you may wish to consider. Ask other companies about used or refurbished systems. In most cases, restaurants don't need so many extensions and features that they demand the latest phone technology, so take advantage of a better price.

## Using e-mail and online services

The restaurant business is slow to adopt technology, but the Internet and e-mail have finally made their way into restaurants. E-mail is now a necessity rather than a novelty. Here are three ways that the Internet and e-mail can benefit your business:

✔ **Customers can contact you:** Providing an additional way for diners to contact you is a benefit. They can use e-mail (and Web sites) to make reservations, communicate satisfaction and dissatisfaction, and place orders for takeout and delivery if this is what you offer too.

If you decide to provide your diners with an e-mail contact, you must respond to their requests in a timely manner. Consider setting up an automated message that responds immediately with a generic thank-you message each time someone e-mails you – something as simple as 'Thanks for using our Web site. Someone will respond to your question as soon as possible.' But you still have to follow up quickly.

✔ **You can contact suppliers:** Having e-mail and Internet access for your managers to contact the outside world can increase efficiency and pro-ductivity, speeding up must-do day-to-day tasks such as purchasing and ordering. Many large food brokers accept orders via e-mail or through their Web sites. If you develop your own spreadsheets, you can often e-mail them to your suppliers to show them which items you need and in what sizes and quantities.

✔ **You can contact customers:** Develop a database of customer e-mail addresses when customers contact you. Then you can send electronic advertising, mailers, special offers, and other promotional material to diners who are likely to take advantage of it. You can even encourage your diners to register to receive promotions in exchange for a draw prize of a free dinner. (Check out Chapter 19 for more info on mailing lists and other ways to build a loyal customer base.)

## *Tracking sales with a point-of-sale system*

Much more than a cash register, a point-of-sale (POS) system can be your time clock, your ordering system, your credit card processing unit, your inventory manager, your calculator for food cost percentages, and so on. Many systems today allow you to manage the business in real time instead of requiring you to analyse them only after the fact. If you can, invest in an integrated system to ease the burden of watching your numbers.

Manual cash registers mean inefficiency and botched cash handling. A *point-of-sale* (POS) system is essential for just about any restaurant or bar. POS sys-tems allow you to track sales of particular items, sales made by particular employees, special orders, and so on. You don't have to be able to perform a hostile takeover of the Bank of England with the thing, and it doesn't even have to be brand-new (if you're trying to save money, look for used systems). At the low end of the operational scale, you simply need something to track the basics, things such as sales, and labour hours. With a good POS system, you know not only how many people ordered the ribeye steak but also how many people ordered it rare with the mustard sauce.

A POS system comes with some basic standard reports. These reports can get you started and allow you to spot and analyse general trends in your business. Generally, they provide a big-picture view of your operation. But you'll likely need more targeted and segmented info so that you can watch specific areas of your business in specific ways. So if you want to track how much fish you're selling compared to beef, you need to add that report. Make sure that the system you buy has some customisation features. Sometimes, you or someone on your team can customise the reports, but often you must work with the POS distributor's programming team to create the specific reports.

Here's a list of some of the data your POS should be able to provide for you:

- **Good basic info:** This category includes info such as bill average (the average total bill for each table), per person average (the average amount each guest spends), per person alcohol sales (the average amount of beer, wine, or other type of alcohol each person orders), dessert average (the average amount of dessert ordered by each person), and average main course price.

- **Sales trends by both major and minor categories:** Say that you have a major category like wine. You'll also have several minor categories, such as white wine by the glass, white wine by the bottle, red wine by the bottle, red wine by the glass, sparkling wine by the glass, sparkling by the bottle, and so on. Your system should be able to break up your sales info in many different ways, like all bottle sales, all glass sales, all red sales, and so on.

- **Sales by different cost centres:** A *cost centre* is a different area of the restaurant that takes in money. Your system should be able to set up each section of the bar as a separate cost centre, each waiter as a separate cost centre, and so on. The system should also be able to combine them to take a look at the bar as a whole, or look at all the waiting staff as a whole. Another feature of the system enables you to see what these groups or individuals sell during specific times and shifts.

As you refine your reporting and better understand your business, look for more specific trends. You may find that a customer who orders a bottle of wine also orders 20 per cent more starters than a customer who doesn't order wine. Maybe when Martin the manager is on duty, you tend to be busier than when John's on. Then you can use the numbers to make adjustments. Jane has a higher bill average than anybody. Don't you want her in the sections that serve the most people? If you discover that you're selling only three steak and kidney pies with mustard mash each night, maybe you should stop offering it. All of this info is available if you track and analyse your sales numbers.

Look for brand names like Micros, Saturn, and Netsuite when you're looking at stock management systems. Many systems can integrate your scheduling, stock management, labour costs, accounts receivable functions, and so on into a single system. (For more on integrating all the electronics in your office, see the 'Interfacing your different systems' section, later in the chapter.)

When shopping, make sure that the paper that works with the POS printers is readily available and relatively inexpensive. If you're saving a ton on the system but spending a fortune in your monthly paper supply, what are you really saving?

## *Interfacing your different systems*

The best time to think about interfacing, or connecting, your systems is before you buy them. The most likely candidates for connectivity are your stock management and sales systems, your scheduling system and time clock, and your online and phone reservations. Think about what you want from your various systems and how you may be able to save time by connecting them. Working with an authorised POS dealer is a great first step. Your sales rep should be able to help you interface anything you're willing to pay for. The easiest way to get your systems talking is to buy software that already works together. Such software isn't always the cheapest way to go, but you can expect that the systems have been tested together and are compatible.

# *Hardware (The Old-Fashioned Variety)*

It may be the information age, but you still have to sit on something. Here are some un-techy things you need for your office:

- ✔ **Desk and chair:** Restaurants are notorious for bad furniture, especially in the office. How much you spend is determined by the importance you place on comfort.

- ✔ **Postage machine with scale:** This item may not be essential, but it's a huge help for posting cheques, marketing materials, and so on. But it pays for itself only if you mail lots of items. Weigh the overall cost against the convenience of having the machine before signing for it.

- ✔ **Calculator:** You'll need a 10-key calculator with a roll of paper that keeps a hard-copy record of your calculations. This old-school device is still the standard for balancing drawers, checking out servers, and so on. It's a must-have item in any restaurant office.

- ✔ **Filing cabinets:** Make sure that they have locks to protect sensitive info, such as employee records.

- ✔ **Safe(s):** The fewer people with the combination the better. Your safe doesn't need to be huge. It should be able to hold however many cash drawers you use plus at least one extra, a supply of gift certificates, credit cards accidentally left by diners, and deposits until you can get to the bank. Some restaurants use a second safe, called a *drop safe* (a safe that functions sort of like a public postbox; you can drop your deposit through the slot, but no one except the security guard who collects it can open it), for holding the deposits. These safes are a good deterrent to guard against employee theft or an inside job robbery (because insiders know you can't get to the money), but they can be very frustrating to an armed robber who may not believe you can't access the money.

Here's a list of some basic office supplies you need to start and will replace as time goes by:

- ✔ **Paper:** You need pads, message pads, the paper you print your menu on (if you do it yourself), letterhead, paper rolls for POS printers and the 10-key calculator, and so on.

- ✔ **Envelopes:** Your supply should include envelopes with or without the company logo, larger envelopes for mailing banquet pricing proposals and press kits, and envelopes to match your cheques.

- ✔ **File folders:** Usually letter-size folders will do the trick.

- ✔ **Forms:** Keep a supply of employment applications and all applicable tax forms, time cards, deposit slips, and so on.

- ✔ **Miscellaneous office stuff:** Don't forget things such as paper clips, scissors, sticky notes, tape, pens, pencils, bins, clipboards, stapler, staples, staple remover, and the like.

- ✔ **Personal trays:** Each manager needs a plastic tray, cubbyhole, or a dedicated office drawer or file. You'll use these to disseminate written info, such as schedules, new policies, and department-specific paperwork.

# Preparing for Payroll

You should have two bank accounts:

- ✔ **Operating account:** You pay all your bills from this account.

- ✔ **Payroll account:** Use the money in this account only to pay your staff. Shuttle money *from* the operating account *to* the payroll account, never the other way around. After you put money into the payroll account, it's gone. Even if it stays there and a casual employee doesn't cash his cheque, that's his business. Resist the urge to 'borrow' from this account even if things seem tight. Many companies pay by BACS, an electronic payment system, for simplicity, the money coming from the payroll account and going direct into the employee's account.

As soon as you employ someone, you need to get the new employee fill out the necessary paperwork, (see Chapter 13 for the list), so that you can properly process their paycheques. You have to pay them if they work for you, but you can't pay them without the right paperwork. This is the *ultimate* case of dotting your i's and crossing your t's. If your records are audited and you don't have the proper paperwork, you could face devastating fines, or worse.

## Farming it out or doing it in-house

Depending on the size of your operation, you may opt to do all the payroll duties yourself from start to finish (or assign it to someone in your operation) or outsource some of the work to a payroll company. If you keep everything in-house, typical duties of the assigned payroll guru for each pay period include the following:

- ✓ **Calculating and verifying hours:** If you use an integrated, computerised system to track hours worked, you should be able to print a report to verify the hours worked by each employee. If not, collect those time cards and start adding.

- ✓ **Confirming employee pay rates:** Computers are only as flawless as the people who program them. Data entry errors are common, so a human needs to do a double-check on this important piece of info if your time clock is computerised.

- ✓ **Crunching the numbers:** You have to calculate gross pay, National Insurance Contributions (NIC), and PAYE for each employee.

- ✓ **Calculating the total deposit for the payroll account:** Work out the full amount of net pay (the amount owed after all the withholding is with-held) that you owe to your employees.

- ✓ **Transferring the payroll deposit from the operations account to the pay-roll account:** In most cases, both your accounts will be held at the same bank, so you can make a phone call or an online transaction to move money from one account to another and post it by the end of the day.

- ✓ **Payroll slip for each employee:** Print a separate slip for each employee. Make sure that each slip includes details about the number of hours the employee worked, his gross pay, and any deductions.

- ✓ **Distributing cheques or payroll slips to employees on payday:** Establish a scheduled time, usually between the lunch and dinner rush, to distribute cheques or payroll slips. You may be paying by BACS in which case you may only need to give them a payroll slip.

Payroll companies generally calculate the amount of tax, National Insurance contributions, and so on and cut the cheques and payroll slips.

But even if you use a payroll company, you still need someone in house to double- (or triple-) check the records and perform the functions listed earlier that the vendor doesn't cover. So decide whether that service is worth the amount of money you'll pay for it. Check with a payroll company such as BACS for quotes and details of the services they can provide. Check out the BACS Web site at www.bacs.co.uk.

## Deciding on a payroll period

There's no right or wrong payroll period, but once a week or every other week is pretty standard for restaurant pay periods. Every choice has its advantages and disadvantages. Pick the period that works best for you. For example:

- **Weekly:** You keep a fairly consistent expense each week, but your payroll management time (verifying hours, preparing money transfers, and so on) increases.

- **Every other week:** You have no payroll expense one week and then a big expense the next week. Paying less often cuts your payroll management time virtually in half compared to paying weekly.

After you pick a pay period, pick a day to hand out or post the cheques or payslips. If your pay period ends on a Saturday, maybe you hand out them the following Wednesday or Thursday. If you're using an outside company to do the work, make sure that they commit to delivering the work by your payday. Also, always deposit money into your payroll account before you hand out the first cheque.

Not paying your employees on time is a telltale sign that the restaurant is in its death throes. If the employees aren't getting paid on time, everyone will know about it. Set a pay period and stick to it.

## Choosing salaries or hourly wages

A *salary* is a regular wage that does not change no matter how many hours the employee works. *Hourly wages* are paid to employees at a set rate for each hour worked. Here's a list to help you decide which system works best for your employees:

- **Salary:** Team members with managerial, supervisory, or accounting-type functions usually are salaried. They include the following positions:

  - **Back-of-the-house employees:** General managers, assistant general managers, accountants, bookkeepers, kitchen managers, head chefs, and sous chefs (see job descriptions in Chapter 13) are in this category.

  - **Front-of-the-house employees:** This category includes front-of-the-house managers, floor managers, bar managers, and possibly cashiers (if you have a dedicated cashier if running a different type of operation such as a combined restaurant/deli) whose cash handling and money management responsibilities are extensive.

✔ **Hourly rate:** Some staff members clock in and out at the beginning and end of each shift.

- **Back-of-the-house employees:** Other unsalaried part-time chefs and kitchen porters are in this category.

- **Front-of-the-house employees:** This group includes waiting and casual bar staff.

# Choosing a method of payment

You have several different payment methods available to you. The most common form of payment is an actual physical cheque, but many restaurants opt for the other forms as well.

### Physical cheques

Cheques are the most mainstream form of payment for restaurants. The cheque should come with the hours worked, taxes deducted such as PAYE and National Insurance, deductions for insurance payments or contributions, and any other deductions relevant to your benefits plan.

### Direct deposit

Direct deposit such as BACS, the electronic payment system, is a service you may want to consider extending to your employees. Instead of a physical, depositable cheque the employee gets a receipt that shows his hours worked, deductions, and the amount automatically deposited in his account. Salaried employees are the best candidates because their pay amounts are the same, and their PAYE, National Insurance Contributions, health insurance, and other deductions are the same in each pay period.

### Cash

Cash is kind of an old-fashioned method of payment, but it's completely legal. Most restaurants are cash businesses. Nowadays, banks charge businesses for converting cheques into cash. If you're doing it the right way, why pay the penalty, also known as the bank charge, and go through a bank? It's almost an incentive to use the cash because you have it. Even if you can work legally in the country, you still might not have a bank account, and cashing a cheque may be tough for an employee, especially one new to the area or the country.

Even if you pay employees in cash, you still must deduct the proper amount of PAYE tax and so on from their pay. Keep good records regarding all of this information because you're required to pay your portion to the government and report all the employees' wages for tax reasons.

## *Opting for bonuses and incentive plans*

Incentive programmes vary from company to company and business to business. Most people recognise incentive plans as a plan to reward employees for doing a specific job at a certain level. Common incentive plans include profit sharing, or a flat amount if managers keep their costs under a certain percentage. Other incentives, like Christmas bonuses, are more like expected gifts, having very little if anything to do with how the business is performing.

The formula or criteria you develop for paying incentives must be fair, consistent, and understood by anyone eligible to receive them. Incentive programmes should be keyed for very specific things, or you may not get the outcome you desire.

If you're thinking long term, you're actually going to pay the incentives that you're promising, so make sure that you can afford whatever you say you will pay. The quickest way to guarantee high turnover of your managers is to tell them that you'll give them a certain thing and then fail to do so. No one's going to stick around if you don't keep your promises.

# *Saving, Storing, and Protecting Records*

Record keeping is an important part of any business. Various government agencies require most businesses to save certain information for a certain period of time. Check out Table 15-1 for our recommendations. Do check with Her Majesty's Revenue and Customs (www.hmrc.gov.uk/employers).

| Table 15-1 | Recommendations for Keeping Records |
|---|---|
| *Records* | *How Long?* |
| Balance sheets | Permanently |
| Bank statements | 5 years |
| Cash receipts | 5 years |
| Cash sales slips | 3 years |
| Credit card receipts | 5 years |
| Contracts: employee, government | Permanently |
| Tax records | 5 years |
| VAT, Equipment leases (after expiration) | 6 years |
| Equipment repair records | Life of equipment |

| *Records* | *How Long?* |
|---|---|
| Accounting records | 3 years (private company) or 6 years (public company) |
| Franchise documents | Permanently |
| General ledger | Permanently |
| Inventory records | 3 years |
| Inspection reports | 5 to 10 years |
| Invoices | 5 years |
| Job applications, nonemployee | 1 year |
| Leases | Permanently |
| Payroll records (after termination) | 4 years |
| Mortgages | Permanently |
| Income statements | 5 years |
| Permits and licenses (fire, alcohol, music, and so on) | Current on file |
| Tax records | 5 years |

Depending on the office and storage space your restaurant offers, the length of time you'll be storing particular documents, and the amount of access you'll need to the document, you can store your records on- or off-site. Wherever you store them, though, remember that temperature and moisture can be the enemy of both paper records and computers. Make sure that your long-term storage area protects them from excessive heat and the possibility of flooding or fire.

You also have to ensure that your data stays out of the wrong hands:

✔ **Secure the office:** You probably keep many records stored in your office, either on the computer or as hard copies in a file cabinet or safe. Job one, then, is to secure this area. Make sure that your door has a heavy-duty lock.

If you have a security system with cameras, you can train one camera on the office itself. You may even consider putting the recording device in a safe in the office so it can't be erased or damaged.

✔ **Lock all filing cabinets:** Ultimately, if someone wants to get into your file cabinet, he will. Locks don't keep criminals and thieves out of your stuff, but they do keep honest people honest. Lock up your employee records, bank account numbers, and credit card numbers.

✔ **Use passwords:** Make access to computers password dependent, and give access to only a limited number of employees. Also, make sure that all managers promptly log off when their computer session is finished.

✔ **Install firewalls:** A *firewall* is a software application that protects the restaurant *and* its clientele from hackers attempting to gain access to your computer records to either destroy them or use the information for illegal gain. Talk to the sales rep who sells you your computer systems about the best plan for protecting your system.

✔ **Secure credit-card transactions:** Hackers can attack your credit card system as well. Use a reputable credit card company and make sure it has protection, insurance, and *encrypted,* or secure, systems. Talk about what services the company can offer, and pick what's best suited for you.

# Chapter 16

# Getting the Word Out

· · · · · · · · · · · · · · · · · · · · · · · · · · · · · · · · · · · · · · · · · · · · · · ·

· · · · · · · · · · · · · · · · · · · · · · · · · · · · · · · · · · · · · · · · · · · · · · ·

*Y*ou may have the most incredible menu, the greatest atmosphere, the most hospitable waiting staff, the most gifted chef, or the best wine list in town. If no one knows about it, however, your restaurant will fail. Getting the word out about your new place isn't as easy as telling your friends and family and waiting for the word to spread around town.

Using *public relations* (PR) and advertising to your advantage is essential to your restaurant's success. Pick the message that you want your potential diners to hear and make sure that it gets to them loud and clear. Of course, you have to live up to your own hype, or they'll never come back. But the first hurdle is getting them in the door. This chapter gives you the details for creating your own marketing machine to bring them in.

Customers return to your business because they like it. You may get them in the first time because you sent out vouchers or offered a buy-one-get-one-at-half-price night, but they probably won't come back unless they enjoyed their first experience. We get them in the door in this chapter. Check out Chapter 19 for tips on how to keep them coming back.

## Defining Your Message

Purposefully crafting your *message* (what you want people to remember about your restaurant) is the key to marketing success or failure. It's understanding *what* you want to say, *who* you want to say it to, *how* you reach this group or groups and *why*, operationally, you're choosing this particular strategy. Create a *marketing plan* to get your message to the group you want to reach.

Success is rarely an accident. It's a function of motivating the buying decision of the potential customer. Efficient operational practices, consistently delicious foods, and an attractive, accessible location don't guarantee success. With all the dining choices available, consumers expect those things at a minimum. You, therefore, have to clearly communicate your message to your audience. Build your message to get these components across:

- Preferred clientele
- Concept
- Competition within that segment
- Desired business outcomes

Simply put in restaurant lingo: It's all about bums in seats. Unless you attract a consistent flow of paying guests to your tables, you'll have a For Sale sign in your windows before you can say, 'Table for . . . none'.

## *Focusing on the consumer*

One size doesn't fit all for restaurant marketing. Just as neighbourhoods and cities feature cultural and economic differences, your marketing plan should address the varied needs and wants of your consumer, whose money you're competing for. Each scenario requires an individualised marketing plan.

The simplest advertising plan is the shotgun effect. You throw it all out there, anywhere, and see what happens. Some consumers don't care, and others will hear it, see it, or read it and then reject it. Still others won't pay any attention. So the most successful ad plans target specific consumers.

Big restaurant companies spend millions to understand the demographic (who customers are) and psychographic (what customers think about) profiles of their consumer. To run your advertising and promotions programme well, you need to understand your targeted clientele as well. In Chapter 4, we provide you with concrete suggestions and resources for researching and defining your potential customer. After you have a handle on who your potential customers are, they become your *target audience* for marketing purposes. You need to craft your message with them in mind.

You can have multiple messages based on the differences of your consumers. You can break them up categorically to focus on gender, geography, income levels, age, interests, or any other demographics of your consumers.

## Communicating your concept

Your concept is the combination of your type of restaurant, your menu and prices, the ambience your offer, and the style of service you provide. We help you establish your initial concept in Chapter 3. And your concept will probably become more concrete as you analyse your local market (we explain how to do this in Chapter 4). But, to get people through your door, you have to tell them who you are, what you're offering, and why they should care. Your message should express these points.

## Keeping up with the competition

You're competing for just one thing – the discretionary amount of money of the consumer who wishes to spend it on restaurants. Those pounds are owned by a spectrum of consumers more or less likely to use your concept, with varying frequency. Your job is to identify your competition and then determine their strengths and their weaknesses and determine your points of difference. (We guide you through both processes in Chapter 4.) Simply put, a *point of difference* is how you're different from your competition. At that point, you're ready to tailor your marketing plan to counter your competitors' strengths or attack their weaknesses in an attempt to attract a segment of the market.

### Emphasising points of difference

Your message can focus on a clear-cut point of difference versus your competition. This tactic is extremely common, but you have to decide how aggressively you want to point out your competition's weaknesses, rather than simply emphasising your own strengths. 'We only use Scotch beef in our burgers' clearly conveys the fact that the others don't, so diners should choose you over them. Or your message could be a more subtle statement of a great feature of your concept that leads the consumers to compare your features with another place: For example, 'We cook our pizza in a wood-fired oven'. You're not saying that the other restaurateur doesn't, but you're leading the customer to think about how the pizza they ate yesterday was cooked and how it could've been better if it had been wood-fired.

When you're defining your own point of difference, think about the burger wars. McDonald's, Burger King, and Wendy's, and all have similar menu items on the surface: burgers and chips, basically. But for years, they've focused their marketing on a point of difference, such as the following:

- **Price:** Enter the 99 pence burger
- **Value:** The combo meal concept is an example.
- **Quantity:** Think super-size.

✔ **Quality:** Flame-grilling versus frying may be the difference.

✔ **New menu offerings:** Examples include healthy salads, Thai chicken, and low-carb dishes.

These companies spend millions each year trying to control their individual points of difference – whether it's their combination of offerings, size of portions, extended hours, kids' toys, co-branding with the hottest new film, or buy-one-get-one-free days – and make it resonate with consumers. They're answering the needs and wants of their targeted consumers and shaping the future of the market by focusing their marketing campaigns on emerging trends and development of new products that their competitors will have to respond to in order to protect market share.

After you're established, don't fall into the trap of just marketing to your strengths. You don't need to target that segment that will visit your restaurant whether you advertise or not. In a competitive marketplace, you must highlight the 'WOW' (the new and exciting parts of your business) to attract a constant flow of new diners looking for variety.

### Facing off – head to head

You can always choose to go head to head with your competition. 'My secret family lasagne recipe will knock the socks off the competition!' Your competitor launches a breakfast sandwich, so you counter with a sausage, egg, and cheese grilled panini. Just don't make the mistake of always being the copycat. Create your own point of difference instead of taking a me-too approach all the time.

Maybe you have pizza on your menu, but you can't make it like Mike's Pizzeria pizza, which has been the favourite in your area for 36 years. Instead of trying to imitate its deep-dish pizza, try focusing on your thinner crust, handmade pizza. You're still doing pizza, but you're offering consumers a different choice in the same type of food. You're not going head to head in a war you may not win.

---

## Introducing the new and improved Us

You can always reinvent yourself if the product you've been serving needs tweaking. An improvement like buying local produce is always a good selling point. Why buy Peruvian asparagus during the English growing season? You can sell it at a premium and even have an asparagus menu of maybe four or five different dishes to choose from.

Become known for your local sourcing rather than buying from the frozen section of the cash and carry. Advertising your new, improved kitchen quality will go down well. Feature it on your advertising boards outside the restaurant too for that extra selling opportunity. And don't forget to add the news to your Web site.

### Conceding strengths

Another approach is to concede a competitor's strength and focus on something it doesn't do at all, such as brunch or afternoon teas with homemade cakes.

In your case, suppose that two identical restaurants are located on the same street, but one offers a 15-minutes-or-it's-free lunch menu. Instead of adding your own 14-minute menu, maybe you offer a lunch buffet.

## Getting tactical

You can also craft your message to achieve strategic results. For example, if you were fortunate enough to buy some excellent wines at a knock-down price (say if a local wine merchant was going out of business and selling stock cheap, or if a new local winery was offering a promotion) and have bought quite a hefty number of bottles, you might design a market strategy to drive sales of this windfall. Make the most of this opportunity to increase customer traffic, maximise publicity and achieve higher profit margins.

Look at your marketing plan as your best opportunity to control the buying decision of your customer. A well-designed, purpose-driven marketing message can both increase your operation's top line by attracting new customers to your restaurant and increase the frequency-of-use by your existing customer base; the same plan can also increase the all-important bottom line by inducing customers (consciously or unconsciously) to select those items on your menu that are the most profitable.

# Using Public Relations

*Public relations,* or PR, means developing a positive public perception of your restaurant with the local community and the media. Here are some examples of PR:

- Stories about you appear in the media, featuring you feeding volunteers at a charitable event.
- A radio station mentions you have the best lobster in town.
- A local restaurant critic reviews your place.
- A magazine includes your Summer Pudding recipe in its summer desserts feature.
- Travel articles mention you and restaurant guides rate you.

Usually, PR is something you don't pay for. The tools to get the PR may cost you, but usually PR doesn't have a direct cost like advertising does. You didn't pay to have the article put in that magazine about your dessert, but the journo who wrote the article came in for lunch and drinks and you paid for it. The chef spent time describing the recipe, and you spent time with him and impressed his friends. Maybe you even paid a PR company to contact him about writing the story, but you didn't pay for the story.

## *Planning for the good and the bad*

Good PR is a fantastic asset. If you have a good PR machine working, you spend less time and money on other promotions, including advertising. If everybody already wants to come in, then you don't need to advertise in the local newspaper every week or hold special events.

But PR can also hurt you. If you have a seafood place making a big deal of selling highly prized species such as cod, growing media concerns about overfishing could hurt you. Sometimes media stories are political, over-hyped, health concerns, but no matter how true or false, they alter public perception, which affects your business. If you get a bad review from a critic, it can hurt. If people haven't been to your restaurant before, this may be this first thing they hear about you. If you don't make a good first impression, you may never get a chance to make another one.

### *Positioning positively: The press kit*

Your *press kit* is the package of promotional materials that you should have at the ready to send to people who want details about your restaurant. It should contain all pertinent info about the restaurant including the phone and fax numbers and Web site and e-mail addresses. Include information about desig-nated contact people, like the chef, general manager, PR person, owner, ban-quet planner, and so on. Any positive press clippings about your place should make an appearance. Add a summary of your restaurant's history or goals and specifics about your cuisine. Detail your mission statement. Include busi-ness cards, a copy of your menu, and something that tells someone what the restaurant's about, such as a postcard if you're in a scenic area. In general, the more distinctive, the better. Anytime you can do something that separates you from everybody else, it's great. Put it all in a sturdy folder, preferably one embossed with your logo. Obviously, for smaller businesses some of these suggestions aren't viable due to cost, but do have cards with details and menus available for picking up in the restaurant. Or hand them out with the bill.

### *Preparing for the worst: Contingency planning*

Drawing attention to yourself is good. But after you're up and running, you become a target. You need to have a game plan for handling negativity, whether it comes from the competition, a disgruntled critic, or a disap-pointed customer. Role play or run through different negative scenarios with your staff and your managers. Ask specific questions related to your concept. Here are a few to get you started:

- ✔ What do we say if people get food poisoning from an oyster? An unwashed salad?
- ✔ What do we do if we have an underage drinker in the bar?
- ✔ How do we handle an aggressive newspaper reporter asking about our employee problem?
- ✔ How do we respond to a less than glowing review? Or do we?

Make it a regular practice to anticipate bad scenarios. The exercise helps you prevent the situation by taking the precautions against it. It heightens awareness of potential issues, improves food safety, and ensures product quality enhancement. And it helps you to be better prepared for dealing with the customer or press questions.

## *Going it alone*

As with most things, you can manage your PR yourself, hire someone to do it, or hire someone to do part of it. Depending on your budget, you may start doing it yourself and then work up to hiring others after you're running a bigger business.

The do-it-yourself (or with your team) approach can work very well. You know your product and your concept, and you can make quick decisions about specials, promotions, and incentives. You save money because your time is paid for already and time because the communication is more direct. The downside: Tons of work and another serving of stress to your already full plate. Plus, you don't get the different perspective of your operation that an outsider can bring – a fresh pair of eyes and some new ideas.

### *Getting noticed in the community*

PR is the public perception of both your restaurant and the most visible people in your restaurant, most likely you. Our best advice is to simply do things the right way. The goal here isn't to avoid attracting negative attention. Your goal should be to make a positive contribution to your community – a positive *visible* contribution to your community. The rewards are twofold: You make a difference, and you generate goodwill for your business.

Have the restaurant participate in charity events, including offering free meals for charity auctions or special dinners. Encourage your chef to teach cooking classes on occasion at the local community college or cookery equipment shop. You can build community relationships and relationships with other restaurant peers.

Make the most of these opportunities to let people try your food. Be present at the major events in your area, like charity events, neighbourhood or community events, or street fairs – whatever is appropriate to your business.

You, personally, have to make the effort as well. Volunteer for a board or join the Chamber of Commerce. Find something that gets you noticed within your clientele group. Or even better, join the group that your clientele wants to be.

### Generating positive PR from the inside

The ideal situation is to have a staff that works as a mini-PR machine. Management extols the virtues of the waiting staff. Waiters talk up the chef. The chef meets people at the tables or has an after-dinner drink in the bar. Good service equals good PR.

These examples aren't only ways to generate good internal PR; they also generate word-of-mouth PR – the good word about your restaurant that spreads outside the restaurant. There is no word of mouth until you start it. Word-of-mouth PR includes diners telling their friends about their experience at your place and talking about your ads, PR, location, and so on. Basically anytime anyone is talking about your establishment, it's word-of-mouth PR.

People gravitate to busy restaurants. If your restaurant is too big, your options include moving to a smaller location (expensive) or building a visible partition to make it look busier. Otherwise, just wait for the axe to fall. Here are some ideas for building the buzz and creating the initial prestige:

- ✔ Get a plug from a writer, DJ, or sporting figure.

- ✔ Make the most of a celebrity sighting in your place. Anonymously leak the information to the local paper. You can also casually mention it to regulars, who in turn (hopefully) pass it on to others.

- ✔ Add expensive cars to your parking area and the occasional limo if you want a higher end clientele. Rent them if you have to.

- ✔ Make it hard to get reservations. But don't make it too hard.

- ✔ If you're serving a particular ethnic cuisine (like Thai, Chinese, or Indian), get diners who are originally from those cultures to frequent your place. Nothing says 'authentic' better.

- ✔ Create buzz about a signature dish by giving free samples to everyone. If you want to be known for the best Thai fish cakes, make sure that each person who comes in the door gets a bite-sized sample. They'll tell their friends how great they are and hopefully order many of them for a first or main course next time.

Courting your neighbours is a good (and necessary) first step because you them on your side. But be careful: Don't exclusively target your neighbourhood unless it can fully support you. You may suffer from 'secret syndrome' – neighbours don't want to share it with the outside world. Long-term success comes from a balance of local support and support from a wider area. If you make your restaurant a destination, as word spreads, it'll become bigger than just a local drop-in. You may risk alienating your core clientele but, if they don't come in their droves, you must become a destination restaurant.

You can generate a ton of talk and a huge buzz, but to move from being the 'in' place of the moment to a perennial favourite, you have to deliver on your promises and exceed your guests' expectations (see Chapter 19).

## Getting some help

A PR company should have connections already. In addition to talking with several people at the firm, speak to the person who's actually handling the account before signing with the company. If you don't feel comfortable with the account rep, pick another person or even a new business. You're looking for someone who's personable and charismatic. If you don't enjoy talking with someone, how will your potential diners feel? But do make sure that you see the press releases and other material they send out; you want to make absolutely sure that they know what they're talking about. Bad PR can make you a laughing stock if those in charge don't understand the restaurant world, food, service, and hospitality.

### Pay someone by event

Say that you're having an event in your restaurant and inviting all the major chefs in town. Or you're having a best local sausage contest and promoting it in the media. A PR rep or firm can help you spread the word. Maybe you're trying to promote a charity dinner, and you just want someone to get this one thing done. Use it as an opportunity to audition a PR company. Start small with a single event and then add a few things to the firm's plate.

Some PR companies specialise in restaurants in large cities. In smaller areas, you may find a more general PR company who may do PR for a local hairdressing salon, charities, a new furniture company, and a few restaurants as well.

### Hire a person or a company for full-time work

Even if you source out your PR work, you must remain actively involved in the process. You get as much out as you put in. A PR professional is the multiplier of your effort. If you put in zero effort, you still get zero out of it. Confirm that everything is meeting your expectations and approval. Review all press releases. Stay on top of things.

A good PR agency probably has a well-oiled PR machine already working and a system already in place and is fitting you in as a client. Such a business won't be reinventing the wheel or using you as a guinea pig. You should be able to get fairly quick results, compared to doing it all on your own.

# *Creating an Advertising Plan*

An *advertising plan,* the plan you use to inform the world about your restaurant, is as unique as your restaurant. Advertising differs from PR in that you always pay for advertising. No one plan works for everyone. And the same formula probably won't work for your restaurant from year to year, or season to season. What works in January doesn't necessarily work in July. Maybe in 2000 your foie gras and lobster starter at £20 was a great idea, but a few years later, the economy was completely different, and people were looking for value.

Developing an advertising plan is an investment in both time and money. Make sure that you're managing advertising like any other expense of time or money. It should be efficient and offer the greatest return on your investment. But unlike other expenses in your business, it's a *speculative* investment, meaning you're rolling the dice and saying, 'I'll make this investment in the hope that I'll see a return by welcoming new customers'.

After you know your target audience to a T (see the 'Focusing on the consumer' section, earlier in the chapter), work out where to reach them. Many of the same sources you initially look at to research these people are the same places you use to reach them – local newspapers, foodie magazines, TV, radio, and other sources we provide you with in Chapter 4.

Make concerted decisions about what outlets you choose to convey your message. You should know which section of the newspaper to put your ad in. If you're opening a sports bar with beer specials and the obligatory 'I ate the whole thing' T-shirt you win for eating the kilo steak, don't waste your ad money in *The Tatler.* Find out enough about your potential consumer. (And if your ad includes a picture, show somebody just like your desired clientele.)

Put together a plan to reach your clientele in as many ways as you can. Think about the reach of really big companies. Ask yourself what age you were when you knew every component of a Big Mac (two all-beef patties, special sauce, lettuce, cheese, pickles, onions, on a sesame seed bun). These successful businesses have reached you since time immemorial. They continue to speak to you, consciously or unconsciously, throughout your life, and it's no accident.

Here are some successful strategies we've used to get people in the door:

✔ **Use incentives:** Send special offer leaflets to your targeted clientele. This approach traditionally works for casual concepts, diners, and family restaurants. You can offer 2-for-1 main courses, a £1 starter or dessert on quiet days, a kids-eat-free meal with paying adult, or anything else relevant to your concept and clientele.

✔ **Place print ads:** Use local newspapers and magazines and dining or entertainment papers. If your potential diners are reading the periodical, let them see your restaurant. Newsletters to customers, past business associates, and old friends are an idea – former classmates may be interested in finding out what you do and come to sample your restaurant.

✔ **Sponsor a local sporting team or event:** This may be for larger restaurants to take on but those T-shirts, banners and other PR material can add to your profile.

✔ **Find exposure on buses, trains, or cabs:** If your potential patrons use these modes of transportation, you may find an interested audience.

✔ **Go global on the Internet:** There are innumerable ways to promote your establishment using ads here. Connecting to other Web sites (cross-pollination), pop-ups, banners, and the like are relatively new and more and more effective.

If you're a new restaurant, your primary advertising objective should be to make people aware of your existence and your offerings. Therefore, your ad has to be informative and educational. Answer all the questions you ask when somebody mentions a restaurant to you that you've never heard of or dined at. Your consumers can then become word-of-mouth advertisers and help spread your message. You want consumers who see your ad to be able to answer specific questions about your restaurants like what you serve, when you're open, and where you're located. They can't talk about you if they don't have anything concrete to say.

Your message should speak to your to your target audience and tell them who you are, where you fit into the local dining scene, and how they should respond to your ad. Figure 16-1 contains our example of a well-rounded ad that addresses each point. Say we're opening The Robin Hood Bar and Grill. From a menu standpoint, we're serving venison, locally made sausages and grills. We plan to focus our drinks sales on specialist beers. The theme is friendly and informal. We're trying to bring in a clientele comprised of either gender between the ages of 18 to 45, middle to upper-middle income, with free nights to spend in our place and disposable income to spend. We also offer jazz nights, free to diners. Who are we competing with in terms of our menu? Our concept? Where else do our customers go to eat? They probably go to gastropubs and bistros or brasseries. We plan to target those who eat out a lot by offering good value food and specialist drinks. This thought process gets us to the point where we can establish our point of difference. Our ads should target the audience we've identified.

The Robin Hood, a just-opened bar and grill in Hoxton, features venison and other game sourced from British moors, mountains and specialist food companies. Grilled venison, beef, pork and lamb sausages plus venison steaks, burgers and crayfish are cooked in the open kitchen by our chefs. Vegetarians also catered for, with a special menu of local, seasonal dishes available.

Our spacious bar offers an ever-changing selection of over 100 local micro-brewery beers, Belgian, Indian and Czech beers in addition to our extensive selection of world wines, whiskies, vodkas and cocktails.

The Robin Hood, next door to the Spitalfield food market on Hoxton Street, also features the best jazz musicians from Britain, Europe and America on Thursday and Saturday nights as well as Sunday Brunch. Free to dining customers. We're open seven days a week from 12 to 12.

www.therobinhoodhoxton.co.uk  0207 444 6789.

**Figure 16-1:**
Sample ad
copy.

# Part IV
# Keeping Your Restaurant Running Smoothly

'Should be an extremely profitable night —
we've got a large party of lawyers in for a
meal this evening.'

Part IV

Keeping Your
Restaurant
Running Smoothly

## In this part . . .

Whether you're currently running a restaurant or you're still in the planning stages, this part is for you as we focus on maintaining and building on your current operation. We offer suggestions that can help you improve your current style of management, attract and retain long-term customers, take another look at cleanliness and safety, and crunch the numbers to improve your financial standing.

# Chapter 17

# Managing Your Employees

*In This Chapter*

▶ Training and motivating your staff

▶ Making quick work of schedules

▶ Establishing company policies

▶ Understanding benefits basics

*B*usiness would be great if it weren't for people. We say this with tongue firmly in cheek, but some days, it definitely feels that way. When you have three waiters clamouring for the same Saturday night off, your kitchen porter didn't show up, and you discover that an expensive bottle of wine is missing, you just might agree. In this chapter, we help you work through some of the common obstacles that come up while managing employees, and we give you tips on how to avoid most of them.

## Selling Employees on Your Restaurant

Whether you're opening your doors for the first time or the ten thousandth time, your success is intrinsically linked to the performance of your staff. And the way to get a top-notch performance out of your employees shift in and shift out is make sure that they feel like they're part of something special. You have to continuously sell your vision, your restaurant, your food, and their vital role in the process to every staff member.

Simply hearing about your enthusiasm for your business and concept only takes you so far with employees. You must talk the talk, but you also have to walk the walk. Make sure they see you consistently exhibiting your standard of guest service, insisting on meeting and exceeding diners' expectations, and maintaining high food-quality standards. Don't just *tell* them how they should perform; *show* them every single day, every single shift.

## *Educating your employees*

Continuous employee education keeps your staff informed about and inter-ested in your business. Correct training from Day 1 is essential (see Chapter 13 for details). But *educating* your employees entails more than initial training programmes. Use weekly, monthly, and daily staff meetings to educate, inform, and motivate your employees. Share as much information about your busi-ness as you can. Investing the time to train and educate them properly shows that you view your employees as an important asset to your business. A good place to start the education process is with the food and drink:

- ✔ **Periodic menu tastings:** If you're just opening your restaurant, have a complete menu tasting. You train two teams at once: The kitchen trains on preparation and presentation, and the waiting staff get lessons on the taste and appearance of the food. Let the waiting staff develop a subjec-tive opinion about the menu by describing, in their own words, how they feel about the offerings. You run the risk that they'll impart personal preferences on the diners' experience, but if they're good salespeople, they can find a pleasant, honest way to describe any dish.

  If the restaurant is in operation, conduct mini-menu tastings on a regular basis. Once a day, or at least a couple times a week, bring out items that are on your regular menu, not just the daily specials. These tastings affect food cost but give your waiting staff more knowledge and confidence in what they're serving, and that leads to better service (and sales).

- ✔ **On-going drinks training:** Any day's a good day for employees to learn more about your drinks programme. Your drink sales reps should be willing to come in and talk with your staff about any category of alcohol, beer, or wine The more your staff knows about a product, the more likely they are to sell it.

  Reps can let the staff taste different wines side by side or introduce your employees to the nuances of vodkas or ports. Ask your wine reps or wine merchants to pair their wines with your food and let your staff taste them together. Wine reps can provide your staff with good basic information about wine, like the terminology used to discuss it, as well as details about the specific wines in their portfolio. Ask your wine rep or wine merchant to give written information to your staff about types of grapes (Sauvignon Blanc, for example and its main characteristics), the main wine regions and the meaning of the amount of alcohol, for example. This way your staff will have a check list to refer to and be well informed enough to converse with customers in a more confident manner.

## *Motivating your staff*

Keep the momentum going by praising your employees often, encouraging them to praise each other, and displaying a positive attitude. Keeping morale up is key. This rather un-British way of doing things may be alien but it works! Don't let negative attitudes affect your staff. Nip negativity in the bud by finding out what their grievances are and acting upon them. The following are ways we've found to be effective in boosting and maintaining morale:

- ✔ **Encourage communication:** Keep an open door policy. Make yourself available to listen to the staff when they have something to say. And encourage them to communicate with each other. Their feedback may not always be positive, but if they get some say in resolving a problem, they're likely to stick with the solution.

- ✔ **Offer constructive criticism:** Clear, concise feedback to employees on their performance is essential, and often, the message is that they need to improve. But don't beat them up with the criticism. Get your point across in a way that also encourages the employee to perform at a higher level.

- ✔ **Praise them:** Pat them on the back for a job well done. If they only receive negative feedback, you're the one doing something wrong. This is a most important part of being a good employer and you'll keep your staff for much longer this way.

- ✔ **Know your staff:** Demonstrate a real interest in (and knowledge of) what's going on in employees' outside life (like tests, school, family and other jobs). You may have a lot of students working for you as well as full time staff. Talk to them and ask specific questions, such as 'How's that Juliet part going?' or 'Did you get to see the Arctic Monkeys gig over the weekend?' Such questions show employees that they matter to you and that you're paying attention. Small things, like acknowledging birthdays, also go a long way to build morale. (Add the birthdays to your calendar as a recurring annual event.)

Asking your staff personal questions also can be a minefield. Don't get too personal or ask questions that could darken their mood. Understand their individuality. What one person may appreciate another may consider an intrusion or an insult.

- ✔ **Encourage camaraderie among your staff:** Look at how the informal hierarchy treats different people, both old and new staff. When new people are treated well, they're much more enthusiastic about their training and tend to stay longer.

The pecking order should have zero impact on how you treat your staff and the amount of respect you pay them. A kitchen can't run without a kitchen porter, and don't forget it.

- ✔ **Don't lose your cool:** Employees (and customers) can smell fear. If they see you act rattled or distressed during busy times – or feel that you're not in total control – your behaviour may be infectious. The people around you may start feeling uncomfortable and become upset. Don't let it show if you feel out of control. Staying composed is half the battle.

## Sure signs of good and bad morale

Morale, both good and bad, trickles through your organisation straight down to your diners. It shows in how the employees treat each other and how they work together as a team. Keep on the lookout for both kinds of morale. Here are examples of both to help you keep your eyes peeled:

**The good:**

✔ The staff goes out together after work.

✔ The chef de partie helps out the kitchen porter when he's overwhelmed with a lot of glasses at the end of the shift.

✔ A waiter sees a group looking around, and even though it's not his table, he helps out to take the order.

✔ Waiters restock service bar glassware. Waiters help kitchen staff take in a delivery order to speed things up before the restaurant becomes full.

✔ Waiters make a new pot of coffee when they take the last cup instead of expecting someone else to do it.

**The bad:**

✔ An employee has a management warning against a co-worker.

✔ A waiter berates a new employee in front of a customer for *any reason*.

✔ A waiter gives the barman an earful because she needs to wait for drinks even though the bartender is trying to break away from a conversation diplomatically.

✔ A waiter doesn't clear a table because it's not his section.

✔ A cook makes a waiter wait for food just to teach him a lesson.

✔ Waiters berate the kitchen staff and vice versa.

✔ **Implement specific staff incentive programmes:** Small-scale incentive programmes are a tried-and-trusted path to boosting morale. Don't focus staff incentive contests on general stats, such as overall sales for a shift. Instead, get your staff focused on specific products or categories of products to build enthusiasm. Do a training session on your wine-by-the-glass programme and coordinate that with sales contests and incentives during the following shifts. Get creative with the prizes: Give them a bottle of your house wine, or an extra day off. Motivating your staff doesn't have to cost you lots of cash.

✔ **Encourage apprenticeships, either formal or informal:** You want experienced staff members to take the new ones under their wing. When possible, give perks, such as preferred schedules or free lunches, to trainers and mentors.

✔ **Watch for animosity between front-of-house (FOH) staff and back-of-house (BOH) staff:** If you've spent more than a minute working in a restaurant, you know that this problem is all too common. The best way to combat it: Keep the lines of communication open. Have meetings that include both FOH and BOH staff to ensure that everyone hears the same info delivered the same way. Don't favour one department over the other. Keep in mind that the chef is more likely to side with the cook rather than a waiter, and a manager is more likely to see the waiter's point of view rather than the cook's. In order to succeed, both departments need to work together.

✔ **Turn the mirror on yourself:** What you do is reflected in what your staff do. You can't expect the cook to be nice to the waiter if you're not nice to the cook. You can't expect a good rapport with your kitchen porter if you're not smiling at him. And don't forget managers are staff, too. How you treat them affects how they treat the rest of the staff.

# Making Staff Schedules

Creating a schedule is a necessary step for any business that relies on shift workers with changing hours. A posted, written schedule communicates who will be working and when they should be in the restaurant. Making schedules for the wait staff in the restaurant is one of the toughest jobs in the working world. You're dealing with part-timers, many of whom have other jobs, attend college, have young children they need to pick up from school, and so on. Many employees may have scheduling needs that change from week to week. Back-of-house employees tend to be a bit more consistent in their schedule expectations.

## Adding it all up

The best way to create your schedules is to start with a job slot list. A *job slot list* is a chart that helps you determine the number of people you need, doing a particular job, at a particular time. Your job slot list will change for different shifts, or meal periods like breakfast, lunch, and dinner, and change based on the days of the week, weeks of the month, and months of the year, just as your business levels change.

Check out the job slot lists in Figures 17-1 and 17-2. These job lists are for the back and front of the house for the fictional restaurant Heather's Bistro on Regent Avenue. First, a bit of background: Heather serves informal bistro-type cuisine to a bustling lunch crowd that comes for her croque monsieur, cassoulet, and tarte Tatin. *Cover counts* (the number of diners in her establishment) for dinner are steady during the week and peak on the weekends, when the pre-theatre rush brings diners looking for steak au poivre, pommes frites, and crème Caramel.

| Job Classification | Monday Average Covers Lunch/Dinner | Tuesday Average Covers Lunch/Dinner | Wednesday Average Covers Lunch/Dinner | Thursday Average Covers Lunch/Dinner | Friday Average Covers Lunch/Dinner | Saturday Average Covers Lunch/Dinner | Sunday Average Covers Lunch/Dinner |
|---|---|---|---|---|---|---|---|
| | | | | Employees Required to Fill Position | | | |
| Kitchen Porter | 5 | 5 | 5 | 10 | 12 | 12 | 10 |
| Head Chef | 5 | 5 | 5 | 10 | 12 | 12 | 10 |
| Sous Chef | 5 | 5 | 5 | 10 | 12 | 12 | 10 |
| Chef de Partie | 5 | 5 | 5 | 10 | 12 | 12 | 10 |
| Larder Chef | 5 | 5 | 5 | 10 | 12 | 12 | 10 |
| Commis Chef | 5 | 5 | 5 | 10 | 12 | 12 | 10 |
| Totals | 30 | 30 | 30 | 60 | 72 | 72 | 60 |

**Figure 17-1:**
Job slot list –
back of the
house.

Heather's Bistro, via Figure 17-1, provides examples of common staffing techniques used to conserve labour and maximise productivity that you may
want to use:

- ✔ **An overall build-up of labour commensurate with anticipated business levels:** Traditionally in the average restaurant market, here's what
  you find:

  - Thursday is busier than other weekdays.

  - Friday and Saturday are busy all day.

  - Sunday is busy early; business then tapers off in the early evening.

- ✔ **Job sharing during slower shifts:** You may only need one waiter or two
  at less busy lunch shifts earlier on in the week, with a full complement
  on weekends.

- ✔ **Concentration of morning prep labour early in the week:** This scheduling gives the kitchen staff time to prep items like salad dressings, desserts,
  and soups for the whole week. And notice that more prep people are
  scheduled for lunch than dinner. Most prep takes place during your slower
  periods so that you can gear up for your busy times. See Chapter 11 for
  details on prep and the stations in the kitchen.

The job slot list in Figure 17-2 is also based on business levels that increase
toward the weekend, through a busy lunch on Sunday but earlier dinner. In
the front of the house, you may make other adjustments as well. For example,
you may need only five waiters to handle your Friday night dinners if they're
experienced and reliable. If you have newer, less experienced people, you
may need seven waiters.

As with the back of the house, always look to save FOH money during traditionally slow shifts. An a.m. waiter could be scheduled on Monday to put
away the big weekly drink order, and then not scheduled again until Friday.

| | Monday | Tuesday | Wednesday | Thursday | Friday | Saturday | Sunday |
|---|---|---|---|---|---|---|---|
| | *Average Covers Lunch/Dinner* | *Average Covers Lunch/Dinner* | *Average Covers Lunch/Dinner* | *Average Covers Lunch/Dinner* | *Average Covers Lunch/Dinner* | *Average Covers Lunch/Dinner* | *Average Covers Lunch/Dinner* |
| *Job Classification* | *Employees Required to Fill Position* | | | | | | |
| Waiting staff | 8 | 8 | 8 | 10 | 12 | 12 | 12 |
| On-call waiting staff | 8 | 8 | 8 | 10 | 12 | 12 | 12 |
| Barman | 8 | 8 | 8 | 10 | 12 | 12 | 12 |
| **Totals** | **24** | **24** | **24** | **30** | **36** | **36** | **36** |

**Figure 17-2:**
Job slot list –
front of the
house.

Schedules aren't set in stone. You can make adjustments later based on experience (yours and theirs) and business levels. During each shift, you cut one or more employees (end their shift early) if your sales don't meet your projections during a certain time of the day. But in doing this, you should ensure that staff members agree. If they would like to stay and work out their hours, they are entitled to and should be paid regardless of how slack business is.

Consider implementing an on-call system if you have very dynamic business levels, especially until you establish some patterns. An *on-call employee* calls into the restaurant an hour or so before a scheduled shift to see whether he or she's working that night. If other employees call in sick or you are busier than expected, having this extra person on the schedule can be a lifesaver. If you don't need that person, she gets a bonus night off. Be sure to rotate this duty, especially if you don't need the on-call staff very often. Most employees work because they need the money.

## *Putting names to numbers*

After you complete your slot lists and know how many people you need for each position, shift, and day, insert specific employees into those slots. At this stage of the game, you turn your attention to employee schedule requests. Decide how you want to run your system for requesting days off. Many people use a master-calendar system combined with a request book. Employees place their names in the request book by the days they want off. Allot space for them to write a reason for a special request, such as a birthday, so that the person writing the schedule can take it into account.

Be consistent in how you resolve conflicts regarding scheduling. Have a policy in place for priority of requests. Many new restaurants use a 'dibs' system, meaning that whoever requests it first gets it. More established places use seniority systems effectively. You can base seniority on either hierarchy or tenure with the company.

Then start filling in the blanks in a table or spreadsheet like the one in Figure 17-3. We use the waiting staff for Saturday at Heather's Bistro as an example. We filled in a couple of names so that you can see how a *double* shows up on the schedule. A double occurs when an employee essentially works straight through, or works two shifts in a single day with a break between them. In this case Steve and Suzie are working both lunch and dinner without a break. Also, this schedule is based on the *first-in, first-out* philosophy.

Save yourself some time by setting up Figure 17-3 in a spreadsheet or other computer program. You can keep track of expected hours worked, planned time off, and so on much more easily.

You have to find a balance between your business levels and staffing levels. While you're getting a feel for business levels, you'll probably be *overstaffed,* or have too many people for a given shift. Try to make corrections as soon as you can.

| Lunch | | |
|---|---|---|
| 1. | Open | 9a.m. - 3p.m. |
| 2. | Open | 9a.m. - 3p.m. |
| 3. | Open | 9a.m. - 3p.m. |
| 4. | Close | 11a.m. - 5p.m. |
| 5. STEVE | Double | 12p.m. - 7p.m. |
| 6. SUZIE | Double | 12p.m. - 7p.m. |
| Dinner | | |
| 1. STEVE | Double | 12p.m. - 7p.m. |
| 2. SUZIE | Double | 12p.m. - 7p.m. |
| 3. | Setup | 4p.m. - 9p.m. |
| 4. | Setup | 4p.m. - 9p.m. |
| 5. | Close | 6p.m. - 11p.m. |
| 6. | Close | 6p.m. - 11p.m. |
| On Call | | |
| 1. | | |
| 2. | | |

**Figure 17-3:** Waiting staff schedule worksheet (Saturday).

Don't get complacent when writing your schedule. You must adjust your schedule to the business on particular weeks or days of the weeks, in particular weather, and so on. Holidays, religious occasions, sporting events, and the like all affect your business, either positively or negatively. The degree to which it affects your business varies from concept to concept. During the World Cup, many restaurants are dead, but if you're a pizza delivery outfit or a sports pub you should be heaving with customers.

# *Setting Up Policies to Live (or Die) By*

The best way to establish your policies is to write them down and then consistently implement them. Be as specific as possible and try to anticipate most potential problems before they happen. When appropriate, make sure to include the consequence for infractions, up to and including termination. Put all your policies together in one easy-to-use reference called your employee manual. (Check out Chapter 13 for details on creating and maintaining your employee manual and getting it to your employees.)

## *Scheduling and attendance*

If you write a schedule and no one shows up for work, you have a problem. Setting an effective attendance policy goes a long way toward minimising employee problems. Figure 17-4 shows an example of an effective, comprehensive attendance policy.

**Attendance Policy**

Being on time and ready for work is part of good attendance. If you are late or plan to be absent, you place an extra burden on fellow employees. If unusual circumstances cause you to be late or absent, you must call your line manager at least two hours in advance so that someone can be located to cover your shift until you arrive. If your line manager isn't available, you should leave the following information with another manager:

- Name
- Reason for absence or lateness
- When you expect to be in
- Phone number where you can be reached

Leaving a message does not relieve you of the responsibility of speaking with your line manager personally. You must continue to call until you make contact with your line manager. Do not rely on friends, relatives, or fellow employees to report your absence or lateness.

Absences of more than one day must be reported daily, and a doctor's certificate of illness may be requested for any absence due to illness. Consecutive absences will require a doctor's note. Absences of more than four days due to illness or disability will require an approved medical leave of absence.

Failure to follow the proper call-in procedure may result in disciplinary action.

**Figure 17-4:**
Sample
employee
attendance
policy.

Develop a policy for handling schedule changes. Generally speaking, employees may suggest replacements to cover their shifts if there is no one else on the payroll who can be called upon, but managers should approve replacements. Managers can refuse replacements for a variety of reasons, including performance difference between the two employees (if the replacement is a brand-new server, he probably can't handle the same workload as the ten-year veteran) or the fact that extra hours worked by the replacement will cause her to get overtime pay.

Post schedules at a consistent time each week. You set the standard for punctuality and respect by keeping this commitment to your employees.

## Employees and smoking

Now that the ban on smoking in public places has come into force (since July, 2007 in England; Wales and Scotland took up the pledge earlier), employees are not allowed to smoke anywhere on your restaurant premises.

They can still smoke outside but, as this is an eyesore to passers-by or those in the restaurant who may see your staff smoking, you will have to come to an arrangement with them, stipulating where they can smoke, preferably out of sight of customers.

Bear in mind that cigarette ends need to be removed, and that the smell of smoke on clothing can be detrimental to your business if customers are aware of it. Staff must wash their hands after smoking. They shouldn't be allowed to take more breaks than non-smoking staff, as this is unfair.

## Drinking or using illegal drugs

You should have a strong, clear, enforceable policy that is in line with the law. Figure 17-5 shows a good example of such a policy.

**Figure 17-5:**
Sample
drug and
alcohol
policy.

### Drug and Alcohol Policy

The illegal use, consumption, possession, distribution, or dispensation of drugs or drug paraphernalia and the unauthorised use, possession, or being under the influence of alcohol, controlled substances, or inhalants on company premises, in company vehicles, or during work hours is prohibited.

# Uniforms and grooming standards

A uniform of some kind is mandatory for most restaurants. Many places don't allow you to work in the clothes you came in, even if it is your uniform. You must change on site, leave your uniform for the company laundry, and pick up a clean, sanitary uniform at your next scheduled shift. This system works best for BOH employees who wear chef whites that are maintained by a laundry service. It can also work in large hotels, or very fine dining restaurants, with a large laundry budget. If you're not providing uniforms, and their cleaning, for your staff, managing this system is tough. You're probably better off requiring that they wear the accepted uniform during their shift, and not worry about when they change.

Far too many restaurants are lax in this regard and allow staff to have scuffed shoes, dirty shirts, inappropriate clothing and jewellery. Don't be one of those restaurants if you value your customers.

Here are a few ideas to keep in mind as you choose uniforms for your employees:

✔ Uniforms for the waiting staff, and bartenders should complement, enhance, and reinforce your concept. Hip, trendy restaurants demand hip, trendy servers with hip and trendy clothes. Other places can get by with more casual uniforms.

Uniforms must be functional to work in. Employees must be able to move freely and carry plates, trays, and the like. Don't dress your waiting staff in high heels, particularly the men. Sure they look good, but stilettos are tough to find in the largest sizes.

✔ In many cases, the restaurant issues and maintains uniforms for kitchen porters and chefs. You should include a policy for handling the uniform and penalties for misuse or abuse.

Your concept and geographic location have lots to do with your grooming standards. You can limit jewellery to no rings except wedding or commitment rings. Decide on your policy for visible tattoos. Make some boundaries for facial hair. Many operations don't allow earrings for men and limit the number for women. Here are a few grooming standards that are non-negotiable:

✔ Employees must restrain hair extending beyond the shoulders.

✔ Nails should be clean.

✔ Employees must not have noticeable body odour.

✔ Employees must not wear an excessive amount of perfume or any at all as it can upset the balance of drinking good wines by customers.

Customers see back-of-the-house (BOH) employees from time to time, so they should be held to the same grooming standards as the front-of-the-house (FOH) employees.

## Disciplinary measures

In some cases, despite your best attempts, rules do get broken. Here's the standard sequence of corrective action:

1. Verbal warning
2. Written warning
3. Suspension
4. Termination of employment

The window of time for a progressive discipline system should be very short. Act promptly if an employee doesn't respond to your progressive discipline system.

Place all written documentation regarding discipline measures in the employee's file. Documentation helps you establish patterns of behaviour over an employee's tenure with your company. The more documentation you have to back you up in the case of a terminated employee who brings a suit against you or your company, the better.

Some offences are cause for immediate termination and don't require progressive discipline. Violence, coming to work impaired by drugs or alcohol, or theft may demand immediate termination. This behaviour is known as *gross misconduct*.

If you've built your organisation right, no one is indispensable. And to an extent, your employees should know it. They should know that every single day, they should do their job to the standard set for them or risk losing it. You've established goals, standards, policies, and so on. You've done the research and developed your concept, which you want your staff to help maintain. If you run into resistance to your standards and policies, eliminate the obstacles, even if that means firing an employee. Don't be afraid to fire employees who don't meet your standards, as long as you have gone through the appropriate steps. Check with the Department of Trade and Industry (www.dti.gov.uk/employment), or ACAS (the Advisory, Conciliation and Arbitration Service; Web site at www.acas.org.uk), or with a reputable legal information Web site (such as www.compactlaw.co.uk), for information on dismissal, redundancy, and other laws.

Employers must give employees a written statement of the main particulars of employment within two months of the beginning of the employment. This should include, among other things, details of pay, hours, holidays, notice period; and an additional note on disciplinary and grievance procedures.

If you sack an employee, follow your written disciplinary policy to the letter. Your policy should include language stating that the employee must turn in all company property on his last day. Make sure that sacked employees know that if company property isn't returned in good condition, you may deduct the cost of it from their last pay cheque.

## Offering Benefits

Decide what benefits you can realistically afford to give to your staff. Each benefit has options. Health insurance plans are available at a wide range of costs, with an equally wide range of coverage. Retirement plans and pensions programs have some flexibility. Consult your insurance agent to determine what benefits you can actually afford.

From an employee's standpoint, taking away or reducing benefits is never a good thing. Make sure that you can afford what you're offering over an extended period of time, at least a year. When your premiums go up the following year (notice that we said *when,* not *if*), decide whether you will pay the difference or pass along some of it to your employees. Breaking the news to employees that they'll have to contribute more out-of-pocket money is always tough, but with the rising costs of various types of insurance and policies, it's the reality of every industry.

If you're a new or small business, you may not be able to afford a pension plan. Don't forget the extra benefits you can give your employees, such as, preferred scheduling, birthdays off, long-term career planning, on-the-job training, and so on. They may not cost you much, but they should matter to your employees. Even the prestige of working in a certain restaurant can be a benefit.

Free or reduced-cost shift meals are a fairly standard restaurant employee perk. Your meal programme may actually be fairly complicated. Maybe employees get free meals when they're working but only a 50 per cent discount when they're not. Often, the free shift meal is served at a specific time and is available to all employees. In other places, employees order off the menu at a discount before or after their shift.

Do arrange with your head chef a cheap, nutritious, well-balanced meal for your staff. They deserve to be treated with respect and not have a miserable meal pawned off on them. Value your staff as you value your customers.

# Chapter 18

# Running a Safe Restaurant

**S**afety first! You hear that from the time you can walk (or run with scissors). The rule about safety is no different in the restaurant business. You just have to consider safety on a broader scale. As a restaurant owner or manager, you're responsible for the safety of everyone on your premises, including your diners, employees, and vendors. No small task! You can implement countless safety measures, but this chapter focuses on a few biggies: cleanliness, food safety, hand washing, and general safety precautions.

## Making Sure Your Food Is Safe

Food safety is one of the most important aspects of running a restaurant. Constant attention to keeping your restaurant clean and organised is the best way to keep food safe. Cleanliness prevents other problems from developing (like vermin or bug infestations) and organisation ensures that food is properly stored and your customers are gastronomically safe.

Some people approach food safety by trying to do the minimum and get away with what they can to avoid the hassle. But our view is simple: *Always follow safety guidelines,* full stop. For one thing, it's the right thing to do – for you, your reputation, and your guests' health. If you have a passion for the business, you want only the best for your customer. Your reputation is reflected in how you treat your food and equipment and in the steps you take to maintain it. Follow your local environmental health department rules and don't give them a reason to fine you.

Contact your local authority for laws that apply to you. Or take a look online at your local authority Web site for details of regulations. The Food Standards Agency Web site (www.food.gov.uk) has regulations on premises, equipment, personal hygiene, cross-contamination, and other issues. There are many booklets available from these sources too.

## Blaming bacteria

Bacteria cause food borne illness. Two of the most common bacteria that cause food borne illness are salmonella and *Campylobacter*. Their symptoms are similar to most food borne illnesses and include fever, abdominal cramps, and intestinal distress. If an individual already has a compromised immune system, is elderly, or is very young, the bacteria can cause a life-threatening infection. Both pathogens are almost always present in raw poultry, but you can easily kill them by:

- ✔ Cooking poultry completely
- ✔ Avoiding *cross-contamination*, or spreading bacteria from one type of food to another through improper handling and storage (see the section 'Preventing cross-contamination', later in this chapter)

*E. coli* is another common bacteria. It lives in the intestines of cattle and makes its way to meat through improper handling. Symptoms (which can be life-threatening if the person isn't treated properly and promptly) usually don't include fever, but *E. coli* can cause vomiting, diarrhoea, and possibly kidney failure, especially in children. *E. coli* infections are often traced back to beef products, most commonly minced beef. But remember that the bacteria can transfer to anything the raw meat comes into contact with, including foods that are rarely if ever cooked, like lettuce.

These are by no means the only bacteria you should be on the lookout for. Botulism can be present in tinned goods. *Vibrio parahaemolyticus* is sometimes present in shellfish. And staphylococcus, commonly called *staph,* can contaminate prepared food in your refrigeration. Some bacteria, like staph and vibrio, can't be killed in the cooking process. So check with your local authority or the Food Standards Agency for a complete list of bacteria you should be aware of and how to avoid them.

## Battling illness – time and temperature

Your two biggest opponents in the war on food borne illness are time and temperature. Foods that need temperature control such a dairy products, fish and meat must be kept either HOT at or above 63 °C or COLD at or below 4.4 °C. Rapidly cool or heat foods so that you can avoid the danger zone of between 4.4 °C and 60 °C for prolonged periods – don't let foods stay in this zone for more than two to four hours. Hold your food, or keep it, at a temperature above or below this zone, at all other times.

Some foods, like raw chicken, arrive at your door contaminated. Count on it. How you handle the food after it enters your restaurant makes the biggest difference. A chicken breast mildly contaminated by salmonella left out at room temperature for 12 hours becomes highly contaminated and can cause illness. But even when contaminated food makes it into your restaurant, you can implement procedures to ensure that it doesn't make it to your customers. Here's a quick list of tips to keep your food safe:

✔ Always store perishable foods at the proper temperature, below 4.4 °C degrees or above 60 °C, depending on the food.

✔ Cool cooked foods that won't be served immediately as quickly as possible. Current laws require you to cool food to 21.1 °C within two hours and 4.4 °C within four hours. Pay particular attention when cooling large quantities of food. Use ice baths, and separate large quantities into smaller containers to cool foods quickly.

✔ Always hold foods at the proper temperature, above 63 °C or below 4.4 °C.

✔ Always cook foods to the proper temperature (see your local authority's requirements for details) before *holding,* or keeping at the proper temperature until service.

✔ Provide access to calibrated, sanitized thermometers to check food temperatures at every point in the production process.

✔ Practice *FIFO* (first in first out). Set up a rotation system so that you're using the oldest products in your inventory first. This process cuts down on waste by reducing spoilage and ensures that you and your staff are in the know about what's on your shelf, how long it's been there, and what condition it's in.

✔ Reheat foods only once. Bin the remainder. Because some bacteria are *heat stable* (meaning heating doesn't kill them), the more often you reheat foods, the more likely they are to be contaminated. If you're binning a lot of food, heat smaller portions until you establish your *levels,* or the amount of a supply (in this case prepared food) you should have on hand for a given period of time (in this case between prep periods). See Chapter 14 for details on establishing your levels.

✔ Always thaw food in a fridge or with a rapid thaw process (such as under running water in a designated sink, if your local authority allows this method). Never leave food out at room temperature to thaw.

You can also make sure that your staff aren't spreading diseases. Institute mandatory, consistent, and enforced hand-washing policies. See the 'Implementing proper hand-washing procedures' section later in the chapter for specifics. Have the kitchen staff use latex gloves whenever working with food. This step protects the food from the people (and their germs) and provides a first line of defence from burns, cuts, and similar injuries. Require your staff to change into work clothes at work to avoid bringing in contaminants from the outside.

## *Preventing cross-contamination*

*Contamination* is the unintended presence of a harmful substance or organism in food. So *cross-contamination* occurs when a bacteria (or other substance or organism) that's present in one food accidentally spreads to another food, usually through improper handling and storage. If you've read the previous section, you're likely on the lookout for the usual contamination suspects, like minced beef and raw chicken. But cross-contamination is probably the single largest food safety problem because the contamination happens accidentally and you may not even be aware of it.

Your best line of defence against cross-contamination is a good attack. Implement proper handling and storage practices, and you're on the road to a restaurant free of food borne illness. Here are a few tips to get you started:

- ✔ Provide plenty of work space for staff working on a variety of foods at the same time.

- ✔ Clean and disinfect knives, utensils, and equipment before and after use.

- ✔ Provide disinfectant buckets with properly concentrated solutions and clean towels. Check with your cleaning product supplier for the details on how to use your particular products.

- ✔ Use hard plastic, wood, or rubber food-grade cutting boards, cleaning and sanitising them between each and every use. Wooden boards have had a bad press – it was said that wooden boards used for cutting allowed bacteria to enter the cracks – but have now been re-habilitated by research. Find out which type of board your local authority prefers you to use.

- ✔ Use separate cutting boards for raw foods, cooked foods, and foods you serve raw, like fruits. Colour code the boards to keep them separate.

## *Monitoring food safety outside the kitchen*

Food safety isn't a concern that stops at the kitchen door. The way you and your front-of-house staff handle dishes after you leave the kitchen affects the safety of your food and your diners. In the front of the house, avoid these potential food safety hazards:

✔ **Waiters touching food or drinks with hands:** They should touch only the plate or glassware, not the contents.

✔ **Waiters with dirty hands:** Some workers may clear and touch dirty dishes and then not wash their hands before returning to the dining room. Effective hand washing is a must for everyone in your organisation. See Figure 18-1, later in the chapter, for the proper hand-washing technique.

✔ **Possible cross-contamination situations:** If a kitchen staff member is slicing lemons, make sure he's not using a slicer that just sliced cooked meats and wasn't cleaned and disinfected afterwards.

✔ **Expired perishables in the bar area:** On a shift-to-shift basis, waiters should check milk, cream, and butter if you store them to be handy in the bar to confirm that they have current use-by dates and that they don't smell 'off.' You especially need to do this check during slow business periods or when you've ignored the rotation schedule.

✔ **Dropped tongs or utensils on buffets:** Watch out for these germ carriers and replace them immediately with clean ones.

✔ **Improper stacking of food:** The bottoms of plates and containers may be contaminated. Create a barrier (a tray, plastic wrap, or the like) to keep bacteria from the bottom of one container from contaminating the top of another.

✔ **Dirty utensils at the dessert station:** Change the ice cream scoop, pie servers, and the like at the servers' dessert station once an hour if you run a buffet-style restaurant or at a designated area in the kitchen, unless you keep the utensils refrigerated.

## *Monitoring food safety outside the restaurant*

Inspect your orders when they arrive to ensure proper product quality (greens and produce are fresh and free from rot and pests, for example). Demand the proper handling by your suppliers. Ensuring proper storage before the food gets to you is just as important as storing it properly in your possession.

If you serve organic or vegan dishes, confirm that your suppliers meet the standards that you've promised to your diners. If the producer is using pesticides, your clientele probably considers that use a food safety issue. Likewise, if you're buying vegan veggie soup that has cream listed as an ingredient, your vegan patrons may be pretty upset.

Some shellfish, such as oysters, can contain illness-causing pathogens, like vibrio, that can make you sick when you eat them raw so make sure you buy them from reputable dealers. Ask pertinent questions before buying such produce. Are your shellfish from a reputable dealer? Have they been stored and handled in a safe manner? Food poisoning can arise if the basics are not carried out properly. Most types of produce, particularly meat, fish, chicken, and eggs, have tracibility attached to them so that you, the consumer, can trace items if you have concerns, and can report it to the authorities.

## Picking up other food safety tools

HACCP (Hazard Analysis Critical Control Point) is a system of tools designed to help restaurants develop cost-effective food safety programmes. The HACCP program focuses on the flow of food from receiving to serving, identifying, monitoring, and removing potential hazards along the way.

Your local authority can become your best partner in implementing food safety programmes. Ask your environmental health officers about programmes that your staff can attend at the department's facility, like Food Hygiene Certificate classes, or consider having a guest speaker at your next staff meeting. Don't be afraid to ask the health department about its training services and facilities.

## Implementing proper hand-washing procedures

From staph infections to hepatitis C to the common cold, employees bring a variety of bacteria and potential pathogens to work with them every day. To reduce the risk of transferring any of these pesky organisms to your guests, facilities, and products, employees must wash their hands with hot water and soap, before and after their shifts, at designated hand sinks (following the proper hand-washing technique, as pictured in Figure 18-1). Employees must also wash their hands at designated hand sinks during their shifts after doing any of the following:

- ✔ Using the toilets
- ✔ Touching their hair, mouths, noses, or other body parts
- ✔ Sneezing or coughing
- ✔ Handling dirty dishes
- ✔ Handling raw food
- ✔ Handling rubbish
- ✔ Eating or drinking

✔ Smoking or using tobacco

✔ Handling animals

✔ Cleaning toilets

✔ Tending to a wound

✔ Coming into contact with bodily fluids

✔ Becoming contaminated in any way

1. Use water hot enough for the hands to stand.

2. Wet hands, soap thoroughly, and lather to the elbow.

3. Use a brush for nails and scrub thoroughly.

**Figure 18-1:** Proper hand-washing technique.

4. Using friction, rub hands together for about 20 seconds.

5. Rinse thoroughly under running water.

6. Dry hands, using a hot air dryer or single service towels.

# Keeping Things Clean

Keeping your restaurant clean is the first step in maintaining food safety. It keeps pests and vermin from sniffing around. Organising your refrigeration helps keep foods from spilling, dripping, or falling into other foods. Regularly moving items to clean behind and under them helps keep your products rotated so that none expire and then get used in your menu items. And using fresh containers and pans ensures that you always know when the food was made and that it's safe to serve to your guests. Label your food with contents, date, who prepped it and sell-by-date. Never put messy containers back in the fridge. Transfer food to a new container and label it.

Cleaning is only as good as your managers. They're ultimately responsible for the cleanliness, health inspection scores, and the processes that make it all work. Hold them to the highest possible standards.

## Getting cleaning supplies

Get the right tools for the job. Buy cleaning products designed for cleaning commercial kitchens. These specialised products cut the kind of grease load a restaurant kitchen puts out, polish stainless steel as only a professional can, and truly disinfect the kind of bacteria and toxins that you find in a kitchen. The typical restaurant kitchen needs these cleaning supplies on hand:

- ✔ All-purpose cleaner
- ✔ Coffee pot and machine cleaner
- ✔ Degreaser
- ✔ Dishwasher detergent
- ✔ Dishwasher rinsing aid
- ✔ Floor cleaner
- ✔ General disinfectant
- ✔ Glass cleaner
- ✔ Hand sanitiser for the hand sinks
- ✔ Oven cleaner
- ✔ Pot and pan soak
- ✔ Silver, copper, or stainless steel polisher
- ✔ Soap for the hand sinks

These chemicals can be very dangerous! Keep the following safety tips in mind as you educate your staff about cleaning supplies:

- ✔ **Keep a Material Safety Data Sheet (MSDS) for all these chemicals on file at all times.** That paperwork contains detailed information on safe handling procedures and instructions for dealing with accidental ingestion, exposure, and contact.

- ✔ **We wish it went without saying, but we'll say it anyway: Never store chemicals near food, including the food in dry storage.** The fumes can permeate things like lettuce. And you run a tremendous contamination risk if something spills, sloshes, or sprays on any food products.

- ✔ **Observe your staff closely until you're comfortable with their use of chemicals.** You must use these chemicals in their proper ratios to maintain the safety of your staff and customers (not to mention your wallet).

In addition to cleaners, you need the tools to use those cleaning products, including mops and mop buckets, a fresh supply of towels, small buckets for disinfectant solution, brooms, squeegees, scrubbing pads, and cleaning brushes.

And just to make sure that we cover everything, here are a few more tips:

- **Consider locking cleaning supplies:** Set up a requisition system, which can benefit you in a couple of ways:

    - You can control the amount of chemicals in use at a given time.

    - You create accountability for proper procedures. If someone has to ask a line manager for the degreaser, you know who's accountable, and you can be reasonably sure they're using it (or not).

    - You limit the opportunity for employees to supplement their home cleaning supplies by borrowing them from your restaurant. Sad but true!

- **Assign different towels different jobs:** You can use one colour for cleaning and dealing with any chemicals, another colour for general kitchen use (like wiping down surfaces), and a third type of towel – of the lint-free variety – solely for wiping down plates and glassware.

- **Never use steel wool or stainless steel scrubbing pads:** As they disintegrate with use, they leave behind bits that get into food.

- **Schedule cleaning for times other than at closing time:** Things can get overlooked when people are trying to get out after work.

## Scheduling your cleaning

The longer you let your kitchen go, the harder it is to clean and the more likely that lack of cleanliness can develop into a bigger problem. Grease erodes paint. Uncovered food invites pests. Old food contaminates new food. Set the standard with exhaustive daily and shift-to-shift cleaning schedules.

Go through your kitchen and note everything that you need to clean and then assign each item a schedule. Don't forget that many items need the occasional heavy-duty cleanup, in addition to daily cleaning. Divide the duties by the employee or job title in a given area to begin to map out your schedule. Base your cleaning schedule on your type of operation. For example, a restaurant featuring fried foods has different cleaning needs from a sushi bar.

Your master cleaning schedule should be part of your operational manual (see Chapter 13). The *master cleaning schedule* should explicitly state what to clean, who should clean it, when to clean it, and how to clean it. Take a look at Table 18-1 for an example schedule based on just one piece of equipment. Create an elaborate cleaning schedule that covers every piece of equipment, every fixture, and every surface in your restaurant.

| Table 18-1 | | Sample Master Cleaning Schedule | |
|---|---|---|---|
| *Who* | *What* | *When* | *How* |
| Commis chef | Fryer | Between every shift and at close | Turn off fryer; allow grease to cool. While oil is cooling, wipe down exterior surfaces, using spray degreaser. Rinse and finish with stainless steel polish. Filter oil. Wipe down the inside of the fryer with a dry towel, removing any food bits. Replace clean, filtered oil. Cover fryer with half sheet pan to prevent light exposure to oil. Run fryer basket through the dish machine. Make sure it's thoroughly dry before use. |
| Commis chef | Fryer | Every Friday | Same as above, but replace old oil with new rather than strain it. |

After you put together your list of things that you need to clean, you decide when to have someone clean them. In the following subsections, we've put together suggested timelines for some of the common kitchen tasks.

Use this section to create your own schedule, but check your equipment for the manufacturer's cleaning recommendations. Some equipment (like combination ovens) have a self-cleaning cycle and recommended cleaning schedule. Always follow the manufacturer's directions.

### Must-do's several times each shift

Here are some things that need to be done several times each shift, as needed:

- ✔ Change water in the washing machine (if this kind of machine).
- ✔ Sweep the prep areas.
- ✔ Change disinfectant.
- ✔ Empty bins if not done at the end of the last shift.
- ✔ Unpack deliveries and place packaging in bins

### Cleaning, shift after shift

You can have workers do these tasks on a shift-by-shift basis:

- ✔ Sweep the kitchen entrance and all kitchen areas.
- ✔ Mop the entire kitchen.

✔ Clean the fryer and ovens.

✔ Filter the fryer oil if it's dirty.

✔ Send the detachable cooker metal parts to the washing machine.

✔ Change disinfectant solution in sanitising buckets.

✔ Clean and disinfect all surfaces (fridge doors, handles, prep tables, and so on).

✔ Hose down mats.

✔ Wipe down walls, surfaces, and hood vents behind hot line.

✔ Empty steam machine if applicable. Clean, and refill with fresh water.

✔ Clean the employee area.

### A cleaning a day . . .

Assign tasks like these on a daily basis:

✔ Empty equipment and hood grease traps.

✔ Change foil linings on catch pans of grill, hobs, and flattops.

✔ Clean the tin opener.

✔ Remove all the hood filters and run them through the washing machine.

✔ Put in a rotating deep-cleaning and maintenance schedule; for example:

  • Monday: Sharpen knives.

  • Tuesday: Oil pans and cast iron cookware.

  • Wednesday: Fill flour, sugar, and other bins in dry storage.

  • Thursday: Apply commercial drain cleaner to floor drains.

  Restrict deep cleaning tasks to Monday to Thursday (or Sunday to Wednesday, depending on your restaurant) because typically the remaining days of the week are too busy, and your staff won't have time for extra cleaning tasks. Just keep up with your daily and shift cleaning on busy days and leave the heavy-duty tasks for slower days.

✔ Create a list of requests for your maintenance staff. Try to assign at least one of these each day during your slower times.

### Week in, week out

Make quick work of these more intense weekly jobs with preventive maintenance throughout the week. Work out your *down days* – days when you have the least amount of stock in the fridges – and detail the produce stored. Sunday or Monday is usually a great day for this process, because your stock is down from the busy weekend.

✔ Empty cupboards and shelves and thoroughly clean and disinfect them. Judge the contents and keep or toss. Reorganise and replace items as needed.

✔ Pull the hot line out, if possible, and clean the walls and floor behind and below the line. This task helps you maintain cleanliness, sanitation, and safety. Grease can build up here and catch on fire.

✔ Descale the sinks, drains, and tap heads.

✔ Clean the coffee machine.

✔ Deep-clean the ovens. Always follow your manufacturer's instructions for cleaning your particular kind of oven. Appropriate cleaning regimens vary greatly, so make sure you know how to clean yours safely.

### That fun monthly cleaning

Break these jobs up between employees and spread them out over the month, doing yourself a favour in the labour category and staving off a mutiny.

✔ Turn the cooler fans off. Remove the covers. Wipe the fans. Clean the covers.

✔ Deep-clean the freezers.

✔ Empty and disinfect the ice machine.

✔ Check all filters, water softeners, and the like.

✔ Calibrate ovens. Place an oven-safe thermometer in your oven; set your oven to 180° C (350 °F). After the oven indicates it's reached the appropriate temperature, wait a few minutes for the thermometer to register the actual oven temperature. Make sure that both the oven and thermometer register 180 °C (350 °F). If not, repeat the test with a different thermometer. If you get similar results, your oven may not be calibrated properly. Call a technician to test the oven and adjust the temperature if necessary.

✔ Calibrate thermometers. Place stick thermometers in a full glass of ice filled with water for one minute to register the correct temperature, which will be 0 °C. If the thermometer doesn't register 0 °C, adjust the small dial under the head of the thermometer until the thermometer reaches 0 °C. Some stick thermometers can't be calibrated. If you find that your thermometer isn't registering the correct temperature and you can't adjust it, throw it out. We recommend that you only buy stick thermometers that can be calibrated.

✔ Sharpen the slicer. (You may have to do this sharpening weekly, depending on the volume of slicing.)

✔ Deep clean walls and ceilings.

✔ Pull everything from dry storage and wipe down the shelves. This cleaning usually coincides with checking your stock. See Chapter 14 for more on stock management.

✔ Change any pest traps.

✔ Restock your first aid kit.

✔ Deep-clean kitchen floors with a motorised floor scrubber.

✔ Update MSDS (Material Safety Data Sheets, which spell out instructions for safely using any chemicals in your business) you're missing.

### *Yearly safety stuff*

You get to take care of the administration of safety stuff once a year. In most cases, you need to hire a professional to come in and do these jobs for you:

✔ Check fire safety systems.

✔ Check fire extinguishers. Make sure you adhere to safety regulations. Contact your local authority for guidance.

✔ Clean hoods twice a year or more, if you're creating a lot of grease.

✔ Clean the pilot lights on all your gas equipment, like your ovens, grills, and ranges. Refer to the cleaning instructions for your particular equipment.

✔ Call for service and maintenance on all your equipment.

✔ Update permits and licences, as necessary. These documents validate your safety compliance.

## *Opening and closing procedures*

Opening and closing procedures are an important part of cleanliness for several reasons. During opening you confirm that everything is in tip-top shape and that the restaurant is ready to safely prepare meals for the day to come. During closing, you preserve any products for the next shift, get rid of vermin-attracting material from the previous shift, and make sure that all surfaces are free from grease to avoid slips and spills for the next shift.

The opening kitchen manager or chef makes sure that everything was cleaned the night before. He's also responsible for ensuring that all the food has made it through the night. And he must make sure that the opening staff is onboard and knows how to start the restaurant day right.

### *Opening procedures*

Here's the short version of the way a manager or chef may start his day:

- ✔ Confirm that refrigerators and freezers are working properly and have been working properly overnight by checking temperatures.
- ✔ Ensure that clean cloths and aprons are available for staff.
- ✔ Read log entries from the previous shift to check that equipment is working properly.
- ✔ Verify that equipment is working properly.
- ✔ Conduct a sweep of all vermin traps.
- ✔ Do a sweep of all food storage areas to make sure that all food is in good order and no food that has gone off is hiding anywhere.

Use this list as a starting point for creating your opening staff's duty list. Add your own food production requirements to finish it off:

- ✔ Pre-clean any surfaces before food prep begins. This step ensures the surface is clean in case it didn't get disinfected the night before.
- ✔ Put out clean disinfectant, buckets, and cloths.
- ✔ Verify that you have sufficient washing machine chemicals to get through the shift.
- ✔ Confirm all ice bins and water wells are clean. Fill them with fresh ice.
- ✔ Make sure that all pans and holding containers are clean. Always use fresh pans, not the ones the food was stored in overnight. If you don't change the pans every day, they eventually become carriers of food borne bacteria over a period of days.
- ✔ Clean and stock the toilets.
- ✔ Line all rubbish bins with fresh bin liners.

### *Closing procedures*

A closing manager or chef has the benefit of the cleaning schedule to keep everyone on track. But she should look for shortcuts that past shifts may have taken. Is the slicer clean underneath the guard? Does the top of the mixer have a dough hook on it? Is the tin opener growing fungus? She should note any equipment problems or deep cleaning required in the log book. Before she leaves, she makes sure that

✔ Doors are closed and locked.

✔ Refrigerators are closed and locked.

✔ All food is labelled and contained properly.

✔ Things that should be covered are covered.

✔ Nothing is improperly stored or dripping cross-contamination.

✔ The washing machine is empty and cleaned.

✔ All rubbish is appropriately disposed of.

✔ No one leaves without checking out with the manager or chef on duty.

# Taking Precautions to Protect Your Customers and Staff

The following sections provide tips on a few of the big safety issues in the restaurant world, including first aid and emergency procedures. Check out Chapter 12 for info on responsible alcohol service.

## First aid

With the number of sharp implements (from knives to slicers to tin openers) and heating elements (including deep fryers, tilt skillets, and even coffee pots) found in restaurants, accidents are bound to happen. Your restaurant needs a basic first aid kit with the following supplies:

✔ Antibiotic ointment

✔ Antiseptic wipes

✔ Assortment of adhesive bandages

✔ Assortment of non-stick pads

✔ Burn gel

✔ Eyewash

✔ Finger cots (latex gloves for one finger)

✔ Gauze

✔ Sterile eye patches

✔ Waterproof first aid tape

Consider training your staff in CPR (cardiopulmonary resuscitation) in case a guest has a heart attack or stops breathing. The Heimlich manoeuvre (designed to help choking victims) is a must-know for restaurant employees. You can find people to provide training at your local St John Ambulance (www.sja.org.uk) or Red Cross (www.redcrossfirstaidtraining.co.uk) organisation, or you can encourage your employees to get training on their own. Give them a complimentary meal if they get certified. Go to the British Safety Council's Web site at www.britishsafetycouncil.co.uk for more information or contact your local authority.

## In the event of an emergency

Your local authority decides how many emergency exits you must have and where you have to put them. Those in charge tell you specifically what kind of doors you have to have, what kind of hardware you should put on the door, which way the door has to swing, and on, and on. Very important stuff. Check with your local authority for the specific ordinances you may be subject to. Here's a general list of good tips to keep in mind regarding emergency exits:

- ✔ They should always be unlocked from the inside.

- ✔ You must clearly mark them. Make sure that you have lighted emergency exit signs.

- ✔ They must be accessible at all times. Never block an emergency exit, even with a movable barrier, like a rubbish bin.

- ✔ If you install *panic hardware* (hardware that sounds an alarm when tripped), make sure that it's properly marked. Nothing is more embarrassing than a diner accidentally tripping an emergency siren.

Make sure that all employees know the escape routes. Instruct your staff to help diners exit your restaurant in the event of an emergency.

Programme your telephones with emergency numbers and post instructions for dialling them. If all else fails, post the emergency numbers so anyone who sees the list knows who to call, even if he can't work out the memory dial.

# Chapter 19

# Building a Clientele

$A$ dvertising and free PR success such as a good restaurant review draw guests to your door. In Chapter 16, we help you design and implement public relations and advertising strategies to get the word out and bring the customers in. But customers are free agents. Just because they give your establishment a try doesn't mean they'll return. How you deliver on your implicit or explicit promises to the customer after they're in their seats makes the difference between one-time customers and a regular *clientele* – patrons you want to have in your restaurant and who put money in your pocket by returning again and again with their friends, family, and colleagues. The best ad campaign in the world won't help you for long if you don't build a strong base of loyal customers by meeting and exceeding expectations.

Establishing a clientele transcends being popular. It's about being permanent. Just like doctors, lawyers, mechanics, and beauticians, you develop a loyal clientele based on how you deliver on their wants, needs, and expectations. You won't survive for long by serving one-time-only customers.

A lot of clientele building is common sense, not rocket science. Most people know the right things to do to make people feel special, important, and valuable. But few people actually do it. That's where we come in. In this chapter, we remind you of the importance of exemplary customer service and outline practical strategies that you can use every day to begin building or expand on your loyal customer base. We shed light on an often-overlooked opportunity to gain a loyal customer – customer complaints. And we outline some long-term clientele-building techniques to keep them coming back.

Any successful restaurant has to innovate and bring new people in the door. The trick is to continue to do it, while you keep your regulars.

# Understanding Who Your Customer Is

After you've researched your target audience (see Chapter 4) and designed the appropriate marketing strategies (see Chapter 16), you get to turn your attention to the actual human beings. In the same way that you have a few dates before you decide to marry someone, you have to get to know your customers and court them before they become your clientele. Understanding your customer begins with listening to what your customer has to say. Talk and *listen* to your guests. Ask the right questions, and they'll give you the keys to their repeat business.

Know the people who eat regularly in your business, and don't underestimate the value of learning and using their names. For some customers, simply saying hello and calling them by name is enough to gain their repeat business.

## Observing and listening

You must get to know your customers in order to figure out what motivates them to pick your restaurant over another one and how to encourage them to come back again and again (with friends). Discover what they want (or think they want) by watching their behaviors, asking questions, and listening to what they have to say. Here are a few ideas to get you started:

✔ What are they eating? Your menu mix analysis and other sales reports can give you the snapshot of what's happening (see Chapter 20). But to understand the complexities of the choices they're making, talk to them. And more importantly, listen to them.

✔ What are they doing besides eating in your restaurant? Get to know your customers, not just their food and drink preferences. Find out what other activities they're involved in. Use that info to find ways to get them to visit you more often. For example, ask yourself the following questions about your customers:

  • Do they have kids, and if so, do they want to bring them in, too, or get away from them for a few hours?

  • Are they health or weight conscious?

- Do they dine in your restaurant before (or after) another activity like shopping, attending the theatre, cinema, or attending sports events?

✔ How does value play a role in their decision-making? Are they looking for the largest portions for the lowest price or high quality at a reasonable price? Or is value not a primary concern as long as the quality is top notch?

✔ How do local preferences and tastes affect their choices? You may have seen the most up-to-date innovative drink at the food and drink show in London. But if you're in a small town where bar orders overwhelmingly consist of beer, you may sell very few pink vodkatinis – regardless of how cool you think they are.

## *Playing on their tendencies*

Consider your customers' wants and desires and incorporate them into your concept to help build a loyal customer base. Take a look at the following list for an idea of how this approach works. If your customers

✔ **Buy mixed drinks:** You can offer a specialty cocktail menu.

✔ **Like live entertainment:** You can offer live music one night a week.

✔ **Order salads and lighter items:** You can offer more choices in this category, at higher margins.

✔ **Read the paper while drinking their morning coffee:** You can have newspapers available.

✔ **Ask for a particular kind of wine:** You can order their favorite wine if they come in often enough.

✔ **Often special-order their breakfast:** You can add a special build-it-yourself menu option.

✔ **Don't like to walk home:** Offer a taxi calling service

✔ **Like to watch sports:** You can buy extra TVs and offer drink promotions during sporting events

✔ **Drink lots of draught beer:** You can expand your draught beer selection.

If you want more of a certain kind of diner, figure out what these types of diners want and give it to them. But you can't please everyone, so make changes to your business and your concept only as a concerted effort to gain the increased patronage of a certain type of diner. If you don't want more children in your restaurant, don't make it especially child friendly.

# *Meeting and Exceeding Expectations*

People come to restaurants ready to spend money. They're not simply browsing or window shopping. They're coming to your restaurant with an expectation of good, wholesome food, efficient service, and courteous treatment. Fewer places deliver those things than you might expect. Because restaurants regularly fall short of their customers' expectations, a pleasant dining experience often is heralded as revolutionary when it does occur. Nowhere is this truer than in Britain, where hospitality is often seen as a necessary evil.

Diners have expectations, regardless of whether you're the owner of a small café on an industrial site or the restaurant of a famous visionary chef. Coauthor Andrew recalls a conversation with a world-class chef, whose commitment to superlative guest service is legendary. The chef said that guests come to his restaurant already expecting and demanding the finest foods, wines, and service in the world. Just delivering on that isn't enough. You have to look at each individual guest and figure out how to exceed his or her expectations, no matter how lofty. And every employee in the restaurant should be committed to delivering this level of customer service, to every diner, every day.

No matter how successful you are, never make customers feel like they're lucky to be in your restaurant.

The minute customers walk in your door, they should experience the best you have to offer. Your host staff is your first exposure to the guest. If you frustrate a diner here, it's tough to turn them around. You have to quote the right waiting times and work the reservation system with enough padding in case you have guests who are lingering over coffee. In fact, you never know what might happen in a restaurant, so giving yourself a little extra time is a good idea. If you quote customers 15 minutes and you seat them in 5 minutes, they love it. But don't exaggerate the waiting time just to exceed their expectations. If you tell them the wait will be an hour, and then seat them in 5 minutes, you don't impress anyone. But remember, there's no reason to tell customers that the wait will be shorter than it is.

Ann and Franco Taruschio were masters of building a clientele at their Welsh restaurant. For 40 years, their dedication, sense of mission, and purpose was evident to anyone who entered The Walnut Tree Inn, their 100 seat restaurant near Abergavenny. They greeted you by name, and welcomed you into their restaurant as if they were inviting you into their home. Neither conveyed a feeling of standing on ceremony and they were personally committed to your individual dining enjoyment. They never ever gave the impression that you would be lucky to be in their restaurant. Rather, they appeared to be overjoyed that you have joined them this evening, and would be delighted to see to your needs. This should be your goal in whatever type of restaurant you run: Hospitality is the name of the game.

Good customer service is *not* a revolutionary concept – that's the way it should be everywhere, all the time. Here are some ways to exceed your customers' expectations:

- ✔ **Do the extras for people in your restaurant.** Don't just tell them where the restroom is; escort them discreetly. Make sure you take their coats and bags for extra comfort and space. Slip a couple two forks when only one orders dessert.

- ✔ **Give them a story to tell.** Give them something positive to talk about the next day at work. Table visits are important to get to know your customers, but move beyond, 'How is everything?' Join them in tasting the new port you just brought in. Talk to them about an upcoming wine and food pairing dinner they may be interested in. Let them know about the local food festival that's on next week and give them flyers.

- ✔ **Find things that matter to them and capitalise.** Don't just serve them dinner. Find out what they enjoy and use that to influence that to create a relationship outside of the restaurant. If a regular diner is into wine and you're going to tour a local vineyard, invite him to come along.

- ✔ **Send cards to your regular clients.** Send handwritten or printed cards or a regular newsletter or e-newsletter to your customers to inform them about the season's events at your restaurant.

- ✔ **Show your customers that they're important to your success.** Invite them to sample new menus, new wines or have a party for regulars to celebrate an anniversary of the restaurant. Make them feel like they have an ownership stake in your restaurant, and they'll share the experience with others, which hopefully means more business for you.

# Turning Unsatisfied Guests into Repeat Customers

Successful restaurateurs attempt to exceed guest expectations 100 percent of the time. *Attempt* is the keyword here because, as hard as you may try, you won't walk away at the end of the day with an unblemished track record.

Every customer service situation is an opportunity to make a customer for life. People remember the bad. If you do it right nine times but mess it up the tenth time, that's what they remember. You need to make the problems go away. You want customers to remember that the tenth time, you fixed it. And they usually do.

Of course, avoiding problems in the first place is the best possible scenario. Prevention is the best option in the restaurant business. With fickle customers, shrinking margins, and limitless dining choices, you need to make it a priority to avoid doing things that result in unsatisfied customers. Here are a few basic things you can do to help ensure happy diners:

- ✔ Make sure that the temperature is right – not too hot and not too cold.

- ✔ Seat guests in the best possible place.

- ✔ Place clean menus, silverware, glassware, and tableware at every table, every time. Never ever give a grubby menu out. This gives off the wrong impressions with the customer thinking 'what's the state of the kitchens?'

- ✔ Keep your toilets in tiptop shape. Again, customers are rightly a picky lot and will assume that your kitchens may be in a poor state too if confronted with loos in a mess.

- ✔ Quote accurate waiting times, and even err on the side of caution. Customers don't get cross if you seat them early.

But, despite your best efforts, problems will occur. So in this section, we provide tips for staying alert and recognising problems and show you how to turn an unsatisfied guest into a repeat customer.

Some guests walk into your restaurant unhappy. Other guests like to show off – they're in the business and want everyone to know it. And some people always complain, like to complain, or just can't help themselves. Whether the gripe is legitimate or not, you have to filter through *all* the complaints, dealing with the bogus ones, to get the opportunity to correct a real problem. One of the worst situations is failing to recognise a genuine problem that a customer is having. You never have the opportunity to correct it. You don't get a second chance. The customer just doesn't come back.

## Recognising unsatisfied guests

If every guest that had a problem said, 'Excuse me I have a problem,' *we'd* have no problem recognising that clear-cut message. But, in the real world, many guests don't let you know. So, you need to perform some detective work to make sure that all's well that seems well. If you see any of the following "clues" from your guests or on tabletops, investigate the problem. Check in with their server to get the whole story before you visit the table.

- ✔ **Human periscopes:** Look for people looking up and around and then back down. Typically, these people need something. It could be a missing menu page, a refill on a soft drink, or extra napkins for a spilled drink. You want to get guests what they need as soon as possible so they can go back to enjoying their time in your restaurant.

✔ **Half-eaten food or food left on a plate:** Maybe the customer has a small appetite – or maybe the food wasn't up to scratch. Ask. You want empty plates going back to the kitchen.

✔ **Empty glasses:** People like full glasses of their drinks, especially non-alcoholic drinks, so replenish the water and other drinks rather than leave you customers to ask for them. Don't fill up wine glasses without asking. What people prefer is to have the wine bottle handy. This way they can monitor their own consumption. Far too many restaurants, keen to sell wine, will constantly get their staff to top up glasses, resulting in too much drinking over a short period of time.

When asking guests about a refill on their alcoholic drinks, by the glass, for example, make it easy for them to say yes. Ask, 'How about another glass of wine?' instead of 'Do you have enough wine?' You can even take the next step and recommend a wine for their next course.

✔ **Watch gazing:** Customers who keep looking at their watches may not be wondering where their food is, but investigate the situation anyway.

✔ **Waving, snapping, and other hand motions:** If you see customers making these gestures, it's not good. Hopefully, you can get to them quickly and fix the problem before they leave. Even if you feel 'attacked' by someone in this agitated state, do your best to maintain your composure and resolve the situation. Also remember that even if you can't win back this customer, other customers are watching to see how you handle the situation. Don't risk losing them as well.

✔ **Aloofness:** If you see people who are laid back in their chair and not looking happy and engaged, this behaviour isn't an automatic problem. Some couples go out and never say a word to each other. Just because they don't appear to be enjoying each other doesn't mean there's anything you can do about it. As you gain experience, you'll be better able to judge the nuances of a diner's body language, but until then, consider stopping by the table to check in with these types of diners.

✔ **'Safe' orders:** If customers order a steak in your seafood restaurant, they may be afraid of the menu and simply need some information about the fish on offer. Don't let them miss what you do best.

## *Making things right*

As corny as it sounds, the customer is always right. Resist the urge to reverse the blame on the customers because they were grumpy or petty. Accept the responsibility for their complaint. And remember, do your best from the start to not give them a reason to complain.

1. **Listen to the guest.** Let your customer tell you what's wrong and even how he thinks you should fix it. Sometimes just having an outlet to vent for a moment can start the process of resolution and calming down.

2. **Apologise or thank the guest, depending on the situation.** A sincere apology can go along way toward resolving your long-term relationship with them. Sometimes guests may just have a recommendation or an idea that can really improve your business, not an actual problem. Thank them for their interest in your business and their patronage.

3. **Fix the current situation.** Figure out how you can correct the current problem. If a customer is completely dissatisfied with her main course or it isn't up to the usual standards, you may consider removing the item from her bill. But giving a free dinner or dessert isn't always the answer. Do what you can to serve customers a quality meal before they leave. If the steak is overdone, get them one that's cooked the way they like it. If their pasta is cold, get them a fresh portion. Or ask them if you can bring them something else. And do it with grace.

Providing a quality meal and service in the face of a problem gives you a huge opportunity: Some of your best, most loyal clients come from what started as a bad situation. The way you handle the situation is what can make the difference in where the relationship goes from here.

4. **Rectify the long-term situation.** Don't patronise or placate your customers. They want to know that someone has heard their problem, fixed it, and will take steps to make sure that it doesn't happen again. If theirs is the fourteenth overcooked steak on the same shift, you probably have a problem with the grill (either the chef manning the station or the equipment itself.) Take the steps necessary to investigate what the true problem is and fix it. Customers hate for someone to listen but at the same time seem to ignore their comments. Give them your name and your card. Tell them to see you the next time they come in. Your sincerity and follow-through are essential in ensuring that they come back again.

# Using Long-Term Loyalty Strategies

Building a clientele requires you to bring in repeat customers, again and again. Sure you can get them in the door. You can even keep them coming for a few months. But how do you keep them interested after you're no longer the hottest new restaurant? You do it by keeping a balance between maintaining what made you popular in the first place and new, exciting events and menu offerings. Give customers an incentive for dining with you more often. Invite them to events at your restaurant. Contact businesses in your area to make sure they know what you offer. The following sections show you how.

## Hosting a diners club

Belonging to a restaurant's diners club is kind of like getting frequent flyer miles for dining. Usually, it's a variation on a common theme: You come enough, and you get a free meal. Fast food, coffee shops and pizza places have loyalty cards. Some restaurants charge a small fee to join their frequent diner club and offer some very high-end perks. After earning a certain amount of points, a customer gets gift certificates, wine, or even spa treatments or other perks.

 The prizes or perks don't have to be extravagant. You could partner up with a good deli shop in town and give discounts on cooking lessons. The more appealing the perks are to *your* customers, the better your response will be.

## Orchestrating theme dinners

A *theme dinner* is an event that you host at your restaurant that's separate from the regular menu and oriented around a theme. The theme is limited only by your imagination. You can plan a theme around the food, beverages, or a combination of the two. Or you may want a dinner that features a celebrity personality, guest chef, or author. Another option is to host a dinner that doubles as a charity event, perhaps including a silent auction.

 You can still make money on a charitable function. But you must donate a portion of the money to charity. Pairing food and wine dinners are a common event for upscale restaurants. Maybe your local chamber of commerce wants to showcase local wines, and the local organic meat business wants to promote their 42-day-old aged beef on restaurant menus. You can get everyone together and host a beef and local wine-pairing combo. You can contact people from your mailing list for advance sale tickets. Here are some other ideas for theme dinners:

- Calendar themes, like St George's Day or Midsummer Evening.

- Ethnic cuisine

- Period dinners, featuring historic, throwback, or retro themes

- Ingredient-focused, such as mushrooms, heritage variety tomatoes, or asparagus.

- Collaborative dinners, in which, for example, several chefs or winemakers work together to put on an event

## Courting local businesses

Every guest isn't created equal. We're not saying that you shouldn't treat each guest with the same amount of courtesy and respect. Just recognise that some customers have the potential to bring in more additional business than others. You can beef up your word-of-mouth advertising exponentially if you treat someone in a dining decision-making position with extra courtesy and an occasional free meal.

For example, maybe the office manager who orders all the catered client lunches at the building next to you comes in a couple times a month. Another guy in accounting from the same company comes in at least once a week for lunch and then occasionally asks for a takeaway. The office manager may be a good candidate for an occasional free lunch. She may not come in as often as the guy from accounting, but she has the potential to mean more money for your business. If she's making the buying decisions for an office, consider giving her a reason to choose you.

A few other specific ideas that may work for your business include:

- ✔ If you're part of a business association, partner with other people in your group to offer each other discounts on products and services.
- ✔ Make the rounds to introduce your business to the concierges of the local hotels. Make sure that they know you're out there with a quality product. Send them an occasional lunch, a nice bottle of wine, or other perk that helps them remember your restaurant first when hotel guests ask for dining suggestions.
- ✔ Make friends with a few taxi drivers, rental car agents, and retail shops. Be known in the places that your customers frequent.

Don't forget the ancillary businesses related to your business. Court your vendors and colleagues. People know they're in the restaurant business and ask them for recommendations. Give them a reason to suggest your place. Don't forget other chefs and restaurateurs in your community who aren't in your direct market segment. If someone asks them where they go for Indian food, you want to be that place, assuming you're an Indian restaurant.

## Laying the foundation for a mailing list

A *mailing list* is a list of your customers that you maintain for the purpose of marketing to them. You can include the following types of content in the material you send to those on your mailing list:

✔ Special events at your restaurant

✔ Periodic discounts to encourage customers to come in

✔ Menu changes

✔ Opinion surveys

✔ Regularly updated newsletters that contain all of the above, along with appealing content such as recipes or wine reviews

The info you request from your clientele for the mailing list can be very detailed or very brief. At a minimum, your mailing list should include the customer's name and address. You can use the addresses to determine where your guests are coming from. But having a list of customers' addresses also lets you know the areas where you're not attracting customers from so you can target those areas with future promotions. To make your mailing list even more useful, consider asking for this information as well:

✔ **E-mail address:** E-mail is a great way to do a fairly inexpensive, quick promotion to your clientele. But remember that not everyone has e-mail and therefore may not be able to receive your newsletter or promotion.

✔ **Birthday or other special dates, such as an anniversary:** Acknowledging special events can make lifelong customers.

✔ **Business address:** This information can be helpful if customers are interested in hearing about business-focused events, like a discount on catering, delivered lunches, and so on.

✔ **Preferences:** Do they like scheduled events? Do they see you only in conjunction with specific holidays? Do they come only for a celebration?

Eventually, you build a picture of your mailing list customers. You can track how long they've been on your list. If they were on your original list, you may like to know that fact eight years down the road. You can also get a sense of how often they visit you.

Ask your customers how they want you to contact them. Typical choices include the following:

✔ Via mail

✔ Via e-mail

✔ Via phone

✔ Don't call me, I'll call you

Although people may be surprised and delighted by a house call from their doctor, they'll be annoyed if their local restaurateur makes a surprise visit. Usually e-mail or snail mail is the way to go.

You can sign people up for your mailing list in many different ways. Here are some ideas:

- ✔ **Web site:** Be sure that your Web site has a place for visitors to sign up for the mailing list.

- ✔ **Comment cards:** Leave a space for customers to include their name and address. Check out Chapter 20 for more info on comment cards.

- ✔ **Mailing list sign-up card:** Customers can fill out this card at the register. It's like a comment card, only without the comments.

- ✔ **Business card drop for a free lunch:** When patrons drop their cards for a drawing for a free lunch, you can add these names to your mailing list.

- ✔ **Customer request by phone or letter:** Some patrons may call or write to ask to be added to the mailing list.

Check your mailing list for duplicate entries to save you some money in mailing costs. You don't want the same person on the list three times.

The people on your mailing list are inviting you to contact them. Don't mess it up. Be courteous and efficient with your communication. And don't forget about them. Use the names you collect to market your business.

Your point-of-sale (POS) company may offer to install some kind of credit card capture and spyware on your system. The basic premise of the software is that by running someone's credit card through your system, you automatically build a database entry for that person, with name, address, and so on, that adds the person to your mailing list. Put yourself in your customer's shoes. If it would violate your privacy to have this information captured about you without your knowledge, you probably don't want to add this functionality to your system. Although this kind of thing happens all the time, as a small business owner, you may not want to feel the wrath of that guest who doesn't appreciate it. Weigh your options carefully.

You can also buy mailing lists from companies that allow you to target a certain demographic group in your area. You can specify income range, geographic location, and so on, and the company provides the information to you for a fee.

# Chapter 20

# Maintaining What You've Created

· · · · · · · · · · · · · · · · · · · · · · · · · · · · · · · · · · · · · · · · · · ·

## In This Chapter

▶ Understanding your restaurant's financial performance

▶ Looking at restaurant-specific factors

▶ Paying attention to feedback

· · · · · · · · · · · · · · · · · · · · · · · · · · · · · · · · · · · · · · · · · · ·

*W*hether you're considering opening a restaurant or you're already up and running, you have to understand how to read the financial numbers to understand how your restaurant's actually doing. If you only watch the money coming in, you may have a very wrong perspective on how successful you truly are (or aren't). Many restaurants bring in lots of money in sales, only to watch it disappear in the bins (waste) or out the back door (theft) before it turns into a profit, while others don't earn the sales they could have had if they had implemented suggestions from their customers and staff.

In this chapter, we help you take a look at your current numbers and work out what they mean. We show you how to listen to suggestions and complaints from all the well-meaning (or bitter) employees, diners, and professionals, in and around your restaurant. And we help you decide how to respond to keep your restaurant running smoothly and profitably.

*Evaluating* your company's financial performance doesn't just mean reading the numbers and looking for changes. Take the next step and find out why numbers are changing, why they match (or don't match) your predictions, and how to get them all going in the right direction.

## Evaluating Financial Performance

Running your business by the numbers is critical. We don't mean for you to throw your common sense out the window. You have to have controls in place, do regular reviews of your numbers, and rely on your brain (and experience if you have some) to dig deeper when the numbers aren't right.

Keep up with your business on a shift-by-shift, daily, weekly, and monthly basis. Don't let the details sneak up and surprise you after it's too late. Don't miss the opportunity to make the corrections. Use the sample worksheets and the figures in this section and throughout the book to keep up with your numbers and the costs they represent.

## Daily business review

Your *daily business review* is a report that you create by recording your sales figures, labour costs, and customer counts (and any other pertinent financial info or business conditions) every day. By recording this info in one place, every day, you build a history of your business that allows you to compare figures across previous days, months, and years to establish patterns and determine whether you've gained or lost ground in individual categories. Graphing this data and cataloguing it over time are essential. You can find a sample in Figure 20-1, but develop your own review that tracks data in the categories important to your particular business.

**Figure 20-1:**
Sample
daily
business
review.

| Daily Business Review<br>Week of | | | | | | | | |
|---|---|---|---|---|---|---|---|---|
| | Monday | Tuesday | Wednesday | Thursday | Friday | Saturday | Sunday | Totals |
| Sales | | | | | | | | |
| Sales | | | | | | | | |
| Food Sales | | | | | | | | |
| Food Sales | | | | | | | | |
| Drink Sales | | | | | | | | |
| Drink Sales | | | | | | | | |
| Labour Cost | | | | | | | | |
| Labour Cost | | | | | | | | |
| Labour % | | | | | | | | |
| Labour % | | | | | | | | |
| Food Cost % | | | | | | | | |
| Food Cost % | | | | | | | | |
| Cover Count | | | | | | | | |
| Cover Count | | | | | | | | |
| Bill Average | | | | | | | | |
| Bill Average | | | | | | | | |
| Food Bill Avg | | | | | | | | |
| Food Bill Avg | | | | | | | | |
| Drink Bill Avg | | | | | | | | |
| Drink Bill Avg | | | | | | | | |
| Food/Drink Mix | | | | | | | | |
| Food/Drink Mix | | | | | | | | |

Your POS (point of sale) system (see Chapter 15) may already have a version of this review built into it. Check your system or check with your salesperson to take advantage of features you may not be using.

Build a history of your business, and you'll benefit in big ways. Here are a few things a daily business review can do for you:

- ✔ Determine whether a current promotional event is affecting your sales compared to last year.

- ✔ Confirm whether your overall volume is increasing over time. Remember, if you want to grow 10 per cent a year, you have to grow 10 per cent a day. (Not literally of course, but you get the picture.)

- ✔ Alert you to the beginning of a problem, but not necessarily what the problem is. For example, you may see that your alcohol sales are down compared to the previous week, but it may not tell you why. You almost always need further investigation to get to the heart of the problem. If you dig deeper into other places, like your logbook, your reservation book, and any other appropriate resources, you discover that you had a large private dinner the previous week that accounts for a jump in your sales last week and now you're actually back to 'normal'.

- ✔ Establish patterns. Over time, you should start to see trends and patterns emerge in your sales figures. For example:

  - Maybe your drinks-to-food mix is dropping on certain nights. Match it up with the staff schedules to see who's working and work out if someone's not selling, or worse.

  - If your labour costs climb because a highly paid sous chef is picking up shifts as a commis chef, talk to the chef about what's up.

  - If your cover count (number of guests in the restaurant for a particular shift) is constant but your bill average plummets, find out whether your chef put a cheap pasta dish as the special.

  - If cover counts remain the same at the bar but your drinks average takes a dip, look for someone giving away free drinks.

## *Income statement*

The *income statement* can also be called a profit and loss (P & L) statement. It summarises your expenses and sales and gives you your bottom line profit for the month. Many restaurants run monthly, quarterly, and annual statements. Some places use abbreviated, concise documents, while others create detailed documents with page after page showing every budget line in a category. For an example, check out the income-statement figure in Chapter 5 for a sample income statement. Use one column of this 6-month statement to get a feel for what your income statement may look like. Again, this statement doesn't diagnose your problems, but it identifies symptoms that can help you discover what the problem is.

The best income statement format provides comparative data in addition to the month's actual data. So, this type of income statement has three columns – the actual numbers, the numbers you projected you'd do, and the historical numbers from the same period last year.

## Cash flow analysis

Keep a constant eye on your *cash flow,* the flow of money coming into (sales) and going out (expenses) of your business. Prepare a report like the one in Chapter 5. Use as many real figures as you can (such as the invoices you know you need to pay next week) and forecast the rest (like what your sales will likely be next weekend) as accurately as possible. A restaurateur must know not only how much money he has at any given time, but also how much he owes (or will owe very soon) in order to stay ahead.

Don't expect to get credit extended to you – especially if you're new to the business. If obtaining credit is tough, keeping control of your cash, receivables, and payables is even more important. Here are some tips:

- ✔ **Weigh the benefits of discounts from suppliers for quick payment versus other uses for the cash.** If you're looking for the money to go out slower than it's coming in, for whatever reason, you may not be able to take advantage of some savings offered by suppliers. Many times you'll get, say, a 5 per cent discount if you pay within 10 days rather than the standard 30 days. But some months require you to hold on to the cash for those extra 20 days instead of taking the discount. Maybe you need to pay your equipment service company for 25 extra hours of labour to repair the cookers. Or maybe you need to upgrade the toilet fixtures.

- ✔ **If your cash flow numbers aren't where you'd like them to be, reducing your stock is a good place to start.** If your money is tied up in extra inventory you don't need, it's not working for you. Keep enough stock to run your business efficiently. Keep the cash flowing your way and pay out as slowly as you can without incurring penalties.

- ✔ **Large parties or banquets can be a boon for your cash flow situation.** If you have to make large, expensive purchases for the party (like cases of champagne or expensive cuts of meat), get at least part of your money in advance. But be careful, if you take money in, say a £5,000 deposit, and count it as a sale two months before the event make sure you spend it on things for the party. Get the money in advance, but use it wisely.

✔ **Beware the danger of tabs.** A *tab* allows individuals or businesses a line of credit and pay it off at regular intervals, such as monthly, instead of paying each time they dine with you. Tabs can go sour quickly, especially as the charges add up. The fact is, in this day of easy plastic money, no one needs a tab. Why wait until the end of the month to get paid (if you get paid at all)? It is advisable not to start tabs for anyone, including staff. If you operate a discount for staff, put it in writing and make them pay when ordering. Your staff may not be taking note of the drinks given to staff or turn a blind eye when others help themselves. Be vigilant.

In Figure 20-2, we map out how your cash flow might look on each day of the month. We use several assumptions (we had to start somewhere), including:

✔ Your sales are constant at £5,000 each day.

✔ Half your diners pay in cash and the other half pay with credit cards.

✔ Your credit card company charges you 3 per cent of the total transaction as a fee. And credit card funds (less the transaction fees) are deposited into your account with a 3-day lag time.

✔ Your operating expenses (includes food costs, labour, and so on) are 88 per cent of sales.

✔ Your rent is £5,000 per month and paid on the 15th of the month.

✔ You're working on a 30-day month.

✔ You pay half of your bills weekly and the other half on the last day of the month.

Your cash flow may look very different depending on things like your sales (which usually fluctuate depending on the day of the week) and your bill payment schedule. But this figure shows you how quickly the money goes even in an efficiently run restaurant.

# Evaluating Operations

*Operational reports* show you other factors that have an impact on your profitability. These reports aren't standard business reports, like the financial reports in the preceding section; instead, they're specific to the restaurant business.

**Understanding Cash Flow**

**Figure 20-2:**
Understanding cash flow on a daily basis.

■ Cash on hand
▨ Expenses paid

## Menu mix analysis

A *menu mix analysis* (like the one in Figure 20-3) is a report used to evaluate the profitability of your menu on an item-by-item basis. It provides data on what's selling (and what's not) and, more importantly, how much money you're making off each item.

**Figure 20-3:**
Example of menu mix analysis.

| Menu Item Name<br><br>Dinner Items | Number Sold | Popularity % | Item Food Cost | Item Sell Price | Item Food Cost % | Item Profit<br><br>*Price-Cost* | Total Cost<br>*Cost x # Sold* | Total Revenue<br>*Price x # Sold* | Total Profit<br>*Revenue -Cost* | Profit Category | Popularity Category | Menu Label |
|---|---|---|---|---|---|---|---|---|---|---|---|---|
| Ribeye | 47 | 15.1% | £4.82 | £18.95 | 25.4% | £14.13 | £226.54 | £ 890.65 | £664.11 | Low | High | **Workhorse** |
| Pasta Marinara | 32 | 10.3% | £1.18 | £9.95 | 11.9% | £ 8.77 | £37.76 | £ 318.40 | £280.64 | Low | High | **Workhorse** |
| Chicken Caesar Salad | 14 | 4.5% | £2.13 | £12.95 | 16.4% | £10.82 | £29.82 | £ 181.30 | £151.48 | Low | Low | **Dog** |
| Roasted Pork Loin | 15 | 4.8% | £3.84 | £18.95 | 20.3% | £15.11 | £57.60 | £ 284.25 | £226.65 | High | Low | **Challenge** |
| Lobster | 15 | 4.8% | £5.84 | £24.95 | 23.4% | £19.11 | £87.60 | £ 374.25 | £286.65 | High | Low | **Challenge** |
| Mixed Grill | 14 | 4.5% | £7.00 | £29.95 | 23.4% | £22.95 | £98.00 | £ 419.30 | £321.30 | High | Low | **Challenge** |
| Grilled Salmon | 23 | 7.4% | £3.25 | £18.95 | 17.2% | £15.70 | £74.75 | £ 435.85 | £361.10 | High | High | **Star** |
| Tiger Prawns | 18 | 5.8% | £6.42 | £24.95 | 25.7% | £18.53 | £115.56 | £ 449.10 | £333.54 | High | Low | **Challenge** |
| Fillet Steak | 46 | 14.8% | £6.58 | £21.95 | 30.0% | £15.37 | £302.68 | £1,009.70 | £707.02 | High | High | **Star** |
| Chicken Risotto | 23 | 7.4% | £3.33 | £17.95 | 18.6% | £14.62 | £76.59 | £ 412.85 | £336.26 | Low | High | **Workhorse** |
| Shrimp Diablo | 26 | 8.4% | £6.42 | £24.95 | 25.7% | £18.53 | £166.92 | £ 648.70 | £481.78 | High | High | **Star** |
| Mozzarella Pizza | 38 | 12.2% | £2.32 | £ 8.95 | 25.9% | £6.63 | £88.16 | £ 340.10 | £251.94 | Low | High | **Workhorse** |
| Total or Overall | 311 | 100% | | | | | £1,361.98 | £5,764.45 | £4,402.47 | | | |
| **Average** | | 8.3% | £4.43 | £19.45 | **20.0%** | £15.02 | | | | | | |

You're looking for your menu to reflect a target overall food cost percentage. (You calculate *food cost percentage* for individual dishes by taking the cost of all the ingredients used to make a dish and dividing it by the menu price.) To come up with the overall percentage, you have to take the overall cost of the food sold and divide it by the overall revenue you received from that food. (Take a look at Chapter 9 if you need more of an explanation on food cost and food cost percentage.)

Use a computer to create your menu mix. Many POS systems come with this functionality. If your system doesn't, create your own by using Excel or another spreadsheet program. Automating this process saves you a lot of time in calculating the figures, leaving you more time to actually analyse them and make changes as appropriate. (Take a look at Chapter 22 for information on where to buy spreadsheets already created for this purpose.)

### *Tracking your menu*

Use your own menu mix analysis (we use the example of Figure 20-3 in our discussion) to answer these questions:

- ✔ **Which items are the most popular?** Our most popular items are our steaks. Both the ribeye and the fillet are best sellers, with 47 and 46, respectively, sold on the night we're looking at.

- ✔ **Which items are bringing in the most revenue?** Notice that it's not usually those that have a low food cost percentage. Pasta marinara has a low food cost percentage but also a comparatively low *profit margin,* or the difference in the cost of the item and its price.

- ✔ **Which items have the highest and lowest profit margins?** Our highest margin item is the mixed grill at $22.95; our lowest is the mozzarella pizza at $6.63.

- ✔ **Are you maximising your sales of your highest profit margin items?** Look at both the cioppino and the mixed grill. They're both high-profit items that are currently low in popularity. Think about ways to improve sales of these items to increase profit. The following are descriptions of the standard menu labels in Figure 20-3:

   - **Star:** Profit is high and popularity is high

   - **Workhorse:** Profit is low and popularity is high

   - **Challenge:** Profit is high and popularity is low

   - **Dog:** Profit is low and popularity is low

   Ultimately, you need to set your own criteria for evaluating your menu mix. Typically, you decide what amount determines high or low profit for your operation. In Figure 20-3, we use the average profit margin of our menu items as the cutoff, £15.02, so anything above £15.02 is considered a high-profit item, and anything below that is a low-profit item.

### *Working with the mix*

Use only similar items when you're comparing them. For example, Figure 20-3 includes only main courses. We don't include desserts, starters, or sandwiches, because not everyone orders one of these items. If you were to evaluate a dinner item compared to a dessert, you'd be comparing apples to oranges (or, more accurately, pasta to cheesecake). Most people who come to your restaurant for dinner will order a main course. Naturally, some people order a starter as a main course, others may split a main course, and someone else wants a sandwich from your lunch menu, but in most cases, they order a main course. After dinner, some guests order desserts, and some don't.

Look at your menu mix over time. Figure 20-3 represents a single dinner shift, but the more info you get over a longer period of time, the more accurately you can view your data. Run menu mixes weekly, monthly, and at intervals that correspond to your business levels. If you have lots of traffic in the summer but not much in the winter, you may run them weekly, monthly, and seasonally. You may see that your summer customers eat very differently than your winter customers, so you may change your menu to match their preferences.

If you're changing your menu quarterly, seasonally, weekly, and so on, save a paper or electronic version of the menu so that you can look back on preparation methods and side dishes. Your POS may just tell you that you sold 18 orders of salmon in a day, but it won't necessarily tell you whether the salmon was grilled, sautéed, or made into a fish pie unless you make each of these separate POS items. This system means more data entry but the informational return will be valuable in evaluating your menu mix. These menu details can complete the picture that your POS starts. Also, save special occasion menus, from holidays such as New Year's Eve, Valentine's Day, and Mother's Day. After you've been in business several years, the holidays blend together, so don't rely on your memory to keep track of it all.

If you run across items that aren't selling, consider the reasons before you decide how to adjust your plan. Here are some questions to get you started:

- **Are you charging too much?** Take a look at Chapter 9 for pricing your menu properly.

- **Is your menu description appealing?** Look at Chapter 9 for tips on making dishes sound like they're worth every penny and more. But don't over-ice the cake by adding too much description. And be aware of hyping up your dishes and selling people short of their expectations.

- **Is the item ideally placed on the menu?** Chapter 9 gives you tips and tricks for placing your high-margin items where diners look most often.

- **Is the item intimidating to your diners?** Pushing the limits is okay if you have a core group of more-adventurous diners. Just keep in mind that the less well-known items may take longer to catch on. Make sure you have the cash reserves to wait it out until they take off.

✔ **Is your staff educated about the item?** Maybe you can do additional training with your staff about these high-margin items, and create an incentive programme to sell them.

At times, raising the price of an item can actually improve its sales. You could cross a price barrier in the consumer's mind (some people won't pay more than £19.95), or you may create prestige and a market for the item (while others won't consider choosing something that isn't over the £20 mark). A price increase is also an incentive for waiting staff that likes to encourage diners to choose higher quality (or additional) menu items. Check out Chapter 9 for info on pricing your menu right the first time.

## Purchasing and inventory analysis

The true test of any purchasing and inventory programme is in how well it performs in the real world and brings you closer to your goal of profitability. You may be purchasing right and pricing your menu right, only to be giving food away because it's not prepared right, ends up in the bin, or walks out the back door. Use a cost of goods sold (COGS) report (see Figure 20-4) to help you figure out how your hard work in this area is really measuring up. In a nutshell, a COGS report measures your true and actual food cost percentage. It won't tell you why the number is too high or too low. You'll definitely need to dig deeper if it doesn't match your expectations.

While you almost always write 'COGS', you never say 'cogs'; instead you always say, 'cost of goods sold'.

|  | Beginning Inventory (A) | Purchases (B) | Ending Inventory (C) | Sales (D) | COGS |
|---|---|---|---|---|---|
| Food | £2,800.00 | £8,700.00 | £2,700.00 | £29,678.00 | 29.65% |
| Liquor | 1,345.00 | 750.00 | 1,296.00 | 4,120.00 | 19.39% |
| Beer | 895.00 | 300.00 | 910.00 | 2,700.00 | 10.56% |
| Wine | 3,200.00 | 350.00 | 2,100.00 | 6,800.00 | 21.32% |
|  |  |  |  |  |  |
| Total | £8,240.00 | £10,100.00 | £7,006.00 | £43,298.00 | 26.18% |

**Figure 20-4:** Sample cost of goods sold (COGS).

To calculate your COGS:

1. **Work out the cost of buying your beginning stock (A).**

2. **Tally your invoices for the products you purchased during the time period you're reporting on (B).**

   Create an *invoice log* to track your invoices and assign the invoices to categories that mirror your COGS categories.

3. **Figure out your ending inventory (C).**

4. **Add your beginning inventory and your purchases (A+B) and subtract your ending inventory from your invoices (A+B-C).**

5. **Divide that total by your sales (D), so [(A+B-C)/D] to get your COGS.**

The more categorised your data is, the more easily you can spot problems, but the tougher it is to get an overall picture. Figure out what's best for your business. You may decide that you want all alcoholic beverages to be included in a single category, rather than in three categories, as in Figure 20-4. Most restaurants count nonalcoholic drinks, like tea, coffee, and soft drinks, in their food costs rather than in their beverage costs. But some restaurants count bottled water, juices, and so on with the beverage or bar costs because these items are often kept in the alcohol storage area. There's no right way to count them, but be consistent no matter how you categorise. Mark the invoice for the item in the same category that you mark the sale.

# *Evaluating and Using Feedback*

Feedback is a blessing and a curse. Every operation must continue to innovate or die, and some of the greatest opportunities for innovation come from feedback. Your employees and your customers are sources of feedback, both positive and negative. But working out what to do with the information you receive isn't always easy. Sometimes, the feedback represents a preference and doesn't really shine light on an actual problem. You have to decide how to sort through all the info and react appropriately.

If you're asking for feedback but you don't act upon it, people can resent it. They may feel that you aren't listening or don't care about their point of view. If at all possible, follow up with them and let them know that you considered their point of view and chose a different path. Choosing to make a different decision is way better than appearing to ignore your employees or customers. If you know that a recommendation won't work, let them know, gently, during the same conversation. You may say something like, 'I agree. The doorframe would look better if it was black. Unfortunately, our landlord requires all the tenants in this building to keep them white gloss'.

# *Paying attention to customer feedback*

Customers provide feedback in all kinds of ways, some formal and some not so formal. Seek out every opportunity you can to get their feedback because, ultimately, their collective opinion matters. Your customers make the final decision on the success of your business.

### *Table talk*

Visit guest tables informally as often as you can. Many guests won't stop you to let you know about something, but if you stop by their table, they may spew a fountain of feedback that you never anticipated. But don't be a pain by being intrusive. After all, they have come to spend time together. Judge carefully who you talk to and who you don't.

Table chats are also a great way to get positive information. Too often, you're called to a table by a frazzled waiter or, even worse, an angry guest. Improve your odds by visiting tables of happy, smiling guests as well. Give your business cards to happy people, who then can tell their friends they 'know' the manager. (See Chapter 19 for more details on building your clientele.) Here are some tips for reading between the lines when you talk to tables:

- ✔ **Find ways to bring yourself into a conversation.** Pour a wine refill if you're passing by and ask how they like their food.

  Watch for signals that indicate a table doesn't want any attention, and then don't bother those diners. Avoid tables where you notice private conversations (people talking quietly with their heads close together) or obvious signs of emotion – crying qualifies.

- ✔ **Keep the tone of your questions positive or at least neutral.** Ask, 'Are you enjoying the sea bass from Cornwall?' or 'How is your fillet?' not 'Is everything okay?' The word *okay* isn't positive in this business. It's never a goal and shouldn't be an acceptable standard.

- ✔ **Ask open-ended, rather than yes/no questions.** You're more likely to get helpful feedback rather than a polite, 'Yes, thanks'.

- ✔ **Be specific.** Know your menu well enough to recognise it half-eaten on a plate. People are impressed when you can ask, 'How's your roast halibut tonight?' instead of 'How's the fish?' Adding extra touches to the conversation helps: 'The pancetta and oyster sauce is the head chef's new one. I had it at lunch today and I think he's on to a winner'.

  If you don't know what guests are eating, don't guess. Confusing two main courses or any other dish can be embarrassing to you.

- ✔ **Remember names and faces.** Remembering regular customers can help build a rapport that can lead to some excellent specific feedback.

### Comment cards

We recommend that you use some form of comment card in your operation as a feedback tool. Figure 20-5 shows a sample comment card. Your comment card may be longer or shorter than the sample shown, depending on what you want to know about your guests' experience. You may prefer to have just general categories (food, service, atmosphere, and so on) rather than specific questions related to each category. Some restaurants add a space for the diner to compare them to other similar restaurants.

Strike a balance between asking every possible thing you want to know and not getting specific, helpful info. This approach works for a couple reasons. People won't fill out a comment card if it's too long. If people do fill it out, they may just be going through the motions rather than providing good, relevant feedback. (For help with dealing with customer complaints, take a look at Chapter 19.)

---

**Guest Comment Card**

Thank you for choosing us. We value your feedback on our service, food and dining with us. Please hand this card to one of the staff.

**Please circle your rating on a scale of 1-10, 1 being the lowest, and 10 being the highest.**

**1. Reception**

| | |
|---|---|
| Courtesy & friendliness of staff at entrance | 1 2 3 4 5 6 7 8 9 10 |
| Waiting time | 1 2 3 4 5 6 7 8 9 10 |
| Service of bar staff | 1 2 3 4 5 6 7 8 9 10 |
| Overall Impression | 1 2 3 4 5 6 7 8 9 10 |

**2. Waiting staff**

| | |
|---|---|
| Courtesy | 1 2 3 4 5 6 7 8 9 10 |
| Speed | 1 2 3 4 5 6 7 8 9 10 |
| Attentiveness | 1 2 3 4 5 6 7 8 9 10 |
| Product Knowledge | 1 2 3 4 5 6 7 8 9 10 |
| Overall Impression | 1 2 3 4 5 6 7 8 9 10 |

**3. Food**

| | |
|---|---|
| Presentation | 1 2 3 4 5 6 7 8 9 10 |
| Temperature | 1 2 3 4 5 6 7 8 9 10 |
| Taste | 1 2 3 4 5 6 7 8 9 10 |
| Overall Impression | 1 2 3 4 5 6 7 8 9 10 |

**4. Overall Dining Experience** 1 2 3 4 5 6 7 8 9 10

_____
_____
_____
_____
_____
_____
_____

**5. How often do you frequent our restaurant?**

First time ☐ 1-4 times a year ☐ monthly ☐ more often ☐

**6. What did you like best about our restaurant?**

_____
_____

**7. Was there anything you didn't like?**

_____
_____

**8. What could we do to make your dining experience better?**

_____
_____

Date _____ Number in Party _____

Occasion _____
(business, entertaining, celebration, etc.)

Your Name _____

Address _____

City _____ County _____ Postcode _____

Telephone _____

Email address _____

Would you like to be on our mailing list? ☐ Yes ☐ No

**Figure 20-5:** Sample comment card.

Don't get so desensitised to the feedback that you ignore people who are sincerely alerting you to an existing problem. Most people aren't trying to gouge you, take advantage of you, or get free stuff. Keep your cynicism in check. Look at each complaint independently and weigh its merits before dismissing it or acting on it.

## Responding to professional criticism and praise

Professional criticism takes many forms, ranging from the local paper's restaurant critic to the colleague sitting next to you at a trade-show conference. You have to grow a thick skin to weather the constant commentary on your business, your lifeblood, your baby.

Take all reviews and criticism with a grain of salt. If a critic praises you, treat it as reinforcement for doing things the right way. If the review is negative, evaluate it and formulate your reaction. But know that if the criticism is public, like a review, others will read it or hear it and form their own opinions. It can mean an increase or a decrease in sales.

As hard as it may be, don't react emotionally if you receive a negative review. Investigate the details in the review objectively, to see if the criticism is valid. Use it as an opportunity to re-evaluate your concept, menu, and processes. And you can always use it as a reason to rally the troops.

The best way to get a good review is to run your business the right way, every day. Sure, if you recognise a food writer, you can go out of your way to treat her well. You may be able to pick a reviewer out if her table orders more food than a party of her size might typically eat, but they often bring in guests as a cover. If you can pick out reviewers, you can do your very best and hope for a good review. But if you don't demand excellence every day in every way, your wave of success will be short lived. If you treat every diner with the same courtesy you show a restaurant critic, you're sure to get a good review.

If you're lucky enough to get a good review, don't put everything on autopilot. Keep doing what got you there. A good review usually means an increase in business. Exceed the new diners' expectations because the bar will be set high.

You have to take advantage of. this big opportunity. Some restaurateurs try to make the money while they're riding the wave by increasing the prices. This approach is strictly a matter of personal choice and management style. If your concept is based on a value-oriented promise, you may not want to increase prices. Instead, you may want to find a way to increase the number of diners you can seat. If exclusivity is essential to your concept, however, increasing prices may be just the thing to do to capitalise on your newfound fame. But don't think it will go unnoticed by your regular customers. Don't alienate them by pricing them out of the market. After all, they are your core clientele whom you attracted in the first place, whereas these new customers could perhaps be fly-by-nights.

Make the most of any industry awards and distinctions – local or national – that you, your restaurant, or your employees receive. If your restaurant gets the vote for the 'Best Fish Restaurant in the South-East', let everyone know about it. If you win a top award from *Decanter* magazine, capitalise on it. Use any public praise or honours as an opportunity to praise yourself and your staff. Include newspaper and magazine clippings in your PR and advertising campaigns (see Chapter 16). Incorporate them into your décor by framing the actual awards and displaying them for diners to see. Tastefully using this info somewhere on your menu or at your entrance (to give a potential patron that little extra nudge) is also a good idea.

## Listening to employee feedback

Talk to your staff at all levels to get feedback. Find opportunities to regularly have one-to-one talks with all your staff. Use formal and informal opportunities to get the word on what's really going on from your employees' standpoint. Keep communication flowing through all the departments in your organisation. Solutions sometimes come from unlikely places. Here are some ways to find out what's going on:

- Use the manager's logbook to communicate problems with service, food, or employees. The more people who know what's going on, the more likely it is that you'll be able to establish patterns and fix the problem. If you notice that waiter Jim constantly serves cold food but no one else does, maybe the problem is really with Jim rather than the kitchen. Maybe he's ordering incorrectly or not serving his food in a timely way.

- Schedule regular staff meetings for the entire staff and departmental meetings as well. You may find that you get very different feedback at each meeting.

- Get a suggestion box. Some employees won't speak up in meetings or come to you directly with a suggestion. The anonymity of the suggestion box can be just the way to pull that next great idea out of them.

Your employees provide customer feedback that's somewhat filtered. It may not be the same information you'd get straight from the customers themselves. An employee, intentionally or not, puts his own spin on the situation and may offer solutions. It's up to you to decide what problems to respond to. If you're talking to different people and you're hearing the same things repeated, consider employees' input.

# Part V
# The Part of Tens

'That was the best omelette I've ever had
in my life — my compliments to the chef.'

## In this part . . .

1t wouldn't be a *For Dummies* book without a Part of Tens. Our take on this part includes ten myths about running a restaurant, resources for restaurant managers and owners, and our favourite stories that provide some insight into the strange world of restaurants.

# Chapter 21

# Ten Myths about Running a Restaurant

. . . . . . . . . . . . . . . . . . . . . . . . . . . . . . . . . . . . . . . . . . . . . . . . . .

*In This Chapter*

▶ Looking behind the scenes

▶ Setting clear expectations for what lies ahead

. . . . . . . . . . . . . . . . . . . . . . . . . . . . . . . . . . . . . . . . . . . . . . . . . .

*O*ne of the biggest reasons people don't stay in the restaurant business is that they don't have realistic expectations of what the job is really like. (The other negatives are that it's really exhausting, time consuming, unappreciated . . . but we digress.) In this chapter, we dispel some of the most common myths while keeping our fingers crossed that we don't scare you away.

## Running a Restaurant Is Easy

The restaurant business captivates and intrigues people. People think it's glamorous and exciting. Customers see you working where they play and assume that it's one big party after another. What these starry-eyed, would-be restaurateurs don't see is what goes on behind the scenes, *each* and *every* day.

A typical chef's or restaurant manager's morning (we're talking before 11 a.m. here) might include all these activities: Getting in at 5 a.m. to inspect and accept deliveries. Starting soups and sauces at 6 a.m. Calling in last-minute orders for tonight's party of 50 that booked yesterday evening. Calling the equipment service technician about the steamer that broke down in the middle of last night's shift. Creating a prep list. Supervising the staff. Finding replacement staff to fill in for late employees, those who rang in sick, and no-shows. Ensuring that the dining room is ready to go before the restaurant opens. Performing a line check to confirm that all food is ready to go before the restaurant opens. Creating specials, such as a soup of the day and what to do with the extra cod to make it a special. Fending off the persistent salesperson who has to talk to you this minute about the new must-have lighting system.

That's quite a to-do list to complete before 11 a.m. But that's not all: Then you handle paperwork about sales, forecast revenue, and pay bills. If the accountant wants to know where you got a case of vodka that's missing from the inventory list, you have to be able to produce the receipt. If the health department is investigating a foodborne illness outbreak related to oysters, you better have traceability for your shellfish on file. If the job centre needs confirmation that an employee quit and wasn't sacked, you need accurate employee files.

If you're building a new business or want to move beyond maintaining an existing one, you spend even more time developing marketing and PR strategies, looking for the best deals from your vendors while preserving the quality of your products, and recruiting a top-notch staff.

If you eat out a lot because you don't like cooking at home, how happy are you going to be creating meals for other people every day, holidays and weekends included, for 14 hours a day? You're at the restaurant before opening *and* after closing. The real world opens, closes, and has a life – all within the hours that make up your workday. Running a restaurant is easy if you do it only one day. Talk to us on day 2, 3, or 1,753.

# I'll Have a Place to Hang Out

Lots of people use this myth as one of the top reasons they should start a restaurant. They picture themselves hanging out and chatting with people at the bar or walking through a kitchen a-buzz with chefs. They imagine getting paid while watching the football in a pub full of their friends. Whatever the specifics of your vision, if you're looking to own a place where you can hang out, you better be willing to pay other people to do the hard work.

It's essential for anyone running a restaurant, either as the owner, chef, or manager, to be in the restaurant and watch what's actually happening. If you're hanging out, you're not seeing what's going on in the supply room, at table 42, or out in the car park. Plus, hanging out socially in the restaurant can be a drain on your finances, especially if you're buying the drinks.

Note the big difference between being friendly with your staff and being friends with your staff. If you're hanging out in the bar with your staff, you're in the danger zone. Ultimately, if you're drinking socially, instead of just testing a wine or having an occasional beer with a regular customer, in your place of business, you're taking a risk. Odds are, eventually, you're going to make a fool of yourself. Whether you believe it now or not, your casualness will change the way employees look at you and respect you.

# I Can Trust My Brother-in-Law

This dilemma – deciding whether to include relatives in your business – isn't unique to the restaurant business. Our general advice is 'Don't get involved in business with your family, because it's hard to get out of business with your family'. Some companies may implement rules against hiring family members because it creates unnecessary complications.

If, for whatever reason, you absolutely, positively must hire your brother-in-law, sister, cousin, or anyone else who shares your family tree, use these tips to minimise miscommunication:

- ✔ **Be very clear about his responsibilities.** Somehow, by virtue of genetic or marital ties, people get strange ideas about what decision-making powers they have and what rights and privileges they enjoy. If they're not partners in your business, explicitly tell them so.

- ✔ **Treat a family member as you would any other employee.** Don't be overly critical or more lenient with them. Watch out for the ' boss's kid' mentality, even though everything they do is a reflection on you. Your staff is always watching, and they do compare notes.

- ✔ **Explicitly go over your expectations with him, especially detailing rules about cash-handling and inventory procedures.** When you mix money with family, people justify a lot, including helping themselves to loans, a case of wine, or a bottle of olive oil. Make sure that family members understand what is acceptable and what isn't. Family members often need even more info about the rules. Also, make sure that the details of his compensation are detailed and clearly defined so that he's not tempted to take liberties he's not entitled to.

Never use family labour as an assumed safety net. If you think that your family will always be available to pitch in at a moment's notice, they may have other ideas on the subject. And don't assume that your kids have a burning desire to follow in your footsteps. Make sure that they share your goals. Your family and your business will suffer if you force family members to give up their own dreams just to keep the family business going.

# The Neighbours Will Love Me

For reasons that you may never know, your neighbours may have preconceived ideas of what you and your business are like. They may have had a bad experience with your predecessor. Maybe it was a noisy bar, or maybe the previous tenant didn't maintain the exterior as they should have.

You can't kill yourself in order to make your neighbours like you. You can, however, be a responsible part of the business community and hope that they return the attitude. Be sensitive about the upkeep in your area, including any common areas you share with other tenants. Let them know about special events that may cause extra noise and traffic, and invite them. If the guy who runs the dry cleaning shop next door is a huge football fan, and, a famous footballer is going to be in for a charity dinner, let him know and invite him to the dinner.

Cultivate friendly relationships with your local police officers and traffic wardens. They're part of the larger community, as well as prospective customers. They usually can't take free food, so don't embarrass them by offering it to them as it may be seen as a bribe, but you could offer a cup of coffee on a cold day or a bottle of water on a hot day. Get to know your area. Many restaurants become sort of a service for diners who want info on local bookstores, cinemas, hot nightspots, and so on. But temper your neighbourliness with good old-fashioned self-interest. If neighbours are looking for a good chef and you have one, don't send them elsewhere.

# I've Been to Catering College, So I'm Ready to Run the Show

Attending catering college is a great head start, but it's just that – a start. You may have had work experience in tandem with your college education but it doesn't mean you know everything. Graduating from catering college is the beginning of your career, not a shortcut. Most students fresh out of college have never hired or fired employees, negotiated with salespeople, placed orders, dealt with local authorities or repaired equipment in the middle of a shift. You don't learn to deal with the controlled chaos of a restaurant in a classroom, not even one that looks like a restaurant.

Attaining the title of chef is akin to becoming a general. You have to live through the battles, suffer losses, and come out on the other side. You have to show fortitude and put in your time. Be patient. When the time comes to assume the mantle of head chef, you'll appreciate it much more. After all, the word *brigade*, used to describe your kitchen staff, comes from the Italian *brigata*, a military term meaning a company or crew. The verb the word comes from is *brigare*, 'to brawl, wrangle, or fight.' But don't let the crew take it too literally!

# I'm Going to Be a Celebrity Chef

The popular media has elevated many restaurant chefs to celebrity status. The work of celebrity chefs has gone a long way to shaping the culinary scene in this country and in the rest of the world. Having talked to many of these chefs, we've found that they think the idea of newfound fame is humorous, in the sense that for years they slaved over a stove for a living. Their careers haven't been all book signings, TV shows, and speaking engagements. People don't see the gruelling hours they've spent cleaning grease traps, being screamed at by pan-wielding temperamental chefs, and mopping the floor. These celebrities didn't attain their status overnight.

Many of these chefs have built wildly successful restaurants and spent thousands of pounds on public relations, agents, and sometimes specialised training just to get their first shot as a media personality. All this media attention takes time away from their restaurants, which sometimes suffer from the celebrity chefs' lack of presence on the scene. On the flip side, many great chefs aren't interested in being media chefs, but that fact doesn't diminish their influence, impact, talent, or passion for their true calling: being a chef first and foremost.

# My Thai-spiced Fishcakes Sing, So I Should Open a Place

Just because you're good at making Thai fishcakes (or anything else, for that matter) for two, four, or six people as a hobby, don't assume that you can turn it into a job. Running a restaurant is so much more than cooking well. It involves being a salesperson, host, buyer, human resources manager, accountant, and efficiency expert all rolled into one. And few places succeed based on the power of a single dish, so it's a little risky to put all your beans on a single plate of fishcakes (they wouldn't really go with them, anyway . . .). But with this warning in mind, remember that all is not lost for your dream of opening that little Thai café. Coffee bars, ice cream parlours, and sandwich bars can all do well, especially with a large population to draw from. Variety isn't always the spice of life. You may get lucky.

# I Can Cut the Advertising Budget

In any business when sales are down, owners and managers naturally begin looking at places to cut the budget. All too often the advertising and marketing budgets are among the first to be cut. Assuming that your advertising is effective, cutting it *will* matter. When sales are down, you need more people coming in the door, and you need the people who are coming in the door to spend more money. Effective advertising can accomplish this goal and more than pay for itself.

Instead of cutting your marketing budget, evaluate how you're currently spending your money and what you're getting in return. If you're placing ads in local publications, review your ad placement. Maybe you should actually spend a bit more and go for the back cover so that more people see it. Evaluate how well the actual ad attracts the customers you're seeking.

# Wraps Are Here to Stay

Trends, by definition, don't last. They're white-hot ideas, that capture the public's interest and then fad . . . er, we mean fade, into the distance. Think wraps, frozen yogurt, over-oaked chardonnay and the £20 hamburger. All still have their place in the hearts of the dining public (maybe not the £20 burger), but they've settled into their proper places on menus everywhere. Wraps gave way to bowls. That oaky chardonnay at best shares the stage with pinot grigio, sauvignon blanc, pinot noir, and shiraz. The list goes on. Don't invest yourself too much in the food equivalent of a 'one-hit wonder'. It's great to get in at the beginning and ride the wave of a trend, but maintain your flexibility and be ready with Plan B when the bottom falls out – because it will.

# I'll Be Home for the Holidays

Home is where the restaurant is. It's a myth that you'll be home for many, if any, of your family's special occasions – not to mention weekends or Tuesday night dinner. You can always find exceptions, like a restaurant located in a business district without much traffic on weekends or holidays. But usually, when people are celebrating special occasions, they often turn to restaurants. So guess where you'll be? You guessed it: working.

Many restaurants, especially those close to retail areas, rely on the weeks running up to Christmas and New Year's Day to turn in their biggest revenue. So if your wife's birthday falls on December 15, you can pretty much forget about taking the day off. You'll probably be working a banquet, catering for an office party, or trying to keep the kitchen from imploding.

As this is the time to make some good money to offset against quiet times in January and February, you'll be taking advantage of the season and working all the days – and nights – you are open. So grin and bear it – make it up to your family at another time of the year.

# Chapter 22

# Ten Sources of Info for Restaurateurs

## In This Chapter

▶ Reviewing a few time-tested titles

▶ Managing magazine subscriptions

▶ Plugging into the power of the Internet

*E*ven though our goal is to present you with a highly readable, very thorough, and (dare we hope) entertaining guide to running a restaurant, we're realists. We can't answer every question in one book, so this chapter provides you with some of the resources we've used at one point or another along the way.

We find inspiration and ideas in just about every cookbook we pick up. The list would get out of control quickly if we listed even just our favourites. Our advice: Read lots and read often. But don't feel like you have to increase your book budget initially. Check out your local library for cookbooks on virtually every style of cuisine and country. After you find your favourites that you go back to again and again, get your own copy for the restaurant.

In addition to reading the business-specific resources in this chapter, keep in touch with what your diners are reading, seeing, and hearing. Don't forget to check out the dining section of your local paper, and the consumer foodie magazines listed later in this chapter.

## Keeping Your Own Logbook

There's no better resource (save one: your customer) than your own personal history and experience with your restaurant. Keep a logbook and update it daily, or even multiple times each day. *The Manager's Red Book* is the industry standard for keeping track of everything – the weather, maintenance and repairs, summaries of guest complaints, ordering notes, and anything else you need to remember for the future. Things change fast, blend together, and are tough to keep track of. The more detailed you can be, the better the resource you build for you, your managers, and the future of your business. Red Book Solutions (www.redbooksolutions.com) also has books such as the *Kitchen Red Book* that brings order, organisation and communication together, but because it is originally an American publication, you may have to change or adapt certain terminology for the British market. The company can custom build the books, which also include the Inspection Red Book for food safety and others.

# *Checking Out a Few Food Books*

By buying the book you're holding now, you've taken a great first step on the road to restaurant management. Here are a few more references in specific areas of the business that can help you make your goal of running a successful, profitable restaurant a reality.

Visit or look at the Web site of 'Books for Cooks' (www.booksforcooks.com), a tiny shop in Notting Hill Gate, which is home to over 8,000 publications that include recipe books plus historical, sociological, nutritional and other types of books on the art of cookery. Known as 'the best smelling shop in the world', due to its small kitchen which tests and develops new recipes, it is possible to eat here too or to see chefs in action.

*The Oxford Companion to Food* by Alan Davidson (Oxford University Press), edited by Tom Jaine, took over 20 years to assemble. The author has brought together no less than 2,650 entries. This 900-plus page book covers every conceivable food item plus cooking methods, history, and significant people in the cookery world and is an outstanding culinary reference and must-have classic.

*The Larousse Gastronomique* by Prosper Montagne (Clarkson Potter) is the definitive reference book for chefs and those interested in good food and cooking. A translated version, it covers world cuisine with, naturally, an emphasis on French cooking.

*On Food and Cooking: The Science and the Lore of the Kitchen* by Harold McGee (Simon & Schuster). This masterpiece combines science, history, gastronomy, and other associated subjects and explains them clearly in the author's own unique style. This bible of food science helped start Heston Blumenthal on his quest for innovative food at the three Michelin starred Fat Duck in Berkshire.

*The New Food Lover's Companion* by Sharon Tyler Herbst (Barron's Educational Series) is the essential guide to 6,000 culinary and dining terms. This resource is a must-have for any culinary or hospitality professional. It gives you easy-to-understand definitions and descriptions of ingredients, techniques, and other food and dining terms. This reference book can help you add pizzazz to your menu, by exploring ingredients you may not be familiar with and by adding dimension to your descriptions of your already-present menu items, without feeling it in your food cost percentage. See Chapter 9 for more details on writing and developing your menu.

# Imbibing Books About Booze

If you're brand-new to the world of wine, *Wine For Dummies,* 3rd Edition, by Ed McCarthy and Mary Ewing-Mulligan (published by Wiley) is a great place to get your passport. It gives you practical information about wine terms, appellations, and vintages. It also gives you essential tips on buying, tasting, ordering, and storing wine. Depending on your experience, your concept, and your goals, this may not be your only wine book, but it should definitely be your first.

Containing nearly 1,000 drink recipes, *Bartending For Dummies,* 2nd Edition, by Ray Foley (published by Wiley) definitely belongs in your restaurant library. Other books that you may want to include are *The Joy of Mixology* by Gary Regan (Clarkson Potter), and *The Bartender's Black Book* by Stephen Kittredge Cunningham (Wine Appreciation Guild). Depending on your clientele, your concept, and so on, you may also want to invest in a specialised book or two. You can find books on scotch, bourbon, and other spirits, as well as titles dedicated to making the best martini or the perfect margarita. Chances are if you specialise in it, someone's written a book that can help.

*The World Atlas of Wine* by Hugh Johnson and Jancis Robinson (Mitchell Beazley). This authoritative book by two of Britain's most respected wine writers covers history, wine-making, storage and enjoyment of wines from all over the world. Regional maps make this beautifully organised book an indispensable resource for anyone who wants to get to grips with this wide subject.

# Finding Out the Fundamentals On Front-of-the-House

*Service That Sells! The Art of Profitable Hospitality* by Phil Roberts (Pencom) is essential reading for anyone who works in the front of the house. Managers, waiting staff, and bar staff can benefit from reading this book. It gives concrete tips for maximising your sales with every guest that walks through the door, which is essential for every profitable restaurant. Get several copies to loan out, or make it part of your new-hire package. The investment will pay for itself in almost no time.

# Consulting Caterer and Hotelkeeper

One magazine which is a must in the trade is *Caterer and Hotelkeeper*. This weekly magazine is essential reading for those in the hospitality industry. It has features, recipes, new product information, business and people profiles including ones on fledgling restaurants and hotels. The magazine also organises a yearly Chef Conference.

# Riffling through Restaurant

Also, have a look at *Restaurant*. Published by William Reed, *Restaurant* is the UK's only magazine for and about the restaurant industry. Published every fortnight, its strapline 'for the professional and the passionate' indicates its appeal not only to those operating within the business, but also restaurant lovers who like to keep abreast of all the news and latest ideas and developments within this constantly changing field.

On *Restaurant*'s site (`www.restaurantmagazine.co.uk`) you will find regular updates from Restaurant magazine, including latest news, a summary of features from the current issue and examples from our extensive photo archive.

You can buy *Restaurant* magazine in some newsagents, but your best bet is to save your shoe leather and invest in a subscription. You can find details of *Restaurant* magazine subscription prices, offers and payment options on the website.

# Checking Out Other Trade Magazines

You may qualify for free subscriptions to some magazines. Some publishers may offer free subscriptions to restaurant industry professionals. Contact them to see if you qualify. Although publishers have the final say on who gets their freebies, they want as many people to have their magazines as possible. Your odds of qualifying are better if you're involved in purchasing decisions at the restaurant.

The great thing about magazines is that most also have Web sites. Even if you can't get a free sub to the printed magazine, many Web sites have free newsletters. Sign up for several freebies and then decide which ones work best for your business.

Like restaurateurs, magazines cater to those who pay the bills – in their case the customer and the advertiser. So take the views and information they present with a grain of sea salt.

# Getting to Know The British Hospitality Association

The British Hospitality Association (BHA) has the Restaurant Association (RA) within its portfolio. For almost 40 years the RA has represented the interests of restaurateurs. Today, with a membership of over 11,500 independent and group restaurants, and as part of the British Hospitality Association it is the foremost organisation in the industry, The Restaurant Association works to protect and enhance the interests of its members, represent the views of members to Government, decision makers, and the media, and to provide professional guidance, cost savings, and essential information to members.

The BHA Web site (www.bha.org.uk) provides a comprehensive range of helplines, publicity, publications and business, sporting and social events. The organisation also provides a full range of advisory and business services and benefits to help members operate their businesses more professionally and profitably, and provide them with essential information through surveys, publications, helplines and general advice.

# Small Business Web Sites

There are many business organisations out there to help the businessman or businesswoman. The ones to search out include

- Business Link (www.businesslink.gov.uk)
- British Chamber of Commerce (www.britishchambers.org.uk)
- The Enterprise Centre (www.enterprise-centre.co.uk)
- The Federation of Small Businesses (www.fsb.org.uk)
- Startups.co.uk (www.startups.co.uk)

All these sites have information on starting, financing, and managing your business with many useful leaflets and publications. You can either contact them to ask advice via email or to download useful advice or some offer free face-to-face advice and information. There are free workshops to consider, seminars on taxation, marketing and bookkeeping and other useful help.

# *Recipe Web Sites*

You'll find a wealth of recipes if you log onto any of the following Web sites:

- ✔ Waitrose Food Illustrated (`www.waitrose.com/inspiration/wfi.aspx`)
- ✔ UKTV Food channel (`uktv.co.uk/food/homepage/sid/566`)
- ✔ The BBC food Web site (`www.bbc.co.uk/food`)
- ✔ *Olive* magazine (`www.olivemagazine.co.uk`)

# Chapter 23

# Ten True Restaurant Stories You Just Couldn't Make Up

. . . . . . . . . . . . . . . . . . . . . . . . . . . . . . . . . . . . . . . . . . . .

## In This Chapter

▶ Keeping your sense of humour no matter what

▶ Recognising you're not in it alone

▶ Finding creative solutions to customer-service situations

. . . . . . . . . . . . . . . . . . . . . . . . . . . . . . . . . . . . . . . . . . . .

*T*he restaurant business has no shortage of colourful characters. Whether it's customers, staff, suppliers, or colleagues, if you look around you can always find something to smile about. Here are a few of our favorites.

## Déjà vu All Over Again

A man called a restaurant and said to the manager, 'I'd like to confirm a reservation that was never made.' The manager repeated what the caller had said, just to make sure he had heard it correctly. 'That's right,' the man said. 'I have a party of ten people coming in tonight at 7:30.' The manager said, 'We'd love to have you, but we can't guarantee that we can take ten of you at that time tonight.' The man said, 'You have to. I'm confirming it.' The manager said, 'But you never made the reservation.' The man said, 'That's what I'm doing now, confirming my reservation that wasn't made.' The manager worked him in later that night, fairly close to 7:30.

## The Eyes Have It

It was a really cold Sunday night. A gregarious man with bottle-bottom glasses was chatting people up and buying them drinks. The manager was in the bar for a while but went to the office to start closing procedures. He was a little wary of the customer, but he wasn't sure why. A short time later, the barman called the office to ask the manager if he'd allow the customer to pay with a cheque. The bartender said, 'I know it's not right, but his girlfriend's got his wallet and she's out shopping. He's got no ID, just a business card.' The manager came out to the bar to discuss the situation with the customer.

The customer informed the manager that he could 'buy and sell this place', that he had an American Express Platinum card. The manager, having some experience with credit cards said to the customer, 'I know Amex will let you get an authorisation over the phone if you give them the right answers to the security questions. Let's call them'. The manager and customer ran the gamut of credit-card companies with no luck. The customer ran through the list of things he could leave as collateral, all virtually worthless.

The manager called the police to help mediate. The police talked with the manager to get his input on how he wanted to handle the situation. The manager said, 'I want some kind of insurance that he's coming back to pay this tab. I want his glasses and his coat'. One policeman said, 'It's below zero! You're sending this bloke out without a coat?' The other policeman said, 'Forget that! Take his shoes, socks, and underwear, too!' The manager was satisfied with just the extra-thick glasses, the coat, and a worthless watch. The customer left the cheque, which turned out to be a forged business one that he had stolen from his employer. The cheque bounced.

# Pie in the Sky

A man walked into a restaurant and helped himself to a piece of pie. The manager politely stopped the 'customer' to ask what was up. The 'customer' said, 'I came for my free pie. The waitress told me to come back for a piece of pie whenever I want, because mine was bad last time. You owe me a piece of pie'. The manager said, 'what was her name? What did she look like?' The 'customer' said, 'I don't know. She was old.' The manager said, 'Do you have any more info, a card, something in writing from her? Can you give me a better description?' The customer said, 'She had grey hair, I think.' That cleared it right up.

Dealing with any customer-service issues on the spot is usually best. If you decide to 'make it right' on the diner's next visit, make sure to give him a signed business card (preferably yours) detailing the specifics of your offer.

# I'll Get My Coat . . .

A man walked up to a restaurant manager and proclaimed, 'My coat's been stolen. My wallet, passport, everything was in it'. The manager headed to the cloakroom to confer with the staff member. The customer stopped him and said, 'No, I hung it over there'. The manager looked where the customer was pointing and saw the hooks by the counter-service area under a big sign that read, 'Leave it at your own risk. We have a cloakroom. Check it in.'

# Chefs Behaving Badly

At a book signing at a food shop owned by a world-renowned restaurateur, an elderly woman pointed out that the black truffle butter was a bit cheaper at the gourmet shop down the street. The chef graciously set down his glass of wine, cleared his throat, and then recommended that she go buy it at the other shop immediately. The lady, familiar with this chef's reputation as a tyrant was flabbergasted and responded that she would tell all her friends how terribly he had treated her.

He paused, looked here directly in the eyes and calmly sneered 'Tell them *both* and get the hell out of my shop'.

# He's Got Marty Feldman Eyes

A visiting restaurant manager elected himself to help an urban restaurant rid itself of a rodent problem, or more correctly, a problem rodent. The chef bragged that he was going to get it with a BB gun, but a couple days later, the problem lingered. Around midnight one night, the visiting manager was coming out of the office and saw the rodent out of the corner of his eye. The huge rat tried to run past him. The manager reached to grab anything to hit it with. As the rat ran past him, it stepped on a glue trap and continued running down the hall with the glue trap stuck to its foot. The manager managed to find a long stick with something heavy on the end. He whacked the rat as it ran past. It turned on him and hissed, going on the offensive. The manager pummeled the rat with his makeshift club, eventually killing it. Still full of adrenaline, the manager decided to create a display worthy of his prize. He rigged up a hanger and some kitchen twine, and then quickly ran to get a witness. He found the night-crew cook who always looked half asleep and usually gave the manager a hard time. The cook came around the corner and, to his now bug-eyed surprise, he saw a dead rat the size of a cat hanging from a rafter in the middle of the office by its tail.

# Ladies' Night

The street level of a primarily residential building was occupied by a fairly busy restaurant. On Sunday afternoons, the management showcased a light jazz band as a way to bring in new business. The third-floor neighbour continuously complained about the noise from the music. After extended discussions, the manager asked the neighbour, ' Madam, can you hear the music when the bus passes? I can't even hear it in the restaurant when the bus passes.' She admitted, 'No, I can't hear the music then, but I'm used to the bus.'

Finally, the management cancelled the Sunday jazz band. The noise-hating neighbour came in about six months later to take advantage of their two-for-one Ladies' Night specials. The barman knew she was the main reason the restaurant no longer played jazz, so he wasn't thrilled to see her. She also had discouraged some of his regular customers from sitting at the bar that night because she was 'saving some seats'. When she got the bill at the end of the night, she questioned the barman. Instead of getting two-for-one drinks, she was charged for all of her drinks. The bartender said, 'There's no mistake. That special is for *ladies*'.

# The Drink's on Me

A waiter was working in a busy restaurant at a resort over Easter weekend. A slew of families were in the restaurant enjoying lunch for the holiday. The waiter was preparing a drink tray full of soft drinks, bar drinks, milk, orange juice. . . . You name it, it was probably on this tray. A waitress working a nearby section asked him, 'Hey, could you serve an orange juice to Table 92 for me?' The waiter happily obliged. When he got to the table, where about 11 people were sitting at a table for 8, he began to set down the juice. As he was setting it down, the guy across the table yelled, 'Look out!' as the entire tray slowly and irretrievably tipped onto a customer. In slow motion, each individual piece of glassware dumped its contents onto the customer before crashing directly on his head. As the waiter tried to help clean up the diner, he knocked over the glass of orange juice that started the avalanche and was the only glass left standing at that point. The table was in absolute hysterics before the last glass even fell. They became regulars and requested the waiter every time.

# Frosty the New Girl

A new manager was training in each of the various stations in the kitchen before assuming the helm. After her kitchen training was completed, her station chefs made her perform one last rite of passage. In their open kitchen concept, it was common to see the line cooks 'flaming' the sauté pans to the delight of the diners. The sauté pans, with a bit of oil, are heated in a line of gas burners. When they're hot, a cook walks down the line and quickly pours water into the hot oil, causing large flames that burn out quickly. The new manager had to perform this traditional manoeuvre before her training was complete. The manager hesitated and let the oil get a little too hot. As the manager poured her water, the flames seemed higher than usual. Suddenly, the fire-suppression system over the range began pouring white puffs of dried chemicals over the range, flooding the dining room with harmless, but very annoying, clouds of chemicals. The entire restaurant had to shut down and wait for a fire inspection and a system reset before opening again.

# Radio Fryer

In a very busy luxury restaurant, a cook considered it his right to blare music in the kitchen. He didn't even turn it down when the chef was in the kitchen trying to talk to the staff. Day after day, for close to a week, he and the chef had the same discussion about the loud radio. The next morning, on the chef's 'day off', the cook turned the radio on once again. He thought he was getting one over on the chef. The chef walked through the door, looked the cook in the eye, but walked past him. He grabbed the radio, placed it into a frying basket and dropped it into the deep fat fryer. Then he walked back to the cook and said, 'When that's done, I need you to clean that fryer', and calmly walked to his office.

# Index

# Notes

# Notes

# Notes

# Notes

# FOR DUMMIES®

## Do Anything. Just Add Dummies

# UK editions

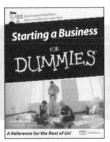

**Buying and Selling a Home**
978-0-7645-7027-8

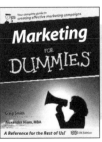

**Renting Out Your Property**
978-0-470-02921-3

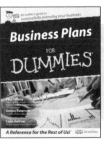

**Buying a Property in Eastern Europe**
978-0-7645-7047-6

## ERSONAL FINANCE

**Investing**
978-0-7645-7023-0

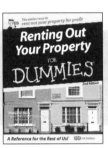

**Personal Finance & Investing**
978-0-470-51510-5

**Bookkeeping**
978-0-470-05815-2

## BUSINESS

**Starting a Business**
978-0-7645-7018-6

**Marketing**
978-0-7645-7056-8

**Business Plans**
978-0-7645-7026-1

Answering Tough Interview Questions For Dummies
(978-0-470-01903-0)

Being the Best Man For Dummies
(978-0-470-02657-1)

Body Language FD
(978-0-470-51291-3)

British History For Dummies
(978-0-470-03536-8)

Buying a Home on a Budget For Dummies
(978-0-7645-7035-3)

Buying a Property in Spain For Dummies
(978-0-470-51235-77)

Cognitive Behavioural Therapy For Dummies
(978-0-470-01838-5)

Cricket For Dummies
(978-0-470-03454-5)

CVs For Dummies
(978-0-7645-7017-9)

Detox For Dummies
(978-0-470-01908-5)

Diabetes For Dummies
(978-0-470-05810-7)

Divorce For Dummies
(978-0-7645-7030-8)

DJing For Dummies
(978-0-470-03275-6)

eBay.co.uk For Dummies
(978-0-7645-7059-9)

Economics For Dummies
(978-0-470-05795-7)

English Grammar For Dummies
(978-0-470-05752-0)

Gardening For Dummies
(978-0-470-01843-9)

Genealogy Online For Dummies
(978-0-7645-7061-2)

Green Living For Dummies
(978-0-470-06038-4)

Hypnotherapy For Dummies
(978-0-470-01930-6)

Life Coaching For Dummies
(978-0-470-03135-3)

Neuro-linguistic Programming For Dummies
(978-0-7645-7028-5)

Parenting For Dummies
(978-0-470-02714-1)

Personal Developmet All-In-One For Dummies
(978-0-470-51501-3)

Pregnancy For Dummies
(978-0-7645-7042-1)

Retiring Wealthy For Dummies
(978-0-470-02632-8)

Self Build and Renovation For Dummies
(978-0-470-02586-4)

Selling For Dummies
(978-0-470-51259-3)

Sorting Out Your Finances For Dummies
(978-0-7645-7039-1)

Starting a Business on eBay.co.uk For Dummies
(978-0-470-02666-3)

Starting and Running an Online Business For Dummies
(978-0-470-05768-1)

The Romans For Dummies
(978-0-470-03077-6)

UK Law and Your Rights For Dummies
(978-0-470-02796-7)

Writing a Novel & Getting Published For Dummies
(978-0-470-05910-4)

# FOR DUMMIES®

## Do Anything. Just Add Dummies

---

## HOBBIES

**978-0-7645-5232-8**

**978-0-7645-5395-0**

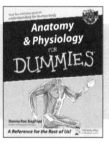

**978-0-7645-5476-6**

**Also available:**

Art For Dummies
(978-0-7645-5104-8)

Aromatherapy For Dummies
(978-0-7645-5171-0)

Bridge For Dummies
(978-0-471-92426-5)

Card Games For Dummies
(978-0-7645-9910-1)

Chess For Dummies
(978-0-7645-8404-6)

Improving Your Memory
For Dummies
(978-0-7645-5435-3)

Massage For Dummies
(978-0-7645-5172-7)

Meditation For Dummies
(978-0-471-77774-8)

Photography For Dummies
(978-0-7645-4116-2)

Quilting For Dummies
(978-0-7645-9799-2)

---

## EDUCATION

**978-0-7645-5434-6**

**978-0-7645-5581-7**

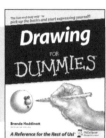

**978-0-7645-5422-3**

**Also available:**

Algebra For Dummies
(978-0-7645-5325-7)

Astronomy For Dummies
(978-0-7645-8465-7)

Buddhism For Dummies
(978-0-7645-5359-2)

Calculus For Dummies
(978-0-7645-2498-1)

Cooking Basics For Dummies
(978-0-7645-7206-7)

Forensics For Dummies
(978-0-7645-5580-0)

Islam For Dummies
(978-0-7645-5503-9)

Philosophy For Dummies
(978-0-7645-5153-6)

Religion For Dummies
(978-0-7645-5264-9)

Trigonometry For Dummies
(978-0-7645-6903-6)

---

## PETS

**978-0-470-03717-1**

**978-0-7645-8418-3**

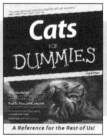

**978-0-7645-5275-5**

**Also available:**

Labrador Retrievers
For Dummies
(978-0-7645-5281-6)

Aquariums For Dummies
(978-0-7645-5156-7)

Birds For Dummies
(978-0-7645-5139-0)

Dogs For Dummies
(978-0-7645-5274-8)

Ferrets For Dummies
(978-0-7645-5259-5)

Golden Retrievers
For Dummies
(978-0-7645-5267-0)

Horses For Dummies
(978-0-7645-9797-8)

Jack Russell Terriers
For Dummies
(978-0-7645-5268-7)

Puppies Raising & Training
Diary For Dummies
(978-0-7645-0876-9)

---

# FOR DUMMIES®

## The easy way to get more done and have more fun

---

## LANGUAGES

**978-0-7645-5193-2**

**978-0-7645-5193-2**

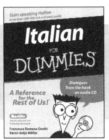

**978-0-7645-5196-3**

### Also available:

Chinese For Dummies
(978-0-471-78897-3)

Chinese Phrases
For Dummies
(978-0-7645-8477-0)

French Phrases For Dummies
(978-0-7645-7202-9)

German For Dummies
(978-0-7645-5195-6)

Italian Phrases For Dummies
(978-0-7645-7203-6)

Japanese For Dummies
(978-0-7645-5429-2)

Latin For Dummies
(978-0-7645-5431-5)

Spanish Phrases
For Dummies
(978-0-7645-7204-3)

Spanish Verbs For Dummies
(978-0-471-76872-2)

Hebrew For Dummies
(978-0-7645-5489-6)

---

## MUSIC AND FILM

**978-0-7645-9904-0**

**978-0-7645-2476-9**

**978-0-7645-5105-5**

### Also available:

Bass Guitar For Dummies
(978-0-7645-2487-5)

Blues For Dummies
(978-0-7645-5080-5)

Classical Music For Dummies
(978-0-7645-5009-6)

Drums For Dummies
(978-0-471-79411-0)

Jazz For Dummies
(978-0-471-76844-9)

Opera For Dummies
(978-0-7645-5010-2)

Rock Guitar For Dummies
(978-0-7645-5356-1)

Screenwriting For Dummies
(978-0-7645-5486-5)

Songwriting For Dummies
(978-0-7645-5404-9)

Singing For Dummies
(978-0-7645-2475-2)

---

## HEALTH, SPORTS & FITNESS

**978-0-7645-7851-9**

**978-0-7645-5623-4**

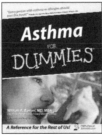

**978-0-7645-4233-6**

### Also available:

Controlling Cholesterol
For Dummies
(978-0-7645-5440-7)

Diabetes For Dummies
(978-0-470-05810-7)

High Blood Pressure
For Dummies
(978-0-7645-5424-7)

Martial Arts For Dummies
(978-0-7645-5358-5)

Menopause FD
(978-0-470-061008)

Pilates For Dummies
(978-0-7645-5397-4)

Weight Training
For Dummies
(978-0-471-76845-6)

Yoga For Dummies
(978-0-7645-5117-8)

---

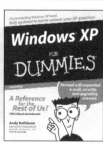